Critical Analysis of Political Policy on National Economies

Critical Analysis of Political Policy on National Economies

Written & Compiled
by

Ashok M. Gadkari

GYAN

ISBN: 978-81-212-2005-7

Published, 2020

Published by

Gyan Publishing House
5, Ansari Road
Daryaganj, New Delhi-110002
Phone: 011-47034999, 9811692060
www.gyanbooks.com
E-mail: books@gyanbooks.com

Printed at: G. Print Process, Delhi.

Contents

Section - I

Section - II
Critical Observations of present status of Countries' Economies

Section - III

Foreword

It is appreciable that Author has completed the second book on Economics within the record time of less than one year. Name of the first book is "Critical Analysis of the External debt on National Economies". The name of this book is "Critical Analysis of Political Policy on National Economies" which shows that Political policy of any country has its impact on its economy. In fact, both Political Science and Economics are two separate social sciences but author has successfully showed that both of them are interdependent on each other. If the political policy of any country is militarily attached another country, then that country will retaliate strongly which will have impact on the country attacking the other country. Superpower country may also support the country which is attacked and impose financial sanctions against the attacking country which will make the economy of the attacking country vulnerable.

Author is of the strong opinion that the world peace is only solution for the welfare of entire mankind and not very happy with the political policies of the super power countries which are practicing wrong policies in competing with each other to prove that they are the most supreme power in the world. They are therefore concentrating to manufacture most sophisticated nuclear weapons, missiles, naval and military strength of all kinds with leisure and other advanced technology.

USA and Russia have 95% of the nuclear weapons which has the power to destroy the whole world ten times. If any accident occurs in their ammunition storage centre, we can image what type of disaster will happened to the world and mankind. It will be more horrible disaster than Chernobyl in Russia.

For the last six months i.e. December 2019 to May 2020, we are experiencing the effect of new disease a virus. This has created economic disaster in the countries and there will be possibility of appearance of great recession after the elimination of this virus. There will be unemployment in all countries substantially about 20% -40% of the present level. In India, 12 crores workers lost their jobs in April 2020 i.e. 20% -21% of unemployment. This will raise to 35% -45% in the next few months.

Author has rightly pointed out that our target is achievement of world peace. For this purpose, we have institutes IMF, World Bank, WTO, WHO and UN etc. after World War II. Superpower like USA, Russia and China have potential to make all countries in the world as welfare states but at present they are concentrated in completion of supremacy among themselves. In such condition, there will be unrest and no peace in the world.

Author is very optimistic that after recovery from the ensuing recession, the Superpowers will realise their mistake and they will strive to make their countries as welfare states and will take initiative and encourage other states to promote their states as welfare states. This will lead to the welfare states all over the world known as "Ram Rajya" which is the ultimate goal of the entire mankind. Author is very optimistic that this goal will accomplish by end 2025.

Book is very informative as it gives substantial knowledge of how economy of various countries like Arab Gulf, Israel, Turkey, Canada, Greece, Italy and African countries are developing. It is a research work which should be valued accordingly and awarded by the Standard Educational Institutions including Noble Committee on Economics in Norway.

Summary of this book is explained very clearly as above. The book is readable for those who are interested in Economics and Politics. This is good book for post graduate students as a **reference** book who are studying Economics Science and Political Science. I was fortunate to work with the author who is authority on foreign exchange dealing operations and government treasury instrument operations. He gave me excellent guidance while working with him on foreign exchange operations. He was the faculty member of the International Training Centre of Grindlays Bank and used to give presentation in Bourse course on foreign exchange dealings.

His presentation skills are excellent. I hope the book will be read by many readers and will be appreciated.

Mr. Manohar Kanchan

Retired Senior Manager in ANZ Grindlays Bank,
Mumbai (now Standard Chartered Bank)

Foreword

The book entitled "Critical Analysis of Political policy on National Economies" is the second book of the author after first book, 'Critical Analysis of External debts on National policies". I am delighted that this book is written on the current topic of the welfare states all over the world. Book is concentrating on the country's ruler interference in the internal affairs of other countries and impact of this interference on economic position on the country's interference.

Ultimate target of the entire mankind is to develop the world as a welfare state. In fact, we have instituted welfare after World War II, such as UN, WHO, IMF, World Bank etc.

India has potential to promote Welfare state and encourage other states to do so. This book is in fact research paper which should be valued accordingly by the standard education Institutes like Cambridge And Oxford Universities and Noble Committee on Economics in Norway and should be awarded accordingly. For example, Cambridge University should award M.A. or Ph.D. honour in Economics to the author. The book gave me good practical knowledge about the economy of above 27 new countries incorporated in the book and their impact of political actions on economies of these countries.

Author is well verse in his subject and a good guide. His presentations in training Institutes are very effective. Though we are retired, we are always in contact with each other.

Mr. Narayan Nerulkar

Retired Manager of ANZ Grindlays Bank
(now the Standard Chartered Bank), Mumbai

List of Abbreviations

ADIA : Abu Dhabi Investment Authority
ADIC : Abu Dhabi Investment Council
APTT : Afghanistan–Pakistan Transit Trade Agreement
AGOA : Africa Growth and Opportunity Act
ANC : African National Congress
BEE : Black Economic Empowerment
BWIs : Bretton Woods Institutions
BSAC : British South Africa Company
CBI : Central Bank of Iraq
CBL : Central Bank of Libya
CNPC : China National Petroleum Corporation
CPI : Consumer Price Index
CAS : Country Assistance Strategy
DIO : Defence Industries Organization
DAI : Development Alternatives, Inc.
DSM : Doha Securities Market
DFM : Dubai Financial Market
DIC : Dubai International Capital
EPZ : Export Processing Zone
EFF : Extended Funding Facility
FDI : Foreign Direct Investment
FTA : Free Trade Agreement
FTAA : Free Trade Area of the Americas
GST : General Sale Tax
GCI : Global Competitiveness Index
GDP : Gross Domestic Product
GCC : Gulf Cooperation Council
HIPC : Heavily Indebted Poor Countries
HRM : Human Resource Management
HDI : Human Development Index
ICAC : Independent Commission Against Corruption
IPPs : Independent Power Projects
INDECO : Industrial Development Corporation
IQ : Industries Qatar

ICT	:	Information and Communication Technologies
IMD	:	Institute for Management Development
ITGI	:	Interconnector Turkey-Greece-Italy
ICC	:	International Chamber of Commerce
IDA	:	International Development Agency
IMF	:	International Monetary Fund
IPIC	:	International Petroleum Investment Company
ILSA	:	Iran and Libya Sanctions Act
IRGC	:	Islamic Revolutionary guard Corps
ISIL	:	Islamic State
IEC	:	Israel Electric Corporation
ISE	:	Istanbul Stock Exchange
JVP	:	Jerusalem Venture Partners
JSF	:	Joint Strike Fighter
LNG	:	Liquefied Natural Gas
MMD	:	Movement for Multiparty Democracy
MDC	:	Mubadala Development Company
MFP	:	Multi-factor Productivity
NOC	:	National Oil Corporation
NCCM	:	Nchanga Consolidated Copper Mines
OPEC	:	Organization of Petroleum Exporting Countrie
PSI	:	Policy Support Instrument
PRGF	:	Poverty Reduction & Growth Facility
PEC	:	Public Electricity Corporation
QCB	:	Qatar Central Bank's
QGPC	:	Qatar General Petroleum Corporation
QIA	:	Qatar Investment Authority
QPMC	:	Qatar Primary Material Company
QTEA	:	Qatar Tourism and Exhibition Authority
REDF	:	Real Estate Development Fund
REIT	:	Rreal Estate Investment trusts
R&D	:	Rresearch and Development
RST	:	Rhodesia Selection Trust
RCM	:	Roan Consolidated Mines
SAGIA	:	Saudi Arabian General Investment Authority
SR	:	Saudi Arabian Riyals
SCA	:	Securities and Commodities Authority
SOC	:	Sirte Oil Company
SADC	:	South Africa Development Countries
SAMP	:	Southern African Migration Project
SMP	:	Staff Monitoring Programme
SCF	:	Standard Cubic Feet
SAIL	:	Steel Authority of India Limited

SAP	:	Structural Adjustment Package
TDM	:	Telecomunicações de Moçambique
TFP	:	Total factor Productivity
UAE	:	United Arab Emirates
USPTO	:	United States Patent and Trademark Office
UPDA	:	Urban Planning and Development Authority
WOC	:	Waha Oil Company
WCO	:	World Customs Organization
WTO	:	World Trade Organization
YR	:	Yemeni Riyal
ZCCM	:	Zambia Consolidated Copper Mines
ZEMA	:	Zambia Environmental Management Agency
ZIMCO	:	Zambia Industrial and Mining Corporation
ZCCM	:	Zambian Consolidated Copper Mines

Section - I

Introduction

In my last book titled "Critical Analysis of the International debts on National Policies", we observed the economy of 12 nations such as India, USA, China, Soviet Union, Soviet Russia, UK, France, Germany, Australia, Japan. Argentina, Mexico and Venezuela from the angle of its impact of international debt on its policy.

Though economy and Political Science are two different subjects, effect of the political policies with that nation's economy is interdependent and therefore the economy and political science are not independent of each other. This book is the extension of author's first book. In this book, we shall observe the political interference of the country's ruler in other country's affairs and its impact on the economic growth of the country initiating interference. The goal of economy of any country is the welfare state and this book will critically analysis how much the state administration has achieved this goal.

In Section II, we shall study thoroughly economy and the political policy of Ian, Iraq, Saudi Arabia, Qatar, UAE, Israel, Syria, Turkey, Italy, Greece, Libya, Gaza Strip, Palestine, Canada, Afghanistan, South Africa and African countries such as Angola, Zambia, Zimbabwe, Malawi, Mozambique, Mauritius and Tanzania.

In the Section III which is the Concluding Part of this book, we shall observe previous 12 countries economy and 23 countries economy incorporated in Section II of this book. We shall show in the concluding section III, the weakness of each country of its political policy and its impact on the economy of that country. We shall also suggest and highlight the remedies which should be implemented on a priority basis by that country to enable it to administer the country in such a way that available resources are distributed equally among the poor and rich citizens with the control of inflation so that all citizens will be happy and comfortable. This will achieve the target of Welfare State which is the ultimate goal of the entire mankind.

Section - II
Critical Observations of present status of Countries' Economies

1

Economy of Qatar

The economy of Qatar is one of the richest in the world based on GDP per capita, ranking between fifth and seventh on world rankings for 2015 and 2016 data compiled by the World Bank, United Nations, and IMF.

Petroleum and natural gas are the cornerstones of Qatar's economy and account for more than 70% of total government revenue, more than 60% of gross domestic product, and roughly 85% of export earnings. Qatar has the world's third largest proven natural gas reserve and is the second-largest exporter of natural gas.

Energy sector

Before the emergence of petrol-based industry, Qatar was a poor pearl diving country. The exploration of oil and gas fields began in 1939. In 1973, oil production and revenues increased dramatically, moving Qatar out of the ranks of the world's poorest countries and providing it with one of the highest per capita incomes in the world.

Qatar's economy was in a downturn from 1982 to 1989. OPEC (Organization of Petroleum Exporting Countries) quotas on crude oil production, the lower price for oil, and the generally unpromising outlook on international markets reduced oil earnings. In turn, the Qatari government's spending plans had to be cut to match lower income. The resulting recessionary local business climate caused many firms to lay off expatriate staff. With the economy recovering in the 1990s, expatriate populations, particularly from Egypt and South Asia, have grown again.

Oil production will not long remain at peak levels of 500,000 barrels (80,000 m) per day, as oil fields are projected to be mostly depleted by 2023. However, large natural gas reserves have been located off Qatar's northeast coast. These offshore gas fields also may contain significant oil and condensate reserves. For example, the state owned Qatar Petroleum found 2 offshore oil fields in the 1960s. At the time production was too expensive. However, technological development led to production over 30 years later.

The gas condensate can be refined to usual oil products in specialized refineries. The costs are a bit higher but it is normal today for companies to use the gas condensate too. Oil offshore production in 2008 for PS-2 and PS-3 blocks was about 31.1 million barrels (84,995 b/d). Joint Ventures facilities (PS-1, ALK, K & A): Combined oil production from these three joint venture production facilities in 2008 was 57.4 million barrels (156,873 b/d). Like with gas fields there are more offshore blocks which need to be explored and could increase the oil output. So the 500,000 bpd peak and a depletion in 2023 is delayed. With higher oil prices it is expected that the offshore exploration of oil and/or natural gas fields will go on. Oil production in June 2016 seemed to be around 670,000 barrels per day, a bit down from February 2016 production of 692,000 barrels per day. Taking all liquids together Qatar is already far beyond a million barrels per day.

Qatar's proved reserves of gas are the third-largest in the world, exceeding 7000 km (250 trillion cubic feet). The economy was boosted in 1991 by completion of the $1.5-billion Phase I of North Field gas development. In 1996, the Qatar gas project began exporting Liquefied Natural Gas (LNG) to Japan. Further phases of North Field gas development costing billions of dollars are in various stages of planning and development.

Qatar's heavy industrial projects, all based in Umm Said, include a refinery with a 50,000 barrels (8,000 m^3) per day capacity, a fertilizer plant for urea and ammonia, a steel plant, and a petrochemical plant. All these industries use gas for fuel. Most are joint ventures between European and Japanese firms and the state-owned Qatar General Petroleum Corporation (QGPC). The U.S. is the major equipment supplier for Qatar's oil and gas industry, and U.S. companies are playing a major role in North Field gas development. 890- Qatar pursues a vigorous program of "Qatarization", under which all joint venture industries and government departments strive to move Qatari nationals into positions of greater authority. Growing numbers of foreign-educated Qataris, including many educated in the U.S., are returning home to assume key positions formerly occupied by expatriates. In order to control the influx of expatriate workers, Qatar has tightened the administration of its foreign manpower programs over the past several years. Security is the principal basis for Qatar's strict entry and immigration rules and regulations.

Industry

The government considers industry to be an integral part of its plan to diversify the economy and maximize its huge natural gas reserves, which serve as the primary feedstock for the sector. Accordingly, careful planning has gone into industrial development. With an eye towards exports, development has been clustered around the ports of Ras Laffan Industrial City and Mesaieed Industrial Area, which are key centers of energy. The result has seen considerable growth over the years. Industries Qatar (IQ), a producer of petrochemicals, fertilizers and steel, is a regional powerhouse, surpassed only in size by Saudi Basic Industries Corporation (SABIC), the Middle East's largest chemical producer. In 2007 the manufacturing sector made the third-largest contribution to GDP among non-oil and gas sectors, equivalent to about 7.5% of GDP.

Petrochemicals and fertilizers supply make up a large portion of the industrial base, along with steel and other construction materials, through Qatar Steel and Qatar Primary Material Company (QPMC). Indeed, over the past few years, demand for construction materials experienced a major surge as the development boom swept the Persian Gulf region. But the global financial crisis has put a significant dent in demand in the region, as project credit lines dry up and investor sentiment remains cautious. The crisis has in fact impacted the whole of the industrial sector – IQ saw its net profit drop in the fourth quarter of 2008 more than 90% over the same period the previous year. But in relative terms, the sector has fared better than most and IQ still managed to post an annual profit of $2billion. Large profit chunks from years past have been channeled into capital investments, which should help the sector ride out the storm. IQ, for example, is pushing several major expansion projects, worth almost $6bn, ahead. Qatar is expected to be one of the fastest growing economies in 2009 – the hope is it will be enough to keep the industrial sector on an upward trajectory.

Financial sector

The Qatari banking sector managed to escape the direct impact of the global subprime fallout, but was not altogether unscathed by its aftershocks. Overall, it was the best performing of the Gulf Cooperation Council markets in the last quarter of 2008 and most banks posted substantial profits for 2008. But the sector is also facing issues of liquidity, declining customer confidence and a forced reluctance to lend. In a bid to strengthen the banks' positions, the Qatar Investment Authority (QIA) announced in early 2009 that it was willing to take a 10-20% stake in any interested local listed banks by way of a capital injection, although this was later reduced to 5% stakes and an additional 5% at the end of 2009.

The Qatari government also announced in March 2009 that it was planning to buy the investment portfolio of the banks in the hope this would encourage them to continue lending. Cautious sector sentiment has also been compounded by the Qatar Central Bank's (QCB's) lending restrictions, which demand a loan-to-deposit ratio of 90%. Given the high level of integration between Qatar's economy and the Persian Gulf region, as well as the wider world, a slowdown in business and banking activity seemed inevitable. Nevertheless, Qatar's banking sector has been faring relatively well, considering the strife experienced in other countries, and insiders are confident that activity will return to its previous brisk pace in the second half of 2009 as confidence slowly rebuilds around the globe.

The International Monetary Fund in its spring assessment 2019 said that Qatar has "successfully absorbed the shocks" of the blockade imposed in 2017 and the dropped oil prices from 2014 to 2016. SHYPERLINK "https://en.wikipedia.org/wiki/S%26P_Global"&HYPERLINK "https://en.wikipedia.org/wiki/S%26P_Global"P Global had marked Qatar's outlook to negative in 2017, but changed it to stable in 2019.

In August 2019, Qatar Central Bank stated that the country's economic growth will see a boost over the next two years amid expectations of stable oil prices and continued strong exports. The GDP is expected to grow at an average rate of 2.8% between 2018 and 2020, with the budget surplus falling to 4.35 billion riyals in 2019, from a surplus of 15.1 billion riyals in 2018. [23]

Islamic finance

The Islamic finance sector enjoyed increased activity in 2008 and is expected to continue to grow into 2009 as more sophisticated financial instruments spark the interest of investors. In addition to Islamic banks, such as Qatar Islamic Bank (QIB), Qatar International Islamic Bank (QIIB) and newcomer Masraf Al Rayyan, conventional banks have also been entering the sharia-compliant sector and are coming to view an Islamic subsidiary as a virtual necessity in order to maintain market standing. Islamic banks currently take the lion's share of sharia-compliant business, though the conventional banks are working hard to take a greater share of market activity. Both Islamic banks and Islamic subsidiaries did remarkably well in the first three quarters of 2008, during which overall financing activity increased by 70.6% compared to the same period in the previous year. The global financial crisis slowed this growth though. Poor market conditions have contributed to a marked slowdown of Islamic bond activity in 2008 throughout the Persian Gulf. But other segments, such as Islamic insurance have not seen a similar downturn. Overall, challenges to further growth remain, including a lack of qualified staff to meet the growing demand for sharia-compliant banking services.

Capital market

The stock market HYPERLINK "https://en.wikipedia.org/wiki/Market_capitalisation"capitalization of listed companies in Qatar was valued at $95,487 million in 2007 by the World Bank. As 2008 drew to a close, no capital markets around the globe, including Qatar's, were immune to the effects of the sub-prime fallout. That said, there is considerable optimism that Qatar's bourse, the Doha Securities Market (DSM), will remain relatively resilient to the ongoing international turbulence. It has followed the same peak-trough trajectory as many others around the globe, hitting record highs in mid-2008, before diving in late 2008 and early 2009. Between December 2006 and July 2008 the DSM Index rose about 117% before the global financial crisis wiped out most of these gains. In the first few months of 2009, the DSM lost about 40% of its value. In an effort to stave off further losses, the government announced in February 2009 that it would step in to buy up shares of troubled banks amounting to about 10% of the market's capitalization. The move improved investor optimism and is hoped to prevent the market from falling further. The proposal to create a single unified regulator as early as 2010 to oversee all banking and financial services is viewed as another promising development that will transform the financial sector for the better.

Tourism

Under the ambitious five-year development plan of the Qatar Tourism and Exhibitions Authority (QTEA), the government aimed to boost the number of visitors from 964,000 as of 2007 to 1.5m by 2010. The funding required to meet this goal was present in sufficient amounts; in 2008 the state allocated some $17bn for tourism development through 2014, most of which was allocated towards hotels, exhibition space and infrastructure. In order to keep up with a rising number of visitors, the government set a goal of increasing hotel capacity 400% by 2012. In addition to financial support, the government has also worked to ease business regulations in a bid to increase private sector activity. A major aspect of expansion plans is the Hamad International Airport, which will have the capacity to handle up to 24m passengers upon the completion of the first phase in 2012.

Other niche tourism segments receiving special focus include cultural tourism on the back of the high publicity opening of Doha's Museum of Islamic Art, and sports tourism, initially spurred by the Asian Games, to which Qatar played host in 2006. The government appears to be committed to long-term expansion plans, but challenges nevertheless remain, including effective marketing to the international community as well as the effect of the financial crisis on global tourism appetite.

Transport

With a fast-expanding population and substantial economic growth over the past decade, a reliable and extensive transportation network is becoming increasingly necessary within Qatar. So far the government, the primary transport developer, has done well in terms of keeping up with demand for new transportation options. In 2008 the Public Works Authority (Ashghal), one of the bodies that oversees infrastructure development, underwent a major reorganization in order to streamline and modernize the authority in preparation for major project expansions across all segments in the near future. Ashghal works in tandem with the Urban Planning and Development Authority (UPDA), the body that designed the transportation master plan, instituted in March 2006 and running to 2025.

Fisheries is a minor sector in Qatar, and production is almost exclusively for domestic consumption.

As driving is the primary mode of transport in Qatar, the road network is a major focus of the plan. Project highlights in this segment include the multibillion-dollar Doha Expressway and the Qatar Bahrain Causeway, which will connect Qatar to Bahrain and Saudi Arabia and is considered a milestone in regional interconnectivity. Mass-transit options, such as a Doha metro, light-rail system and more extensive bus networks, are also under development to ease road congestion. In addition, the railway system is being significantly expanded and could eventually form an integral part of a GCC-wide network linking all the Arab states of the Persian Gulf. The airport, too, is expanding capacity to keep up with rising visitor numbers. The New Doha International Airport is one of the largest projects in Qatar today and will boast a capacity of 50m passengers upon completion in 2015. Finally, port infrastructure is seen as an integral part of Qatar's economic development as it focuses on LNG and industrial exports. The port at Mesaieed is undergoing expansion. While the financial crisis may present challenges to infrastructure development, once all projects are completed Qatar will have one of the most advanced and modern transport infrastructures in the region.

Macro-economic trend

Qatar is now the richest country in the world, on a per person basis. Current GDP per capita registered a world record-breaking peak growth of 1,156% in the 70s. This became quickly unsustainable and Qatar's current GDP per capita contracted 53% in the 80s. But rising global oil demand helped current GDP per capita to expand 94% in the 90s. Diversification is still a long-term issue for this over-exposed economy.

For purchasing power parity comparisons only, the US Dollar is exchanged at 3.67 Qatari Riyals. Mean wages were $59.99 per man-hour in 2009.

In February 2012, the International Bank of Qatar reported that GDP grew by 19.9% in 2011, but estimated that 2012 growth would slow to 9.8%

Critical Observations of present status of Economy of Qatar

- Being abundant storage of proven petroleum oil, the economy of Qatar is one of the richest in the world.
- Petroleum and natural gas are two cornerstones of Qatar economy. It earns 70% of total government revenue, 60% of GDP and 85% of total exports.
- Before the emergence of petrol-based industry, Qatar was poor pearl diving country. Exploration of oil and gas fields began in 1939. In 1973, oil production and revenues increased dramatically. It was in downturn from 1982 to 1990. OPEC quotas on crude oil production, lower price of oil, negative outlook on international markets reduced oil earnings .Spending plan cut to match lower income. The resulting recessionary local business climate caused many firms to lay off the expatriate staff. With the economy recovering from 1990s, expatriate population from Egypt and South Asia have grown again.
- Oil production was 500000 bpd. Storage of oil is expected to last 2023. Natural gas located off Qatar's northeast coast. These are significant oil and condensate reserves. Gas condensate can be refined to usual oil products in specialized refineries. In June 2016, oil production was 670000 bpd down from February 2016 692000 bpd.
- Qatar's proved reserves of gas is 250 trillion cubic feet (7000km). Economy was boosted in 1991. Liquefied natural gas exported to Japan.
- Qatari Banking Sector managed to escape the direct impact of the global surprise fall out, but was not together unscathed by it's after-shocks. Issue of liquidation declining customer confidence and forced reluctant to lend.
- Government encouraged banks to lend by buying the investment portfolio of the banks. Loan to deposit ratio was as high as 90%.
- In August 2019, Qatar Central Bank stated that Qatari economy will boost on account of stable oil prices and strong exports.
- In addition to Islamic banks, Conventional banks were also entering in Qatar with sophisticated instruments/

- Stock Market capitalization was \$95.487 billion in 2007.
- Under the ambitious five year development plan, Qatar Tourism and Exhibition Authority (QTEA), government aimed to boost the number of visitors from 964000 in 2007 to 1.5 million in 2010. The funding required to meet this goal was present in sufficient amounts. In 2008, the state allocated 17 billion for tourism development. Hotels, Exhibition Space and Infrastructure were developed. Hotel capacity raised to 400% by 2012 to help rising number of visitors. Qatar eased the business regulations to increase private sector activities. Hamad International Airport has the capacity of handling 24 million passengers on its completion phase I in 2012.
- With fast expanding population and substantial economic growth over the past decade, extensive transportation network is becoming necessary within Qatar.
- Public Works Authority underwent major reorganization in order to streamline and modernize the preparation of major project expansion across all segments.
- Fisheries is a minor sector. Fishery output is exclusively used for domestic consumption.
- Road network is the major focus. Multi billion dollars spent to develop Doha Expressway and Qatar Bahrain Causeway to connect Qatar to Bahrain and Saudi Arabia. This will be milestone in regional interconnectivity. Doha International Airport will accommodate 50 million passengers. Port infrastructure is Qatar's integral part.
- Exchange rate for Qatari Riyal is 3.65 Riyals per US dollar. PPP US dollar rate is Riyals 3.67 =US dollar 1.
- International Bank of Qatar reported 19.9% GDP growth in February 2011 but it will be 9.8% in 2012.
- Currency: Qatari Riyal
- Trade Organization: WTO
- Country Group: Developing/Emerging, High income economy
- Population: 2.782 million
- GDP: \$191.849 billion Nominal & \$365.835 billion PPP in 2019
- GDP growth: 1.6% in 2017, 1.5% in 2018, 0.5% in 2019 and 1.5% in 2020 Forecast
- GDP per Capital: \$69688 Nominal & \$ 132886 PPP

- GDP by Sector: Agriculture 0.2%, Industry 50.3%, Services 49.5% in 2019
- Inflation: 2.2% in 2020 & 3.8% in 2019
- Population below poverty level: 0%
- Labour Force: 2.129 million. Labour force of the country should be 1.5 million domestic and 0.6 million from expatriate in other countries like Egypt and South Asia
- Main Industries: liquefied natural gas, crude oil, ammonia, fertilizers, petrochemicals, steel, cement, construction, ship repairs
- Exports: $86.51 billion (2018, Imports: $26.69 billion Trade Surplus: $59.82 billion
- Gross external debt: $168 billion 87.57% of GDP
- Public debt: 56.5% of GDP
- Revenues: $ 95.35 billion Expenses: $ 55.81 Fiscal Surplus: $40.46 billion. Budget expenditure should be raised substantially to improve infrastructure speedily.
- Credit Rating: S & P's AA(Domestic), AA (Foreign)

  AA+, Outlook: Stable (T&C), Moody's Aa2, Outlook: Stable.
- Qatar was isolated by Saudi Arabia and UAE on account of secretly assisting Iran but it has no impact on Qatar. Qatar employs large amount of expatriate labour from Egypt and South Asia as its labour force may not exceed 1.4 million out of the small population of 2.782 million.
- Country is well managed as a welfare state.

2

Economy of Saudi Arabia

The economy of Saudi Arabia is one of the top twenty economies in the world (G20). It is dependent on oil as the country has the second-largest proven petroleum reserves, and the country is the largest exporter of petroleum in the world. It also has the fifth-largest proven natural gas reserves and is considered an "Energy Superpower". With a total worth of US$33.2 trillion, Saudi Arabia has the second most valuable natural resources in the world.

In 2016 the Saudi Government launched its Saudi Vision 2030 to reduce the country's dependency on oil and diversify its economic resources. Saudi Arabia has the largest economy in the Arab world and the Middle East. In the first quarter of 2019, Saudi Arabia's budget has accomplished its first surplus since 2014. This surplus that is accounted for $10.40 billion has been achieved due to the increase of the oil and non-oil revenues.

Economic overview

Saudi oil reserves are the second largest in the world, and Saudi Arabia is the world's leading oil exporter and second largest producer. Proven reserves, according to figures provided by the Saudi government, are estimated to be 260 billion barrels (41 km^3), which is about one-quarter of world oil reserves. Petroleum in Saudi Arabia is not only plentiful but under pressure and close to the earth's surface. This makes it far cheaper and thus far more profitable to extract petroleum in Saudi Arabia than in many other places. The petroleum sector accounts for roughly 87% of Saudi budget revenues, 90% of export earnings, and 42% of GDP. Saudi Arabia's oil reserves and production are largely managed by the state-owned corporation Saudi Aramco.

Another 40% of GDP comes from the private sector. An estimated 7.5 (2013) million foreigners work legally in Saudi Arabia, playing a crucial role in the Saudi economy, for example, in the oil and service sectors. The government has encouraged private sector growth for many years to lessen the kingdom's dependence on oil, and to increase employment opportunities for the swelling Saudi population. In recent decades the government has begun to permit private sector and foreign investor participation in sectors such as power generation and telecom, and acceded to the WTO. During much of the 2000s, high oil prices enabled the government to post budget surpluses, boost spending on job training and education, infrastructure development, and government salaries.

With its absolute monarchy system of government, large state sector and supply of welfare benefits, the Saudi economy has been described as a bewildering (at least to outsiders) combination of a feudal fealty system and a more modern political patronage one. At every level in every sphere of activity, Saudis maneuver through life manipulating individual privileges, favors, obligations, and connections. By the same token, the government bureaucracy is a maze of overlapping or conflicting power center under the patronage of various royal princes with their own priorities and agendas to pursue and dependents to satisfy.

The gross domestic product of Saudi Arabia fluctuates dramatically according to the price of oil (see below).

Year	*Gross Domestic Product (GDP) (in billions of current USD)*	*GDP per capita (in current USD)*	*US Dollar Exchange (in millions of Saudi Riyals)*	*Inflation Index (2000=100)*	*Population (millions)*	*Per Capita Income (as % of USA)*
1970	5.3773	921.35	4.50		5.836	
1975	46.7734	6,296.30	3.52		7.429	
1980	164.5417	16,892.36	3.59	95	9.741	43.84
1985	103.8978	7,877.54	3.62	92	13.189	49.33
1990	117.6303	7,204.73	3.74	91	16.326	33.13
1995	143.3430	7,650.74	3.74	101	18.736	28.29
2000	189.5149	9,126.95	3.74	100	20.764	26.50
2005	328.4596	13,739.83	3.74	100	23.906	32.53
2010	528.2072	19,259.59	3.75		27.426	
2015	654.2699	20,732.86	3.75		31.557	
2017	688.586	21,113.957	3.75	104.168	32.613	
2018	786.522	23,538.940	3.75	106.562	33.414	
2019	779.289	22,865.178	3.75	105.441	34.082	

Market prices estimated by the International Monetary Fund and other sources, with figures in millions of Saudi Arabian Riyals (SR). Mean wages were $14.74 per man-hour in 2009.

Data

The following table shows the main economic indicators in 1980–2017. Inflation below 2% is in green.

Year	*GDP (in Bil. US$ PPP)*	*GDP per capita (in US$ PPP)*	*GDP growth (real)*	*Inflation rate (in Percent)*	*Government debt (in % of GDP)*
1980	360.3	38,665	▲5.6 %	▲4.4 %	n/a
1985	▼271.2	▼22,793	▼−9.8 %	▼−2.3 %	n/a
1990	▲448.0	▲29,500	▲15.2 %	▼−1.0 %	n/a
1995	▲600.8	▼33,128	▲0.2 %	▲5.3 %	▲74.2 %
2000	▲708.9	▲34,624	▲5.6 %	▼−1.1 %	▼86.7 %
2005	▲969.3	▲41,548	▲5.6 %	▲0.5 %	▼37.3 %
2010	▲1,217.3	▲44,163	▲4.8 %	▲3.7 %	▼8.4 %
2015	▲1,704.5	▲54,956	▲4.1 %	▲1.3 %	▲5.8 %
2016	▲1,755.1	▲55,292	▲1.7 %	▲2.0 %	▲13.1 %
2017	▲1,773.6	▼54,777	▼−0.7 %	▼−0.8 %	▲17.3 %

History

Saudi Arabia was a subsistence economy until the 1930s. In 1933, the Saudi government signed an oil concession agreement with Standard Oil Company of California. Development of oil fields continued in Saudi Arabia, managed mainly by Aramco, company formed by the partnership of Texaco and Chevron. In 1951, the first offshore field in the Middle East was found by the Arabian American Oil Company (Aramco) at Ra's Al-Saffâniyyah area. In the same year, by 1949, Saudi oil production reached 500,000 bpd, and rose rapidly to 1 million bpd in 1954. Moreover, in 1951, Aramco started operating Trans-Arabian Pipeline that used to transform oil from the eastern region of Saudi Arabia to the Mediterranean Sea, passing by Jordan, Syria and Lebanon. However, in 1981 the operations in this line was ceased as a new one was put into operation that linked between Jubail on the Persian HYPERLINK "https://en.wikipedia.org/wiki/Persian_Gulf" Gulf and Yanbu on the Red Sea which highly contributed in shortening the destination of oil transform. In 1960, OPEC was created with Saudi Arabia as one of its founding members. During the 1973 oil crisis, the price of oil rose from $3 per barrel to nearly $12, and the Saudi economy began to grow rapidly, with GDP increasing from approximately $15 billion in 1973, to approximately $184 billion by 1981. After gradually purchasing Aramco's assets, the Saudi government nationalized the company in 1980. In 1988, Saudi Aramco was established to take over the responsibilities of Aramco.

In 1980, the price of oil peaked, and demand began to fall as a result of recessions in industrialized nations and more efficient use of oil which produced surpluses. This created a worldwide oil glut, with the price of oil dropping from approximately $36 per barrel in 1980, to approximately $14 by 1986. Saudi oil production, which had increased to almost 10 million barrels (1,600,000 m) per day during 1980–81, dropped to about 2 million barrels per day (320,000 m^3/d) in 1985. Budgetary deficits developed, and the government drew down its foreign assets. As a result of the oil glut and the pressures of declines in production, after 1985 Saudi Arabia began enforcing production quotas more harshly for OPEC members.

In June 1993, Saudi Aramco absorbed the state marketing and refining company (SAMAREC), becoming the world's largest fully integrated oil company. Most Saudi oil exports move by tanker from oil terminals at Ras Tanura and Ju'aymah in the Persian Gulf. The remaining oil exports are transported via the east–west pipeline across the kingdom to the Red Sea port of Yanbu. A major new gas initiative promises to bring significant investment by U.S. and European oil companies to develop non-associated gas fields in three separate parts of Saudi Arabia. Following final technical agreements with concession awardees in December 2001, development should begin in 2002.

However, beginning in late 1997, Saudi Arabia again faced the challenge of low oil prices. Due to a combination of factors—the East Asian economic crises, a warm winter in the West caused by El Niño, and an increase in non-OPEC oil production—demand for oil slowed and pulled oil prices down by more than one-third.

Saudi Arabia was a key player in coordinating the successful 1999 campaign of OPEC and other oil-producing countries to raise the price of oil to its highest level since the (Persian) Gulf War by managing production and supply of petroleum. That same year, Saudi Arabia established the Supreme Economic Council to formulate and better coordinate economic development policies in order to accelerate institutional and industrial reform.

Saudi Arabia acceded to the WTO (World Trade Organization) in 2005 after many years of negotiations.

Foreign investment

The mid-1980s was also the time that foreign ownership of business was allowed. In the mid-1990s, foreign ownership rules were relaxed again, with investment sought in telecommunications, utilities, and financial services. In 2000, 100% foreign-owned businesses were allowed in the kingdom.

Since 2008, extensive land investment has taken place, especially in Africa - see paragraph Non-petroleum sector.

As per the report released by UNCTAD in June 2018, Saudi Arabia's foreign direct investment was only $1.4 billion in 2017, down from $7.5 billion the year before and as much as $12.2 billion in 2012. The fall in investment is attributed to negative intra-company loans by foreign multinationals and various divestment. In the first quarter of 2018, net capital outflows were running at approximately 5% of GDP, compared to less than 2% of GDP in late 2016. However, according to a report published in Trading Economics, in the second quarter of 2018, foreign direct investment in the country raised by $882 million. Moreover, SAGIA's data indicate that licenses provided to foreign investment have been increased by 130% in the first quarter or 2018 as a result to the current reforms in economy.

After the finance budget was released for 2019, Saudi Arabia planned to issue bonds worth approx. 120 billion riyals ($32 billion) in order to cover up for its 4.2% GDP deficit of 131 billion riyals.

In January 2019 itself the kingdom sold bonds worth $7.5 billion. Saudi Arabia turned towards international debts following a decline in its oil income. In almost two and a half years, bonds worth $60 billion have been sold by Saudi, becoming one of the biggest borrowers globally.

The foreign investments in the Kingdom have witnessed a rapid increase in the first quarter of 2019. The number of new licenses approved for foreign businesses has grown by 70% compared with 2018. Most licenses were approved for British and Chinese companies which have driven this increase. In the first quarter of 2019, foreign investment in Saudi Arabia has jumped by 28%.

Diversification and the development plans

The government has sought to allocate its petroleum income to transform its relatively undeveloped, oil-based economy into that of a modern industrial state while maintaining the kingdom's traditional Islamic values and customs. Although economic planners have not achieved all their goals, the economy has progressed rapidly. Oil wealth has increased the standard of living of most Saudis. However, significant population growth has strained the government's ability to finance further improvements in the country's standard of living. Heavy dependence on petroleum revenue continues, but industry and agriculture now account for a larger share of economic activity. The mismatch between the job skills of Saudi graduates and the needs of the private job market at all levels remains the principal obstacle to economic diversification and development; about 4.6 million non-Saudis are employed in the economy.

Saudi Arabia first began to diversify its economy to reduce dependency on oil in the 1970s as part of its first five-year development plan. Basic petrochemical industries using petroleum byproducts as feedstock were developed. The fishing villages of al-Jubail on the Persian Gulf and Yanbu on the Red Sea were developed. However, their effect on Saudi Arabia's economic fortunes has been small.

Saudi Arabia's first two development plans, covering the 1970s, emphasized infrastructure. The results were impressive—the total length of paved highways tripled, power generation increased by a multiple of 28, and the capacity of the seaports grew tenfold. For the third plan (1980–85), the emphasis changed. Spending on infrastructure declined, but it rose markedly on education, health, and social services. The share for diversifying and expanding productive sectors of the economy (primarily industry) did not rise as planned, but the two industrial cities of Jubail and Yanbu—built around the use of the country's oil and gas to produce steel, petrochemicals, fertilizer, and refined oil products—were largely completed.

In the fourth plan (1985–90), the country's basic infrastructure was viewed as largely complete, but education and training remained areas of concern. Private enterprise was encouraged, and foreign investment in the form of joint ventures with Saudi public and private companies was welcomed. The private sector became more important, rising to 70% of non-oil GDP by 1987. While still concentrated in trade and commerce, private investment increased in industry, agriculture, banking, and construction companies. These private investments were supported by generous government financing and incentive programs. The objective was for the private sector to have 70% to 90% ownership in most joint venture enterprises.

The fifth plan (1990–95) emphasized consolidation of the country's defenses; improved and more efficient government social services; regional development; and, most importantly, creating greater private-sector employment opportunities for Saudis by reducing the number of foreign workers.

The sixth plan (1996–2000) focused on lowering the cost of government services without cutting them and sought to expand educational training programs. The plan called for reducing the kingdom's dependence on the petroleum sector by diversifying economic activity, particularly in the private sector, with special emphasis on industry and agriculture. It also continued the effort to "Saudiize" the labor force.

The seventh plan (2000–2004) focuses more on economic diversification and a greater role of the private sector in the Saudi economy. For 2000–04, the government aims at an average GDP growth rate of 3.16% each year, with projected growths of 5.04% for the private sector and 4.01% for the non-oil sector. The government also has set a target of creating 817,300 new jobs for Saudi nationals.

Advertising expenditures have reached new peaks due to emphasis on value-added manufacturing.

The main investing countries in Saudi Arabia in 2016 were the US, UAE, France, Singapore, Kuwait and Malaysia. They mainly invested in chemical industry, real estate, tourism, fossil fuels, automobiles and machinery. As part of its diversification, Saudi Arabia has been inking major refinery contracts with Chinese and other companies.

As Saudi Arabia became a member of the World Trade Organization (WTO) in 2005, an improvement took place in the overall environment of foreign investment in Saudi Arabia due to many reasons including, the stable economy, the fact that the kingdom has the largest oil reserves worldwide, the high power of expenditure, the good infrastructure system, reinforced finance and a good banking system. Since that time and pursuant to its commitment to the WTO, Saudi Arabia has been developing trade-related policies and legislations. Moreover, foreign investment has been highly encouraged recently with the announcement of The Saudi vision 2030 as it promises of a better economic diversification.

Since 2017, in order to boost the economy and decrease the country's dependency on oil, Mohammed bin Salman has brought in multiple changes, including the raising of prices of gasoline and electricity, introduction of new taxes, and policy of Saudi workers over foreign workers. However, the government officials said the policies were causing serious effects on the economy. Saudi businessmen reported a decline in sales for 2018, blaming the government.

In 2019, Financial Times reported that the plans to float state-owned oil beneficiary Saudi Aramco were stranded between the company's attachment to the ministry and the need to meet the International standards. A person close to the firm stated, "The IPO is seen as a sensible way to clear up the company." On the other hand, Energy Minister Khalid Al Falih has long maintained that the Aramco's association with the state is a "win-win policy" for both parties.

Future plans

Saudi Arabia has announced plans to invest about $47 billion in three of the world's largest and most ambitious petrochemical projects. These include the $27 billion Ras Tanura integrated refinery and petrochemical project, the $9 billion Saudi Kayan petrochemical complex at Jubail Industrial City, and the $10 billion Petro Rabigh refinery upgrade project. Together, the three projects will employ more than 150,000 technicians and engineers working around the clock. Upon completion in 2015–16, the Ras Tanura integrated refinery and petrochemicals project will become the world's largest petrochemical facility of its kind with a combined production capacity of 11 million tons per year of different petrochemical and chemical products. The products will include ethylene, propylene, aromatics, polyethylene, ethylene oxide, chlorine derivatives, and glycol.

Saudi Arabia had plans to launch six "economic cities" (e.g. King Abdullah Economic City, to be completed by 2020) in an effort to diversify the economy and provide jobs. They are being built at a cost of $60bn (2013) and are "expected to contribute $150bn to the economy". As of 2013 four cities were being developed.

Privatization program, a part of Crown Prince Mohammad bin Salman's Vision 2030, is running behind the schedule. The oil prices have gone up by double since the government began to consider the program in 2015. Delay in Aramco's initial public offering further highlights the less urgency in privatization, even though in July 2018, the International Monetary Fund urged to accelerate the process.

According to many reports, the Saudi government is greatly interested in giving more liberty to the foreign investment system and in giving a 100% allowance to the foreign investors to work in the wholesale and retail sector in particular cases.

The Saudi Ministry of Commerce and Investment expects the Kingdom will witness an increase in the GDP per capita from US$20,700 to 33,500 by 2020.

As Vision 2030 has been recently adapted by the Saudi government several reforms has been undertaken including improving the business environment and reform in the financial sector. Moreover, the government has been seeking to achieve greater transparency by issuing a draft law regarding the involvement of private sector. Another reform move has been undertaken to increase the number of national manpower working in the private sector.

Employment

As of 2008, roughly two thirds of workers employed in Saudi Arabia were foreigners, and in the private sector approximately 90%. In January 2014, the Saudi government claimed it had lowered the 90% rate, doubling the number of Saudi citizens working in the private sector employment to 1.5 million. (This compares to 10 million foreign expatriates working in the kingdom.)

According to Reuters, economists "estimate only 30–40 percent of working-age Saudis hold jobs or actively seek work," although the official unemployment rate is only around 12 percent. Most Saudis with jobs are employed by the government, but the International Monetary Fund has warned the government cannot support such a large wage bill in the long term. The government has announced a succession of plans since 2000 to deal with the imbalance by "Saudizing" the economy, however, the foreign workforce and unemployment continued to grow. Since the beginning of 2017, however, Saudi Arabia has seen record numbers of foreign workers leaving the country as the Saudi government imposed higher fees on expatriate workers, with more than 677,000 foreigners leaving the kingdom. This has done little to lower the unemployment rate, which rose to 12.9 percent, it's highest on record.

One obstacle is social resistance to certain types of employment. Jobs in service and sales are considered totally unacceptable for citizens of Saudi Arabia—both potential employees and customers.

Non-petroleum sector

Saudi Arabia has natural resources other than oil, including small mineral deposits of gold, silver, iron, copper, zinc, manganese, tungsten, lead, Sulphur, phosphate, soapstone and feldspar. The country has a small agricultural sector, primarily in the southwest where annual rainfall averages 400 mm (16"). The country is one of the world's largest producers of dates. For some years it grew very expensive wheat using desalinated water for irrigation, but plans to stop by 2016. As of 2009, livestock population amounted to 7.4 million sheep, 4.2 million goats, half a million camels and a quarter of a million cattle.

Although jobs created by the roughly two million annual *hajj* pilgrims do not last long, the hajj employs more people than the oil industry—40,000 temporary jobs (butchers, barbers, coach drivers, etc.)—and US$2–3 billion in revenue.

In 2008, the "Initiative for Saudi Agricultural Investment Abroad" was launched, leading to extensive billion-dollar purchases of large tracts of land around the world: Ethiopia, Indonesia, Mali, Senegal, Sudan and others. Critics see cases of land-grabbing in various instances that also lead to uproars in the respective countries. Competing industrializing nations with food security problems in the quest for agricultural land are China, South Korea and India as well as the Gulf States Kuwait, Qatar and the UAE.

In 2016, Mohammad bin Salman announced Saudi Vision 2030, a plan to reduce Saudi Arabia's dependence on oil, diversify its economy, and develop public service sectors such as health, education, infrastructure, recreation and tourism.

Real estate

One of the fastest growing sectors in the country has been real estate supported by the introduction of real estate investment trusts (REITs) market which has witnessed a significant growth in the number of REITs, although this is yet to achieve its full potential despite some shortages in both residential and commercial real estate. A number of regional experts believe that most issues will be resolved as the market becomes more mature.

Real estate plays a fundamental role in the country's non-oil economy. In 2016, the value of real estate transactions including sales of existing units amounted to $74.91 billion from October 15 to September 16. That is a major drop compared to the number of transactions recorded a decade earlier, which reached $239.93 billion. The real estate sector has been driven recently by strong local demand fundamentals and only a small amount by speculation.

Ownership of land property in Saudi Arabia is generally restricted to Saudis, but this is subject to certain qualifications. For example, Gulf Cooperation Council ('GCC') nationals and GCC companies have certain rights to own land, subject to a number of restrictions. Foreigners (being non-GCC nationals) are entitled to ownership and investment of in real estate with some conditions. A foreign company needs to have a foreign investment licence from the Saudi Arabian General Investment Authority ('SAGIA') and the owned real estate must be related to particular investment project for property development. Where a foreign individual needs to have a normal legal residency status and a permit from the Ministry of the Interior to own a land or property.

The major expansion in this sector attracted the top real estate consultancies such as Jones Lang LaSalle, Knight Frank and Cluttons to the country who have now opened offices in the country. Beyond this, demand for professional real estate services is attracting regional educators such as DREI to provide courses on Saudi real estate, and even dedicated books focused on the market such as Saudi Real Estate Companion.

Real Estate plays an important role in the Saudi Vision 2030 which maps out significant commitments by the Saudi Government relating to housing and the development of land for a variety of uses. In particular, Vision 2030 states: 'Where it exists in strategic locations, we will also capitalize on the government's reserves of real estate. We will allocate prime areas within cities for educational institutions, retail, and entertainment centres, large areas along our coasts will be dedicated to tourist projects and appropriate lands will be allocated for industrial projects.

In 2016, new rules were introduced by the Capital Market Authority to form REITs. This aims at opening the real estate market to a wide range of investor. The REITs consist of units representing the ownership of the underlying real estate. These units are offered to the public and traded on the Saudi Stock Exchange.

The introduction of REITs was a part of the National Transformation program, one of the Saudi Arabia's Vision 2030 programs, and has targets of

- Increasing the real estate sector contribution from GDP five per cent to 10 per cent annually.
- Supporting the construction of 1.5 million homes by providing the required private capital.
- Establishing partnerships with private sector developers to develop government land for housing projects.
- Establishing fast-track licenses and special finance packages to encourage private sector investment in housing projects.

Private sector

Saudi Arabia's private sector is dominated by a handful of big businesses in the service sector, primarily in construction and real estate— Olayan, Zamil, Almarai, Mobily, STC, SABIC, Sadara, Halliburton, Baker Hughes, Flynas, Hilton, Zain, Yanbu Cement, Alhokair, MBC, Mahfouz, Al Rajhi and Alfanar. These firms are "heavily dependent on government spending", which is dependent on oil revenues.

From 2003–2013, "several key services" were privatized—municipal water supply, electricity, telecommunications—and parts of education and health care, traffic control and car accident reporting were also privatized. According to Arab News columnist Abdel Aziz Aluwaisheg, "in almost every one of these areas, consumers have raised serious concerns about the performance of these privatized entities."

To provide the best support for the private sector and entrepreneurs, The Kingdom announced a decision approved by the Saudi Cabinet, In July 2019, allowing businesses in the country to be given the option to remain open 24 hours a day.

Trade

In recent years, Saudi Arabia sought to join the World Trade Organization. Negotiations have focused on the degree to which Saudi Arabia is willing to increase market access to foreign goods and services and the timeframe for becoming fully compliant with World Trade Organization obligations.

In April 2000, the government established the Saudi Arabian General Investment Authority to encourage foreign direct investment in Saudi Arabia. Saudi Arabia maintains a negative list of sectors in which foreign investment is prohibited, but the government plans to open some closed sectors such as telecommunications, insurance, and power transmission/distribution over time. As of November 2005, Saudi Arabia was officially approved to enter World Trade Organization. Saudi Arabia became a full WTO Member on 11 December 2005. In 2019, the government established the General Authority for Foreign Trade to enhance the kingdom's international commercial and investment activities.

List of trade organizations

World Trade Organization (WTO)

- International Monetary Fund (IMF)
- International Chamber of Commerce (ICC)
- International Organization for Standardization (IOS)
- World Customs Organization (WCO)
- Gulf Cooperation Council (GCC)

Challenges

Among the challenges to Saudi economy include halting or reversing the decline in per capita income, improving education to prepare youth for the workforce and providing them with employment, diversifying the economy, stimulating the private sector and housing construction, diminishing corruption and inequality. In answer to the question of why the Saudi economy is so dependent on foreign labor, the UN Arab Human Development Report blamed stunted social and economic development inhibited by lack of personal freedom, poor education and government hiring based on factors other than merit, and exclusion of women.

Income drop

Despite possessing the largest petroleum reserves in the world, per capita income dropped from approximately $18,000 at the height of the oil boom (1981) to $7,000 in 2001, according to one estimate. As of 2013, due to the rapid population growth of Saudi Arabia, per capita income in Saudi was "a fraction of that of smaller Persian Gulf neighbors", even less than petroleum-poor Bahrain.

Unlike most developed countries where gross domestic product growth is a function of increases in productivity and inputs such as employment, in Saudi the fluctuation of oil prices is the most important factor in the growth or decline of domestic production. "Saudi reserves are steadily being depleted, and no significant new discoveries have been found to replace them," according to Middle East journalist Karen House. Saudi population grew sevenfold from 1960 to 2010, and petrol prices are subsidized and cost users less than equivalent quantities of bottled water. With production stagnant, growth in population and domestic energy consumption means a decline in per capita income unless oil prices rise to match that growth.

Demographics

Saudi population is young. About 51% are under the age of 25 (as of Feb 2012). According to a 2013 report by the International Monetary Fund, up to 1.6 million young nationals of the Persian Gulf countries (of which Saudi Arabia is the largest) will enter the workforce from 2013 to 2018, but the economies of those countries will have jobs in the private sector for less than half (approximately 600,000).

Education

According to *theHYPERLINK "https://en.wikipedia.org/wiki/The_Economist" Economist* magazine, the Saudi government has attempted in years past to raise employment by forcing "companies to fill at least 30% of their positions" with Saudi citizens. However, "employers complained bitterly about the lack of skills among young locals; years of rote-learning and religious instruction fail to prepare them for the job market." As a consequence, "the quota has now been dropped and replaced with a more flexible system."

According to another source (scholar David Commins), the kingdom depends "on huge numbers of expatriates workers to fill technical and administrative positions" in part because of an educational system that in spite of "generous budgets", has suffered from "poorly trained teachers, low retention rates, lack of rigorous standards, weak scientific and technical instruction and excessive attention to religious subjects".

Another statistic conducted by Bayt.com shows that over a quarter (28%) of professionals believe that there is a skills shortage in their country of residence. This belief is more prominent among respondents in Saudi Arabia (39%).

Innovation

Saudi has not been a hotbed of technological innovation. The number of Saudi patents registered in the United States between 1977 and 2010 came to 382—less than twelve per year—compared to 84,840 patents for South

Korea or 20,620 for Israel during that period. However, in 2017 Saudi Arabia was granted 664 patents by the United States Patent and Trademark Office (USPTO) ranking the 23rd among 92 countries. The number of granted patents was double that of all Arab countries combined during the same period. Saudi hopes to increase technological innovation, particularly with the King Abdullah University of Science and Technology, and thus to stimulate the economy.

Legal system

Saudi Arabia's legal system is based on Shariah (Islamic law), which comes from interpretations from the Quran and the Sunnah.

The author of a book on the Saudi legal system (Frank Vogel) bemoaned the "unpredictability of decisions; obscure if not occult doctrine; dissonance between many Saudi commercial norms and those prevailing nearly everywhere else ... huge costs on the Saudi economy. That the king and government have not been inclined, or able, to impose a solution to this widely known difficulty is an apt measure of the cultural and political influence of fiqh and ulama and of the centrality of the shari'a ideal for Saudi life public and private."

Bureaucracy

A business journalist (Karen House) criticizing the Saudi bureaucracy complained that someone seeking to start a business in Saudi Arabia has to complete innumerable applications and documents at multiple layers of multiple ministries, which invariably requires seeking favors from various patronage networks and accumulating obligations along the way, most probably including having to hire less-than-competent dependents of his patrons. Then, for any business of any size, government contracts, not private competition, are the financial lifeblood. So this means more patrons, more favors, and more obligations. Not surprisingly, Saudi businesses that can compete outside the protected Saudi market are few.

Corruption

The cost of maintaining the Royal Family is estimated by some to be about US$10 billion per year. A 2005 survey by the Riyadh Chamber of Commerce found 77% of businessmen polled felt they had to 'bypass' the law to conduct their operations. Since then "businessmen say it has only gotten worse."

Saudi Arabia has been severely criticized for failing to tackle money laundering and international terrorism financing. A report released by the Financial Action Task Force on 24 September 2018, says, "Saudi Arabia is not effectively investigating and prosecuting individuals involved in larger scale or professional [money laundering] activity" and is "not effectively confiscating the proceeds of crime".

Poverty

Estimates of the number of Saudis below the poverty line range from between 12.7% and 25%. Press reports and private estimates as of 2013 "suggest that between 2 million and 4 million" of the country's native Saudis live on "less than about $530 a month" – about $17 a day – considered the poverty line in Saudi Arabia.

The Saudi state discourages calling attention to or complaining about poverty. In December 2011, days after the Arab Spring uprisings, the Saudi interior ministry detained reporter Feros Boqna and two colleagues (Hussam al-Drewesh and Khaled al-Rasheed) and held them for almost two weeks for questioning after they uploaded a 10-minute video on the topic (*Mal3ob 3alena*, or 'We are being cheated') to YouTube. Authors of the video claim that 22% of Saudis are considered to be poor (2009) and 70% of Saudis do not own their houses. Statistics on the issue are not available through the UN resources because the Saudi government does not issue poverty figures. Observers researching the issue prefer to stay anonymous because of the risk of being arrested, like Feras Boqna.

Housing

50% of Saudi Arabia's citizens own their own home, compared to the international average rate of 70% ownership, even though, it is beneath the international average, but it raised from 30% in 2011 according to the most recent census results. In 2011, analysts estimated 500,000 new homes/year were needed to match the growth in Saudi population, but as of early 2014 only 300,000 to 400,000 houses/year were being built.

One problem is that the government Real Estate Development Fund (REDF)—which provides 81% of all loans for housing—had an 18-year waiting list for loans due to pent-up demand. Another is that the REDF's maximum loan is 500,000 SR ($133,000), while in 2012 the average price for a small free-standing home in Riyadh is more than double that—1.23 million SR ($328,000). However, as a part of the economic reforms that has been undertaken by the government to enhance the living standards within the country, new funding solutions have been established to boost the mortgages for existing and new borrowers in order to help financing their housing plans. This was announced in August 2018 by the minister of Housing Mr. Majed Al-Hogail.

A major reason for the high cost of housing is the high cost of land. In urban areas the price of land has been bid up because nearly all of it is owned by the Saudi elite (members of the royal family or other wealthy Saudis), who have lobbied the government for land "giveaways". Landlords have seen prices rocket by 50% from 2011 to 2013. The owners benefit from these price increases as they hold the land for future development. To deal with the key "land banking" issue the Housing Minister suggested in 2013 that landowners of vacant within city limits could be subject to a tax. However, no firm plans for any tax have been unveiled.

Further diversification

According to journalist Karen House, "every" Saudi five-year plan "since the first one in 1970" has called for diversifying the economy beyond oil, but with marginal success.

As of 2007, manufacturing outside of the petroleum industry contributed 10% to Saudi Arabian GDP and less than 6% of total employment.

Private Sector Growth

In 2018, an imposition of 5% value-added tax brought the private-sector growth to a halt. Consumer spending was also restrained after a sharp increase in prices for energy, electricity and water earlier in 2018. The kingdom witnessed a mass departure of around 750,000 foreign workers after imposing new government levies on expat workers. The government is also forcing small-business owners to hire Saudi nationals at comparatively higher wages than the foreign workers. Gaining money from large foreign direct investments is also not working in the favor of the government. Rich Saudis are reluctant to invest within the kingdom due to the fear of triggering government scrutiny.

Investment

Saudi Arabia has two stock exchanges, the Tadawul and The Saudi Parallel Market (Nomu) whose financial markets are regulated by the Capital Market Authority. The stock market HYPERLINK "https://en.wikipedia.org/wiki/Market_capitalisation"capitalization of listed companies in Saudi Arabia was valued at $646 billion in 2005 by the World Bank. According to the International Institute for Management Development (IMD), Business competitiveness in Saudi Arabia has witnessed an improvement better than any other country in the world as the Kingdom has jumped to 26th in the world with respect Business competitiveness.

Doing business

Saudi Arabia is among the countries with the most notable improvement in doing business according to the World Bank Group's Doing Business 2020 report. The country jumped 30 places to rank 62nd in ease of doing business compared to the last year.

According to the World Bank, Saudi Arabia has conducted several reforms. These reforms have been made in eight business areas which are: starting a business, getting construction permits, getting electricity, getting credit, protecting minority investors, trading across borders, enforcing contracts, and resolving insolvency.

Previously, the country rated as the 92nd for ease of doing business, according to the World Bank in its annual "Doing Business" report issued for 2018. Since 2013, the Kingdom has declined in the overall Doing Business rankings, from 22nd to 92nd.

Saudi Arabian companies dominate 2009's "MEED 100", with companies listed on the Tadawul, accounting for 29 out of the region's 100 biggest publicly quoted companies ranked by market capitalization. Just three of the 20 companies that have dropped out of the top 100 over the past year are listed on the Saudi stock exchange.

Foreigners are allowed to wholly own limited liability companies in the majority of industries. Non-Saudi nationals are required to obtain a foreign capital investment license from the Saudi Arabian General Investment Authority (SAGIA).

With a total of 291 foreign investor licenses were issued in the second quarter of 2019, the Kingdom has witnessed an increase in international investment, reflecting the economic reforms under the Saudi Vision 2030. Obtaining a foreign investor license became more straightforward as it requires only two documents, and it is processed in three hours.

Companies

Saudi ARAMCO

Saudi Aramco (officially the Saudi Arabian Oil Co.), is a Saudi Arabian national petroleum and natural gas company based in Dhahran, Saudi Arabia. Saudi Aramco has been listed for public trading on 10th December 2019 and has a valuation as of US$2 trillion as of 12th December 2019.

Saudi Aramco has both the largest proven crude oil reserves, which it claims to be more than 260 billion barrels (4.1×10^{10} m^3), and largest daily oil production. Headquartered in Dhahran, Saudi Arabia, Saudi Aramco operates the world's largest single hydrocarbon network, the Master Gas System. Its yearly production is 3.479 billion barrels (553,100,000 m), and it managed over 100 oil and gas fields in Saudi Arabia, including 284.8 trillion standard cubic feet (SCF) of natural gas reserves. Saudi Aramco owns the Ghawar Field, the world's largest oil field, and the Shaybah Field, another one of the world's largest oil fields.

SABIC

The Saudi Arabian Basic Industries Corporation SABIC was established by a royal decree in 1976 to produce chemicals, polymers, and fertilizers. In 2008, SABIC was Asia's largest (in terms of market capitalization) and most profitable publicly listed non-oil company, the world's fourth-largest petrochemical company, ranked 186th as world's largest corporation on the Fortune Global 500 for 2009, the second largest producer of ethylene glycol and methanol in the world, the third largest producer of polyethylene and overall the fourth-largest producer of polypropylene and polyolefin. Standard HYPERLINK "https://en.wikipedia.org/wiki/Standard_%26_Poor%27s"&HYPERLINK "https://en.wikipedia.org/wiki/Standard_%26_Poor%27s" Poor's and Fitch Ratings claimed SABIC to be the world's largest producer of polymers and the Persian Gulf region's largest steel producer for 2005 and assigned SABIC an "A" corporate credit rating. In 2008, Fortune 500 ranking records SABIC revenues at $40.2 billion, profits at $5.8 billion and assets standing at $72.4 billion.

Ma'aden (company)

Ma'aden was formed as a Saudi Joint Stock Company on 23 March 1997 for the purpose of facilitating the development of Saudi Arabia's mineral resources. Ma'aden's activities have focused on its active gold business which has grown in recent years to include the operation of five gold mines: Mahd Ad Dahab, Al Hajar, Sukhaybarat, Bulghah, and Al Amar. Ma'aden is now expanding its activities beyond its gold business with the development of phosphates, aluminum, and other projects. In addition, since its formation, Ma'aden (through the Ministry of Petroleum and Mineral Resources) has collaborated with the government and local legislators to develop a regulatory framework for the governance of the mining industry.

ICT Services

Saudi Arabia is currently enjoying a massive boom in its personal computer industry since the deregulation of 2002. PC per capita has exploded to nearly 43% of the population in 2005 from just 13% in 2002 leapfrogging over the rest of West Asia. The electrical and electronic market was estimated to be around $3.5 billion in 2004.

The Saudi ICT sector has grown significantly over the last decade and is still showing strong growth. In 2012, ICT sector spending was recorded at SAR 94 billion, with 13.9% annual growth, and reached approximately SAR 102 billion in 2013, with approximately 14% annual growth.

The e-commerce market was estimated at just over $1 billion in 2001.

Critical Observation of the present status of Economy of Saudi Arabia

- The economy of the Saudi Arabia is one of the top twenty economies in the world. It is dependent on oil as country has second largest proven petroleum reserves, and the country is the largest exporter of petroleum in the world. Natural gas reserves are fifth largest in the world. Saudi is considered "energy Superpower" with a total worth of $33.2 trillion. Saudi has the second most valuable natural resources in the world.
- The country has diversified in 2015 Saudi vision 2030 in cement, construction, fertilizers and aircraft repairs, ship repairs, plastic and metal.
- Saudi has 260 billion barrels, one fourth of the world's oil reserves. Saudi is not only plentiful but under pressure and close to the earth's surface. This makes it far cheaper and more profitable to extract petroleum in Saudi than in many countries. Petroleum sector accounts for roughly 87% of Saudi's budget resource, 90% of exports and 42% of GDP. Saudi's oil reserves and production are largely managed by the state owned corporation Saudi Aramco. Another 40% of GDP come from private sector. An estimated 7.5 million foreign workers work legally in Saudi, playing a crucial role in Saudi's economy. Government has encouraged private sector growth for many years to reduce the kingdom's dependence on oil and to increase the employment opportunities to the swelling Saudi population. It has permitted private sector and foreign investor participation in sectors such as power generation and telecom, and acceded to WTO.
- In 2000s, oil prices enabled the government to post budget surplus, both spending on job training, education, infrastructural development and government salaries.
- Saudi Arabia was a subsistence economy till 1930. In 1933, Saudi government signed an oil Concession agreement with Standard Oil Company of California. Development of oil fields continued in Saudi Arabia, managed by Saudi Armco formed by partnership of Texaco and Chevron. Production was 50000 bpd in 1949 and raised to 1 million in 1954.
- Foreign ownership of business was allowed by mid-1980s. In mid-1990s, foreign ownership rules were relaxed with investment

sought in telecommunications, utilities and financial services. In 2000, 100% foreign owned businesses were allowed in the kingdom.

- In the Report of UNCTAD released in June 2018, Saudi's FDI was $ 1.4 billion only in 2017, down from $ 7.5 billion and in 2016, and $ 12.2 billion in 2012.
- Diversification from 1970s, fishing villages of Jubal on Persian Gulf and Yanbu on Red Sea were developed. Total length of paved highways tripled. Power generation increased by multiple of 28. Capacity of seaports grew tenfold.

  In third plan (1980-85), emphasis changed. There was less spending on infrastructure. Spending rose markedly on education, health and social services.

In forth plan (1985-90), infrastructure was completed but education and training remained area of concerns. Private enterprise was encouraged, foreign investment in the form of joint ventures with Saudi public and private companies were welcome. Private sector became more important rising to 70% of non-oil GDP by 1987. Private sector concentrated in trade and commerce. Private investment increased in agriculture, industry, banking and construction companies.

The main investing countries in Saudi in 2016 were USA, UAE, France, Singapore, Kuwait and Malaysia. They mainly invested in real estate, tourism, fossil fuels, automobiles and machinery. As a part of diversification, Refinery contracts with Chinese and other companies were made.

- Saudi announced plans to invest $47 billion in three of world's largest and most ambitious petrochemical projects: $27 billion Ras Tanura, and $90 billion Saudi Keyan, $10 billion Petro Rabigh. 150000 technicians and engineers will be appointed.
- Saudi Arabia became a member of WTO in 2005. Environment of foreign investment in Saudi Arabia improved due to stable economy, high power of expenditure, good infrastructure, good reinforced finance and banking system.
- In 2008, two-third workers employed in Saudi were foreigners. Private sector employed 90% of expatriates. This was lowered by compelling private sector to double the Saudi nationals to 1.5 million. (10 million foreign workers were working in Saudi). Economists estimate only 30-40 percent of working age Saudis hold jobs or actively seek work although official unemployment rate was around 12%. Most Saudis with jobs are employed in

government. IMF warned no support for such government large bill in the long term. Foreign workforce and employment grew. Heavy fee on expatriate resulted in 677000 foreigners leaving the jobs. Employment rose to 12.9%.

- Real estate plays a fundamental role in the country's non-oil economy. In 2016, value of real estate transactions including sale of existing units accounted to $74.91 billion from October 15 to September 16. In 2017, there was major drop. In earlier decade, it was $239.97billion. Ownership of land property is restricted to Saudis, Gulf Corporation Council nationals and companies have certain rights to own land. Foreigners are entitled to ownership with conditions.
- There are two handful of business i.e. construction and real estate.
- Saudi is willing to increase the access to foreign goods and services within the specific time frame.
- Halting or reversing the decline in capital incom, improving education to prepare youth for work force, providing them employment, diversifying the economy, stimulating private sector and housing construction, diminishing corruption and inequality are challenges before the Saudi government.
- The UN Arab Development Report blamed stunted social and economic development inhibited by the lack of personal freedom, poor education and government hiring based on factors other than merit, and exclusion of women.
- Income per capita dropped from $18000 in 1981 to $7000 in 2001 due to rapid growth of population during the period.
- Saudi population is young with 51% of population is under age of 25. Only 1.6 million nationals are employed. Private sector jobs are 600000 but only for expatriate from Persian Gulf. This will result in unrest among the Saudi nations. Government should give education to all nationals speedily to match with knowledge of jobs to avoid giving employment to expatriates from Egypt and South Asia.
- Saudi government forced the private sector employers to take 30% of the Saudi nationals in their employment. But these employers complained bitterly about lack of skills among young locals. Quota system was dropped and flexible system was introduced. Kingdom depends on huge numbers of expatriate workers to fill technical and administrative positions.

- The number of Saudi patents registered in USA between 1977 and 2010 came to 382 – less than 12 per year compared to 84640 patents for South Korea. Saudi Arabia granted 664 patents by US Patents and Trademark office.
- Legal system is based on Shariah (Islamic law) which comes from interpretation from Quran and Sunnah.
- Number of applications are required to be made to get permission to start new business and favors required from many ministries.
- Cost of maintaining Royal family is estimated @ $10 billion per year. 77% of businessmen felt they had to "bypass" the law to conduct their operations. To tackle money laundering and interacts, the country is not sufficiently investigating and prosecuting individuals involved in money laundering for tourism financing.
- Population below poverty line is estimated between 2 million and 4 million of the country's natives live in less than about $530 per month and $17 per day –considered poverty in Saudi Arabia.
- 50% of Saudi Arabians own house. Government Real Estate Development Fund which provides 81% of all loans for housing has waiting list of 18 years for loans due to pent up demand. Maximum loan is offer at SR 500000-($133000-). High cost of land in urban area makes it difficult to buy a house at SR50000-
- 5% value added tax halted private sector growth. 75000 private enterprises left and departed.
- Rich Saudis are reluctant to invest due to inquiry.
- Stock Exchange capitalization is $646 billion in 2005.
- Saudi Arabian Basic Industries Corporation was established by a Royal Decree in 1976. To produce chemicals, polymers and fertilizers. It was Asia's profitable publicly listed non-oil company in 2008.
- Ma'aden was Saudi Stock Exchange Company formed on 23 March 1997, for the purpose of facilitating Saudi Arabia's mineral resources. Ma'aden activities have been focused on gold mines and it developed phosphates, aluminum and other mineral projects.
- PC per capita has exploded to nearly 43% of population in 2005 from just 13% in 2002. ICI is spending SAR 94 billion with 13.9% annual growth. Spending was SAR102 billion in 2013 with 14% growth. The e-commerce market was estimated over $1 billion in 2001.

- Currency: Saudi Riyal (SAR)
- Fiscal Year: Calendar year
- Trade Organizations: WTO, OPE, G-20 Major economies, BIS, ICS, IOS, WCO, and GCC
- Country Group: Developing/Emerging, high income economy
- Population 34.173 million (3.42 crores)
- GDP : $ 779.289 billion Nominal (2019) & $1.899 trillion PPP in 2018
- GDP growth: 0.7% in 2017, 2.4% in 2018, 0.4% in 2019 & 1.9% in 2020 Forecast
- GDP per capita: $ 22865 Nominal & $55704 PPP
- GDP by Sector: Agriculture 2.6%, Industry$$.2% and Services 53.2% in 2017
- Inflation 2.2%
- Labour Force: 13.8 million - 3.1 million Saudis(about 10% of Population), 10.7 million non-Saudis 52.4% employment rate in 2018
- Labour force by occupations: agriculture 5.7%, industries 21.4% and 72.9%
- Unemployment: 6% in 2017
- Main Industries: Crude oil products, petroleum refineries, petrochemical, ammonia, industrial gases, sodium hydroxide, cement, fertilizers, plastic, metal, ship repairs, aircraft repairs, construction, foodstuff
- Exports: $221.1 billion Imports; $119.3 billion Trade Surplus: $ 101.8 billion
- Current account: $119.3 billion in 2017
- Gross external debt: $205.1 billion in 2017
- Public debt: 17.2% of GDP
- Budget deficit: -8.9%
- Revenue $181 billion & Expenses 241.8 billion in 2017 Fiscal deficit:$60.8 billion i.e. &.80% of GDP high
- Foreign reserves: 500.588 billion
- Current rating: S & P‘s A- (Domestic & Foreign), A (T & C), Outlook: Stable Moody's A1 Outlook Stable. Fitch A+ outlook: Stable

- There are internal conflict between Royal family members especially Princesses about who will become the next king. Recently there was fierce fight internally and many ambitious princesses were locked in jail. They were then released on their agreement not to contest the King position.
- Royal family is not administrating the country properly. Why the country requires foreigners to work in its country. Why they cannot educate and train skill workers. Why only 50% of the Saudis own house when country is one of richest in the world. Why real estate is in the hands of Royal family. Why the prices of house cannot be brought down. Why there is population under poverty line of 20% and 40% as per the country's standards of poverty. These challenges should be addressed and resolved speedily by the country. Otherwise there will be unrest like Arab spring in the country.
- Saudi is unnecessarily involving in the internal affairs of many countries. Hothi in Yemen air attached with dropping missiles with the military assistance of Iran recently on the Oil refinery and oil storage tanks. It resulted in heavy losses to Saudi and has to stop exporting oil for some days. Saudi should divert its attention to the challenges before it as mentioned above and should not dominate other countries.
- Of late, it was reported that 15 Royal members are Corona virus patients.

3

Economy of Yemen

The economy of Yemen is under-developed and poorest in the world. At the time of unification, South and North Yemen were both had under-developed economy and vast difference which resulted in civil war between the Ruling Hathi rivals Hothi.

Saudi- Arabia and Kuwait have given large financial aid to Yemen. About more than million Yemen workers were employed by the Saudi-Arabia and Yemen used to get substantial amount of foreign remittances from Saudi –Arabia. In spite to this, Yemen supported Iraq in Gulf War, 1990. Saudi-Arabia, in retaliation, expelled about one million workers of Yemen. Saudi Arabia and Kuwait also reduced significantly financial aid they used to give to Yemen. This resulted in weakening and collapsing the Yemen economy.

Since the economy has scattered, people in the country were discontents. The difference between South Yemen and North Yemen also added fuel to the fire. This resulted in Conflict between Hathi and Hothi tribes and resulted in Civil War since 1994... Saudi Arabia supported ruling party Hathi and fought against Hothi continually. In this process, Saudi incurred heavy losses on oil refinery area in its country from Hothi soldiers. UAE and Sudan who were supporting Saudi Arabia have reduced their support on account of heavy losses by Hothi and Iran who is supporting Hothi.

In 2019, Saudi Arabia, Government of Yemen and UAE made agreement by which "Socotra Island" has been given to UAE for 95 years on rental basis. Even though, UAE has reduced its cooperation and support to fight Hothi against Hathi to Saudi Arabia, it has not abandoned its control over Socotra Island. US Marines provides Saudi Arabia and UAE military support for fighting Hothi soldiers in the form of Patriate missiles system. These missiles system has been set up in Socotra Island. It is reported that US wants to use Socotra Island as its military Base. In this field China and

Russia are speeding their military activities and US want them to control their activities in this region.

The economy of Yemen is one of the poorest and least-developed in the world. At the time of unification, South Yemen and North Yemen had vastly different but equally struggling underdeveloped economic systems. Since unification, the economy has been forced to sustain the consequences of Yemen's support for Iraq during the 1990–91 Persian Gulf War: Saudi Arabia expelled almost 1 million Yemeni workers, and both Saudi Arabia and Kuwait significantly reduced economic aid to Yemen. The 1994 civil war further drained Yemen's economy. As a consequence, for the past 24 years Yemen has relied heavily on aid from multilateral agencies to sustain its economy. In return, it has pledged to implement significant economic reforms. In 1997 the International Monetary Fund (IMF) approved two programs to increase Yemen's credit significantly: the enhanced structural adjustment facility (now known as the poverty reduction and growth facility, or PRGF) and the extended funding facility (EFF). In the ensuing years, Yemen's government attempted to implement recommended reforms—reducing the civil service payroll, eliminating diesel and other subsidies, lowering defense spending, introducing a general sales tax, and privatizing state-run industries. However, limited progress led the IMF to suspend funding between 1999 and 2001.

In late 2005, the World Bank, which had extended Yemen a four-year US$2.3 billion economic support package in October 2002 together with other bilateral and multilateral lenders, announced that as a consequence of Yemen's failure to implement significant reforms it would reduce financial aid by one-third over the period July 2005 through July 2008. A key component of the US$2.3 billion package—US$300 million in concessional financing—has been withheld pending renewal of Yemen's PRGF with the IMF, which is currently under negotiation. However, in May 2006 the World Bank adopted an assistance strategy for Yemen under which it will provide approximately US$400 million in International Development Association (IDA) credits over the period FY 2006 to FY 2009. In November 2006, at a meeting of Yemen's development partners, a total of US$4.7 billion in grants and concessional loans was pledged for the period 2007–10. At present, despite possessing significant oil and gas resources and a considerable amount of agriculturally productive land, Yemen remains one of the poorest of the world's low-income countries; more than 80 percent (2018) of the population lives in poverty. The influx of an average 1,000 Somali refugees per month into Yemen looking for work is an added drain on the economy, which already must cope with a 20 to 40 percent rate of unemployment. Yemen remains under significant pressure to implement economic reforms or face the loss of badly needed international financial support.

In the north, disruptions of Civil War (1962–1970) and frequent periods of drought had dealt severe blows to a previously prosperous agricultural sector. Coffee production, formerly the north's main export and principal form of foreign exchange, declined as the cultivation of khat increased. Low domestic industrial output and a lack of raw materials made the Yemeni Arab Republic dependent on a wide variety of imports.

Black market fuel for sale in Sanaa during the ongoing civil war.

The Yemeni Civil War and air bombing campaign by the coalition during the Saudi-led intervention have devastated the Yemeni economy further.

As a result of Civil War, Yemen is suffering from inflation and devaluation of Yemeni HYPERLINK "https://en.wikipedia.org/wiki/Yemeni_rial"riHYPERLINK "https://en.wikipedia.org/wiki/Yemeni_rial" yaHYPERLINK "https://en.wikipedia.org/wiki/Yemeni_rial"l, and Yemen's economy contracted by 50% from the start of the civil war in 19 March 2015 to October 2018.

Macro-economic trend

This is a chart of trend of gross domestic product of Yemen (since unification) at market prices estimated by the International Monetary Fund with figures in millions of Yemeni riyals.

Year	*Gross domestic product*	*US dollar exchange*	*Inflation index (2000=100)*
1989	125,562	11.70 Yemeni Riyals	5.10
1995	516,643	40.49 Yemeni Riyals	51
2000	1,539,386	161.00 Yemeni Rials	100
2005	2,907,636	191.37 Yemeni Rials	175

For purchasing power parity comparisons, the US Dollar is exchanged at 150.11 Yemeni Rials only. Mean wages were $1.06 per man-hour in 2009.

Remittances from Yemenis working abroad and foreign aid paid for perennial trade deficits. Substantial Yemeni communities exist in many countries of the world, including Yemen's immediate neighbors on the Arabian Peninsula, Indonesia, India, East Africa, the United Kingdom, and the United States. Beginning in the mid-1950s, the Soviet Union and People's Republic of China provided large-scale assistance to the YAR. This aid included funding of substantial construction projects, scholarships, and considerable military assistance.

Integration issues

In the south, pre-independence economic activity was overwhelmingly concentrated in the port city of Aden. The seaborne transit trade, which the port relied upon, collapsed with the closure of the Suez Canal and Britain's withdrawal from Aden in 1967. Only extensive Soviet aid, remittances from south Yemenis working abroad, and revenues from the Aden refinery (built in the 1950s) kept the PDRY's centrally planned Marxist economy afloat. With the dissolution of the Soviet Union and a cessation of Soviet aid, the south's economy basically collapsed.

Since unification, the government has worked to integrate two relatively disparate economic systems. However, severe shocks, including the return in 1990 of approximately 850,000 Yemenis from the Persian Gulf states, a subsequent major reduction of aid flows, and internal political disputes culminating in the 1994 civil war, hampered economic growth.

Industries

Agriculture and fishing

Agriculture is the mainstay of Yemen's economy, generating more than 20 percent of Gross Domestic Product (GDP) since 1990 (20.4 percent in 2005 according to the Central Bank of Yemen) and employing more than half (54.2 percent in 2003) of the working population. However, a U.S. government estimate suggests that the sector accounted for only 13.5 percent of GDP in 2005. Numerous environmental problems hamper growth in this sector—soil erosion, sand dune encroachment, and deforestation—but the greatest problem by far is the scarcity of water. As a result of low levels of rainfall, agriculture in Yemen relies heavily on the extraction of groundwater, a resource that is being depleted. Yemen's water tables are falling by approximately two meters a year, and it is estimated that Sanaa's groundwater supplies could be exhausted by 2008. The use of irrigation has made fruit and vegetables Yemen's primary cash crops. With the rise in the output of irrigated crops, the production of traditional rain-fed crops such as cereals has declined. According to the Central Bank of Yemen, in 2005 the production of khat, a mildly narcotic and heavily cultivated plant that produces natural stimulants when its leaves are chewed, rose 6.7 percent and accounted for 5.8 percent of GDP; its usage in Yemen is widespread. According to the World Bank and other economists, cultivation of this plant plays a dominant role in Yemen's agricultural economy, constituting 10 percent of GDP and employing an estimated 150,000 persons while consuming an estimated 30 percent of irrigation water and displacing land areas that could otherwise be used for exportable coffee, fruits, and vegetables.

Although Yemen's extensive territorial waters and marine resources have the potential to produce 840,000 tons of fish each year, the fishing industry is relatively underdeveloped and consists largely of individual fishermen in small boats. In recent years, the government has lifted restrictions on fish exports, and production has reached one-quarter of capacity, yielding revenues valued at US$260 million in 2005. Fish and fish products constitute only 1.7 percent of Yemen's GDP but are the second largest export. In December 2005, the World Bank approved a US$25 million credit for a Fisheries Management and Conservation Project to be launched in all coastal governorates along the Red Sea and the Gulf of Aden. This project is expected to improve fish landing and auction facilities, provide ice plants for fish preservation, and enable Yemen's Ministry of Fisheries to undertake more effective research, resource management planning, and regulatory activities.

Oil & Gas

Yemen is a small oil producer and does not belong to the Organization of the Petroleum Exporting Countries (OPEC).

Unlike many regional oil producers, Yemen relies heavily on foreign oil companies that have production-sharing agreements with the government. Income from oil production constitutes 70 to 75 percent of government revenue and about 90 percent of exports. Yemen contains proven crude oil reserves of more than 4 billion barrels (640,000,000 m), although these reserves are not expected to last more than 9 years, and output from the country's older fields is falling, a concern since oil provides around 90% of the country's exports. The World Bank predicts that Yemen's oil and gas revenues will plummet during 2009 and 2010, and fall to zero by 2017 as supplies run out, and UK's Royal Institute for International Affairs warns that instability there could expand a zone of lawlessness from northern Kenya to Saudi Arabia, while describing Yemen's democracy as "fragile" and pointing to armed conflicts with Islamists and tribal insurgents. Thus western and other diplomats and leaders are concerned to preserve Yemen's stability and to avert adverse outcomes. According to statistics published by the Energy Information Administration, crude oil output averaged 413,300 barrels per day (65,710 m^3/d) in 2005, a reduction from 423,700 bbl/d (67,360 m^3/d) in 2004. For the first eight months of 2006, crude oil output was flat, averaging 412,500 bbl/d (65,580 m^3/d).

Following a minor discovery in 1982 in the south, an American company found an oil basin near Ma'rib in 1984. A total of 27,000 m^3 (170,000 barrels) of oil per day were produced there in 1995. A small oil refinery began operations near Ma'rib in 1986. A Soviet discovery in the southern governorate of Shabwah has proven only marginally successful even when taken over by a different group. A Western consortium began exporting oil from Masila in the Hadhramaut in 1993, and production there reached 67,000 m^3 (420,000 barrels) per day in 1999. More than a dozen other companies have been unsuccessful in finding commercial quantities of oil. There are new finds in the Jannah (formerly known as the Joint Oil Exploration Area) and east Shabwah blocks. Yemen's oil exports in 1995 earned about US$1 billion.

Marib oil contains associated natural gas. In September 1995, the Yemeni Government signed an agreement that designated Total of France to be the lead company for a project for the export of Liquefied Natural Gas (LNG). In 1997, Yemen Gas Company joined with various privately held companies to establish Yemen LNG (YLNG). In August 2005 the government gave final approval to three LNG supply agreements, enabling YLNG to award a US$2 billion contract to an international consortium to build the country's first liquefaction plant at Balhat on the Arabian Sea coast. The project is a $3.7 billion investment over 25 years, producing approximately 6.7 million tons of LNG annually, with shipments likely to go to the United States and South Korea. Production of LNG began in October 2009. The Yemen government expects the LNG project to add US$350 million to its budget and enable it to develop a petrochemicals industry.

Industry and manufacturing

The U.S. government estimates that Yemen's industrial sector constitutes 47.2 percent of gross domestic product. Together with services, construction, and commerce, industry accounts for less than 25 percent of the labor force. The largest contributor to the manufacturing sector's output is oil refining, which generates roughly 40 percent of total revenue. The remainder of this sector consists of the production of consumer goods and construction materials. Manufacturing constituted approximately 9.5 percent of Yemen's gross domestic product in 2005. In 2000 Yemen had almost 34,000 industrial establishments with a total of slightly fewer than 115,000 workers; the majority of the establishments were small businesses (one to four employees). Almost half of all industrial establishments are involved in processing food products and beverages; the production of flour and cooking oil has increased in recent years. Approximately 10 percent of the establishments are classified as manufacturing mixed metal products such as water-storage tanks, doors, and windows.

Services and tourism

Economists have reported that Yemen's services sector constituted 51.7 percent of Gross Domestic Product (GDP) in 2002 and 52.2 percent of GDP in 2003. The U.S. government estimates that the services sector accounted for 39.7 percent of gross domestic product in 2004 and 39.3 percent in 2005.

Yemen's tourism industry is hampered by limited infrastructure as well as serious security concerns. The country's hotels and restaurants are below international standards, and air and road transportation is largely inadequate. Kidnappings of foreign tourists remain a threat, especially outside the main cities, and, coupled with terrorist bombings at the Port of Aden in 2000 and 2002, present a significant deterrent to tourism. As recently as September 2006, tribesmen in the Shabwa province, east of Sanaa, kidnapped four French tourists on their way to Aden. They were freed two weeks later. In October 2006, the U.S. Department of State reiterated previous warnings to U.S. citizens, strongly urging them to consider carefully the risks of traveling to Yemen. Britain's Foreign Office has issued a similar advisory. Recent statistics for tourist arrivals in Yemen are not available, but in 2004 the number rose to 274,000 from 155,000 in 2003.

Labor

According to the U.S. government, the agriculture and herding sector employs the majority of Yemen's working population (54.2 percent in 2003). Industry, together with services, construction, and commerce, accounts for less than 25 percent of the labor force.

According to the World Bank, Yemen's Civil Service is characterized by a large, poorly paid work force and inadequate salary differential between high and low skilled jobs to attract and retain qualified workers. In 2004 the government increased civil service salaries by 20 to 40 percent in order to alleviate the impact of anticipated economic reforms that were never implemented. The result was a 20 percent rise in wage costs; civil service wages constituted 7 percent of gross domestic product in 2004. The 2005 budget reduced economic subsidies but in exchange required the government to make various concessions, including increasing civil service wages another 10 to 15 percent by 2007 as part of a national wage strategy.

The economic assistance package the International Monetary Fund (IMF) pledged to Yemen is contingent on the implementation of civil service reform, which the government has resisted because of the country's estimated 20 to 40 percent unemployment rate. In 2004 the government claimed to have reduced the civil service labor force through retirements and layoffs, but it appears that the large salary increases have lessened the impact of any reforms. The IMF has stated that civil service salaries as a component of gross domestic product should be reduced 1 to 2 percent, a level that can only be achieved with continued reductions in the size of the civil service. It is unclear whether the national wage strategy, which may succeed in streamlining the system and removing irregularities, will in fact be able to reduce employment costs.

Currency, exchange rate, and inflation

Yemen's currency is the Yemeni Riyal (YR), which was floated on the open market in July 1996. Periodic intervention by the Central Bank of Yemen has enabled the riyal to gradually depreciate approximately 4 percent per year since 1999. It's valued averaged YR191.5 per US$1 in 2005, and has averaged YR197.5 in 2006. In late November 2006, the exchange rate was about YR198 per US$1.

During the years immediately following unification (1990–96), Yemen experienced a very high average rate of inflation—40 percent. Economic reforms brought this rate down to only 5.4 percent in 1997, but high oil prices and cuts in the fuel subsidy in recent years have had a negative impact on the inflation rate, which has generally been on the rise despite some fluctuations. In 2004 efforts by the Central Bank of Yemen to tighten the money supply were offset by a weakening US$, to which the Yemeni riyal is linked in a managed float, and by rising global commodity prices, resulting in an inflation rate of 12.5 percent. In July 2005, the government succumbed to public opposition and lowered the new general sales tax from 10 to 5 percent. This tax, coupled with reductions in government fuel subsidies and higher import prices, is expected to result in an estimated inflation rate of 15 percent in 2006, up from 11.8 percent in 2005.

Banking and finance

According to economists, Yemen's financial services sector is underdeveloped and dominated by the banking system. Yemen has no public stock exchange. The banking system consists of the Central Bank of Yemen, 15 commercial banks (nine private domestic banks, four of which are Islamic banks; four private foreign banks; and two state-owned banks), and two specialized state-owned development banks. The Central Bank of Yemen controls monetary policy and oversees the transfer of currencies abroad. It is the lender of last resort, exercises supervisory authority over commercial banks, and serves as a banker to the government. Since end 2005 and up to the end of 2010, Tadhamon International Islamic Bank has maintained the top spot between all banks in Yemen (Commercial and Islamic) in terms of total assets, capital and trade business. The largest commercial bank, the Credit and Agricultural Cooperative Bank, which is state-owned, and the Yemen Bank for Reconstruction and Development, which is majority state-owned, are currently being restructured with the goal of eventual privatization. Because of fiscal difficulties in both banks, in 2004 Yemen's government adopted a plan to merge them; the new publicly owned Development Bank will have a minimum capital of US$50 million. Till end April 2011 this step has yet to materialize.

The large volume of non-performing loans, low capitalization, and weak enforcement of regulatory standards hamper Yemen's banking sector as a whole. Numerous banks are technically insolvent. Because many debtors are in default, Yemen's banks limit their lending activities to a select group of consumers and businesses; as a result, the entire banking system holds less than 60 percent of the money supply. The bulk of the economy operates with cash. Legislation adopted in 2000 gave the Central Bank the authority to enforce tougher lending requirements, and in mid-2005 the Central Bank promulgated several new capital requirements for commercial banks aimed at curtailing currency speculation and protecting deposits.

Energy

Yemen's state-owned Public Electricity Corporation (PEC) operates an estimated 80 percent of the country's electricity generating capacity (810–900 megawatts) as well as the national power grid. Over the past 10 years, the government has considered various means of alleviating the country's significant electricity shortage, including restructuring the PEC, integrating the power sector through small-scale privatization of power stations, creating Independent Power Projects (IPPs), and introducing gas-generated power plants to free up oil supplies for export. However, because of inadequate infrastructure, large-scale IPPs and privatization proposals have failed to materialize, although several smaller-scale projects in Makala and Aden have been completed, and contracts have been signed for future projects. In 2004 Yemen's diesel-run power plants generated 4.1 billion kilowatt-hours of electricity, a level of production that is insufficient to maintain a consistent supply of electricity. Although demand for electricity increased 20 percent between 2000 and 2004, it is estimated that only 40 percent of the total population has access to electricity from the national power grid, and supply is intermittent. To meet this demand, the government plans to increase the country's power generating capacity to 1,400 megawatts by 2002.

Government budget

In 1995, in order to comply with conditions stipulated by the International Monetary Fund (IMF), Yemen began an economic reform program, one component of which is fiscal policy reform aimed at reducing deficits and expanding the revenue base. However, the government has failed to significantly reduce its primary expenditure—subsidies, especially the fuel subsidy. In January 2005, Yemen's parliament narrowly adopted a 2005 budget that forecast a reduced budget deficit of about 3 percent of gross domestic product (GDP). The budget was predicated on the adoption of a reform package that included a broad-based, 10 percent general sales tax (GST) and a 75 percent reduction in the fuel subsidy. Strong public opposition to these reforms led the government in July 2005 to defer the 10 percent GST for 18 months, adopting instead a hybrid 5 percent GST, and to modify the fuel subsidy reduction. Nonetheless, the cost of subsidies, primarily for fuel, rose dramatically (almost 90 percent) in 2005, accounting for the largest share (almost 25 percent) of total government expenditures and approximately 9 percent of GDP. These costs, coupled with a 24 percent increase in civil service wages and salaries and a 42 percent increase in defense spending, resulted in a government budget deficit of US$350.8 million, or more than 2 percent of GDP, in 2005. The government has budgeted a sharp (41 percent) rise in overall spending for 2006, which economists estimate will result in a fiscal deficit of US$800 million, or 4.2 percent of GDP.

Foreign economic relations

History and overview

During the 1990–91 Persian Gulf War, Yemen supported Iraq in its invasion of Kuwait, thereby alienating Saudi Arabia and Kuwait, which both had provided critical financial assistance to Yemen. In addition to withdrawing this aid, Saudi Arabia expelled almost 1 million Yemeni workers. The resultant fall in expatriate remittances had a disastrous impact on Yemen's governmental budget. The civil war of 1994 further drained the economy, and in 1995 Yemen sought the aid of multilateral agencies. In 1996 the International Monetary Fund (IMF) granted Yemen a US$190 million stand-by credit facility, and the following year it approved two funding facilities that increased the country's credit by approximately US$500 million. The funding was contingent on Yemen's adoption of stringent economic reforms, a requirement that the country had limited success in fulfilling. As a result, the IMF suspended lending to Yemen from late 1999 until February 2001. The extension of the two funding facilities, particularly the Poverty

Reduction and Growth Facility (PRGF), through October 2001 was again contingent on Yemen's commitment to economic reform. Because of Yemen's failure to comply sufficiently with the terms imposed by the IMF, since 2002 the IMF has withheld US$300 million in concessional financing. Discussions over the renewal of the PRGF are ongoing. In 2000 Kuwait and Saudi Arabia resumed financial aid to Yemen.

In October 2002, bilateral and multilateral lenders led by the World Bank agreed to give Yemen a four-year economic support package worth US$2.3 billion, 20 percent in grants and 80 percent in concessional loans. This funding is almost eight times the amount of financial support Yemen received under the IMF's PRGF. However, in December 2005 the World Bank announced that because of the government's continued inability to effect significant economic reforms and stem corruption, funding would be reduced by more than one-third, from US$420 million to US$240 million for the period July 2005 – July 2008. In May 2006, the World Bank adopted a new Country Assistance Strategy (CAS) for Yemen for the period FY 2006 to FY 2009, providing a blueprint for fostering the country's fiscal and human development improvement. The bank pledged to contribute approximately US$400 million in International Development Association (IDA) credits over the CAS time frame. At present, Yemen owes approximately US$264 million to Japan, one of its largest donors. In December 2005, the Japanese government pledged to write off US$17 million of the debt. That same month, Germany pledged to increase its annual aid to Yemen to US$83.6 million over the next two years; funding will go primarily to education and water improvement projects. In November 2006, the United Kingdom announced that aid to Yemen would increase 400 percent, to US$222 million through 2011.

Yemen is a member of the Arab Fund for Economic and Social Development, which since 1974 has contributed to the financing of economic and social development in Arab states and countries through loans and guarantees. In March 2004, the Arab League provided US$136 million to Yemen to finance infrastructure improvements. At a mid-November 2006 meeting in London, a group of bilateral and multilateral donors pledged US$4.7 billion over four years (2007–10) to fund economic development in Yemen. The goal of the meeting, which was jointly chaired by the World Bank and the government of Yemen, was to provide sufficient economic aid to Yemen to enable it to qualify for future Gulf Cooperation Council (GCC) membership. More than 55 percent of the aid, which is primarily in the form of grants, will come from the GCC. Yemen was granted observer status at the World Trade Organization (WTO) in 1999, and its application for full membership was under negotiation as of December 2006.

Foreign trade

Imports totaled an estimated US$4.7 billion in 2005 and are projected to increase to US$5 billion in 2006 and to US$5.4 billion in 2007. Yemen is a net importer of all major categories of products except fuels. Principal imports are machinery and transport equipment, food and livestock, and processed materials. According to the United Nations, Yemen imports more than 75 percent of its main dietary staple—wheat. The principal source of Yemen's imports in 2005 was the United Arab Emirates (13.4 percent of total imports); the bulk of these imports are actually re-exports from the United States and Kuwait. Yemen received 10.6 percent of its total imports from Saudi Arabia and 9 percent from China.

In 2005 Yemen's exports totaled US$6.4 billion. Exports are expected to increase to reach a record US$8.6 billion in 2006 as a result of strong oil revenues. Petroleum is Yemen's main export, accounting for 92 percent of total exports in 2004 and 87 percent in 2005. Yemen's non-oil exports are primarily agricultural products, mainly fish and fish products, vegetables, and fruits. In 2005 Asia was the most important market for Yemen's exports, primarily China (37.3 percent of total exports), Thailand, and Japan. Chile was also a primary export market (19.6 percent of total exports).

Yemen's import and export values have increased and decreased dramatically in the past 10 years owing to shifts in global oil prices. As a result, the country's trade balance has fluctuated significantly from a deficit of almost US$800 million in 1998 to a surplus of US$1 billion in 2000. Rising oil prices resulted in a surplus of US$817 million in 2004 and a surplus of US$1.7 billion in 2005.

In recent years, Yemen has reported increasing non-merchandise deficits. These deficits have, however, been offset by record export earnings, which have resulted in large enough trade surpluses to keep the current account in surplus—US$175.7 million in 2003, US$524.6 million in 2004, and US$633.1 million (about 4 percent of gross domestic product) in 2005.

External debt

In 1990 the newly unified Republic of Yemen inherited an unsustainable debt burden amounting to roughly 106 percent of gross domestic product. Debt rescheduling by the Paris Club creditor countries in the 1990s coupled with assistance from the World Bank's International Development Agency resulted in a drop in Yemen's debt stock to US$5.4 billion (an estimated 39 percent of gross domestic product) by year-end 2004. According to the Central Bank of Yemen, Yemen's debt stock was US$5.2 billion (an estimated 33 percent of gross domestic product) by year-end 2005.

According to the U.S. government, Yemen's reserves of foreign exchange and gold were US$6.1 billion in 2005.

Foreign investment

Yemen does not have a stock exchange (Though it does have plans that have been ruined by the on-going war), therefore limiting inward portfolio investment. Portfolio investment abroad is also very limited, with the result that portfolio flows are largely unrecorded by authorities. In the early 1990s, net direct investment was at its peak as foreign investors tapped Yemeni oil reserves, but since 1995 net direct investment flows have been negative because cost recovery for foreign oil companies has exceeded new direct investment. A five-year US$3 billion Liquid Natural Gas (LNG) construction project involving a consortium of foreign companies is planned following government approval in August 2005. Such a project raises the prospect of increased foreign investment in the future as LNG facilities are built.

Critical Observations of present status of economy of Yemen

(1) The Economic of Yemen is one of the poorest and least developed in the world.

(2) South Yemen and North Yemen were two parts which were vastly different but both were equally struggling underdeveloped economic systems. South and North Yemen were unified in 1990. This led to civil war between ruling party Hathi and Hothi, an opposition party which still exists. Hathi has been supported by US, EU, Saudi Arabia and UAE. Hothi is mainly supported actively by Iran. Recently Iran in the name of Hothi air attacked with missiles in Saudi Arabia which resulted in tremendous loss to Saudi Arabia crude oil tankers. UAE and Sudan reduced their support to Saudi Arabia after the loss.

(3) In 2019, there was an Agreement between Yemen government, Saudi Arabia and UAE in which Yemen's Socotra Island has been given to UAE for 95 years on rent. Though UAE has reduced its support to Saudi Arabia recently, it has not left its occupation of Socotra Island. US Marines has provided the Patriot missile system in this Island. It is reported that US Marines want to set up Military Base in Socotra Island to control the increasing military activities of Russia and China in this region.

(4) Unified Yemen unnecessary supported Iraq in the Persian Gulf War. This resulted in Saudi Arabia expelling 1 million employees of Yemen working in Saudi Arabia. Kuwait and Saudi Arabia were granting significant economic aids to Yemen which was

substantially reduced. This made the Yemen's economy scattered and vulnerable. Conflict between ruling Hathi and Opposite Hothi further weakened the Yemen economy.

(5) In 1997, IMF approved two programs to increase Yemen's credit significantly, the enhanced structural adjustment facility (now known as the poverty reduction and growth facility PRGF) and Extended Funding Facility (EFF). In the ensuing years, Yemen's government attempted to implement recommended reforms – reducing the civil service payroll, eliminating diesel and other subsidies, lowering defence spending, introducing a general sale tax, and privatizing state-run industries. However, limited progress led the IMF to suspend funding between 1999 and 2001.

(6) In late 2000s, the World Bank which had extended Yemen a four year $2.3 billion economic support package in October 2002 together with other bilateral and multilateral lenders out of which 20% was Grants and 80% commercial loans. World Bank announced that as a consequences of Yemen's failure to implement significant reforms, it would reduce financial aid by third over the period of July 2005 through July 2008. A key component of the of the $2.3 billion package- $230 million in concessional financing – has been withheld pending renewal of PRGF with IMF, which is currently under negotiation. However, in 2006, the World Bank adopted an assistance strategy for Yemen under which it will provide approximately $400 million in International Development Agency (IDA) credit over the period FY 2006 to FY 2009. In November 2006, at a Meeting of Yemen's Development Partners, a total of $4.7 billion in Grants and concessional loans were pleaded for the period of 2007-10. But in spite of significant oil and gas resources and considerably agricultural productive land, Yemen remained the one of the poorest of the world's low income countries. At present Yemen owes $264 million to Japan. Japan wrote off $17 million in 2005. German granted aid $83.6million over next two years for education and water improvement projects. UK announced aid $222 million through 2011. Arab League provided $136 million to Yemen to improve infrastructure. Bilateral and Multilateral donors pledged $4.7 billion over 2007-2010 to fund economic development in Yemen.

(7) The influx of an average 1000 Somali refugees per month into Yemen looking for work I an added drain on the economy. Yemen is under unemployment level of 20% to 40%. Yemen is under

constant pressure to implement economic reforms or face the loss of badly needed international financial support.

(8) Continuous disruption on account of Civil War and frequently draught had several blows for previously prosperous agricultural sector. Coffee production which was significant share of foreign exchange declined as the cultivation of khat increased. Low domestic industrial output and a lack of new materials made the Yemeni Arab Republic dependent on wide variety of imports.

(9) Yemen Civil War and air bombing campaign by the coalition during the Saudi-led intervention has devastated the Yemeni economy further. Yemen is suffering from inflation and devaluation of Yemen Riyal, and Yemen's economy contracted by 50% from the start of Civil war in 19-03-2015 to October 2018. In 1989, Yemen Riyal 11.70 =$1. But in 2005, Yemeni Riyal is YR 197.37 =$1. For purchasing parity comparison, US dollar is exchanged @150.11 Yemeni Riyals. Mean wages were $1.06 per man hour in 2009.

(10) Remittances from Yemeni working abroad and financial aid paid for persistent trade deficit. Substantial Yemeni exist in many countries of the world. Beginning in mid-1950s, the Soviet Union and China provided large scale assistance to the YAR. This aid included funding of substantial construction projects, scholarships and considerable military assistance.

(11) In the South, pre-independence economic activity was overwhelmingly concentrated in the port of Aden. The Seaborne transit trade, which the part relied upon, collapsed with the closure of Suez Canal and the Britain's withdrawal from Aden in 1967.

(12) Extensive Soviet aid, and remittances from South Yemenis working abroad, and revenues from the Aden refinery (built in 1950) kept foe PDRY's centrally planned Marxist economy afloat. With the dissolution of the Soviet Union and cessation of Soviet aid, the South economy basically collapsed.

(13) Since unification, the government has worked to integrate two relatively desperate economic systems. However, severe shocks, including the returns in 1990 of approximately 850000 Yemenis from Saudi Arabia, and a subsequent major reduction of aid flows, and internal political disputes culminating in 1994 Civil War, hampered economic growth.

(14) Agriculture is generating 20% of GDP. According to US government, it is 13.5% of GDP in 2005. Soil erosion. Sand dune encroachment and deforestation with scarcity of water are problems hindering the agricultural growth. On account of low rainfall, Agriculture depends on extraction of groundwater, a resource that is being depleted. Yemen's water tables are falling by approximately 2 meters a year. Sana's groundwater supplies have been exhausted in 2008. Cash crops in Yemen are fruits and vegetables which are grown on water irrigation. Cultivation of khat plays a dominant role in agricultural economy; 10% of GDP and employs 150000 persons by consuming 30% of irrigation water and displacing land area that would otherwise be used for exportable coffee, fruits, vegetables.

(15) Fishing industry is underdeveloped and assists largely individual fishermen in small boats. Export of fish released capacity is 840000 of fish per year. Revenues of $260 million is earned in 2005. It constitutes 1.17% of GDP. In December 2005, the World Bank approved $25 million credit for a fisheries Management and Conservation Project to be launched in all costal alongwith the Red Sea and Gulf of Aden.

(16) Yemen is a small oil producer country and does not belong to the OPEC. Yemen heavily relies on foreign oil companies that have production sharing agreement with the government. Income from oil production constitutes 70% -75% of the government proven crude oil reserves of more than 4 billion barrels (640000000m), although these reserves are not expected to last more than 9 years. Output from the country's older fields is falling. It is predicted that by the World Bank that oil and gas revenue will plummet during 2009 and 2010 and fall to zero in 2017.

(17) The US government estimates that Yemen's industrial sector constitutes 47.2% of GDP. Together with Services, Construction and Commerce, industry accounts for less than 25% of the labour force. Oil refining is the largest contributor of the manufacturing sector. Manufacturing consists of 95% of GDP in 2005. Yemen had 134000 industrial establishments with 115000 workers.

(18) Yemen's Services sector constituted 51.7% of GDP. US, however, estimated that Services sector accounts for 39.7% of GDP in 2003 and 39.3% in 2005.

(19) Tourism sector is hampered by limited infrastructure as well as serious security concerns. Hotels are below international standards.

Roads & air transportation is largely inadequate. Kidnapping of foreign tourists remain a threat. Terrorist bombings at Port of Aden in 2000 & 2002 significantly deterrent to tourism. In 2004, tourists rose to 274000 from 155000 in 2003.

(20) According to the US government, the agriculture & herding sector employs the majority of Yemen's working force (54.2% in 2003). Industry together with services, construction and commerce accounts for less than 25% of the labour force. Yemen Civil Service is poorly paid work force and inadequate salary differential between high and low skilled jobs to attract and retain qualified workers. In 2004, the government increased civil service salaries by 20% to 40%. Economic reforms were never implemented. 20% increase in work costs, civil service wages constituted 7% of GDP in 2005. IMF wanted salary cost of civil servants to be 1% to 2% of GDP. This can be achieved by continuously reducing size of Civil Service. This will of course increase unemployment level.

(21) Yemen Riyal is floated on the open market in July. 1996. Its value average was YR 191.5 =$1 in 2005 and YR 197.5 =$1 in November 2006.Following unification, Yemen experienced a very high inflation of 40%. Economic reforms brought down inflation to 5.4% in 1997 but high oil prices and cut in fuel subsidy in recent years had a negative impact on the inflation rate. In 2004, Central Bank of Yemen tightened the many supply which was offset by a weakening US $ to which the Yemeni Riyal is linked in a managed float. This rose global commodity prices and inflation rate was 12.5%. Sale tax was reduced to 5% in July 2005 resulting in inflation rising to 15% in 2006.

(22) Yemen's Financial Services Sector is underdeveloped and dominated by the banking system. Yemen has no public Stock Market. The banking system consists of the Central Bank of Yemen, 15 commercial banks (nine private banks, four of which are Islamic bank. Four private banks and two state owned banks). Central Bank of Yemen controls monetary policy and oversees the transfer to currency abroad. It is the lender of last resort, exercises supervisory authority over commercial banks and serves as a bank to the government. Total assets, capital and business of Tadhamon International Islamic Bank were the highest during 2005 to 2010. The largest commercial bank, the Credit & Agriculture Co-operative Bank, which is state owned and the Yemen Bank for Reconstruction & Development which is majority state owned bank are currently

being restructured with the goal of eventual privatization. Both will be merged into one bank. The new publicly owned Development Bank will have a minimum capital of US$ 50 million. But till 2011, this step was not materialized. he large volume of non-performing loans, low capitalization and weak enforcement of regularity standards hamper Yemen's banking system as a whole. Numerous banks are technically insolvent. Entire banking system holds less than 60% of money supply. Bulk of the economy operates on cash. Lending is restricted to select group of consumers and business as many debtors are in default. Legislation adopted in 2000 gave the Central Bank the authority to enforce tougher requirements, and in mid-2005, the Central Bank promulgated several new capital requirements for commercial banks aimed at curtailing speculation and protecting deposits.

(23) State-owned Public Electricity Corporation operates an estimated 80% of the country's electricity generating capacity (810-900 megawatts) as well as the national power grid. Over last ten years, country has considered various plans to alleviating the country's electric shortage. It is estimated that only 40% of the total population has access to electricity from the national power grid, and supply is intermittent. To meet the demand, the government plans to increase the country's power generating capacity to 1400 megawatts by 2002.

(24) In 1995, as per requirements of IMF, Yemen began an economic reform program, one component of which is fiscal policy reforms aimed at reducing deficits and expanding the revenue base. But government failed to reduce its primary expenditure- subsidies especially for fuel. In 2005, budget deficit expected to be 3% of GDP. The budget was predicted on adoption of a reform package that included 10% General Sale Tax (GST) and a 75% reduction in the fuel subsidy. Strong public opposition to these reforms led the government to modify the fuel subsidy reduction and general sale tax. Hybrid 5% GST was instead, levied. Subsidy reduction was postponed to 18 months in 2005. Still cost of subsidies rose dramatically to 90% in 2005 accounting for the largest share of government expenditure (25%). These cost coupled with 20% increase in Civil Services and 42% increase in defence spending resulted in government budget deficit $350.8 million a more than 2% of GDP. In 2005, Government increased sharp 41% rise in fiscal deficit of $800 million or 4.2% of GDP.

(25) Imports was $4.7 billion in 2005. Projected to increase to $5 billion in 2006, $5.6 billion in 2007. Import goods are machinery and equipment, food & livestock, process materials. Yemen imports more than 75% of its main dietary staple- wheat. Main source was UAE. Exports was $6.4 million in 2005, $8.6 billion in 2006. Strong oil revenues about 92% of total exports comes from oil 2001 and 87% in 2005. Export goods are fruits & vegetables, fisheries etc. Foreign loan was 106% of GDP. Debt rescheduled by the Paris Club creditors countries with assistance from the World Bank's IDA resulted in a drop in Yemen's debt stock to $5.4 billion i.e. 39% of GDP by 2004. Yemen's reserves in foreign exchange and gold was $6.1 billion in 2005.

(26) Portfolio flows are largely unrecorded. Five year $3 billion liquid gas construction project with a consortium of foreign company was planned and approved by the government in 2005. Such project raises the prospect of increased foreign investment in the fuel as LNG facilities building ambitious.

(27) Currency: Yemen Riyal

(28) Fiscal Year: Calendar year

(29) Trade Organizations: WTO, GAFTA

(30) Country Group: Underdeveloped/low income economy

(31) Population: 2.90 crores

(32) GDP: $27.591 billion Nominal & $69.439 billion PPP in 2018

(33) GDP Growth: -5.1% in 2017, 0.8% in 2018, 2.1% in 2019 2% in 2020 forecast

(34) GDP per capita : $951 Nominal & $ 2379 PPP

(35) GDP by Sector: 20.3% in agriculture, Industry 11.8% and Services 67.9%

(36) Inflation 27.60%

(37) Population under poverty line: 48.6%

(38) Labour Force: 68.14 lacs

(39) Labour Force by employment : 23.50% in agriculture and herding, Construction and other services 25%and rest in industry

(40) Unemployment:12.8% in 2019

(41) Main Industries: crude oil, production of petroleum refining, leather goods, food processing, handicrafts, aluminum, commercial ship repairs, natural gas production.

(42) Exports: $384.5 million in 2017

(43) Export Goods: crude oil, coffee, dried and salted fish, liquid gas

(44) Imports: $4.079 billion in 2017 Deficit $3.695 billion or 13.39 % of GDP. Export figures are not looking correct.

(45) Import goods: food and livestock, machinery & equipment and chemicals

(46) External debts: $7.068 billion. Rescheduled by Paris Club Yemen's huge foreign loan.

(47) Public loan: 74.5% of GDP in 2017 high

(48) Budget deficit: 5.2% of GDP. It should not be exceeding 4% of GDP

(49) Revenue: $2.821 billion Expenses: $4.458 billion Fiscal Deficit: $1.637

(50) Economic Aid: $2.3 billion (2003-2007 disbursement)

(51) Foreign Reserve: $245.4 million in December 2017

Conclusion

Yemen is an underdeveloped country depending on significant foreign aid by Saudi Arabia and Kuwait. About 1 million workers of Yemen were employed in Saudi Arabia. In spite of this, Yemen supported Iraq in Gulf/ Persian War in 1990. This led to retaliation by Saudi Arabia and Kuwait. Saudi Arabia expelled 1 million workers of Yemen which came to. This led to retaliation by Saudi Arabia and Kuwait. Saudi Arabia expelled 1 million workers of Yemen. This workforce came to Yemen for employment. Yemen was unable to extend employment to these unemployed people. Saudi Arabia and Kuwait also reduced substantial aid to Yemen. This created economy crisis in Yemen and Yemen's economy was scattered.

Unification of South and North Yemen was artificial as both have different and opposition structure. Unification resulted in clashes between two provinces and led to civil war between Hathi and Hothi group. This again ruined the economy. Hathi were supported by US, EU, Saudi Arabia, UAE and Sudan. Hothi were supported by Iran. It is reported that recently Hothi with the military assistance of Iran ruthlessly air attacked and threw missiles which seriously damaged Saudi's Oil Tankers and Saudi had to stop exporting oil for some days/period.

Socotra Island has been granted by Yemen government in 2019 to UAE for 95 years on rent basis. US marines have set up patriot missile system in the Island. It is reported that US Marines wants to set up the Military Base in the Island to control military activities of China and Russia in this area.

Yemen government is unable to take reform measures and reduce subsidies and increase sale tax as IMF has directed. Their reported figures on economic data are also not accurate compared with US records. Corruption is also at high level in Yemen.

4

Economy of Canada

The economy of Canada is a highly developed market economy. It is the 10th largest GDP by nominal and 16th largest GDP by PPP in the world. As with other developed nations, the country's economy is dominated by the service industry which employs about three quarters of Canadians. Canada has the fourth highest total estimated value of natural resources, valued at US$33.2 trillion in 2016. It has the world's third largest proven petroleum reserves and is the fourth largest exporter of petroleum. It is also the fourth largest exporter of natural gas. Canada is considered an "energy superpower" due to its abundant natural resources and a small population of 37 million inhabitants relative to its land area.

According to the Corruption Perceptions Index, Canada is one of the least corrupt countries in the world, and is one of the world's top ten trading nations, with a highly globalized economy. Canada historically ranks above the U.S. and most western European nations on The Heritage Foundation's index of economic freedom, and experiencing a relatively low level of income disparity. The country's average household disposable income per capita is "well above" the OECD average. The Toronto Stock Exchange is the ninth-largest stock exchange in the world by market capitalization, listing over 1,500 companies with a combined market capitalization of over US$2 trillion.

In 2018, Canadian trade in goods and services reached CA$1.5 trillion. Canada's exports totalled over CA$585 billion, while its imported goods were worth over CA$607 billion, of which approximately CA$391 billion originated from the United States, CA$216 billion from non-U.S. sources. In 2018, Canada had a trade deficit in goods of CA$22 billion and a trade deficit in services of CA$25 billion.

Canada is unusual among developed countries in the importance of the primary sector, with the logging and oil industries being two of Canada's most important. Canada also has a sizable manufacturing sector, based in

Central Canada, with the automobile industry and aircraft industry being especially important. With the world's longest coastline, Canada has the 8th largest commercial fishing and seafood industry in the world. Canada is one of the global leaders of the entertainment software industry. It is a member of the APEC, NAFTA, G7, G20, OECD and WTO.

With the exception of a few island nations in the Caribbean, Canada is the only major Parliamentary system in the Western Hemisphere. As a result, Canada has developed its own social and political institutions, distinct from most other countries in the world. Though the Canadian economy is closely integrated with the American economy, it has developed unique economic institutions.

The Canadian economic system generally combines elements of private enterprise and public enterprise. Many aspects of public enterprise, most notably the development of an extensive social welfare system to redress social and economic inequities, were adopted after the end of World War II in 1945.

Canada has a private to public (Crown) property ratio of 60:40 and one of the highest levels of economic freedom in the world. Today Canada closely resembles the U.S. in its market-oriented economic system and pattern of production. As of 2019, Canada has 56 companies in the Forbes Global 2000 list, ranking ninth behind South Korea and ahead of Saudi Arabia.

Tree-map of Canada's goods exports in 2017

International trade makes up a large part of the Canadian economy, particularly of its natural resources. In 2009, agriculture, energy, forestry and mining exports accounted for about 58% of Canada's total exports. Machinery, equipment, automotive products and other manufactures accounted for a further 38% of exports in 2009. In 2009, exports accounted for about 30% of Canada's GDP. The United States is by far its largest trading partner, accounting for about 73% of exports and 63% of imports as of 2009. Canada's combined exports and imports ranked 8th among all nations in 2006.

About 4% of Canadians are directly employed in primary resource fields, and they account for 6.2% of GDP. They are still paramount in many parts of the country. Many, if not most, towns in northern Canada, where agriculture is difficult, exist because of a nearby mine or source of timber. Canada is a world leader in the production of many natural resources such as gold, nickel, uranium, diamonds, lead, and in recent years, crude petroleum, which, with the world's second-largest oil reserves, is taking an increasingly prominent position in natural resources extraction. Several of Canada's largest companies are based in natural resource industries, such as Encana, Cameco, Goldcorp, and Barrick Gold. The vast majority of these products are exported, mainly to the United States. There are also many secondary and service industries that are directly linked to primary ones. For instance one of Canada's largest manufacturing industries is the pulp and paper sector, which is directly linked to the logging business.

The reliance on natural resources has several effects on the Canadian economy and Canadian society. While manufacturing and service industries are easy to standardize, natural resources vary greatly by region. This ensures that differing economic structures developed in each region of Canada, contributing to Canada's strong regionalism. At the same time the vast majority of these resources are exported, integrating Canada closely into the international economy. Howlett and Ramesh argue that the inherent instability of such industries also contributes to greater government intervention in the economy, to reduce the social impact of market changes.

Natural resource industries also raise important questions of sustainability. Despite many decades as a leading producer, there is little risk of depletion. Large discoveries continue to be made, such as the massive nickel find at Voisey's Bay. Moreover, the far north remains largely undeveloped as producers await higher prices or new technologies as many operations in this region are not yet cost effective. In recent decades Canadians have become less willing to accept the environmental destruction associated with exploiting natural resources. High wages and Aboriginal land claims have also curbed expansion. Instead many Canadian companies have focused their exploration, exploitation and expansion activities overseas where prices are lower and governments more amenable. Canadian companies are increasingly playing important roles in Latin America, Southeast Asia, and Africa.

The depletion of renewable resources has raised concerns in recent years. After decades of escalating overutilization the cod fishery all but collapsed in the 1990s, and the Pacific salmon industry also suffered greatly. The logging industry, after many years of activism, has in recent years moved to a more sustainable model, or to other countries.

Data

The following table shows the main economic indicators in 1980–2018. Inflation under 2 % is in green.

Year	GDP (in bn. US$ PPP)	GDP per capita (in US$ PPP)	GDP growth (real)	Inflation rate (in Percent)	Unemployment (in Percent)	Government debt (in % of GDP)
1980	287.3	11,739	▲2.1 %	▲10.2 %	7.5 %	45.1 %
1986	▲440.4	▲16,894	▲2.2 %	▲4.2 %	▼9.6 %	▲70.1 %
1990	▲561.0	▲20,302	▲0.2 %	▲4.8 %	▲8.2 %	▲74.5 %
1991	▲567.3	▼20,271	▼−2.1 %	▲5.6 %	▲10.3 %	▲81.5 %
2000	▲910.9	▲29,723	▲5.2 %	▲2.7 %	▼6.8 %	▼80.7 %
2001	▲948.2	▲30,615	▲1.8 %	▲2.5 %	▲7.2 %	▲81.8 %
2002	▲991.7	▲31,676	▲3.0 %	▲2.3 %	▲7.7 %	▼79.9 %
2010	▲1,353.1	▲39,844	▲3.1 %	▲1.8 %	▼8.0 %	▲81.1 %
2011	▲1,424.3	▲41,524	▲3.1 %	▲3.1 %	▼7.5 %	▲81.9 %
2012	▲1,475.9	▲42,537	▲1.7 %	▲1.5 %	▼8.1 %	▲85.5 %
2013	▲1,536.8	▲43,787	▲2.3 %	▲0.9 %	▼7.1 %	▲86.2 %
2014	▲1,609.1	▲45,345	▲2.9 %	▲1.9 %	▼6.9 %	▼85.7 %
2015	▲1,642.8	▲45,884	▲0.7 %	▲1.1 %	→6.9 %	▲91.3 %
2016	▲1,678.9	▲46,569	▲1.1 %	▲1.4 %	▲7.0 %	▲91.8 %
2017	▲1,761.4	▲48,273	▲3.0 %	▲2.1 %	▼6.3 %	▼90.1 %
2018	▲1,838.3	▲49,690	▲1.9 %	▲2.2 %	▼5.8 %	▼89.9 %

Unemployment rate

Province	Unemployment rate percentage of labour force as of November 2018[50]
Newfoundland and Labrador	12.2
Prince Edward Island	8.5
New Brunswick	7.9
Nova Scotia	7.0
	6.3
Manitoba	5.7
Saskatchewan	5.5
Quebec	5.4
Ontario	5.6
British Columbia	4.4
Canada (national)	5.6

Export trade

Export trade from Canada measured in US dollars. In 2018, Canada exported over US$450 billion.

Partner	Value	Fraction
United States	$338.2 billion	75.0%
China	$21.3 billion	4.7%
United Kingdom	$12.6 billion	2.8%
Japan	$10.0 billion	2.2%
Mexico	$6.3 billion	1.4%
South Korea	$4.5 billion	1.0%
Germany	$3.7 billion	0.8%
Netherlands	$3.7 billion	0.8%
India	$3.3 billion	0.7%

(Contd...)

Hong Kong	$3.0 billion	0.7%
Belgium	$2.9 billion	0.6%
France	$2.7 billion	0.6%
Italy	$2.3 billion	0.5%
Norway	$1.9 billion	0.4%
Brazil	$1.7 billion	0.4%

Import trade

Import trade in 2017 measured in US dollars.

Partner	*Value*	*Fraction*
United States	$222.0 billion	51.3%
China	$54.7 billion	12.7%
Mexico	$27.4 billion	6.3%
Germany	$13.8 billion	3.2%
Japan	$13.5 billion	3.1%
United Kingdom	$6.9 billion	1.6%
South Korea	$6.7 billion	1.5%
Italy	$6.3 billion	1.5%
France	$4.8 billion	1.1%
Vietnam	$3.9 billion	0.9%

Measuring productivity

Productivity measures are key indicators of economic performance and a key source of economic growth and competitiveness. The Organization for Economic Co-operation and Development (OECD)'s. *Compendium of Productivity Indicators*, published annually, presents a broad overview of productivity levels and growth in member nations, highlighting key measurement issues. It analyses the role of "productivity as the main driver of economic growth and convergence" and the "contributions of labour, capital and MFP in driving economic growth". According to the definition above "MFP is often interpreted as the contribution to economic growth made by factors such as technical and organizational innovation" (OECD 2008.November). Measures of productivity include Gross Domestic Product (GDP) (OECD 2008, 11) and multifactor productivity.

Multifactor productivity

Another productivity measure, used by the OECD, is the long-term trend in Multifactor Productivity (MFP) also known as Total Factor Productivity (TFP). This indicator assesses an economy's "underlying productive capacity ('potential output'), itself an important measure of the growth possibilities of economies and of inflationary pressures". MFP measures the residual growth that cannot be explained by the rate of change in the services of labour, capital and intermediate outputs, and is often interpreted as the contribution to economic growth made by factors such as technical and organizational innovation. (OECD 2008, 11)

According to the OECD's annual economic survey of Canada in June 2012, Canada has experienced weak growth of Multi-factor Productivity (MFP) and has been declining further since 2002. One of the ways MFP growth is raised is by boosting innovation and Canada's innovation indicators such as business R&D and patenting rates were poor. Raising MFP growth is "needed to sustain rising living standards, especially as the population ages".

Bank of Canada

The mandate of the central bank—the Bank of Canada is to conduct monetary policy that "preserves the value of money by keeping inflation low and stable".

Monetary Policy Report

The Bank of Canada issues its bank rate announcement through its Monetary Policy Report which is released eight times a year. The Bank of Canada, a federal crown corporation, has the responsibility of Canada's monetary system. Under the inflation-targeting monetary policy that has been the cornerstone of Canada's monetary and fiscal policy since the early 1990s, the Bank of Canada sets an inflation target. The inflation target was set at 2 per cent, which is the midpoint of an inflation range of 1 to 3 per cent. They established a set of inflation-reduction targets to keep inflation "low, stable and predictable" and to foster "confidence in the value of money", contribute to Canada's sustained growth, employment gains and improved standard of living.

In a January 9, 2019 statement on the release of the Monetary Policy Report, Bank of Canada Governor Stephen S. Poloz summarized major events since the October report, such as "negative economic consequences" of the US-led trade war with China. In response to the ongoing trade war "bond yields have fallen, yield curves have flattened even more and stock markets have repriced significantly" in "global financial markets". In Canada, low oil prices will impact Canada's "macroeconomic outlook". Canada's housing sector is not stabilizing as quickly as anticipated.

Inflation targeting

During the period that John Crow was Governor of the Bank of Canada—1987 to 1994— there was a worldwide recession and the bank rate rose to around 14% and unemployment topped 11%. Although since that time inflation-targeting has been adopted by "most advanced-world central banks", in 1991 it was innovative and Canada was an early adopter when the then-Finance Minister Michael Wilson approved the Bank of Canada's first inflation-targeting in the 1991 federal budget. The inflation target was set at 2 per cent. Inflation is measured by the total Consumer Price Index (CPI). In 2011 the Government of Canada and the Bank of Canada extended Canada's inflation-control target to December 31, 2016. The Bank of Canada uses three unconventional instruments to achieve the inflation target: "a conditional statement on the future path of the policy rate", quantitative easing, and credit easing.

As a result, interest rates and inflation eventually came down along with the value of the Canadian dollar. From 1991 to 2011 the inflation-targeting regime kept "price gains fairly reliable".

Following the Financial crisis of 2007–08 the narrow focus of inflation-targeting as a means of providing stable growth in the Canadian economy was questioned. By 2011, the then-Bank of Canada Governor Mark Carney argued that the central bank's mandate would allow for a more flexible inflation-targeting in specific situations where he would consider taking longer "than the typical six to eight quarters to return inflation to 2 per cent".

On July 15, 2015, the Bank of Canada announced that it was lowering its target for the overnight rate by another one-quarter percentage point, to 0.5 per cent "to try to stimulate an economy that appears to have failed to rebound meaningfully from the oil shock woes that dragged it into decline in the first quarter". According to the Bank of Canada announcement, in the first quarter of 2015, the total Consumer Price Index (CPI) inflation was about 1 per cent. This reflects "year-over-year price declines for consumer energy products". Core inflation in the first quarter of 2015 was about 2 per cent with an underlying trend in inflation at about 1.5 to 1.7 per cent.

In response to the Bank of Canada's July 15, 2015 rate adjustment, Prime Minister Stephen Harper explained that the economy was "being dragged down by forces beyond Canadian borders such as global oil prices, the European debt crisis, and China's economic slowdown" which has made the global economy "fragile".

The Chinese stock market had lost about US$3 trillion of wealth by July 2015 when panicked investors sold stocks, which created declines in the commodities markets, which in turn negatively impacted resource-producing countries like Canada.

The Bank's main priority has been to keep inflation at a moderate level. As part of that strategy, interest rates were kept at a low level for almost seven years. Since September 2010, the key interest rate (overnight rate) was 0.5%. Since September 2010, the key interest rate (overnight rate) was 0.5%. In mid-2017, inflation remained below the Bank's 2% target, (at 1.6%) mostly because of reductions in the cost of energy, food and automobiles; as well, the economy was in a continuing spurt with a predicted GDP growth of 2.8 percent by year end. Early on 12 July 2017, the bank issued a statement that the benchmark rate would be increased to 0.75%.

Key industries

In 2017, the Canadian economy had the following relative weighting by industry, as percentage value of GDP:

Industry	*Share of GDP*
Real estate and rental and leasing	13.01%
Manufacturing	10.37%
Mining, quarrying, and oil and gas extraction	8.21%
Finance and insurance	7.07%
Construction	7.07%
Health care and social assistance	6.63%
Public administration	6.28%
Wholesale trade	5.78%
Retail trade	5.60%
Professional, scientific and technical services	5.54%
Educational services	5.21%
Transportation and warehousing	4.60%
Information and cultural industries	3.00%
Administrative and support, waste management and remediation services	2.46%
Utilities	2.21%
Accommodation and food services	2.15%
Other services (except public administration)	1.89%
Agriculture, forestry, fishing and hunting	1.53%
Arts, entertainment and recreation	0.77%
Management of companies and enterprises	0.62%

Service sector

The service sector in Canada is vast and multifaceted, employing about three quarters of Canadians and accounting for 70% of GDP. The largest employer is the retail sector, employing almost 12% of Canadians. The retail industry is concentrated mainly in a small number of chain stores clustered together in shopping malls. In recent years, there has been an increase in the number of big-box stores, such as Wal-Mart (of the United States), Real Canadian Superstore, and Best Buy (of the United States). This has led to fewer workers in this sector and a migration of retail jobs to the suburbs.

The Financial District in Downtown Vancouver. Canadian business services are largely concentrated in large urban areas of Canada.

The second largest portion of the service sector is the business service and hire only a slightly smaller percentage of the population. This includes the financial services, real estate, and communications industries. This portion of the economy has been rapidly growing in recent years. It is largely concentrated in the major urban centres, especially Toronto, Montreal and Vancouver (see Banking in Canada).

The education and health sectors are two of Canada's largest, but both are largely under the influence of the government. The health care industry has been quickly growing, and is the third largest in Canada. Its rapid growth has led to problems for governments who must find money to fund it.

Canada has an important high tech industry, and a burgeoning film, television, and entertainment industry creating content for local and international consumption (see Media in Canada). Tourism is of ever increasing importance, with the vast majority of international visitors coming from the United States. Casino gaming is currently the fastest-growing component of the Canadian tourism industry, contributing $5 billion in profits for Canadian governments and employing 41,000 Canadians as of 2001.

Manufacturing

Ford's Oakville Assembly in the Greater Toronto Area. Central Canada is home to several auto factories of the major American and Japanese automakers.

The general pattern of development for wealthy nations was a transition from a raw material production based economy to a manufacturing based one, and then to a service based economy. At its World War II peak in 1944, Canada's manufacturing sector accounted for 29% of GDP, declining to 10.37% in 2017. Canada has not suffered as greatly as most other rich, industrialized nations from the pains of the relative decline in the importance of manufacturing since the 1960s. A 2009 study by Statistics Canada also found that, while manufacturing declined as a relative percentage of GDP from 24.3% in the 1960s to 15.6% in 2005, manufacturing volumes between 1961 and 2005 kept pace with the overall growth in the volume index of GDP. Manufacturing in Canada was especially hit hard by the financial crisis of 2007–08. As of 2017, manufacturing accounts for 10% of Canada's GDP, a relative decline of more than 5% of GDP since 2005.

Central Canada is home to branch plants to all the major American and Japanese automobile makers and many parts factories owned by Canadian firms such as Magna International and Linamar Corporation.

Steel

Arcelor Mittal Dofasco, view from Burlington Street

Canada was the world's nineteenth-largest steel exporter in 2018. In year-to-date 2019 (through March), further referred to as YTD 2019, Canada exported 1.39 million metric tons of steel, a 22 percent decrease from 1.79 million metric tons in YTD 2018. Canada's exports represented about 1.5 percent of all steel exported globally in 2017, based on available data. By volume, Canada's 2018 steel exports represented just over one-tenth the volume of the world's largest exporter, China. In value terms, steel represented 1.4 percent of the total goods Canada exported in 2018. The growth in exports in the decade since 2009 has been 29%. The largest producers in 2018 were Arcelor Mittal, Essar Steel Algoma, and the first of those alone accounted for roughly half of Canadian steel production through its two subsidiaries. The top two markets for Canada's exports were its NAFTA partners, and by themselves accounted for 92 percent of exports by volume. Canada sent 83 percent of its steel exports to the United States in YTD 2019. The gap between domestic demand and domestic production increased to -2.4 million metric tons, up from -0.2 million metric tons in YTD 2018. In YTD 2019, exports as a share of production decreased to 41.6 percent from 53 percent in YTD 2018.

Energy

Syncrude's Mildred Lake plant site at the Athabasca oil sands in Alberta.

Canada is one of the few developed nations that is a net exporter of energy—in 2009 net exports of energy products amounted to 2.9% of GDP. Most important are the large oil and gas resources centered in Alberta and the Northern Territories, but also present in neighbouring British Columbia and Saskatchewan. The vast Athabasca oil sands give Canada the world's third largest reserves of oil after Saudi Arabia and Venezuela according to USGS. In British Columbia and Quebec, as well as Ontario, Saskatchewan, Manitoba and the Labrador region, hydroelectric power is an inexpensive and relatively environmentally friendly source of abundant energy. In part because of this, Canada is also one of the world's highest per capita consumers of energy. Cheap energy has enabled the creation of several important industries, such as the large aluminum industries in British Columbia and Quebec.

Historically, an important issue in Canadian politics is the interplay between the oil and energy industry in Western Canada and the industrial heartland of Southern Ontario. Foreign investment in Western oil projects has fueled Canada's rising dollar. This has raised the price of Ontario's manufacturing exports and made them less competitive, a problem similar to the decline of the manufacturing sector in the Netherlands. Also, Ontario has relatively fewer native sources of power. However, it is cheaper for Alberta to ship its oil to the western United States than to eastern Canada. The eastern Canadian ports thus import significant quantities of oil from overseas, and Ontario makes significant use of nuclear power.

The National Energy Policy of the early 1980s attempted to force Alberta to sell low-priced oil to eastern Canada. This policy proved deeply divisive, and quickly lost its importance as oil prices collapsed in the mid-1980s. One of the most controversial sections of the Canada–United States Free Trade Agreement of 1988 was a promise that Canada would never charge the United States more for energy than fellow Canadians.

Agriculture

Canada is also one of the world's largest suppliers of agricultural products, particularly of wheat and other grains. Canada is a major exporter of agricultural products, to the United States and Asia. As with all other developed nations the proportion of the population and GDP devoted to agriculture fell dramatically over the 20th century. The agriculture and agro-food manufacturing sector created $49.0 billion to Canada's GDP in 2015, accounting for 2.6% of total GDP.

As with other developed nations, the Canadian agriculture industry receives significant government subsidies and supports. However, Canada has been a strong supporter of reducing market influencing subsidies through the World Trade Organization. In 2000, Canada spent approximately CDN$4.6 billion on supports for the industry. Of this, $2.32 billion was classified under the WTO designation of "green box" support, meaning it did not directly influence the market, such as money for research or disaster relief. All but $848.2 million were subsidies worth less than 5% of the value of the crops they were provided for.

Free-trade agreements

Canada

Free-trade areas

Free-trade agreements in force

Source: Canada–U.S. Free Trade Agreement (Signed 12 October 1987, entered into force 1 January 1989, later superseded by NAFTA)

North American Free Trade Agreement (Entered into force 1 January 1994, includes Canada, U.S. and Mexico)

Canada–Israel Free Trade Agreement (Entered into force 1 January 1997, modernization ongoing)

Canada–Chile Free Trade Agreement (Entered into force 5 July 1997)

Canada–Costa Rica Free Trade Agreement (Entered into force 1 November 2002, modernization ongoing)

Canada–European Free Trade Association Free Trade Agreement (Iceland, Norway, Switzerland and Liechtenstein; entered into force 01-Jul-2009)

Canada–Peru Free Trade Agreement (Entered into force 1 August 2009)

Canada–Colombia Free Trade Agreement (Signed 21 November 2008, entered into force 15 August 2011; Canada's ratification of this FTA had been dependent upon Colombia's ratification of the "Agreement Concerning Annual Reports on Human Rights and Free Trade Between Canada and the Republic of Colombia" signed on 27 May 2010)

Canada–Jordan Free Trade Agreement (Signed on 28 June 2009, entered into force 1 October 2012)

Canada–Panama Free Trade Agreement (Signed on 14 May 2010, entered into force 1 April 2013)

Canada–South Korea Free Trade Agreement (Signed on 11 March 2014, entered into force 1 January 2015)

Canada–Ukraine Free Trade Agreement (concluded 14 July 2015, entered into force 1 August 2017)

Comprehensive and Progressive Agreement for Trans-Pacific Partnership (signed 8 March 2018, entered into force 30 December 2018)

Free-trade agreements concluded

Source:

Trans-Pacific Partnership (concluded 5 October 2015, superseded by CPTPP)

Comprehensive Economic and Trade Agreement (concluded 5 August 2014)

United States–Mexico–Canada Agreement (to supersede NAFTA, concluded 30 November 2018)

Ongoing Free Trade Agreements negotiations

Source:

Canada is negotiating bilateral FTAs with the following countries respectively trade blocs:

Caribbean Community (CARICOM)

Guatemala, Nicaragua and El Salvador

Dominican Republic

India

Japan

Morocco

Singapore

Andean Community (FTA's are already in force with Peru and Colombia)

Canada has been involved in negotiations to create the following regional trade blocks:

Canada and Central American Free Trade Agreement

Free Trade Area of the Americas (FTAA)

Political issues

Relations with the U.S.

Canada and the United States share a common trading relationship. Canada's job market continues to perform well along with the US, reaching a 30-year low in the unemployment rate in December 2006, following 14 consecutive years of employment growth.

The United States is by far Canada's largest trading partner, with more than $1.7 billion CAD in trade per day in 2005. In 2009, 73% of Canada's exports went to the United States, and 63% of Canada's imports were from the United States. Trade with Canada makes up 23% of the United States' exports and 17% of its imports. By comparison, in 2005 this was more than U.S. trade with all countries in the European Union combined, and well over twice U.S. trade with all the countries of Latin America combined. Just the two-way trade that crosses the Ambassador Bridge between Michigan and Ontario equals all U.S. exports to Japan. Canada's importance to the United States is not just a border-state phenomenon: Canada is the leading export market for 35 of 50 U.S. states, and is the United States' largest foreign supplier of energy.

Bilateral trade increased by 52% between 1989, when the U.S.–Canada Free Trade Agreement (FTA) went into effect, and 1994, when the North American Free Trade Agreement (NAFTA) superseded it. Trade has since increased by 40%. NAFTA continues the FTA's moves toward reducing trade barriers and establishing agreed-upon trade rules. It also resolves some long-standing bilateral irritants and liberalizes rules in several areas, including agriculture, services, energy, financial services, investment, and government procurement. NAFTA forms the largest trading area in the world, embracing the 405 million people.

The largest component of U.S.–Canada trade is in the commodity sector.

The U.S. is Canada's largest agricultural export market, taking well over half of all Canadian food exports. Nearly two-thirds of Canada's forest products, including pulp and paper, are exported to the United States; 72% of Canada's total newsprint production also is exported to the U.S.

At $73.6 billion in 2004, U.S.-Canada trade in energy is the largest U.S. energy trading relationship, with the overwhelming majority ($66.7 billion) being exports from Canada. The primary components of U.S. energy trade with Canada are petroleum, natural gas, and electricity. Canada is the United States' largest oil supplier and the fifth-largest energy producing country in the world. Canada provides about 16% of U.S. oil imports and 14% of total U.S. consumption of natural gas. The United States and Canada's national electricity grids are linked, and both countries share hydropower facilities on the western borders.

While most of U.S.-Canada trade flows smoothly, there are occasionally bilateral trade disputes, particularly in the agricultural and cultural fields. Usually these issues are resolved through bilateral consultative forums or referral to World Trade Organization (WTO) or NAFTA dispute resolution. In May 1999, the U.S. and Canadian governments negotiated an agreement on magazines that provides increased access for the U.S. publishing industry to the Canadian market. The United States and Canada also have resolved several major issues involving fisheries. By common agreement, the two countries submitted a Gulf of Maine boundary dispute to the International Court of Justice in 1981; both accepted the court's 12 October 1984 ruling which demarcated the territorial sea boundary. A current issue between the United States and Canada is the ongoing softwood lumber dispute, as the U.S. alleges that Canada unfairly subsidizes its forestry industry.]

In 1990, the United States and Canada signed a bilateral Fisheries Enforcement Agreement, which has served to deter illegal fishing activity and reduce the risk of injury during fisheries enforcement incidents. The U.S. and Canada signed a Pacific Salmon Agreement in June 1999 that settled differences over implementation of the 1985 Pacific Salmon Treaty for the next decade.

Canada and the United States signed an aviation agreement during Bill Clinton's visit to Canada in February 1995, and air traffic between the two countries has increased dramatically as a result. The two countries also share in operation of the St. Lawrence Seaway, connecting the Great Lakes to the Atlantic Ocean.

The U.S remains Canada's largest foreign investor and the most popular destination for Canadian foreign investments. In 2018, the stock of U.S. direct investment in Canada totaled $406 billion, while the stock of Canadian investment in the U.S totaled $595 billion, or 46% of the overall CDIA stock for 2018. This made Canada the second largest investing country in the U.S for 2018 US investments are primarily directed at Canada's mining and smelting industries, petroleum, chemicals, the manufacture of machinery and transportation equipment, and finance, while Canadian investment in the United States is concentrated in manufacturing, wholesale trade, real estate, petroleum, finance, and insurance and other services.

Debt issue

Government debt as a percent of GDP by IMF (2018)

Central Government Debt

The OECD reports the Central Government Debt as percentage of the GDP. In 2000 Canada's was 40.9 percent, in 2007 it was 25.2 percent, in 2008 it was 28.6 percent and by 2010 it was 36.1 percent. The OECD reports net financial liabilities measure used by the OECD, reports the net number at 25.2%, as of 2008, making Canada's total government debt burden as the lowest in the G8. The gross number was 68% in 2011.

The CIA World Factbook, updated weekly, measures financial liabilities by using gross general government debt, as opposed to net federal debt used by the OECD and the Canadian federal government. Gross general government debt includes both "intragovernmental debt and the debt of public entities at the sub-national level". For example, the CIA measured Canada's public debt as 84.1% of GDP in 2012 and 87.4% of GDP in 2011 making it 22nd in the world.

Household Debt

Household debt, the amount of money that all adults in the household owe financial institutions, includes consumer debt and mortgage loans. In March 2015, the International Monetary Fund reported that Canada's high household debt was one of two vulnerable domestic areas in Canada's economy; the second is its overheated housing market.

According to Statistics Canada, total household credit as of July 2019 was CAD$2.2 trillion. According to Philip Cross of the Fraser Institute, in May 2015, while the Canadian household debt-to-income ratio is similar to that in the US, however lending standards in Canada are tighter than those in the United States to protect against high-risk borrowers taking out unsustainable debt

Mergers and Acquisition

Since 1985 63,755 deals in- and outbound Canada have been announced. This cumulates to an overall value of 3700.5 billion USD. Almost 50% of the targets of Canadian companies (outbound deals) have a parent company in the US. Inbound deals are 82% percent from the US.

Critical Observations of present status of economy of Canada

(1) Canada had clashes with India when the Sikh activities were initiated from Canada during the Sikhs Independent Agitation supported by Pakistan to dis-stabilize India. India strongly objected to Canadian activities. Otherwise Canadian relationship with India are cordial.

(2) Unlike other Gulf countries, Canada did not show political dominance on other countries. Its Administrators are engaged to promote the welfare and economic growth of their country. There were no wasteful resources for military interference and all resources were utilized for the economic improvement of the country.

(3) Canada is strong follower of U.S. Apart from the high trade partnership between Canada and U.S., there is a strategic partnership between U.S. and Canada. U.S. provides Canada advanced military equipments including nuclear weapons and have built up strong military Base in Canada. Communist countries such as Soviet Russia and China has no dominance in Canada. Country has therefore been peacefully making economic growth and improvement without interference/obstructions from other countries.

(4) The economy of Canada is highly developed market economy. It is the 10th largest GDP by Nominal and 16th largest GDP PPP economy in the world.

(5) The country's economy is dominated by the service industry which employs 75% of the Canadian workforce.

(6) Canada has the fourth highest total estimated value of natural resources valued @ $ 33.2 trillion in 2016 with small population of 3.7 crores.

(7) It has the third largest proven petroleum resources and it is the fourth largest exporter of the natural gas.

(8) Canada is one of the least corrupt countries in the world and is one of the world's top ten trading nations, with a highly globalized economy.

(9) Canada historically ranks above the U.S. and most western European nations on the Heritage Foundation's index of economic freedom, and experiencing a relatively low level of income disparity. The country's average household disposable income per capita is "well above" the OECD" average.

(10) Toronto Stock Market is the ninth largest Stock Market in the world by market capitalization, listed over 1500 companies with the combined market capitalization over $2 trillion.

(11) U.S. is main trading partner of Canada. Trade was resulting in adverse balance of trade to U.S. till 2016. U.S. therefore stopped implementing NAFTA with Canada. In 2017, fresh NAFTA was signed which gave more favourable trade terms to U.S. and its adverse trade balance with Canada was reduced. U.S. is the main trade partner of Canada with 75% of the exports goes from Canada to U.S.

(12) Canadian Trade deficit of goods was Can$ 22 billion and trade deficit in services Can$ 25 billion recently.

(13) Canada's primary sector with oil industries is the largest with the manufacturing sector based on automobile industry and aircraft industry. It has the world's largest coastline and the largest commercial fishing and seafood industry. It is also the global leader of software industry. It has natural resources such as gold, nickel, uranium, diamonds, lead, crude petroleum and natural gas.

(14) In 1987-1994 recession Bank rate was 14% and unemployment 11%.

(15) Inflation has been reduced from 10.2% in 1983 to 2.2% in 2018 and unemployment from 7.5% to 5.8% and Domestic debt from 45.1% to 89.9% during the same period. This shows that Canada is spending high on welfare of the citizens of the state.

(16) Canada has currency Canadian Dollar. Its Fiscal year is financial year i.e. 1st April – 31st March.

(17) Trade Organisations are NAFTA, OECD, and WTO.

(18) Country Group: Developed/Advanced High Income Economy

(19) Population 3.80 crores

(20) GDP $ 1.731 trillion Nominal and $1.900 trillion PPP in 2018

(21) GDP Rank: 10th Nominal 13th PPP

(22) GDP growth 3% in 2017, 1.9% in 2018, 1.5% in 2019 and 1.8% in 2020 (Forecast)

(23) GDP per capita $46213 Nominal & $50275 PPP

(24) GDP per capita rank 17th

(25) GDP by Sector Agriculture 1.6%, Industries 28.2% and Services 70.2%

(26) Inflation 2%

(27) Unemployment 5.6% in 2019. 11.1% youth under employed and 1.143 million unemployed. With small population of 3.8 crores and labour force 2.03 crores this seems very high. Priority should be given to tackle this issue satisfactorily.

(28) Population below poverty line 9.4% Satisfactory.

(29) Average Gross salary $1042 weekly.

(30) Main Industries Transport equipments, chemical, minerals, food products, wood & paper, fish products, petroleum and natural gas

(31) Exports $ 585 billion

(32) Export Goods Motor vechicles and parts, industrial machinery, aircrafts, chemicals, plastics fertilizers, timber, crude petroleum, natural gas, electricity

(33) Imports $607 billion Trade Deficit $ 22 billion

(34) Import Goods: Machinery equipment, motor vechicles & parts, crude oil, chemicals, electricity, durable goods

(35) Current Account $17.3 billion

(36) Gross external debt: $1.791 trillion 103.47% of GDP. Country is spending high. Needs to be controlled to avoid hyperinflation followed by recession.

(37) Public debt 89.7% of GDP. Servicing debt problem needs to be resolved satisfactorily.

(38) Budget deficit -1% of GDP with Revenue$649.6 billion, Expenses $ 665.7 billion

(39) Economic Aid Donor ODA $3.96 billion in 2016 and Foreign Reserves $ 86.3 billion. Comfortable

(40) Credit Rating S & Ps AAA Outlook stable, Moody's AAA Outlook Stable & Finch AAA Outlook Stable. Credit Rating is good.

5

Economy of Zambia

The economy of Zambia is one of the fastest growing economies in Africa and its capital, Lusaka is the fastest growing city in the Southern African Development Community (SADC). Zambia itself is one of Sub-Saharan Africa's most highly urbanized countries. About one-half of the country's 16 million people are concentrated in a few urban zones strung along the major transportation corridors, while rural areas are under-populated. Unemployment and underemployment are serious problems. National GDP has actually doubled since independence, but due in large part to high birth rates and AIDS per capita annual incomes are currently at about two-thirds of their levels at independence. As of 2018, Zambia's GDP per capita, PPP (current international dollars) stands at $4,216.46.

For the first time since 1989 Zambia's economic growth reached the 6%-7% mark (in 2007) needed to reduce poverty significantly. Copper output has increased steadily since 2004, due to higher copper prices and the opening of new mines. The maize harvest was again good in 2005, helping boost GDP and agricultural exports. Cooperation continues with international bodies on programs to reduce poverty, including a new lending arrangement with the IMF in the second quarter of 2004. A tighter monetary policy will help cut inflation, but Zambia still has a serious problem with high public debt.

Economic policies soon after independence

GDP per capita (current), compared to neighbouring countries (world average = 100)

The British South Africa Company (BSAC, originally set up by the British imperialist Cecil Rhodes) retained commercial assets and mineral rights that it acquired from a concession signed with the Litunga of Barotseland in 1892. Only by threatening to expropriate the BSAC, on the eve of independence, did the incoming Zambian government manage to get the BSAC to relinquish the mineral rights. The Federation's government assigned roles to each of the three territories: Southern Rhodesia was assigned the responsibility of providing managerial and administrative skills; Northern Rhodesia provided copper revenues; and Nyasaland provided the Black labour.

After independence, Zambia instituted a program of national development plans, under the direction of a National Commission for Development Planning: the Transitional Development Plan (1964–66) was followed by the First National Development Plan (1966–71). These two plans, which provided for major investment in infrastructure and manufacturing, were largely implemented and were generally successful. This was not true for subsequent plans

The Mulungushi Economic Reforms (1968)

A major switch in the structure of Zambia's economy came with the Mulungushi Reforms of April 1968: the government declared its intention to acquire equity holdings (usually 51% or more) in a number of key foreign-owned firms, to be controlled by a parastatal conglomerate named the Industrial Development Corporation (INDECO). By January 1970, Zambia had acquired majority holding in the Zambian operations of the two major foreign mining corporations, the Anglo American Corporation and the Rhodesia Selection Trust (RST); the two became the Nchanga Consolidated Copper Mines (NCCM) and Roan Consolidated Mines (RCM), respectively. The Zambian government then created a new parastatal body, the Mining Development Corporation (MINDECO). The Finance and Development Corporation (FINDECO) allowed the Zambian government to gain control of insurance companies and building societies. However, foreign-owned banks (such as Barclays, Standard Chartered and Grindlays) successfully resisted takeover. In 1971, INDECO, MINDECO, and FINDECO were brought together under an omnibus parastatal, the Zambia Industrial and Mining Corporation (ZIMCO), to create one of the largest companies in sub-Saharan Africa, with the country's president, Kenneth Kaunda as Chairman of the Board. The management contracts under which day-to-day operations of the mines had been carried out by Anglo American and RST were ended in 1973. In 1982 NCCM and RCM were merged into the giant Zambia Consolidated Copper Mines Ltd (ZCCM).

In 1973 a massive increase in the price of oil was followed by a slump in copper prices in 1975, resulting in a diminution of export earnings. In 1973 the price of copper accounted for 95% of all export earnings; this halved in value on the world market in 1975. By 1976 Zambia had a balance-of-payments crisis, and rapidly became massively indebted to the

International Monetary Fund (IMF). The Third National Development Plan (1978–83) had to be abandoned as crisis management replaced long-term planning.

By the mid-1980s Zambia was one of the most indebted nations in the world, relative to its gross domestic product (GDP). The IMF was insisting that the Zambian government should introduce programs aimed at stabilizing the economy and restructuring it to reduce dependence on copper. The proposed measures included: the ending of price controls; devaluation of the kwacha (Zambia's currency); cut-backs in government expenditure; cancellation of subsidies on food and fertilizer; and increased prices for farm produce. Kaunda's removal of food subsidies caused massive increases in the prices of basic foodstuffs; the country's urbanized population rioted in protest. In desperation, Kaunda broke with the IMF in May 1987 and introduced a New Economic Recovery Programme in 1988. However, this did not help him and he eventually moved toward a new understanding with the IMF in 1989. In 1990 Kaunda was forced to make a major policy volte-face: he announced the intention to partially privatize the parastatals. Time, however, was running out for him. Like many African independence leaders Kaunda tried to hang on to power but unlike many he called multiparty elections and lost them (to the Movement for Multiparty Democracy (MMD) and abided by the results. Kaunda left office with the inauguration of MMD leader Frederick Chiluba as president on 2 November 1991.

Chiluba's economic reform

Zambia's Economic System of Government is Unitary because of that the Frederick Chiluba government (1991–2001), which came to power after democratic multi-party elections in November 1991, was committed to extensive economic reform. The government privatized many state industries, and maintained positive real interest rates. Exchange controls were eliminated and free market principles endorsed. It remains to be seen whether the Mwanawasa government will follow a similar path of implementing economic reform and undertaking further privatization. Zambia has yet to address issues such as reducing the size of the public HYPERLINK "https://en.wikipedia.org/wiki/Public_sector"sector, which still represents 44% of total formal employment, and improving Zambia's social sector delivery systems.

After the government privatized the giant parastatal mining company Zambian Consolidated Copper Mines (ZCCM), donors resumed balance-of-payment support. The final transfer of ZCCM's assets occurred on March 31, 2000. Although balance-of-payment payments are not the answer to

Zambia's long-term debt problems, it will in the short term provide the government some breathing room to implement further economic reforms. The government has, however, spent much of its foreign exchange reserves to intervene in the exchange rate mechanism. To continue to do so, however, would jeopardize Zambia's debt relief. Zambia qualified for HIPC debt relief in 2000, contingent upon the country meeting certain performance criteria, and this should offer a long-term solution to Zambia's debt situation. In January 2003, the Zambian Government informed the International Monetary Fund and World Bank that it wished to renegotiate some of the agreed performance criteria calling for privatization of the Zambia National Commercial Bank and the national telephone and electricity utilities.

Copper

The Zambian economy has historically been based on the copper-mining industry. The industrialization of the copper industry is owed partly to Frederick Russell Burnham, the famous American scout who worked for Cecil Rhodes. By 1998, however, output of copper had fallen to a low of 228,000 tonnes, continuing a 30-year decline in output due to lack of investment, and until recently, low copper prices and uncertainty over privatization. In 2001, the first full year of a privatized industry, Zambia recorded its first year of increased productivity since 1973. The future of the copper industry in Zambia was thrown into doubt in January 2002, when investors in Zambia's largest copper mine announced their intention to withdraw their investment. However, surging copper prices from 2004 to the present day rapidly rekindled international interest in Zambia's copper sector with a new buyer found for KCCM and massive investments in expanding capacity launched. China has become a major investor in the Zambian copper industry, and in February 2007, the two countries announced the creation of a Chinese-Zambian economic partnership zone around the Chambishi copper mine.

Today copper mining is central to the economic prospects for Zambia and covers 85% of all the country's exports, but concerns remain that the economy is not diversified enough to cope with a collapse in international copper prices.

In January 2013, the Zambia Environmental Management Agency (ZEMA) approved 27 mining and exploration licences, with more rumored to be confirmed.

Inflation

Lack of balance-of-payment support meant the Zambian government did not have resources for capital investment and periodically had to issue bonds or otherwise expand the money supply to try to meet its spending and debt obligations. The government continued these activities even after balance-of-payment support resumed. This has kept interest rates at levels that are too high for local business, fueled inflation and burdened the budget with domestic debt payments, while still falling short of meeting the public payroll and other needs, such as infrastructure rehabilitation. The government was forced to draw down foreign exchange reserves sharply in 1998 to meet foreign debt obligations, putting further pressure on the kwacha and inflation. Inflation held at 32% in 2000; consequently, the kwacha lost the same value against the dollar over the same period. In mid- to late 2001, Zambia's fiscal management became more conservative. As a result, 2001 year-end inflation was below 20%, its best result in decades. In 2002 inflation rose to 26.7%. However, in 2007 inflation hit 8%, the first time in 30 years that Zambia had seen single digit inflation.

On January 27, 2011, it was reported by the Central Statistical Office that inflation rose to 9%.

Agriculture

The agriculture sector represented 20% GDP in 2000. Agriculture accounted for 85% of total employment (formal and informal) for 2000. Maize (corn) is the principal cash crop as well as the staple food. Other important crops include soybean, cotton, sugar, sunflower seeds, wheat, sorghum, pearl millet, cassava, tobacco and various vegetable and fruit crops. Floriculture is a growth sector, and agricultural non-traditional exports now rival the mining industry in foreign exchange receipts. Zambia has the potential for significantly increasing its agricultural output; currently, less than 20% of its arable land is cultivated. In the past, the agriculture sector suffered from low producer prices, difficulties in availability and distribution of credit and inputs, and the shortage of foreign exchange.

Growth

There are, however, positive macroeconomic signs, rooted in reforms implemented in the early and mid-1990s. Zambia's floating exchange rate and open capital markets have provided useful discipline on the government, while at the same time allowing continued diversification of Zambia's export sector, growth in the tourist industry, and procurement of inputs for growing businesses. Some parts of the Copper Belt have experienced a significant revival as spin-off effects from the massive capital reinvestment are experienced.

Salaula

Standard economic theory and empirical data indicates that second-hand clothing import can have positive effects in a country like Zambia (one of the least developed countries in the world). The *salaula* market reduces the proportion of income that a family has to spend on clothing. It also helps to keep employments like repairs and alterations in business and forces tailors to proceed into more specialize production of styled garments.

There is a downside to such imports, however; the massive importation of used clothing from the developed world has resulted in a near-total collapse of the Zambian indigenous textile industry. In the face of cheap used clothing, tailors' specialized production may be irrelevant - customers will buy the least expensive clothing available, irrespective of style. Those who might otherwise work at textile mills or clothing factories are left jobless, or else make significantly less money in the salaula resale business.

Critical Observation of Present Status of Economy of Zambia

(1) Zambia is one of the fastest growing economies in Africa and its capital Lusaka is fastest growing city in South Africa Development Countries (SADC)

(2) One half of the population i.e. 80 lacs are residing in urban areas and rural areas are underpopulated. Zambia is one of the Sub-Saharan Africa's most highly urbanized country.

(3) Unemployment and underemployment are serious problems. High birth rate and AIDS have resulted in lower per capita annual income to about two-third of their levels at independence in spite of National GDP has actually doubled since independence in 1964.

(4) IN 2007, the economic growth reached 6%-7% though the average growth rate is 3% from 2017 onwards. Copper is the main export and agriculture is only 20% of GDP. There is no diversification of economy.

(5) Co-operation continues with international bodies on programs to reduce poverty, including new pending arrangement with these bodies.

(6) Zambian government's plan to gain control over insurance companies and building was successfully resisted by banks like Barclays, Standard Chartered and Grindlays.

(7) By the mid-1980, Zambia was one of the most indebted nations in the world, relative to its GDP. IMF was insisting that the Zambian

government should introduce programs aimed at stabilizing economy and restructuring it to reduce dependence on copper. The proposed measures included: the ending of price controls, devaluation of kwacha, cut-backs in government expenditure, cancellation of subsidiaries on food and fertilizers and increased prices for farm produces.

(8) After independence, country was ruled by Kaunda till 1991, then by Frederick Chiluba (1991-2001). They introduced reforms under planning and privatized many state industries, maintained positive interest rates. Exchange controls were eliminated and free market principles introduced.

(9) Currency is Zambian kwacha which is floating currency. To stabilize the exchange rate, foreign reserves were utilized and the Kwacha was devalued to resolve Balance of Payment issue.

(10) Zambia qualified for HIPC debt relief in 2000 contingent upon the country meeting certain performance criteria and this should offer a long term solution. In January 2003, the Zambian government informed the IMF and World Bank that it wishes to renegotiate some of the agreed performance criteria calling for privatization of Zambia National commercial Bank, national telephone and electricity utilities.

(11) Calendar Year is the fiscal year.

(12) Trade organizations: AU, SADC, WTO.

(13) GDP $26.720 billion Nominal 2018 and $ 73.186 billion PPP 2018

(14) GDP per capita $1503 Nominal & $4118 PPP

(15) GDP by Sector: Agriculture 8.6%, Industry 35.3% and Service 61%

(16) Inflation: 6.993% Slightly high

(17) Unemployment: 7.2%. In 2000s, it was 20% has since been reduced.

(18) Population 1.60 crores and Labour force 69 lacs

(19) Labour Force by Occupation: Agriculture 85% Industry 5% and Services 8%

(20) Main Industries Copper mining and processing, Construction, foodstuff and beverage

(21) Exports: $6.316 billion. Export goods are copper/cobalt 64%, Electricity and tobacco. Economy is not diversified and this results in economic crisis in case of drop in copper prices.

(22) Imports: $6.798 billion Import Goods: Machinery, transportation equipment, petroleum, fertilizers and foodstuff

(23) Balance of Payment -0.482 billion

(24) Public debts is $ 21.73 billion i.e. 81.32% of GDP Nominal. Public debt is taken at very high interest rates. Lack of balance of payment support means the Zambian government did not have resources for capital investment and periodically had to issue bonds or expand money supply to meet its spending and debt obligations. This policy continued even after balance of payment support resumed.

(25) Revenue: $3.643 billion Expenses: $5.189 Billion.

Fiscal Deficit $1.546 billion which is high @5.79% of Revenue. Very high and needs to be controlled.

6

Economy of Zimbabwe

The economy of Zimbabwe is mainly made of tertiary industry which makes up to 60% of the total GDP as of 2017. Zimbabwe has the second biggest informal economy as a share of its economy which has a score of 60.6%. Agriculture and mining largely contribute to exports. The economy of Zimbabwe grew at average of 12% from 2009 to 2013 making it one of the fastest growing economies in the world recovering from negative growth from 1998 to 2008 before it slowed to 0.7% growth in 2016.

The country has reserves of metallurgical-grade chromite. Other commercial mineral deposits include coal, asbestos, copper and nickel, gold, platinum and iron ore.

Current economic conditions

Since 2000, Zimbabwe has seized and forcibly redistributed most of the country's white-owned, commercial farms. The new occupants, mainly consisting of indigenous citizens and several prominent members of the ruling ZANU-PF administration, were usually inept, inexperienced, or uninterested in farming – thereby failing to retain the labour-intensive, highly efficient management of previous landowners. Short term gains were achieved by selling the land or equipment. The contemporary lack of agricultural expertise triggered severe export losses and negatively affected market confidence. Idle land is now being utilized by rural communities practicing subsistence farming. Production of staple foodstuffs, such as maize, has recovered accordingly – unlike typical export crops including tobacco and coffee. Zimbabwe has also sustained the 30th occurrence of recorded hyperinflation in world history.

Government spending is 29.7% of GDP. State enterprises are strongly subsidized. Taxes and tariffs are high. State regulation is costly to companies. Starting or closing a business is slow and costly. Labour market is highly regulated, hiring a worker is cumbersome and firing a worker is difficult. By 2008 unemployment had risen to 94%.

A 2014 report by the Africa Progress Panel found that, of all the African countries looked at when working out how many years it would take to double per capita GDP, Zimbabwe fared the worst, and that at its current rate of development it would take 190 years for the country to double its per capita GDP. Uncertainty around the indigenization HYPERLINK "https://en.wikipedia.org/wiki/Indigenisation_and_Economic_Empowerment_Act" programme, the perceived lack of a free press, the possibility of abandoning the US dollar as official currency, and political uncertainty following the end of the government of national unity with the MDC as well as power struggles within ZANU-PF have increased concerns that the country's economic situation could further deteriorate.

In September 2016 the finance minister identified "low levels of production and the attendant trade gap, insignificant foreign direct investment and lack of access to international finance due to huge arrears" as significant causes for the poor performance of the economy.

Transportation

Zimbabwe has adequate internal transportation and electrical power networks, however maintenance has been neglected over several years. Poorly paved roads link the major urban and industrial centers, and rail lines managed by the National Railways of Zimbabwe tie it into an extensive central African railroad network with all its neighbors.

Energy

The Zimbabwe Electricity Supply Authority is responsible for providing the country with electrical energy. Zimbabwe has two larger facilities for the generation of electrical power, the Kariba Dam (owned together with Zambia) and since 1983 by large Hwange Thermal Power Station adjacent to the Hwange coal field. However, total generation capacity does not meet the demand leading to rolling blackouts. The Hwange station is not capable of using its full capacity due to old age and maintenance neglect. In 2006, crumbling infrastructure and lack of spare parts for generators and coal mining lead to Zimbabwe importing 40% of its power - 100 megawatts from the Democratic Republic of Congo, 200 megawatts from Mozambique, up to 450 from South Africa, and 300 megawatts from Zambia. In May 2010 the country's generation power was an estimated 940MW against a peak demand of 2500MW. Use of local small scale generators is widespread.

Telephone

The telephone service is problematic, and new lines used to be difficult to obtain. With TelOne, however, Zimbabwe has only one fixed line service provider. Cellular phone networks are an alternative. Principal mobile phone operators are Telecel, Net*One, Econet.

Agriculture

Exports in 2010

A chart of Zimbabwe's import and export products from 2010.

Agriculture in Zimbabwe can be divided into two parts: commercial farming of crops such as cotton, tobacco, coffee, peanuts and various fruits, and subsistence farming with staple crops such as maize or wheat.

Commercial farming was almost exclusively in the hands of the white minority until the controversial land redistribution program began in 2000. Land was forcibly seized from white farmers and redistributed to black settlers, justified by Mugabe on the grounds that it was meant to rectify inequalities left over from colonialism. The new owners did not have land titles, so they did not have the collateral necessary to access bank loans. The small-scale farmers also did not have experience with commercial-scale agriculture.

After land redistribution, much of Zimbabwe's land went fallow and agricultural production decreased steeply. The University of Zimbabwe estimated in 2008 that between 2000 and 2007 agricultural production decreased by 50%. Production of tobacco, Zimbabwe's main export crop, decreased by 79% from 2000 to 2008.

Tobacco production recovered after 2008 thanks to the contract system of agriculture and growing Chinese demand. International tobacco companies, such as British American Tobacco and China Tobacco, supplied farmers with agricultural inputs, equipment, and loans, and supervised them in growing tobacco. By 2018, tobacco production had recovered to 258 million kg, the second largest crop on records Instead of large white-owned farms selling mostly to European and American companies, Zimbabwe's tobacco sector now consists of small black-owned farms exporting over half of the crop to China. Tobacco farming accounted for 11% of Zimbabwe's GDP in 2017, and 3 million of its 16 million people depended on tobacco for their livelihood.

Land reform has found considerable support in Africa and a few supporters among African-American activists but Jesse Jackson commented during a visit to South Africa in June 2006, "Land redistribution has long been a noble goal to achieve but it has to be done in a way that minimizes trauma. The process has to attract investors rather than scare them away. What is required in Zimbabwe is democratic rule, democracy is lacking in the country and that is the major cause of this economic meltdown.

Mining sector

As other southern African countries, Zimbabwean soil is rich in raw materials, namely platinum, coal, iron ore, and gold, and lately also diamonds have been found in considerable deposits. Copper, chromite and nickel deposits also exist, though in lesser amounts. The Marange diamond fields, discovered in 2006 are thought to be among the richest in the world.

In March 2011, the government of Zimbabwe implemented laws which required local ownership of mining companies; following this news, there were falls in the share prices of companies with mines in Zimbabwe.

Gold production year	*kg*
1998	27,114
2007	7,017
2015	18,40

It has been reported by various NGOs that the diamond sector in Zimbabwe is rife with corruption; a November 2012 report by NGO Reap What You Sow revealed a huge lack of transparency of diamond revenues and that Zimbabwe's elite are benefiting from the country's diamonds. This followed former South African President Thabo Mbeki's warning days earlier that Zimbabwe needed to stop its "predatory elite" from colluding with mining companies for their own benefit. Also in that month, the Associated Press reported that at least $2 billion worth of diamonds had been stolen from Zimbabwe's eastern diamond fields and had enriched Mugabe's ruling circle and various connected gem dealers and criminals.

In January 2013, Zimbabwe's mineral exports totalled $1.8 billion.

As of October 2014, Metallon Corporation was Zimbabwe's largest gold miner. The group is controlled by its Chairman Mzi Khumalo.

Education

The state of education in Zimbabwe affects the development of the economy while the state of the economy can affect access and quality of teachers and education. Zimbabwe has one of Africa's highest literacy rates at over 90%. The population is usually better educated than the African average, making the people one of the greatest assets of the country. The crisis since 2000 has however diminished these achievements because of general lack of resources and the exodus of teachers and specialists (e.g. doctors, scientists, engineers) to other countries. Also, the start of the new curriculum in primary and secondary sections has drastically affected the state of the once strong state of the education sector.

Science and technology in Zimbabwe

Zimbabwe's *Second Science and Technology Policy* (2012) cites sectorial policies with a focus on biotechnology, information and communication technologies (ICTs), space sciences, nanotechnology, indigenous knowledge systems, technologies yet to emerge and scientific solutions to emergent environmental challenges. The policy makes provisions for establishing a National Nanotechnology Programme.

Zimbabwe has a *National Biotechnology Policy* which dates from 2005. Despite poor infrastructure and a lack of both human and financial resources, biotechnology research is better established in Zimbabwe than in most sub-Saharan countries, even if it tends to use primarily traditional techniques.

The *Second Science and Technology Policy* asserts the government commitment to allocating at least 1% of GDP to research and development, focusing at least 60% of university education on developing skills in science and technology and ensuring that school pupils devote at least 30% of their time to studying science subjects.

History

1980–2000

At the time of independence, annual inflation was 5.4 percent and month-to-month inflation was 0.5 percent. Currency of Z$2, Z$5, Z$10 and Z$20 denominations were released. Roughly 95 percent of transactions used the Zimbabwean dollar. Following the Lancaster House Agreement in December 1979, the transition to majority rule in early 1980, and the lifting of sanctions, Zimbabwe enjoyed a brisk economic recovery. Real growth for 1980-1981 exceeded 20%. However, depressed foreign demand for the country's mineral exports and the onset of a drought cut sharply into the growth rate in 1982, 1983, and 1984. In 1985, the economy rebounded strongly due to a 30% jump in agricultural production. However, it slumped in 1986 to a zero growth rate and registered negative of about minus 3% in 1987, primarily because of drought and the foreign exchange crisis faced by the country. Zimbabwe's GDP grew on average by about 4.5% between 1980 and 1990

In 1992, a World Bank study indicated that more than 500 health centres had been built since 1980. The percentage of children vaccinated increased from 25% in 1980 to 67% in 1988 and life expectancy increased from 55 to 59 years. Enrolment increased by 232 per cent one year after primary education was made free and secondary school enrolment increased by 33 per cent in two years. These social policies lead to an increase in the debt ratio. Several laws were passed in the 1980s in an attempt to reduce wage gaps. However, the gaps remained considerable. In 1988, the law gave women, at least in theory, the same rights as men. Previously, they could only take a few personal initiatives without the consent of their father or husband.

The government started crumbling when a bonus to independence war veterans was announced in 1997 (which was equal to 3 percent of GDP) followed by unexpected spending due to Zimbabwe's involvement in the Second Congo War in 1998. In 1999, the country also witnessed a drought which weakened the economy more; the economy could not recover, which ultimately led to the country's bankruptcy in the next decade. In the same year, 1999, Zimbabwe experienced its first defaults on its IMF, World Bank, and African Development Bank debts in addition to debts taken out with Western lenders.

2000–2009

In recent years, there has been considerable economic hardship in Zimbabwe. Many western countries argue that the Government of Zimbabwe's land reform program, recurrent interference with, and intimidation of the judiciary, as well as maintenance of unrealistic price controls and exchange rates has led to a sharp drop in investor confidence.

Between 2000 and December 2007, the national economy contracted by as much as 40%; inflation vaulted to over 66,000%, and there were persistent shortages of hard currency, fuel, medicine, and food. GDP per capita dropped by 40%, agricultural output dropped by 51% and industrial production dropped by 47%.

The Mugabe Government attribute Zimbabwe's economic difficulties to sanctions imposed by the Western powers. It has been argued that the sanctions imposed by Britain, the US, and the EU have been designed to cripple the economy and the conditions of the Zimbabwean people in an attempt to overthrow President Mugabe's government. These countries on their side argue that the sanctions are targeted against Mugabe and his inner circle and some of the companies they own. Critics point to the so-called "Zimbabwe Democracy and Economic Recovery Act of 2001", signed by Bush, as an effort to undermine Zimbabwe's economy. Soon after the bill was signed, IMF cut off its resources to Zimbabwe. Financial institutions began withdrawing support for Zimbabwe. Terms of the sanctions made it such that all economic assistance would be structured in support of "democratization, respect for human rights and the rule of law." The EU terminated its support for all projects in Zimbabwe. Because of the sanctions and US and EU foreign policy, none of Zimbabwe's debts have been cancelled as in other countries.

Other observers also point out how the asset freezes by the EU on people or companies associated with Zimbabwe's Government have had significant economic and social costs to Zimbabwe.

As of February 2004, Zimbabwe's foreign debt repayments ceased, resulting in compulsory suspension from the International Monetary Fund (IMF). This, and the United Nations World Food Programme stopping its food aid due to insufficient donations from the world community, has forced the government into borrowing from local sources.

Hyperinflation 2004–2009

Zimbabwe began experiencing severe foreign exchange shortages, exacerbated by the difference between the official rate and the black market rate in 2000. In 2004 a system of auctioning scarce foreign currency for importers was introduced, which temporarily led to a slight reduction in the foreign currency crisis, but by mid-2005 foreign currency shortages were once again severe. The currency was devalued by the central bank twice, first to 9,000 to the US$, and then to 17,500 to the US$ on 20 July 2005, but at that date it was reported that that was only half the rate available on the black market.

In July 2005 Zimbabwe was reported to be appealing to the South African government for US$1 billion of emergency loans, but despite regular rumors that the idea was being discussed no substantial financial support has been publicly reported.

The official Zimbabwean dollar exchange rate had been frozen at Z$101,196 per U.S. dollar since early 2006, but as of 27 July 2006 the parallel (black market) rate has reached Z$550,000 per U.S. dollar. By comparison, 10 years earlier, the rate of exchange was only Z$9.13 per USD.

In August 2006 the RBZ revalued the Zimbabwean Dollar by 1000 ZWD to 1 (revalued) dollar. At the same time Zimbabwe devalued the Zim Dollar by 60% against the USD. New official exchange rate revalued ZWD 250 per USD. The parallel market rate was about revalued ZWD 1,200 to 1,500 per USD (28 September 2006).

In November 2006, it was announced that sometime around 1 December there would be a further devaluation and that the official exchange rate would change to revalued ZWD 750 per USD. This never materialized. However, the parallel market immediately reacted to this news with the parallel rate falling to ZWD 2,000 per USD (18 November 2006) and by year end it had fallen to ZWD 3,000 per USD.

On 1 April 2007, the parallel market was asking ZWD 30,000 for US$1. By year end, it was down to about ZWD 2,000,000. On 18 January 2008, the Reserve Bank of Zimbabwe began to issue higher denomination ZWD bearer cheques (a banknote with an expiry date), including $10 million bearer cheques - each of which was worth less than US$1.35 (70p Sterling; 0.90 Euro) on the parallel market at the time of first issue. On 4 April 2008 the Reserve Bank of Zimbabwe introduced new $25 million and $50 million bearer cheques. At the time of first issue they were worth US$0.70 & US$1.40 on the parallel market respectively.

On 1 May 2008, the RBZ announced that the dollar would be allowed to float in value subject to some conditions.

On 6 May 2008, the RBZ issued new $100 million and $250 million bearer cheques. At the date of first issue the $250 million bearer cheque was worth approximately US$1.30 on the parallel market. On 15 May 2008, a new $500 million bearer cheque was issued by the RBZ. At time of first issue it was worth US$1.93. In a widely unreported parallel move, on 15 May 2008, the RBZ issued three "special agro-cheques" with face values $5 billion (at time of first issue - $19.30), $25 billion ($96.50) & $50 billion ($193). It is further reported that the new agro-cheques can be used to buy any goods and services like the bearer cheques.

On 30 July 2008, the Governor of the RBZ, Gideon Gono announced that the Zimbabwe dollar would be redenominated by removing 10 zeroes, with effect from 1 August 2008. ZWD10billion became 1 dollar after the redenomination.

More banknotes were issued since Gono vowed to continue printing money: $10,000 and $20,000 (29 September); $50,000 (13 October); $100,000, $500,000 and $1 million (3 November); $10 million (2 December); $50 million and $100 million (4 December); $200 million (9 December); $500 million (11 December); $10 billion (19 December); $1 trillion (17 January 2009)

On February 2, 2009 a final denomination was implemented, cutting 12 zeroes, before the Zimbabwe dollar was officially abandoned on April 12, 2009. Pending economic recovery, Zimbabwe relied on foreign currency rather than introducing a new currency.

Dollarization: 2009–present

In February 2009, the newly installed national unity government (which included the opposition to Mugabe) allowed foreign currency transactions throughout the economy as a measure to stimulate the economy and end inflation. The Zimbabwean dollar quickly lost all credibility, and by April

2009, the Zimbabwean dollar was suspended entirely, to be replaced by the US dollar in government transactions. In 2014 there were eight legal currencies - US dollar, South African rand, Botswana pula, British pound sterling, Australian dollar, Chinese yuan, Indian rupee and Japanese yen.

Dollarization reversed inflation, permitting the banking system to stabilize and the economy to resume slow growth after 2009. Dollarization also had other consequences, including:

- Reduced taxation and financial transparency, as people continued to keep their money out of the formal banking system.
- Extremely high real interest rates due to lack of capital.
- Government forced into a "pay as you go" system, unable to spend more than it takes in.
- Deficits of coinage for everyday transactions, leading to the adoption of South African rand coins, sweets, airtime for mobile phones or even condoms for small change.
- Counterfeiting currencies with which Zimbabweans are not familiar.
- 10% growth of the economy a year up to 2012

In January, 2013 Finance Minister Tendai Biti announced that Zimbabwe's national public account held just $217. The election budget for the July 2013 presidential election was $104 million and government budget for 2013 was $3.09 billion at a projected economic growth of 5 per cent. The Economist described the 2013 election as "rigged" and how, after regaining full control of the government, the Mugabe government doubled the civil service and embarked on "...misrule and dazzling corruption.

In August 2014, Zimbabwe began selling treasury bills and bonds to pay public sector salaries that have been delayed as GDP growth weakens while the economy experiences deflation. US$2 million was sold in July through private placements of Six-month Treasury bills at an interest rate of 9.5%. According to IMF data, GDP growth was forecast to be 3.1% by the end of 2014, a major decline from an average rate of 10% between 2009 and 2012, while government data showed that consumer prices declined for five consecutive months by the end of June. By mid-2016, the net benefits of dollarization seemed to have run out, leading to protests and political instability.

In February 2019, John Mangudya, through a monetary policy presentation introduced a new currency, the RTGS dollar which consists of electronic balances in banks and mobile wallets, bond notes and bond coins.

Government of National Unity: 2009–2013

In response to the negative long term economic situation the three parliamentary parties agreed on a Government of National Unity. Despite serious internal differences this government made some important decisions that improved the general economic situation, first of all the suspension of the national currency, the Zimbabwean Dollar, in April 2009. That stopped hyperinflation and made normal forms of business possible again, by using foreign currency such as the US American Dollar, the South African Rand, the EUs Euro or the Botswana Pula. The former finance minister Tendai Biti (MDC-T) tried to hold a disciplined budget. In 2009 Zimbabwe recorded a period of economic growth for the first time in a decade.

Post-Government of National Unity: 2013–present

Following ZANU-PF's landslide electoral victory in the 2013 general elections, Patrick Chinamasa was appointed finance minister. Policies encouraging the indigenization of the economy were fast tracked and laws requiring that 51% or more of non-black Zimbabwean owned companies had to be handed over to black Zimbabweans were implemented. This has been credited with creating further uncertainty in the economy and negatively impacting investment climate in the country. Although legislation dealing with the indigenization of the Zimbabwean economy has been in development since 2007 and actively initiated by ZANU-PF in 2010 the policy has continued to be accused of being unclear and a form of "racketeering by regulation." The government doubled the civil service and embarked on what the Economist described as "...misrule and dazzling corruption."

In April 2014, Chinamasa admitted that the country was heavily in debt and that the country needed to better attract foreign direct investment. Officially Zimbabwe's debt is $7 billion, or over 200% of the country's GDP. However, this figure is disputed, with figures as high as $11 billion being quoted, once debts to other African countries and China are included. As of May 2014, it has been reported that Zimbabwe's economy was in decline following the period of relative economic stability during the Government of National Unity. It is estimated that Zimbabwe's manufacturing sector requires an investment of roughly US$8 billion for working capital and equipment upgrades.

In 2016 Tendai Biti, an opposition politician estimated the government was running a deficit of up to 12% of GDP and Zimbabwe began experiencing a significant shortage of US dollars partly due to a consistent trade deficit. This prompted the Zimbabwean government to limit cash withdrawals from banks and change exchange-control regulations in order to try to promote exports and reduce the currency shortage. In June and July 2016, after Government employees had not been paid for weeks, police had set up road blocks to coerce money out of tourists and there were protests throughout Zimbabwe, Patrick Chinamasa, the finance minister, toured Europe in an effort to raise investment capital and loans, admitting "Right now we have nothing". In August 2016 the government announced that it would be laying off 25,000 civil servants (8% of the country's 298,000 civil servants), cut the number of embassies and diplomatic expenses and cut ministerial expenses in an attempt to save $4 billion in annual wages and secure help from the World Bank and the IMF.

At the same time, the government sought to improve women's access to microfinance via the Zimbabwe Women Microfinance Bank Limited, which began operations 29 May 2018. The Bank operates under the supervision of the Ministry of Women's Affairs, Gender and Community Development.

Re-adoption of the Zimbabwe Dollar

In mid-July 2019 inflation had increased to 175% following the adoption of a new Zimbabwe dollar and banning the use of foreign currency thereby sparking fresh concerns that the country was entering a new period of hyperinflation. The Zimbabwean government stopped releasing inflation data in August 2019. By September 2019 monetary economist Steve Hanke estimated that the inflation rate had exceeded 900% a year.

Poverty and unemployment

Poverty and unemployment are both endemic in Zimbabwe, driven by the shrinking economy and hyper-inflation. Poverty rates in 2007 were nearly 80%, while the unemployment rate in 2009 was ranked as the world's largest, at 95%.

As of January 2006, the official poverty line was ZWD 17,200 per month (US$202). However, as of July 2008 this had risen to ZWD 13 per month (US$41.00). Most general laborers are paid under ZWD 200 Billion (US 60c) per month. A nurse's salary in September was Z$12,542 (12 US cents), less than the cost of a soft drink.

The lowest 10% of Zimbabwe's population represent 1.97% of the economy, while the highest 10% make 40.42%. (1995) the current account balance of the country is negative, standing at around US -$517 million. The negative economic environment since the year 2000 has also impacted

Zimbabwean entrepreneurs with a large number of them going bankrupt between 2000 and 2014.

Government response

2007 Empowerment Bill to increase local ownership of economy was drafted for presentation to parliament in July 2007. It was signed into law by President Mugabe on 7 March 2008. The law requires all White or foreign owned business to hand over 51 percent of their business to indigenous Zimbabweans. In response to inflation, the government has introduced price controls, but enforcement has been largely unsuccessful Police have been sent in to enforce requirements that shopkeepers sell goods at a loss. This has resulted in hundreds of shop owners being arrested under accusations of not having lowered prices enough. Because of this, basic goods no longer appear on supermarket shelves and the supply of petrol is limited. This has diminished public transport. This has not been a significant problem during the term of Reid. However, goods can usually be purchased for a high rate on the black market

In January 2010, Finance Minister Tendai Biti announced that Zimbabwe would seek highly indebted poor country (HIPC) status in order to cancel the country's $6 billion debt. Despite criticism from some government officials and economists, Biti stated that, among other strategies considered, seeking HIPC status was the best option. In addition to debt forgiveness, HIPC status (which is attained from the International Monetary Fund (IMF) and World Bank) would also allow Zimbabwe access to World Bank resources and loans through the IMF's Poverty Reduction and Growth Facility.

Critical Observations of the present status of Zimbabwe

(1) Currency: RTGS dollar. During 1980-2000, there was wide and dangerous fluctuation in the official exchange rate leading to exchange crisis. Sanctions were imposed by USA, England and European Union. Mugabe Government implemented the redistribution of land. This land reforms policy failed miserably which led to the economic sanctions by USA, EU and England. IMF and above countries refused to give Moratorium for $6 billion debt which these institutions approved for other countries under Highly Indebted Country Program. There was Black Market where the exchange rate was more than double the official exchange rate.

(2) Zimbabwe is developing/Emerging country with lower-middle Income Economy. At times, it was highly indebted Country which

was not approved $6billion debt like other African countries due to the country's wrong economic policies in the Land Reforms.

(3) Its population is 1.44 crores and Labour Force 70 lacs.

(4) GDP is $ 20.997 billion and external debt is $ 9.357 billion which is 44.56% of GDP.

(5) GDP per capita is $ 1434 Nominal & $ 2908 PPP

(6) GDP growth is 4.7% in 2017, 3.5% in 2018, -7.5% in 2019 and 2.7%in 2020 (forecast). This shows that GDP growth is fluctuating widely and is not stable.

(7) Inflation is 10.3% which rose dangerously to a very high level in previous years showing that economy is crippling.

(8) Unemployment was 10.3% which is high. Country was not able to pay Week's wages to the employees frequently and compelled the government to reduce employment resulting in further unemployment.

(9) Main Industries are Mining- coal, gold, platinum, copper and nickel.

(10) Exports are $ 4.53 billion and Imports are $5. 472 billion resulting in trade deficit $0.942 billion.

(11) Main exports are Platinum, cotton, tobacco, ferroalloys, textiles and clothing.

(12) Main imports are machinery and transport equipment, other manufacturing, chemicals and fuel.

(13) Current Account is $-7.16 million.

(14) Revenue is $3.8 billion, Expenses $5.5 billion with fiscal deficit is $1.7 billion which is 8.10 %. Of GDP. Needs to be substantially reduced.

(15) Gross external debt $ 9.357 is very high compared to the other countries and the fact that there will be no waiver of external debt by IMF.

(16) Foreign Reserves are $431.8 million.

(17) Taxes and tariffs are high. Government spending is 29.7% of GDP. State enterprises are strongly subsidized. Starting or Closing of business is slow and costly. Hiring a worker is cumbersome and firing a worker is difficult. By 2008, unemployment was risen to 94%.

(18) In doubling per GDP from the present stage, Zimbabwe faired worst. It takes 190 years for the country to double its per capita GDP. Very slow growth.

(19) Though Zimbabwe has adequate internal transport and electrical power network, maintenance was neglected over several years.

(20) Democracy is lacking in the country and this is the main cause of the economic meltdown.

(21) There were falls in the share prices of mining companies in Zimbabwe when the government of Zimbabwe implemented laws which required local ownership of mining companies.

(22) Economic growth was 20% in 1980-81. Drought cut sharply into the growth rate in 1982-84. In 1985, it bounced to 30% due to jump in agricultural production.

(23) Bonus to independence war veterans was announced in 1997 (3% of GDP) followed by unexpected spending due to the involvement in Second Congo War in 1998, drought in 1999 weakened the economy. This leads to the country's bankruptcy in the next decade. In 1999 Zimbabwe experienced its 1st defaults in IMF, World Bank, African Development Bank debts in addition to the debts taken out from Western lenders.

(24) Land Reforms by Mugabe, recurrent interference with judiciary, failure to main price controls and exchange rates led to sharp drop in investor's confidence.

(25) Mugabe Government attributes Zimbabwe's economic difficulties to sanctions imposed by Britain, US and EU which results in crippling the economy and conditions of the people in an attempt to overthrow President Mugabe's government. IMF cut off resources to Zimbabwe. Because of sanctions by US and EU foreign policy, no debts have been cancelled (Memorandum) as in other countries. It also stopped food and forced the government into borrowing from local sources.

7

Economy of Angola

The country Angola was ruled mainly by the Portugal and Dutch colonies. There was war for Independence from Portugal from 1961-75. In 1975, the country was free from Portugal colonies. But after the Independence of Angola, there was civil war from 1975 to 2002.

Despite extensive oil and gas resources, diamonds, hydroelectric potential, and rich agricultural land, Angola remains poor, and a third of population relies on subsistence agriculture. In 2002, when the 27 year civil war ended, government policies prioritized the repair and improvement of infrastructure and strengthening of political and social institutions. During the first decade of 21st century, Angola was one of the fastest growing in the world, with reported annual average GDP growth of 11.1 percent from 2001 to 2010. High international oil prices and rising oil production contributed to strong economic growth, although with high inequality, at that time. Corruption is rife throughout the economy and the country remained heavily dependent on the oil sector, which in 2017 accounted for over 90 percent of export by value and 64 % of government revenue. With this end of the oil boom from 2015 Angola entered into a period of economic contraction.

History of Angola

Angola's history traces in the Portuguese reaching the Angola coast in 1484 and began to found trading posts and forts along with the shore. Paulo Dias de Novais found Sao Paulo de Loanda (Luanda) in 1575 followed by discovery of Beguines in 1587.

The principal early trade was in slaves. Portugal merchants purchased the slaves from the local Inbangala and Mbundu peoples, notably slave hunters and sold them to the sugarcane plantations in Brazil. Brazilian ships were frequent visitors to Luanda and Beguines and Angola functioned as a kind of colony of Brazil, with Brazilian Jesuits active in its religious and educational centres.

The Portuguese empire was neglected during the period of Iberian Union, which lasted from 1590 to 1640. The Dutch, bitter enemies of their former master in Spain, invaded many Portuguese overseas possessions. During the separation War against Spain, the Dutch occupied Luanda from 1640 to 1648.The Dutch used the territory to supply their own slaves to the sugarcane planters of Northeastern Brazil.

Portugal expanded their territory but did not control much of the interior prior to the late 19th century. Portuguese started to develop townships, trading posts, logging camps and small possessing factories. From 1764 onwards, there was a gradual change from the slaved based society to one based on production for domestic consumption and exports in 1844, Angola's ships were opened to foreign shipping. In 1850, Portuguese cities in the vast Portuguese Empire exporting peanut oil, coal, timber and cocoa. The principal exports of post-slave economy in the 19th century were rubber, beeswax, and ivory, maize, tobacco, dried meats and cassava flour also began to be locally produced. Prior to 1st World War exportation of coffee, palm kernels and oil. Cotton, cattle leather and hides, and salt fish joined the principal exports.

From 1920 to 1960, strong economic growth, abundant natural resources and development of infrastructure led to the arrival of even more Portuguese settlers. Petroleum was known to exist as early as the mid-19th century, but modern exploitation did began after 1955.

United Nations Angola Verification Mission III and MONUA spent USD 5 billion overseeing implementation of the 1994 peace accord which ultimately failed to end civil war. Protocol prohibited UNITA from buying foreign arms, a provision the United Nations largely did not enforce, so both sides continued to build up stockpile. In spite the increase in civil warfare, the country exported diamonds worth $1.72 billion and the economy grew by an estimate of 4% in 1999. The government introduced new currency denominations in 1999, including a 1 and 5 kwanza.

In 2000, Angola ranked 160 of 174 nations in the United Nations Human Development Index. In April 2000, Angola started an International Monetary Fund Staff Monitoring Programme. (SMP). Government of Angola succeeded in unifying exchange rates and has raised fuel, electricity, and water rates. The civil war internally displaced 3.8 million people, 32% of the population, by 2001.The security brought about by the 2002 peace settlement which has led to the resettlement of 4 million displaced persons, thus resulting in large scale increase in agricultural production. Angola produces 3 million carats (600 kilograms) of diamonds in 2003 and the production was expected to grow 10 million carats (2000 kilograms) per year by 2007. In 2004 China's Exim-Bank approved $2billion line of credit to Angola to rebuild infrastructure. The economy increased by 18% in 2005 and growth was expected to reach 26% in 2006 and stay above 10% for the rest of the decade.

Construction Industry

The construction industry is taking advantage of the growing economy, with various housing project simulated by the government initiatives. Not all construction projects were functional. The new satellite town of Luanda consisting of housing facilities for several hundreds of thousands of people, was completely uninhabited for over four years because of skyrocketing prices, but completely sold out after the government decreased the original price and created mortgage plans at around the election time thus made it affordable for middle-class people.

Despite the abundant natural resources, output per capita is showing the world's lowest. Subsistence agriculture provides the main livelihood for 85% of the population. Oil production and supporting activities are vital to the economy, contributing about 45% to GDP and 90% of exports. Growth is almost entirely driven by rising oil production which surpassed 1.4 million barrels per day in late 2008 and which is expected to grow to 2 million barrels per day by 2007. Control of the oil industry is consolidated in Sonangol Group a conglomerate owned by the Angolan government. With revenues booming from oil exports, the government has started to implement ambitious development programs to build roads and other basic infrastructure to the nation.

In the last decade of the colonial period, Angola was a major African food exporter but now imports almost all its food. Severe wartime conditions, including extensive planning of landmines throughout the countryside have brought agricultural activities to a near-standstill. Some efforts to recover have gone forward, however, notably in fisheries. Coffee production, though fraction of its pre-1975 level, is sufficient for domestic needs and some exports. Expanding oil production is now almost half of GDP and 90% of exports, at 800 thousand barrels per day. Diamonds provided much of the revenue for Jonas Savimbi's UNITA rebellion through illicit trade. Other rich resources and development gold, forest products, fisheries, irn ore, coffee, and fruits.

Economic Indicators

Year	*GDP in billion $*	*GDP per capita*	*GDP Growth*	*Inflation rate in percent*	*Govt. debt in percent of GDP*
1980	20.3	2373	2.4%	46.7%	n/a
2000	50.8	2966	3.1%	325%	133.5%
2007	119.1	5655	14%	12.2%	21%
2014	194	7489	4.8%	7.3%	39.8%
2015	197.9	7417	0.9%.	9.2%	57.1%
2017	193.6	6835	-2.5%	29.8%	65%

Foreign Trade

Exports in 2004 was $10.530 billion. Out of which 92% export was in petroleum products and $785 million worth of diamonds, 7.5% exports were sold abroad that year. In 2006, Angola became the main exporter of oil to China. Trade between Angola and South Africa exceeded $300 million in 2007. From 2000s, Chinese have settled at startup business.

Petroleum

Angola produces and exports more petroleum than any other region in sub-Saharan Africa surpassing Nigeria in 2000s.

UN has criticized the Angolan government for using torture, rape, summary execution, and disappearances, action which Angolan Government has justified on the need to maintain oil output.

Oil makes up over 80% of Angolan exports.

Diamond

Angola is the third large producer of diamonds and has only explored 40% of diamond-rich territory within the country, but has had difficulty in attracting foreign investment because of corruption, human rights violations, and diamond smuggling. Production rose by 30% in 2006. It expects production to increase by 8% in 2007 to 10 million carats annually. The government is trying to attract foreign companies to invest for exploring diamond mines in the country. Angola government loses $375 million annually from diamond smuggling.

Diamond accounted for 1.14% of Angolan exports in 2014.

Iron

Under Portuguese rule, Angola began mining iron in 1967, producing 1.2 million tons in 1967 and 6.2 million tons by 1971. In the early 1970s, 70% of Portuguese Angola iron exports went to Western Europe and Japan. After Independence in 1975, the Angolan Civil War (1975-2002) destroyed most of the territory's mining infrastructure. The redevelopment of Angolan mining industry started in the late 2000s.

Critical Observations of Economy of Angola

(1) The country was ruled by the Portuguese colony and Dutch Colony. It got Independence in 1975 from Portuguese.

(2) Portugal and Dutch oppressed the country by buying slaves from Angola and sold them to Brazil for working them on plant cultivation.

(3) Angola was not fortunate to start effective administration after independence. Civil War started in 1975 and lasted for 27 years to end in 2002. UN provided financial assistance to Angola for settlement of Civil War in 1990 but was not successful in abolishing it.

(4) After end of Civil War, Government started effective administration for the welfare and prosperity of the country. These rulers effectively improved agricultural production, mining and industries. During the civil war, 3.8 million were displace but after the good administration, 4 million people were resettled after end of civil war in 2004.

(5) Most important thing is that rulers administered the country and developed agriculture, diamonds industry, petroleum products, gold etc. These rulers did not show their supremacy to other countries by setting military base in that country and providing military equipments to the country. It did not show aggressive nature while dealing with other countries. Non-interference in the political and military affairs of other countries resulted in economic growth of that country.

(6) Angolan Kwanza is the currency of exchange of Angola. It has population of 30,809,762 in 2018. GDP was $ 91.527 billion with GDP per capita income was$3038 in 2019. Inflation rate was slightly high @15% but at times, it rose to 40% in 2008. Population below poverty line was 36.6% which is on high side. Labour Force was approximately 13.8 million which is 45% of the population.

(7) Exports were $33 billion in 2017 with crude oil, diamonds refined petroleum products coffee, fish and fish products, timber and cotton as main export goods. Imports were $19 .5 billion showing surplus of balance of trade which is $13.5 billion. Good Performance.

(8) Public debt is 65% of GDP and Gross external debt is $42 which is 46% of GDP $91 billion. In fiscal policy, expenditure is $45.44 billion and revenues are 37.02 billion which shows $ 8 billion fiscal deficit which is 8%. Seems high. Foreign reserves $17.29 billion and economic aids #383 million look comfortable.

(9) Overall economy of Angola looks comfortable but influenced by oil, diamond, agriculture which are dependent on vagaries of monsoon and wide inflections in oil prices. This may look unstable at times.

8

Economy of Malawi

The economy of Malawi is predominantly agricultural, with about 80% of the population living in rural areas. The landlocked country in south central Africa ranks among the world's least developed countries. In 2017, agriculture accounted for about one-third of GDP and about 80% of export revenue. The economy depends on substantial inflows of economic assistance from the IMF, the World Bank, and individual donor nations. The government faces strong challenges: to spur exports, to improve educational and health facilities, to face up to environmental problems of deforestation and erosion, and to deal with the problem of HIV/AIDS in Africa.

Agriculture

Agriculture in Malawi

See also: Tobacco industry

Malawi's most important export crop is tobacco, which accounted for a third (30%) of export revenue in 2012. In 2000, the country was the tenth-largest producer in the world. The country's heavy reliance on tobacco places a heavy burden on the economy as world prices decline and the international community increases pressure to limit tobacco production. Malawi's dependence on tobacco is growing, with the product jumping from 53% to 70% of export revenues between 2007 and 2008

A Malawi tea estate

The country also relies heavily on tea, sugarcane and coffee, with these three plus tobacco making up more than 90% of Malawi's export revenue. Tea was first introduced in 1878. Most of it is grown in Mulanje and Thyolo. Other crops include cotton, corn, potatoes, sorghum, cattle and goats. Tobacco and sugar processing are notable secondary industries.

Traditionally Malawi has been self-sufficient in its staple food, maize (corn), and during the 1980s it exported substantial quantities to its drought-stricken neighbors. Nearly 90% of the population engages in subsistence farming. Smallholder farmers produce a variety of crops, including maize, beans, rice, cacassava, tobacco and groundnuts (peanuts). Financial wealth is generally concentrated in the hands of a small elite. Malawi's manufacturing industries are situated around the city of Blantyre.

Lake Malawi and Lake Chilwa provide most of the fish for the region. For many Malawians, fish is the most important source of proteins. Dried fish is not only consumed locally, but also exported to neighboring countries. Most fishing is done on small scale by hand. However, Maldeco Fisheries owns several commercial fishing boats and operates fish farms in the southern part of Lake Malawi.

Dried fish on Likoma Island

Malawi has few exploitable mineral resources. A South-African Australian consortium exploits uranium at a mine near Karonga. Coal is being extracted in Mzimba District. Malawi's economic reliance on the export of agricultural commodities renders it particularly vulnerable to external shocks such as declining terms of trade and drought. High transport costs, which can comprise over 30% of its total import bill, constitute a serious impediment to economic development and trade. Malawi must import all its fuel products. Other challenges include a paucity of skilled labor, difficulty in obtaining expatriate employment permits, bureaucratic red tape, corruption, and inadequate and deteriorating road, electricity, water, and telecommunications infrastructure which hinder economic development in Malawi. However, recent government initiatives targeting improvements in the road infrastructure, together with private sector participation in railroad and telecommunications, have begun to render the investment environment more attractive.

Roadside vendor in Blantyre

The following are Malawi's top 20 agricultural production values and volumes for 2009. (Unofficial figures derived from FAO statistics)

Commodity	*Production in International dollars (1000)*	*Production in tonnes*	*FAO source*
Maize	462,330	3,582,500	
Cassava	404,764	3,823,240	
Tobacco	331,542	208,155	
Groundnuts	116,638	275,176	
Bananas (excluding plantains)	95,152	400,000	F
Sugar cane	82,093	2,500,000	F
Indigenous cattle meat	80,688	0	
Pigeon peas	80,274	184,156	

(Contd...)

Beans, dry	75,706	164,712	
Fresh fruit	74,456	213,321	Im
Plantains	72,634	351,812	Im
Indigenous pig meat	68,788	0	
Tea	55,895	52,559	P
Indigenous goat meat	53,512	0	
Mangoes, mangosteens and guavas	49,527	82,659	Im
Cotton lint	39,017	27,300	F
Paddy rice	36,896	135,988	
Fresh vegetables	30,530	162,012	Im
Indigenous chicken meat	25,713	0	
Cow peas	18,073	72,082	

Key: F: FAO estimate, Im: FAO data based on imputation methodology, P: Provisional official data.

Industry

In 2013, Malawi's manufacturing sector contributed 10.7% of GDP. The main industries are food processing, construction, consumer goods, cement, fertilizer, ginning, furniture production and cigarette production.

The government's attempts to diversify the agriculture sector and move up the global value chain have been seriously constrained by poor infrastructure, an inadequately trained work force and a weak business climate. In order to help companies adopt innovative practices and technologies, the *National Export Strategy* adopted in 2013 affords companies greater access to the outcome of international research and better information about available technologies; it also helps companies to obtain grants to invest in such technologies from sources such as the country's Export Development Fund and the Malawi Innovation Challenge Fund. In parallel, the government has raised its investment in research and development to 1% of GDP.

Food and beverages

Most fruits and vegetables are exported raw, while processed food is imported mainly from South Africa. Carlsberg opened its first brewery outside of Denmark in Blantyre in 1965. The brewery also bottles Coca-Cola products under licence. A mango processing plant for the export of fruit concentrate opened in Salima in 2013. Universal Industries operates several food factories in Blantyre, where it produces sweets, crisps, biscuits, milk powder, soy products and baby food. Coffee and tea are processed by half a dozen of different companies in the regions of Thyolo, Mulanje and around Mzuzu.

Pharmaceutical companies

Malawi has four pharmaceutical companies. They manufacture a limited range of drugs, particularly those that are in great demand on the local market. These are Pharmanova Ltd which is the biggest pharmaceutical manufacturer in Malawi, followed by SADM, Malawi Pharmacies (Pharmaceuticals Limited) and Kentam Products Limited.

Forestry

Lady carrying a solar panel.

Large man-made pine tree forests are located in the Viphya Mountains, around Mulanje and Zomba. Timber production for building materials and furniture is an important industry for these regions. However, most areas in Malawi suffer from deforestation due to illegal logging for charcoal production and the use of firewood.

Electricity

Malawi's sole power supplier is the state owned Electricity Supply Commission of Malawi (ESCOM), which generates almost all its power from hydroelectric plants along the Shire River. The installed is approximately 351MW. About 12% of the country's population has access to electricity, according to 2014 World Bank figures.

The country has been suffering from intermittent power outages as a result of an ongoing drought that has halved power output as water levels of the Shire River dropped significantly. The river usually generates 300MW of electricity, accounting for 98% of Malawi's total supply. However, the drought reduced that capacity to 160MW, according to ESCOM.

Services

The service sector accounts for 51.7% of Malawi's national GDP. Notable industries are tourism, retail, transport, education, health services, telecommunication and the banking sector. The Government of Malawi holds shares in many important companies, such as Malawian Airlines (51%) and Press Corporation Limited. Press Corporation Ltd. is the country's biggest company, with subsidiaries in the tobacco, banking, sugar, fishing, ethanol production, steel production, retail, telecommunication and petrol sectors.

International support

Malawi has undertaken economic structural adjustment programs supported by the World Bank (IBRD), the International Monetary Fund (IMF), and other donors since 1981. Broad reform objectives include stimulation of private sector activity and participation through the elimination of price controls and industrial licensing, liberalization of trade and foreign exchange, rationalization of taxes, privatization of state-owned enterprises, and civil service reform. Malawi qualified for Heavily Indebted Poor Country (HIPC) debt relief and is in the process of refining its poverty reduction strategy.

Malawi has bilateral trade agreements with its two major trading partners, South Africa and Zimbabwe, both of which allow duty-free entry of Malawian products into their countries. The government faces challenges such as the improvement of Malawi's educational and health facilities — particularly important because of the rising rates of HIV/AIDS — and environmental problems including deforestation, erosion, and overworked soils.

Former President Bingu WA Mutharika of Malawi spoke about the country's recent unilateral agricultural reforms at the World Economic Forum on Africa at the United Nations, September 2008.

Move towards economic independence

In 2006, in response to disastrously low agricultural harvests, Malawi, through an initiative by the late President Bingu Mutharika, an economist by profession, began a program of fertilizer subsidies that were designed to re-energize the land and boost crop production. It has been reported that this program, championed by the country's president, is radically improving Malawi's agriculture, and causing Malawi to become a net exporter of food to nearby countries.

Economic grievances though took a downward slide during Mutharika's second term. Economic grievances were a catalyst that resulted in the 2011 economic protests in Malawi in July.

Critical Observations of the present status of Economy of Malawi

(1) The Malawi is the least developed country in the South Central African region. It has the Population of 2 crores and workforce 80 lacs which is 39.1% of the population.

(2) 90% of the population is living on agriculture. Country produces tobacco, cotton, coffee and tea which amounts for 80% of the country's exports with tobacco along amounts to 30% of exports.

(3) Country is dependent on substantial inflows of economic assistance from IMF, World Bank and other individual donors.

(4) Today exchange rate of South African rand is 97 rand =$1.

(5) Fiscal year is 1st April to 31st March

(6) Service sector accounts for 51.3% which includes tourism, retail, transport, education, telecommunication and banking sector.

(7) In foreign trade, the country has exports $1.443 billion and imports $2.386 billion thus trade deficit is about $ 1 billion.

(8) Fiscal deficit is almost nil and external debt 1.86 billion which is about 25% and Public debt is 50.8% of GDP. Both are manageable.

(9) Per capita income is $371 of GDP Nominal GDP is $7.522 billion (Nominal) and $ 25.167 billion in PPP.

(10) Inflation is 8.4% which is high. Unemployment rate is not available. Population below poverty line is 51.35%.

(11) The country is politically on-alignment country. Rulers are concentrating on welfare of the Society with available resources.

(12) Timber production for building construction and furniture is available.

(13) GDP growth varies from 4% in 2017, 3.5% in 2018, and 4.4% in 2019 and is forecast 4.8% in 2020 (forecast).

9

Economy of Mauritius

The economy of Mauritius is a mixed developing economy based on agriculture, exports, financial services, and tourism. It is a sub-Saharian African country but has made great progress in the economy due to the diversification. It got its independence in 1968. Since the 1980s, the government of Mauritius has sought to diversify the country's economy beyond its dependence on just agriculture, particularly sugar production. In terms of energy, Mauritius' endowment with alternative energy resources and good governance makes it one of the potential winners in the global transition to renewable energy and the country is ranked no. 8 among 156 nations in the index of geopolitical gains and losses after energy transition.

Overview

In 1961, Professor James Meade painted a bleak picture of the economic prospects of Mauritius, which then had a population of 650,000. All the disadvantages associated with smallness of island states weighed heavily in his conviction that Mauritius was caught in a Malthusian trap and, therefore, if economic progress could at all be achieved, it would be to a very limited extent. Since independence in 1968, Mauritius has developed from a low-income, agriculturally based economy to a middle-income diversified economy with growing industrial, financial, ICT and tourist sectors. For most of the period, annual growth has been roughly 4%. This compares very favorably with other sub-Saharan African countries and is largely due to sustained progress in economic conditions; between 1977 and 2008, growth averaged 4.6% compared with a 2.9% average in sub-Saharan Africa. Also important is that it has achieved what few fast growing economies achieve, a more equitable income distribution and inequality (as measured by the Gini coefficient) fell from 45.7 to 38.9 between 1980 and 2006.This remarkable achievement has been reflected in increased life expectancy, lowered infant mortality, and a much-improved infrastructure. Sugarcane is grown on about 90% of the cultivated land area and accounts for 25% of export earnings. The government's development strategy centers on expanding local financial institutions and building a domestic information telecommunications industry. Mauritius has attracted more than 9,000 offshore entities, many aimed at commerce in India and South Africa, and investment in the banking sector alone has reached over $1 billion. Mauritius, with its strong textile sector, has been well poised to take advantage of the Africa Growth and Opportunity Act (AGOA).

Mauritius has attracted US$10.98 billion in foreign HYPERLINK "https://en.wikipedia.org/wiki/Foreign_direct_investment" direct investment inflows. Top sectors attracting FDI inflows from Mauritius (from January 2000 to December, 2005) are electrical equipment, telecommunications, fuels, cement and gypsum products and services sector (financial and non-financial).

With a well-developed legal and commercial infrastructure and a tradition of entrepreneurship and representative government, Mauritius is one of the developing world's most successful democracies. The economy has shown a considerable degree of resilience, and an environment already conducive to dynamic entrepreneurial activity has moved further toward economic freedom. The island's institutional advantages are noticeable. A transparent and well-defined investment code and legal system have made the foreign investment climate in Mauritius one of the best in the region. Taxation is competitive and efficient. The economy is increasingly diversified, with significant private-sector activity in sugar, tourism, economic processing zones, and financial services, particularly in offshore enterprises. The government is trying to modernize the sugar and textile industries, which in the past were overly dependent on trade preferences, while promoting diversification into such areas as information and communications technology, financial and business services, seafood processing and exports, and free trade zones. Agriculture and industry have become less important to the economy, and services, especially tourism, accounted for over 72 percent of GDP. The government still owns utilities and controls imports of rice, flour, petroleum products, and cement.

Policies for success

Recent reports on progress on the Millennium Development Goals by the Overseas Development Institute indicated four key reasons for economic success.

(1) Heterodox liberalization and diversification
(2) Concerted strategy of nation building
(3) Strong and inclusive institutions
(4) High levels of equitable public investment

Heterodox liberalization and diversification

Mauritius has followed a pragmatic development strategy in which liberalization process was sequenced and tailored to its competitive advantages and weaknesses. The export-orientated approach has encouraged liberalization supported by strong state involvement as a facilitator (of the enabling environment for the private sector); as operator (to encourage competition); and as regulator (to protect the economy as well as vulnerable groups and sectors from shocks). Strategies were evidence-based and adapted according to results. There has been consistency and stability, regardless of which political party is in power.

Liberalization occurred in phases that were initiated to build on advantages the economy enjoyed on the international market.

- 1970s: Mauritius profited from sugar rents, established an export processing zone EPZ and successfully attracted capital and foreign investment in manufacturing.
- 1980s–1990s: EPZ expanded and led to a significant increase in Foreign Direct Investment (FDI) and tourism. Preferential access to sugar and clothing markets amounted to 7% of GDP in the 1980s and 4.5% in the 1990s, capital and current accounts were liberalized, contributing to an investment and employment boom and the high inflow of FDI brought with it managerial skills.
- 1990s–2010: Further diversification, liberalization and investment.

Concerted strategy of nation building

A concerted strategy of nation building since Independence created the foundations for sustained growth. Partnerships across ethnic groups allowed economic redistribution to be negotiated and the resulting better balance of economic and political power allowed strong and independent institutions. The emerging political system encouraged a consultative approach to policy formation that allowed strategies for growth to be continued regardless of changes in the parties in power.

Strong and inclusive institutions

Strong institutions are critical in ensuring country's competitiveness, economic resilience and stability. They have supported development strategies and ensured that export earnings are reinvested in strategic and productive sectors. In the financial sector they have built a regulated and well-capitalized banking and financial system that protected it from toxic assets prior to the 2008 global financial crisis.

Corruption laws

In 2002, the government adopted the Prevention of Corruption Act, which led to the setting up of an Independent Commission Against Corruption (ICAC) a few months later. The ICAC has the power to detect and investigate corruption and money-laundering offenses and can also confiscate the proceeds of corruption and money laundering. Corruption is not seen as an obstacle to foreign direct investment. Mauritius ranks 45th out of 168 countries in Transparency International's Corruption Perceptions Index for 2015. Mauritius is one of Africa's least corrupt countries.

High levels of equitable public investment

Mauritius has a strong human capital foundation developed through consistent and equitable investment in human development. This enabled Mauritius to exploit advantages, learn from expertise brought in through FDI and maintain competitiveness in a fast evolving international market. Education and health services are free and have been expanded in recent years, in order to create further employment opportunities and ensuring inclusive growth. The educated and adaptable workforce were essential elements of 1980s export-orientated growth. Around 90% of entrepreneurs in the Export Processing Zone (EPZ) and in the manufacturing sector were Mauritian nationals, businesspeople had the human capital, education and knowledge needed to exploit market opportunities. According to the Government of Mauritius the general outlook for the manufacturing sector is positive, as the country offers many opportunities to entrepreneurs across the various value chains but insufficient skilled labour and limited research and development will remain impediments to potentially higher growth in this sector.

Financial services

Mauritius provides an environment for banks, insurance and reinsurance companies, captive insurance managers, trading companies, ship owners or managers, fund managers and professionals to conduct their international business. The economic success achieved in the 1980s engendered the rapid growth of the financial services sector in Mauritius. The following types of offshore activities can be conducted in Mauritius:

- Offshore Banking
- Offshore Insurance
- Offshore Funds Management
- International Financial Services
- Operational Headquarters
- International Consultancy Services

- Shipping and Ship Management
- Aircraft Financing and Leasing
- International Licensing and Franchising
- International Data Processing and Information Technology Services
- Offshore Pension Funds
- International Trading
- International Assets Management

Information and communication technology

Since 2002, Mauritius has invested heavily into the development of a hub in Information and Communication Technology (ICT). The contribution of the ICT sector accounts for 5.7% of the GDP. The ICT Sector employs 15,390 people. In 2016, two students from Mauritius became finalists in Google Code-in. In 2017, Mauritius got its first grand prize winner. In 2012, Mauritius participated for the first time in Google Summer of Code. In 2018, the cyberstorm.mu team from Mauritius led three tracks during the Internet Engineering Task Force Hackathon in Bangkok.

Statistical Data

Name	*Source*	*Year*	*Macroeconomic statistics[edit]Notes*	*Ref*
GDP (PPP)	International Monetary Fund	2012	GDP (PPP) is $20.200 billion	[1]
	World Bank	2012	GDP (PPP) is $19,245,631,329	[2] [3]
	The World Facebook	2012	GDP (PPP) is $20,950,000,000	[4]
GDP (PPP) per capita	International Monetary Fund	2012	GDP (PPP) per capita is $15,591.974	[5]
	World Bank	2012	GDP (PPP) per capita is $14,902	[6]
	The World fact book	2013	GDP (PPP) per capita is $16,100	[7]
GDP (PPP) per person employed	World Bank	1990-2010		[8]
	The World fact book	2012		[9]
GDP (nominal)	United Nations	2012	GDP (nominal) is $10,086,649,093	[10]
	International Monetary Fund	2013	GDP (nominal) is US$11.930 billion	[11]
	World Bank	2012	GDP (nominal) is $10,486,037,634	[12] [13]
	The World fact book	2013	GDP (nominal) is $11.9 billion	[14]

(*Contd...*)

GDP (nominal) per capita	United Nations	2012		[15]
	International Monetary Fund	2013	GDP (nominal) per capita is US$9,159.681	[16]
	World Bank	2012		[17]
	The World fact book	2013		[18]
Gross national income (Atlas method)	World Bank	2012	Gross national income is US$11,070 million	[19]
GNI per capita (Atlas method and PPP)	World Bank	2012	Average national income (PPP) of US$8,570 per person/Year	[20]

Critical Observations of Present Status of economy of Mauritius.

(1) Mauritius is a small tiny island in Sub Saharan African country. It is a mixed economy based on agriculture, exports, financial services, and tourism. It got its independence in 1968.

(2) In 1961, Professor James Meade painted a bleak picture of the economic prospects of Mauritius. Government of Mauritius however made good progress by diversification the country's economy beyond its dependence on just agriculture, particularly sugar production. It achieved better progress than other sub-Saharan African countries and is largely due to sustained progress in economic conditions. During 1977 and 2008, growth averaged 4.6% compared with 2.9% average in sub-Saharan Africa.

(3) Also important is that it has achieved what few growing economies achieve, a most equitable income distribution and inequality fell from 45.7% to 38.9% between 1980 and 2006. This remarkable achievement has been reflected in increased life expectancy, lower infant mortality, and a much-improved infrastructure. The country is well governed by the leaders of the country. Sugarcane is produced on 90% of cultivated land and accounts for 25% of the country's exports.

(4) Government's development strategy expanded local financial institutions and industry. Mauritius has attracted $10.9 billion in FDI inflows in electric equipments, telecommunications, fuels, cement and gypsum products and services sector.

(5) Exchange rate of Mauritius rupee was 30.12 per US dollar on 26-03-2014 from 29.96 in 2002 and 29.13 in 2001. There was no large devaluation of Mauritius rupee per Us Dollar during 2001-2014.

(6) Mauritius rulers, unlike any other country, have not shown their false domination to the other countries but concentrated in good governing the country and therefore made remarkable economic progress in spite of very few opportunities to them to make this progress in the fields of agriculture, telecommunication and other sectors. It diversified from Command Economy to Market Economy.

(7) Mauritius is a small country with population of 12.65 lacs people out of which Labour Force is 6.07 lac. Unemployment is 6.8% and inflation is 3.23%.

(8) Its Financial year is 1July -3o June.

(9) GDP is $14.277 billion Nominal and $ 29.004 billion PPP with GDP per Capita $11280 Nominal and $23669 PPP as per 2018 estimates.

(10) Exports were $2.36 billion and imports $4.986. Trade Deficit is $2.626 billion which is too high. External debt of $19.99 billion as at 31-12-2017 works out to 162% of GDP. This may result in Loan Servicing trap and will need the country to apply for rescheduling for Loan instalments and interest payment frequently to IMF which will be approved with stringent conditions. The external debt should be reduced substantially to the level of 40% of GDP to avoid debt servicing problems.

(11) Public debt is 64% of GDP i.e. 9.14 billion looks slightly high.

(12) Budgetary deficit 0 .3% with Revenue $2.994 billion and Expenses $3.018 billion is negligible.

(13) Economic Aids and Foreign reserves are comfortable.

10

Economy of Mozambique

The end of the Mozambican Civil War (1977–1992). In 1987, the government embarked on a series of macroeconomic reforms designed to stabilize the economy. These steps, combined with donor assistance and with political stability since the multi-party elections in 1994, have led to dramatic improvements in the country's growth rate. Inflation was brought to single digits during the late 1990s although it returned to double digits in 2000–02. Fiscal reforms, including the introduction of a value-added tax and reform of the customs service, have improved the government's revenue collection abilities. In spite of these gains, Mozambique remains dependent upon foreign assistance for much of its annual budget. Subsistence agriculture continues to employ the vast majority of the country's workforce. A substantial trade imbalance persists although the opening of the MOZAL aluminum smelter, the country's largest foreign investment project to date has increased export earnings. Additional investment projects in titanium extraction and processing and garment manufacturing should further close the import/export gap. Mozambique's once substantial foreign debt has been reduced through forgiveness and rescheduling under the International Monetary Fund's Heavily Indebted Poor Countries (HIPC) and Enhanced HIPC initiatives, and is now at a manageable level.

Although the Portuguese participated in the trading networks of East Africa as early as the 16th century, they did not establish hegemonic (total) colonial dominance over the entire territory that now comprises Mozambique until the 19th century. Portugal founded settlements, trading posts, forts and ports. Cities, towns and villages were founded all over the territory by the Portuguese. Others were expanded and developed greatly under Portuguese rule. By this time, Mozambique had become a Portuguese colony, but administration was left to the trading companies (like Mozambique Company and Niassa Company) who had received long-term leases from Lisbon. By the mid-1920s, the Portuguese succeeded in creating a highly exploitative and coercive settler economy, in which African natives were forced to work on the fertile lands taken over by Portuguese settlers. Indigenous African peasants mainly produced cash crops designated for sale in the markets of Portugal. Major cash crops included cotton, cashews, tea and rice. This arrangement ended in 1932 after the takeover in Portugal by the new António de Oliveira Salazar government. Thereafter, Mozambique, along with other Portuguese colonies, was put under the direct control of Lisbon. In 1951, it became an overseas province. The economy expanded rapidly during the 1950s and 1960s, attracting thousands of Portuguese settlers to the country. It was around this time that the first nationalist guerrilla groups began to form in Tanzania and other African countries. The strong industrial and agricultural development that did occur throughout the 1950s, 1960s and early 1970s was based on Portuguese development plans, and also included British and South African investment.

In 1959–60, Mozambique's major exports included cotton, cashew nuts, tea, sugar, copra and sisal. The expanding economy of the Portuguese overseas province was fueled by foreign direct investment, and public investment which included ambitious state-managed development plans. British capital owned two of the large sugar concessions was controlled by England and the United States. In 1948 the petroleum concessions which were controlled given to the Mozambique Gulf Oil Company. At Maotize coal was mined; the industry was chiefly financed by Belgian capital. 60% of the capital was held by the Societe Miniere ET Geologique Belge, 30% by the Mozambique Company, and the remaining 10% by the Government of the territory. Three banks were in operation, the Banco Nacional Ultramarino, Portuguese, Barclays Bank, D.C.O., British, and the Banco Totta e Standard de Moçambique (a joint-venture between Standard Bank of South Africa and Banco Totta HYPERLINK "https://en.wikipedia.org/wiki/Banco_Totta_ % 26_A%C3%A7ores"&HYPERLINK "https://en.wikipedia.org/wiki/Banco_Totta_%26_A%C3%A7ores" Açores of the Portuguese mainland). Nine out of the twenty-three insurance companies were Portuguese. 80% of life-insurance was in the hands of foreign companies which testifies the openness of the economy. The Portuguese overseas province of Mozambique was the first territory of Portugal, in the sisal plantations Swiss capital was invested, and in copra concerns, a combination of Portuguese, Swiss and French capital was invested. The large availability of capital from both Portuguese and international origin, allied to the wide range of natural resources and the growing urban population, lead to an impressive growth and development of the economy. From the late stages of this notable period of high growth and huge development effort started in the 1950s, was the construction of Cahora Bassa dam by the Portuguese, which started to fill in December 1974 after construction was commenced in 1969. In the face of intransigent Portuguese ruling authorities, the main nationalist movement, FRELIMO, began a guerrilla war which gradually wrested control of parts of the northernmost regions of the territory from the Portuguese. The Mozambican War of Independence came to an end in 1974 following a leftist military coup in Portugal. The new left-wing government in Lisbon had no wish to maintain an empire and negotiations on the country's independence began immediately. In 1975, after the leftist military coup of 24 April 1974 in Portugal that overthrew the Estado Novo regime which had governed the nation and its overseas territories, the colonial wars that raged in the various Portuguese African territories since the early 1960s ended. At independence, Mozambique's industrial base was well-developed by Sub-Saharan Africa standards, thanks to a boom in investment in the 1960s and early 1970s. Indeed, in 1973, value-added in manufacturing was the sixth highest in Sub-Saharan Africa. However, further industralisation was stopped by the hasty exodus of 90 percent of the ethnic Portuguese citizens during and after the independence process which was concluded on June 25, 1975. Portuguese population's rapid exodus left the Mozambican economy in disarray. The situation was exacerbated by the Mozambican Civil War (1977–1992) during the following years that destroyed the remaining wealth and left the former Portuguese Overseas Province in a state of absolute disrepair.

Independent Mozambique

GDP per capita (current), compared to neighbouring countries (world average = 100)

Mozambique became an independent state in 1975. The exodus of trained Portuguese and the eruption of the Mozambican Civil War in 1977 opposing RENAMO to FRELIMO, drove the country to absolute chaos. Mozambique became an independent nation and the Frente de Libertacao de Mocambique (FRELIMO), the socialist guerrilla organization that had fought the colonial war against Portugal, assumed power....... Over the next several years, FRELIMO pursued numerous socialist policies, including nationalization of land and large industries, centralized planning, and heavy funding for the national educational and health systems, which however, remained weak for decades in independent Mozambique, and still are among the most ineffective and underfunded in the world. The exodus (mass departure) of the Portuguese following independence in 1975 facilitated the takeover of many shops by Mozambicans. Unfortunately, the exodus, which totaled over 275,000 ethnic Portuguese, also led to a huge loss of professionals, productive machinery, entrepreneurs, and skilled workers. By the early 1980s, Mozambique became what Joseph Hanlon—author of Peace without Profit: How the IMF Blocks Rebuilding in Mozambique —

called a "Cold War battlefield." The term refers to the situation in which socialist FRELIMO, with Soviet backing, was forced to fight a lengthy civil war (Mozambican Civil War) against a counterinsurgency movement of Mozambicans named RENAMO, funded and directed by the neighboring white minority states of apartheid South Africa and Rhodesia. The cold war was defined by animosity between capitalist and socialist world powers, and though there was never an outright military conflict between the former and the latter, each respectively funded counterinsurgency movements against governments they disfavored. The capitalist governments of South Africa and Zimbabwe feared that a successfully ruled African socialist system might send a message of revolution and self-rule to citizens in contemporaneous majority rule African countries, such as their own.

The political pressure of the ideologically charged civil war, in conjunction with the excruciating need for aid and funds to finance imports, compelled FRELIMO to negotiate its first Structural Adjustment Package (SAP) with the World Bank and the International Monetary Fund (IMF) in 1986 (commonly referred to as the Bretton Woods Institutions or International Financial Institutions—IFIs). The series of SAPs that followed thereafter, required privatization of major industries, less government spending, deregulation of the economy, and trade liberalization. The SAPs, therefore, have essentially focused on the implementation of an unfettered free market economy.

Today, the economy of Mozambique continues to be dominated by agriculture. Major exports include prawns, cotton, cashew nuts, sugar, citrus, copra and coconuts, and timber. Export partners, in turn, include Spain, South Africa, Portugal, the United States, Japan, Malawi, India, and Zimbabwe. Imports, such as farm equipment and transport equipment, are capital goods that are worth more than agricultural products, hence Mozambique's large trade deficit. The country also imports food, clothing, and petroleum products. Import partners include South Africa, Zimbabwe, Saudi Arabia, Portugal, the United States, Japan, and India. In the past several years, the value of imports outweighed the value of exports by 5 to 1 or more—a factor that obliges Mozambique to depend heavily on foreign aid and loans by foreign commercial banks and the Bretton Woods Institutions (BWIs). In 1995 alone, Mozambique received $1.115 billion in aid. In 1999, the total external debt stood at $4.8 billion. Fortunately, in the same year significant economic recovery did occur, as the real GDP growth rate reached 10 percent.

Sectors

All economic sectors ranging from manufacturing and agriculture to tourism and finance, declined sharply after independence from Portugal in 1975, but picked up in the 2000s after the end of the Mozambican Civil War, although they are still performing well below potential.

Gas and oil reserves

Recent oil and gas discoveries across East Africa, most notably in Mozambique and Tanzania, have seen the region emerge as a new player in the global oil and gas industry.

The discoveries have driven billions of dollars in annual investment to the region. According to BMI estimates, the finds in the last few years are more than that of any other region in the world, and the discoveries are expected to continue for the next few years.

Agriculture, fishing and forestry

In Mozambique, agriculture is the mainstay of the economy and the country has a great potential for growth in the sector. Agriculture employs more than 80 percent of the labour force and provides livelihoods to the vast majority of over 23 million inhabitants. Agriculture contributed 31.5 percent of the GDP in 2009, while commerce and services accounted for 44.9 percent. By contrast, 20 percent of the total export value in 2009 originated from the agriculture sector, mostly through the export of fish (mainly shrimps and prawns), timber, copra, cashew nuts and cotton, coconuts, tea and tobacco.

Agricultural potential is high, particularly in the fertile northern regions, which accounts for the bulk of the country's agricultural surplus. The main cash crops are sugar, copra, cashew nuts, tea, and tobacco. Total sugar production was expected to rise by 160% in the 2000s, which would make the country a major net exporter for the first time since independence. All the plantations and refineries have been privatized. Marine products, particularly prawns, are Mozambique's largest single export. There is an abundance of marine resources that are not fully exploited. After the Mozambican Civil War, the return of internally displaced persons and the gradual restoration of rural markets have enabled Mozambique to increase agricultural production dramatically.

Food security, vulnerability and risk management

Mozambique's diverse soils and climatic conditions, influenced by latitude, variations in altitude, topography and the proximity to the coast, offer a wide range of production opportunities; agricultural potential is high despite frequent droughts and floods. Water resources are relatively plentiful and the country is traversed by a number of perennial rivers and enjoys considerable mineral reserves. Nevertheless, Mozambique is a highly indebted, poverty-stricken country.

Mozambique net importer of food. Total annual cereal import requirements average 0.89 million tons (0.14 million of maize, 0.39 of rice and 0.36 of wheat). Mozambique must also import substantial quantities of meat and livestock products.

Mining and semi-processing

There are large mineral deposits, but exploration has been constrained by the civil war (1977–1992) and poor infrastructure. The World Bank has estimated that there was the potential for exports worth US$200m by 2005 – in the late 1990s they totaled US$3.6m, some 1% of total exports, and a contribution of less than 2% of GDP. Minerals currently being mined include marble, bentonite, coal, gold, bauxite, granite, titanium and gemstones. Illegal exports from artisanal production are estimated at US$50 million.

Mozambique exported its first batch of coal in 2011 and expects to become the world's largest coal exporter. It is also spending about US$50 billion in infrastructure projects to access its coal reserves. Mozambique is reported to have the fourth largest reserves of natural gas in the world, after Russia, Iran, and Qatar.

Manufacturing

Although very well developed during the 1960s and early 1970s, industralisation declined rapidly with the loss of most Portuguese after independence. Since 1995 production has increased sharply and was expected to grow by 33% in 2001 due to the expansion (costing US$860m) of the Mozal aluminum smelter which was approved in mid-2001. The country's largest ever foreign investment, Mozal has little impact on employment, but is making a substantial contribution to balance of payments through taxes generated. Exports generated in the first quarter of 2001 were worth US$85.3, the primary factor for the 172% expansion in Mozambique's exports for the period. Completion of the smelter resulted in aluminum accounting for up to 70% of exports. Construction materials, agricultural processing, beverages, and consumer goods were the main sub-sectors.

Tourism

This sector declined sharply after independence from Portugal, but has been developed, although it is still performing well below potential. The national strategy is to promote high-value, low-volume tourism. The first section of the "Peace Park" initiative which links with Kruger Park in

South Africa, and Gonarezhou in Zimbabwe, was a project aimed at the development of tourism.

Telecommunication

Immediately after a long civil war ended in 1992 the country started to reform telecommunication sector. The mobile sub-sector has experienced excellent growth rates following the introduction of competition in 2003 between Vodacom Mozambique and mCel, the incumbent mobile subsidiary of the national telco, Telecomunicações de Moçambique (TDM). The government is intent on introducing competition to the fixed-line sector as well, but it is hesitating to privatize TDM. All other services are open to competition, subject to licensing by the industry regulator, INCM. Internet usage in the country has been hampered by the inadequate fixed-line infrastructure and the high cost of international bandwidth, but this market sector has started to accelerate following the introduction of various kinds of broadband services including ADSL, cable modems, WiMAX wireless broadband and mobile data services, and then the landing of the first international submarine fibres optic cable in the country (SEACOM) in 2009. Further improvements can be expected from the ongoing rollout of 3G mobile services and a national fibres backbone network as well as the landing of the second international fibres (EASSy) in 2010. The lower cost of bandwidth has already started to trickle down to lower consumer prices in some service segments, while others have remained unchanged.

Finance

The banking system collapsed after independence from Portugal in 1975. From an earlier position (in the 1980s) of central government control of the economy, Mozambique has initiated rapid reforms in recent years, accelerating the implementation of market-based economic policies, and committing to a policy of fiscal and monetary discipline. In 1995 the government introduced its medium-term economic growth, strategy which it continues to pursue. Since the late 1990s, both national and international banking, established an environment for rapid economic growth and development of the financial system. On 11 December 2012, the Mozambican Government acquire the Portuguese shares of BNI Banco Nacional de Investimento, owning 100% of the bank and turning it into the country's development bank and nominated a former Governor of the Bank of Mozambique, Adriano Maleiane as CEO.

Macroeconomic review

Alleviating poverty: at the end of the civil war in 1992, Mozambique ranked among the poorest countries in the world. It still ranks among the least developed countries, with very low socioeconomic indicators. In the last decade, however, it has experienced a notable economic recovery. Per capita GDP in 2000 was estimated at $222; in the mid-1980s, it was $120. With a high foreign debt (originally $5.7 billion at 1998 net present value) and a good track record on economic reform, Mozambique was the first African country to receive debt relief under the initial Heavily Indebted Poor Country (HIPC) Initiative. In April 2000, Mozambique qualified for the Enhanced HIPC program as well and attained its completion point in September 2001. This led to the Paris Club members agreeing in November 2001 to substantially reduce the remaining bilateral debt. This will lead to the complete forgiveness of a considerable volume of bilateral debt, including that owed to the United States.

Rebounding growth

The resettlement of war refugees and successful economic reform have led to a high growth rate: the average growth rate from 1993 to 1999 was 6.7%; from 1997 to 1999, it averaged more than 10% per year. The devastating floods of early 2000 slowed GDP growth to a 2.1%; estimates point to a full recovery in 2001. The government projects have caused the economy to continue to expand between 7%-10% a year for the next 5 years, although rapid expansion in the future hinges on several major foreign investment projects, continued economic reform, and the revival of the agriculture, transportation, and tourism sectors. More than 75% of the population engages in small scale agriculture, which still suffers from inadequate infrastructure, commercial networks and investment. Yet 88% of Mozambique's arable land is still uncultivated; focusing economic growth in this sector is a major challenge for the government.

Low inflation

The government's tight control of spending and the money supply, combined with financial sector reform, successfully reduced inflation from 70% in 1994 to less than 5% from 1998–99. Rates spiked in 2000, however, to a rate of 12.7% due to economic disruptions stemming from the devastating floods. Starting 2001 the inflation was in the range of 5%-12%.

2003 - 5.2%; 2004 - 7.5%; 2005 - 7.6%; 2006 - 11.8%; 2007 - 7.4%; 2008 - 8.4%; 2009 - 4.2%; 2010 - 10.0%; 2011 - 11.1%

Extensive economic reform

Economic reform has been extensive. Over 1,200 state-owned enterprises (mostly small) have been privatized. Preparations for privatization and/or sector liberalization are underway for the remaining parastatals, including telecommunications, electricity, water service, airports, ports, and the railroads. The government frequently selects a strategic foreign investor when privatizing a parastatal. Additionally, customs duties have been reduced, and customs management has been streamlined and reformed. The government introduced a highly successful value-added tax in 1999 as part of its efforts to increase domestic revenues. Plans for 2001-02 include Commercial Code reform; comprehensive judicial reform; financial sector strengthening; continued civil service reform; improved government budget, audit, and inspection capability; and introduction of the private management of water systems in major cities. The process of liberalization in Mozambique was an initiative from the World Bank. In the Mid 1990s, World Bank made it necessary for the nation to liberalize their *cashew* sector. The lifting of protectionist measures for the cashew industry in Mozambique was an attempt to increase the incomes of cashew farmers and reduce poverty in the country. This policy of liberalization has been one of the most contentious policies.

Improving trade imbalance

In recent years, the value of imports has surpassed that of exports by almost 2:1, an improvement over the 4:1 ratio of the immediate post-war years. In 2000 imports were $1,217 million, and exports were $723 million. Support programs provided by development partners have largely compensated for balance of payments shortfalls. The medium-term outlook for exports is encouraging, since a number of foreign investment projects should lead to substantial export growth and a better trade balance. MOZAL, a large aluminum smelter that commenced production in mid-2000, has greatly expanded the nation's trade volume. Traditional Mozambican exports include cashews, shrimp, fish, copra, sugar, cotton, tea, and citrus fruits. Most of these industries are being rehabilitated. Mozambique is becoming less dependent on imports for basic food and manufactured goods due to steady increases in local production.

Critical Observations of the present status of Economy of Mozambique

(1) After the end of the Civil war in 1992, the country started making growth and development. In 1987, Government embarked on a series of macroeconomic reforms. Through donors assistance. Political stability was established after multi-party elections in 1994. Dramatic improvement was brought. Inflation was brought down to single digit in 1990s but again rose to double digit in 2000-2002.

(2) Foreign debts has been reduced through forgiveness (moratorium) and rescheduling under IMF Heavily Indebted Poor Countries and Enhanced initiatives. External debt is now at manageable level.

(3) Portuguese participated in the trading network of East Africa in 16th century but did not establish total colonial dominance over the entire territory that now comprises Mozambique until the 19th century.

(4) Portugal's contributions in the growth and development was very high. Portugal founded settlements, trading posts, forts, ports, cities, towns and villages all over the territory. Others were expanded and developed greatly under Portugal rule. By this, Mozambique had become a Portugal Colony but administration was left to the trading companies who received long term leases from Lisbon.

(5) By Mid-1920, the Portuguese succeeded in creating a highly exploitative and coercive settler economy, in which African natives are forced to work on the fertile lands taken over by the Portuguese settlers. Indigenous African peasants mainly produced cash cops designed for sale in the market of Portugal (cotton, cashews, tea and rice.)

(6) Mozambique like other Portugal colonies was put under the direct control of Lisbon. It became an overseas province in 1951. Economy expanded rapidly in 1950-60 attracting thousands of settlers to the country group. Nationalist guerrilla group began to form in Tanzania and other African countries. The strong industrial and agricultural development that did occur throughout the 1950-60 and early 1970 as based on Portuguese development plans and included British and South African investment. The expanding economy of the Portuguese overseas province was fueled by foreign direct investment which included ambitious state-managed development plan. British capital owned by two of the large sugar concession was controlled by England and US in 1948. Petroleum concession was given to the Mozambique gulf coal mine was mainly financed by Belgian capital.

(7) Swiss and French capital was invested. Large availability of capital both from Portuguese and international origin led to impressive growth and development of the economy. Construction of Cahora Bassam dam was started in 1969 and completed in December 1974.War of Independent was fought in 1974 and Mozambique got independence in 1975. But Civil war started in

1977 to 1992. There was hasty exodus of 90% of the ethnic Portugal citizens. Civil war in 1977-1992 destroyed developments made by Portugal.

(8) Mozambique currency is Mozambican metical (MZN) which is 23-25 MZM=$1.

(9) Fiscal year is Calendar year

(10) Trade Organizations are AU, AFCFTA, SADC, World Bank, IMF, WTO, and Group of 77

(11) It is low income country as well as developing/ emerging country.

(12) GDP is $14.396 billion (Nominal, 2018 and $ 39.183 billion PPP in 2018

(13) GDP Growth was 3.7% in 2017, 3.4% in 2018 2.0% in 2019 and 3.7% in 2020 forecast

(14) Inflation is 3.91% in 2018

(15) Population about 2 crore and Labour force 1.01 crore

(16) Population below poverty line was 55% too high

(17) Unemployment 17% Very high

(18) Main Industries are Aluminum, coal, petroleum chemicals, fertilizers, textiles, tobacco and food processing

(19) Exports are in aluminum, coal, bulk electricity, cotton, prawn and main imports are fuel, chemicals, fertilizers, machinery, vehicles, metal products, textile and food. Trade deficit $2.698 billion. Exports $3.469 billion and Imports $6.167 billion. Very high trade deficit. Imports should be curtailed and exports to be raised.

(20) Revenues are $4.315 billion and expenses $4.905 billion. Fiscal deficit is maintainable.

(21) External debt is $7.79 billion which is above 54% of GDP. This is excessive and should be substantially reduced to avoid restructuring of external debt by IMF or Moratorium.

(22) Domestic loan is 34.6% of GDP which is well manageable and credit rating is satisfactory.

11

Economy of Tanzania

The economy of Tanzania is the second largest in the East African Community and the tenth Africa. Tanzania is largely dependent on agriculture for employment, accounting for about half of the employed workforce. The economy has been transitioning from a command economy to a market economy since 1985. Although total GDP has increased since these reforms began, GDP per capita dropped sharply at first, and only exceeded the pre-transition figure in around 2007.

Following the rebasing of the economy in 2014, the GDP increased by a third to $41.33 billion.

History

Significant measures have been taken to liberalize the Tanzanian economy along market lines and encourage both foreign and domestic private investment. Beginning in 1986, the Government of Tanzania embarked on an adjustment program to dismantle the socialist (Ujamaa) economic controls and encourage more active participation of the private sector in the economy. The program included a comprehensive package of policies which reduced the budget deficit and improved monetary control, substantially depreciated the overvalued exchange rate, liberalized the trade regime, removed most price controls, eased restrictions on the marketing of food crops, freed interest rates, and initiated a restructuring of the financial sector.

Current GDP per capita of Tanzania grew more than 40 percent between 1998 and 2007. In May 2009, the International Monetary Fund (IMF) approved an Exogenous Shock Facility for Tanzania to help the country cope with the global economic crisis. Tanzania is also engaged in a Policy Support Instrument (PSI) with the IMF, which commenced in February 2007 after Tanzania completed its second three-year Poverty Reduction and Growth Facility (PRGF), the first having been completed in August 2003. The PRGF was the successor program to the Enhanced Structural

Adjustment Facility, which Tanzania also participated in from 1996–1999. The IMF's PSI program provides policy support and signaling to participating low-income countries and is intended for countries that have usually achieved a reasonable growth performance, low underlying inflation, an adequate level of official international reserves, and have begun to establish external and net domestic debt sustainability.

Tanzania also embarked on a major restructuring of state-owned enterprises. The program has so far divested 335 out of some 425 parastatal entities. Overall, real economic growth has averaged about 4 percent a year, much better than the previous 20 years, but not enough to improve the lives of average Tanzanians. Also, the economy remains overwhelmingly donor-dependent. Moreover, Tanzania has an external debt of $7.9 billion. The servicing of this debt absorbs about 40 percent of total government expenditures. Tanzania has qualified for debt relief under the enhanced Heavily Indebted Poor Countries (HIPC) initiative. Debts worth over $6 billion were canceled following implementation of the Paris Club 7 Agreement. Height measure studies for Tanzania show that welfare increased through the years of colonization, with a decline during the 1930s. This is due to epidemics in that period of time.

Macro-economic trend

This is a chart of trend of Gross Domestic Product of Tanzania at market prices estimated by the International Monetary Fund with figures in millions of Tanzanian Shillings.

Year	*Gross Domestic Product*	*US Dollar Exchange*
1980	45,749	8.21 Shillings
1985	115,006	17.87 Shillings
2005	13,713,477	1,127.10 Shillings
2010	–	1,515.10 Shillings

Mean wages were $0.52 per man-hour in 2009. The economy saw continuous real GDP growth of at least 5% since 2007.

The following table shows the main economic indicators in 1980–2017. Inflation below 5% is in green.

Year	*GDP (in bil. US$ PPP)*	*GDP per capita (in US$ PPP)*	*GDP growth (real)*	*Inflation rate (in Percent)*	*Government debt (in % of GDP)*
1980	11.0	592	▲3.3%	▲30.2%	n/a
1981	▲12.1	▲633	▲0.5%	▲25.7%	n/a
1982	▲13.0	▲657	▲0.6%	▲28.9%	n/a
1993	▲27.4	▲1,009	▲1.2%	▲26.1%	n/a
1994	▲28.4	▲1,016	▲1.6%	▲37.9%	n/a

(*Contd...*)

1995	▲30.0	▲1,044	▲3.6%	▲26.8%	n/a
1996	▲32.0	▲1,081	▲4.5%	▲21.0%	n/a
1997	▲33.7	▲1,108	▲3.5%	▲16.1%	n/a
1998	▲35.3	▲1,132	▲3.7%	▲12.8%	n/a
1999	▲37.6	▲1,174	▲4.8%	▲7.9%	n/a
2000	▲40.3	▲1,228	▲4.9%	▲6.0%	n/a
2001	▲43.7	▲1,298	▲6.0%	▲5.1%	50.2%
2002	▲47.4	▲1,377	▲6.9%	▲4.6%	▼47.0%
2003	▲51.4	▲1,447	▲6.4%	▲4.4%	▼44.3%
2004	▲56.6	▲1,548	▲7.2%	▲4.1%	▲44.6%
2005	▲62.1	▲1,651	▲6.5%	▲4.4%	▲46.8%
2006	▲66.9	▲1,732	▲4.7%	▲7.3%	▼32.8%
2014	▲128.7	▲2,754	▲7.0%	▲6.1%	▲33.8%
2015	▲139.1	▲2,918	▲7.0%	▲5.6%	▲37.2%
2016	▲150.4	▲3,091	▲7.0%	▲5.2%	▲38.0%
2017	▲162.5	▲3,247	▲6.0%	▲5.3%	▼37.0%

Agriculture

Main article: Agriculture in Tanzania

Farmers clearing a rice field using their hands.

The Tanzanian economy is heavily based on agriculture, which accounts for 24.5 percent of gross domestic product, provides 85 percent of exports and accounts for half of the employed workforce; the agricultural sector grew 4.3 percent in 2012, less than half of the Millennium Development Goal target of 10.8 percent. 16.4 percent of the land is arable, with 2.4 percent of the land planted with permanent crops.

This strong dependence on agriculture, makes Tanzania's economy highly vulnerable to weather shocks and fluctuating commodity prices. 76% of Tanzania's population subsist thanks to agriculture and, due to the lack of knowledge and infrastructure to develop and implement some kind of agricultural technology, any droughts, floods, or temperature shocks can severely damage the living standards of those people and create huge increases in unemployment, hunger, and malnutrition rates, as well as, in really severe case, mortality rates due to starvation.

Industry

Industries are a major and growing component of the Tanzanian economy, contributing 22.2 percent of GDP in 2013. This component includes mining and quarrying, manufacturing, electricity and natural gas, water supply, and construction.

Mining

Main article: Mining industry of Tanzania

Mining contributed 3.3 percent of GDP in 2013. The vast majority of the country's mineral export revenue comes from gold, accounting for 89 percent of the value of those exports in 2013. It also exports sizable quantities of gemstones, including diamonds and tanzanite. All of Tanzania's coal production, which totalled 106,000 short tons in 2012, is used domestically.

Minerals

Other minerals exploited in Tanzania include;

1. Pozzolana
2. Salt
3. Gypsum
4. Kaolinite
5. Silver ore
6. Copper
7. Phosphate
8. Tin
9. Graphite
10. Bauxite.

Modern gold mining in Tanzania started in the German colonial period, beginning with gold discoveries near Lake Victoria in 1894. The first gold mine in what was then Tanganyika, the Sekenke Gold Mine, began operation in 1909, and gold mining in Tanzania experienced a boom between 1930 and World War II. By 1967, gold production in the country had dropped to insignificance but was revived in the mid-1970s, when the gold price rose once more. In the late 1990s, foreign mining companies started investing in the exploration and development of gold deposits in Tanzania, leading to the opening of a number of new mines, like the Golden Pride mine, which opened in 1999 as the first modern gold mine in the country, or the Buzwagi mine, which opened in 2009.

Buzwagi Gold Mine

Nickel reserves amounting to 290,000 tonnes were discovered in October 2012 by Ngwena Company Limited, a subsidiary of the Australian mining company IMX Resources. An initial investment of around USD $38 million has been made since exploration began in 2006, and nickel should start being mined at the end of 2015.

Chinese firms have been showing major interest in Tanzania's mineral deposits; an announcement was made in late 2011 of a plan by the Sichuan Hongda Group, to invest about USD3 billion to develop the Mchuchuma coal and Liganga iron ore projects in the south of the country. It was also announced in August 2012 that China National Gold Corp are in talks to purchase mining assets in Tanzania from African Barrick Gold, in a deal that could be worth more than £2 billion.

In November 2012, the Tanzanian government announced investigations into allegations that mining investors in the country were harassing and on some occasions, killing residents around mining sites.

Electricity

The government-owned Tanzania Electric Supply Company Limited (TANESCO) dominates the electric supply industry in Tanzania. The country generated 6.013 billion kilowatt hours (kWh) of electricity in 2013, a 4.2 percent increase over the 5.771 billion kWh generated in 2012. Generation increased by 63 percent between 2005 and 2012; however, only 15 percent of Tanzanians had access to electric power in 2011.Almost 18 percent of the electricity generated in 2012 was lost because of theft and transmission and distribution problems. The electrical supply varies, particularly when droughts disrupt hydropower electric generation; rolling blackouts are implemented as necessary. The unreliability of the electrical supply has hindered the development of Tanzanian industry. In 2013, 49.7 percent of Tanzania's electricity generation came from natural gas, 28.9 percent from hydroelectric sources, 20.4 percent from thermal sources, and 1.0 percent from outside the country. The government is building a 532 kilometres (331 mi) gas pipeline from Mnazi Bay to Dar es Salaam, with a scheduled completion in 2015. This pipeline is expected to allow the country to double its electricity generation capacity to 3,000 megawatts by 2016. The government's goal is to increase capacity to at least 10,000 megawatts by 2025.

Natural gas

According to PFC Energy, 25 to 30 trillion cubic feet of recoverable natural gas resources have been discovered in Tanzania since 2010. The value of natural gas actually produced in 2013 was US$52.2 million, a 42.7 percent increase over 2012.

Commercial production of gas from the Songo Island field in the Indian Ocean commenced in 2004, thirty years after it was discovered there. Over 35 billion cubic feet of gas was produced from this field in 2013, with proven, probable, and possible reserves totaling 1.1 trillion cubic feet.

The gas is transported by pipeline to Dar es Salaam. Of 27 August 2014, TANESCO owed the operator of this field, Orca Exploration Group Inc., US$50.4 million, down from US$63.8 million two months earlier.

A newer natural gas field in Mnazi Bay in 2013 produced about one-seventh of the amount produced near Songo Island but has proven, probable, and possible reserves of 2.2 trillion cubic feet. Virtually all of that gas is being used for electricity generation in Mtwara.

The Indian Ocean, off the coast of Mozambique and Tanzania, is proving to be a rich hunting ground for natural gas exploration. According to US Geological Survey estimates, the combined gas reserves of Mozambique and Tanzania could be as high as 250 trillion cubic feet. In Mozambique alone, proven gas reserves have increased dramatically from a mere 4.6 trillion cubic feet in 2013 to 98.8 trillion cubic feet as of mid-2015. Given continued offshore discoveries and the size of discoveries to date, continued growth in proven gas reserves is likely to continue into the foreseeable future.

New exploration on more frontier blocks, however, will likely be slowed as oil and gas prices fall and companies apply increasing caution to investing in frontier markets with nascent industries, poor infrastructure and long lead times.

External trade and investment

Tanzania's history of political stability has encouraged foreign direct investment. The government has committed itself to improve the investment climate including redrawing tax codes, floating the exchange rate, licensing foreign banks, and creating an investment promotion center to cut red tape. Tanzania has mineral resources and a largely untapped tourism sector, which might make it a viable market for foreign investment.

The stock market HYPERLINK "https://en.wikipedia.org/wiki/Market_capitalisation"capitalization of listed companies in Tanzania was valued at $588 million in 2005 by the World Bank.

Zanzibar's economy is based primarily on the production of cloves (90% grown on the island of Pemba), the principal foreign exchange earner. Exports have suffered from the downturn in the clove market.

The Government of Zanzibar has been more aggressive than its mainland counterpart in instituting economic reforms and has legalized foreign exchange bureaus on the islands. This has loosened up the economy and dramatically increased the availability of consumer commodities. Furthermore, with external funding, the government plans to make the port of Zanzibar a free port. Rehabilitation of current port facilities and plans to extend these facilities will be the precursor to the free port. The island's manufacturing sector is limited mainly to import substitution industries, such as cigarettes, shoes, and process agricultural products. In 1992, the government designated two export-producing zones and encouraged the development of offshore financial services. Zanzibar still imports much of its staple requirements, petroleum products, and manufactured articles.

Critical Observations of present status of the Economy of Tanzania

(1) Tanzania is the Second largest economy in the East African Community and the tenth largest in Africa.

(2) It depends on agriculture for employment

(3) The economy is seen transitioning from a command economy to a market economy. GDP increased by a third to 43.33 billion.

(4) Significant measures have been taken to liberalize the Tanzanian economy along market lines and encouraged both foreign and domestic private investment. Beginning in 1986, Government of Tanzania embarked on an adjustment program to distribute the Socialist economic control to encourage more participation of the private sector. It included a comprehensive package of policies to reduce the budget deficit and improve monetary control, depreciation in overvalued exchange rate, liberalized the trade regime, removed most price controls, free interest rate, ease restrictions on marketing of food crops, restructuring of financial sector.

(5) In May 2009, IMF approved an Exogenous Shock Facility for Tanzania to help the country cope with the global economic crisis. Tanzania also is engaged with Policy Support Instrument (PSI) with IMF which commenced in February 2007. Second three year Poverty Reduction & Growth Facility (PRGF) completed in August 2003.

(6) Tanzania embarked on a major restructuring of state owned enterprises. Economic growth of 4% remains overwhelmingly donor dependent. External debt was $7.9 billion. Servicing of the debt was 40% of the total expenditure. Debts worth $6 billion were cancelled following implementation of Paris Club & Agreement. This is Moratorium.

(7) Exchange rate of Tanzanian shilling widely fluctuated from 8.21 Shilling =$1 in 1980to shilling 17.87 =$1 in 1985 and Shilling 1515.10 =$1 in 2010.

(8) Agriculture income is 24.5% of GDP. Agriculture grew 2 4.5% but target was 10.8%. 16.4% land is arable and 2.4% of land planted with permanent crops. Dependent on Agriculture leads vulnerable to weather shocks.

(9) Industry production accounts to 22.2% of GDP.

(10) Mining exports comes from gold which is 89% of the exports. Other exports are gemstone, diamond, coal gypsum. Coal Production is 106000 tons. Gold mines boom was experienced in 1930 and during World War II.

(11) Chinese firms are showing major interest in Tanzania's plan for the Sichuan Hong da Group plans to invest $3billion to develop the project. Mozambique's capacity of natural gas expanded from 4.6 trillion cubic feet to 98.8 trillion cubic feet by Middle of 2015.

(12) GDP Nominal $163 billion. GDP growth 7.2% Population 6 crores and GDP per capita $1100-

(13) Labour Force 2.36 crores

(14) Unemployment 2.2% and Inflation 3.5%

(15) Exports $5.6685 billion and imports $10.441 billion Current Trade Deficit $4.002 billion

(16) External debt $15.4 billion and Public debt $472.7% Billion which is 290% of the GDP Nominal.

(17) Fiscal Deficit is $1.18 billion with Revenue $7.117 billion and Expenditure $8.917billion is normal

(18) Foreign Reserves are $4.83 million (4-5 months of imports)

12

Economy of South Africa

When we think of the economy of South Africa, we are reminded of the ruthless treatment given by the South Africa to our young Barrister Mr. Mohandas Karmachand Gandhi in late ninetieth century when he was travelling in Railways first AC coach in South Africa. When white Ticket Checker found him, he prohibited Gandhi from travelling in First Class coach and threw his luggage on the Station as well as forced him to delight from train on that Station. Gandhi started peaceful protest against this injustice but was ruthlessly beaten up. This news spread all over the world and there was heavy criticism all over the world of South Africa and economic sanctions against South Africa internationally for its race-based policy named Apartheid. Elections in the State were also taken on racial basis. South Africa was ruled by Colonies like Dutch, French, German and British. The cricket was widely spread and promoted in colonized countries like South Africa, India and West Indies. But South Africa was playing cricket matches only with England, Australia and New Zealand but not with India, West Indies till recently. Country, however, changed its racial policy lately and is now playing Cricket Test matches with India, West Indies, Pakistan and Ceylon on racial division.

The economy of South Africa is the second largest in the Africa, after Nigeria. As a regional manufacturing hub, it is the most industrialized and diversified economy on the continent. South Africa is an upper-middle-income economy – one of only eight such countries in Africa. Since 1996, at the end of over twelve years of international sanctions, South Africa's Gross Domestic Product almost tripled to peak at $400 billion in 2011, but has since declined to roughly $385 billion in 2019. In the same period, foreign exchange reserves increased from $3 billion to nearly $50 billion creating a diversified economy with a growing and sizable middle class, within two decades of ending apartheid. South African state owned enterprises play a significant role in the country's economy with the government owning a share in around 700 SOEs involved in a wide array of important industries. In 2016 the top five challenges to doing business in the country were (1) inefficient government bureaucracy, (2) restrictive labour regulations, (3) a shortage of skilled workers, (4) political instability, and (5) corruption, whilst the country's strong banking sector was rated as a strongly positive feature of the economy. The nation is among the G20, and is the only African member of the group.

History

The formal economy of South Africa has its beginnings in the arrival of Dutch settlers in 1652, originally sent by the Dutch East India Company to establish a provisioning station for passing ships. As the colony increased in size, with the arrival of French Huguenots and German citizens, some of the colonists were set free to pursue commercial farming, leading to the dominance of agriculture in the economy.

At the end of the 19th century, the British annexed the colony. This led to the Great Trek, spreading farming deeper into the mainland, as well as the establishment of the independent Boer Republics of Transvaal and the Orange Free State.

In 1870 diamonds were discovered in Kimberley, while in 1886 some of the world's largest gold deposits were discovered in the Witwatersrand region of Transvaal, quickly transforming the economy into a resource-dominated one. The British annexed the area as a result of the Boer War which witnessed the placement of Boer women and children in British-built concentration camps. The country also entered a period of industrialization during this time, including the organization of the first South African trade unions.

The country soon started putting laws distinguishing between different races in place. In 1948 the National Party won the national elections, and immediately started implementing an even stricter race-based policy named Apartheid, effectively dividing the economy into a privileged white one, and an impoverished black one. The policy was widely criticized and led to crippling sanctions being placed against the country in the 1980s.

South Africa held its first multi-racial elections in 1994, leaving the newly elected African National Congress (ANC) government the daunting task of trying to restore order to an economy harmed by sanctions, while also integrating the previously disadvantaged segment of the population into it. The 1994 government inherited an economy wracked by long years of internal conflict and external sanctions.

The government refrained from resorting to economic populism. Inflation was brought down, public finances were stabilized, and some foreign capital was attracted. However, growth was still subpar. At the start of 2000, then President Thabo Mbeki vowed to promote economic growth and foreign investment by relaxing restrictive labour laws, stepping up the pace of privatization, raising governmental spending and cutting interest rates sharply from 1998 levels. His policies faced strong opposition from organized labour. From 2004 onward economic growth picked up significantly; both employment and capital formation increased.

In April 2009, amid fears that South Africa would soon join much of the rest of the world in the late-2000s recession, Reserve Bank Governor Tito Mboweni and Minister of Finance Trevor Manuel differed on the matter: whereas Manuel foresaw a quarter of economic growth, Mboweni predicted further decline: "technically," he said, "that's a recession." In 2009 the Nobel-Prize-winning economist Joseph Stiglitz warned South Africa that inflation targeting should be a secondary concern amid the global financial crisis of 2007–2009.

South Africa, unlike other emerging markets, has struggled through the late 2000s recession, and the recovery has been largely led by private and public consumption growth, while export volumes and private investment have yet to fully recover. The long-term potential growth rate of South Africa under the current policy environment has been estimated at 3.5%. Per capita GDP growth has proved mediocre, though improving, growing by 1.6% a year from 1994 to 2009, and by 2.2% over the 2000–09 decade, compared to world growth of 3.1% over the same period.

The high levels of unemployment, at over 25%, and inequality are considered by the government and most South Africans to be the most salient economic problems facing the country. These issues, and others linked to them such as crime, have in turn hurt investment and growth, consequently having a negative feedback effect on employment. Crime is considered a major or very severe constraint on investment by 30% of enterprises in South Africa, putting crime among the four most frequently mentioned constraints.

In April 2017, political tensions in the country arose over the sacking of nine cabinet members including Minister of Finance Pravin Gordhan by the president Jacob Zuma. The finance minister was seen as central to efforts to restore confidence in South Africa. As a result of the tensions, S&P Global cut South Africa's credit rating to junk status on Monday 3 April 2017. Fitch Ratings followed suit on Friday 7 April 2017 and cut the country's credit status to the sub-investment grade of BBB-. The South African rand lost more than 11% in the week following the cabinet Reshuffling.

Historical Statistics 1980-2017

Year	*GDP in $bil*	*GDP per capita PPP*	*GDP growth real*	*Inflation rate*	*uneployment*	*Govt. debts(% of GDP)*
1980	134.7	4631	6.6%	14.2%	9.2%	-
1990	235.4	6398	-0.03%	14.2%	18.8%	
2000	345.8	7701	4.3%	5.4%	23%	42.2%
2010	600.8	11818	5%	4.3%	24.9%`	34.7%
2015	728.8	13311	1.3%	4.6%	25.4%	49.3%
2017	765.6	13544	1.3%	5.3%	27.5%	52.7%

The following table shows the main economic indicators in 1980–2017. Inflation under 5% is in green.

South Africa Export Treemap by Product (2014) from Harvard Atlas of Economic Complexity.

South Africa has a comparative advantage in the production of agriculture, mining and manufacturing products relating to these sectors. South Africa has shifted from a primary and secondary economy in the mid-twentieth century to an economy driven primarily by the tertiary sector in the present day which accounts for an estimated 65% of GDP or $230 billion in nominal GDP terms. The country's economy is reasonably diversified with key economic sectors including mining, agriculture and fisheries, vehicle manufacturing and assembly, food processing, clothing and textiles, telecommunication, energy, financial and business services, real estate, tourism, transportation, and wholesale and retail trade.

Seasonally adjusted and annualized quarterly value added (Q1 2013)	
Industry	*Value added (R billion, 2004 prices)*
Agriculture, forestry and fishing	43.382
Mining and quarrying	97.096
Manufacturing	296.586
Electricity, gas and water	33.951
Construction	59.943
Wholesale and retail trade, hotels and restaurants	246.584
Transport, storage and communication	178.591
Finance, real estate and business services	422.850
General government services	271.209
Personal services	107.690
Taxes less subsidies on products	215.668
GDP at market prices	1,973.552

Natural resources

See also: Mining industry of South Africa

Mining has been the main driving force behind the history and development of Africa's most advanced economy. Large-scale and profitable mining started with the discovery of a diamond on the banks of the Orange River in 1867 by Erasmus Jacobs and the subsequent discovery and exploitation of the Kimberley pipes a few years later. Gold rushes to Pilgrim's Rest and Barberton were precursors to the biggest discovery of all, the Main Reef/Main Reef Leader on Gerhardus Oosthuizen's farm Langlaagte, Portion C, in 1886, the Witwatersrand Gold Rush and the subsequent rapid development of the gold field there, the biggest of them all.

South Africa is one of the world's leading mining and mineral-processing countries. Though mining's contribution to the national GDP has fallen from 21% in 1970 to 6% in 2011, it still represents almost 60% of exports. The mining sector accounts for up to 9% of value added.

In 2008, South Africa's estimated share of world platinum production amounted to 77%; kyanite and other materials, 55%; chromium, 45%; palladium, 39%; vermiculite, 39%; vanadium, 38%; zirconium, 30%; manganese, 21%; rutile, 20%; ilmenite, 19%; gold, 11%; fluorspar, 6%; aluminum, 2%; antimony, 2%; iron ore, 2%; nickel, 2%; and phosphate rock, 1%. South Africa also accounted for nearly 5% of the world's polished diamond production by value. The country's estimated share of world reserves of platinum group metals amounted to 89%; hafnium, 46%; zirconium, 27%; vanadium, 23%; manganese, 19%; rutile, 18%; fluorspar, 18%; gold, 13%; phosphate rock, 10%; ilmenite, 9%; and nickel, 5%. It is also the world's third largest coal exporter.

The mining sector has a mix of privately owned and state-controlled mines, the latter including African Exploration Mining and Finance Corporation.

Agriculture and food processing

The agricultural industry contributes around 5% of formal employment, relatively low compared to other parts of Africa, as well as providing work for casual laborers and contributing around 2.8% of GDP for the nation. However, due to the aridity of the land, only 13.5% can be used for crop production, and only 3% is considered high potential land. The sector continues to face problems, with increased foreign competition and crime being two of the major challenges for the industry. The government has been accused of either putting in too much effort, or not enough effort, to tackle the problem of farm attacks as opposed to other forms of violent crime.

Maize production, which contributes to a 36% majority of the gross value of South Africa's field crops, has also experienced negative effects due to climate change. The estimated value of loss, which takes into consideration scenarios with and without the carbon dioxide fertilization effect, ranges between tens and hundreds of millions of Rands.

According to FAOSTAT, South Africa is one of world's largest producers of: chicory roots (4th); grapefruit (4th); cereals (5th); green maize and maize (7th); castor oil seed (9th); pears (9th); sisal (10th); fibre crops (10th). In the first quarter of 2010, the agricultural sector earned export revenues for R10.1 billion and used R8.4 billion to pay for imported agricultural products, therefore earning a positive trade balance of R1.7 billion.

The most important agricultural exports of South Africa include: edible fruit and nuts, beverages, preserved food, tobacco, cereals, wool not carded or combed, miscellaneous food, sugar, meat, milling products, malt and starch. These products accounted for over 80% of agricultural export revenue in the first quarter of 2010. The most important agricultural imports, which accounted for over 60% of agricultural import value during the same period, include: cereals, meat, soya-bean oil cake, beverages, soya-bean oil and its fractions, tobacco, palm oil and its fractions, miscellaneous food, spices, coffee, tea, and preserved food.

The dairy industry consists of around 4,300 milk producers providing employment for 60,000 farm workers and contributing to the livelihoods of around 40,000 others.

The food sub-sector is the largest employer within the agro-processing sector – contributing 1.4% to total employment, and 11.5% within the manufacturing sector. In 2006, the agro-processing sector represented 24.7% of the total manufacturing output. Although the economy as a whole gained 975,941 jobs between 1995 and 2006, the agro-processing sector lost 45,977 jobs. The competitive pressures from abroad, particularly from China and India, played a role in the decline of exports for the food, textiles and paper sub-sectors, as firms in these sectors increasingly compete with lower cost producers. Increased exports from the beverages, tobacco, wood and leather sub-sectors over the period are probably due to the presence of large dominant firms within these sectors in South Africa, that have managed to remain competitive.

Manufacturing

The manufacturing industry's contribution to the economy is relatively small, providing just 13.3% of jobs and 15% of GDP. Labour costs are low, but not nearly as low as in most other emerging markets, and the cost of the transport, communications and general living is much higher.

The South African automotive industry accounts for about 10% of South Africa's manufacturing exports, contributes 7.5% to the country's GDP and employs around 36,000 people. Annual production in 2007 was 535,000 vehicles, out of a global production of 73 million units in the same year. Vehicle exports were in the region of 170,000 units in 2007, exported mainly to Japan (about 29% of the value of total exports), Australia (20%), the UK (12%) and the US (11%). South Africa also exported ZAR 30.3 billion worth of auto components in 2006.

BMW, Ford, Volkswagen, Daimler-Chrysler, General Motors, Nissan and Toyota all have production plants in South Africa. Large component manufacturers with bases in the country are Arvin Exhaust, Bloxwitch, Corning and Senior Flexonics. There are also about 200 automotive component manufacturers in South Africa, and more than 150 others that supply the industry on a non-exclusive basis. The industry is concentrated in two provinces, the Eastern Cape and Gauteng. Companies producing in South Africa can take advantage of the low production costs and the access to new markets as a result of trade agreements with the European Union and the Southern African Development Community.

After a steep decline of 10.4% in 2009, the manufacturing sector performed well in 2010, growing by 5%, though this rebound was limited to the automotive, basic chemicals, iron and steel and food and beverages industries. The performance of this sector remains curtailed by the low demand in South Africa's main export markets in the developed world.

Service industry

Telecommunications in South Africa and Tourism in South Africa

The domestic telecommunications infrastructure provides modern and efficient service to urban areas, including cellular and internet services. In 1997, Telkom, the South African telecommunications parastatal, was partly privatized and entered into a strategic equity partnership with a consortium of two companies, including SBC, a U.S. telecommunications company. In exchange for exclusivity (a monopoly) to provide certain services for 5 years, Telkom assumed an obligation to facilitate network modernization and expansion into the unserved areas. A Second Network Operator was to be licensed to compete with Telkom across its spectrum of services in 2002, although this license was only officially handed over in late 2005 and has recently begun operating under the name, Neotel. Five mobile-phone companies provide service to over 20 million subscribers, with South Africa considered to have the 4th most advanced mobile telecommunications network worldwide. The five major cellular providers are Vodacom, MTN, Cell C, 8ta (owned by the parastatal, Telkom) and Virgin Mobile.

Business process outsourcing

Over the last few decades, South Africa and particularly the Cape Town region has established itself as a successful call centre and business process outsourcing destination. With a highly talented pool of productive labour and with Cape Town sharing cultural affinity with Britain, large overseas firms such as Lufthansa, Amazon.com, ASDA, The Carphone Warehouse, Delta Airlines and many more have established inbound call centres within Cape Town as a means of utilizing Cape Town's low labour costs and talented labour force.

Tourism

South Africa is a popular tourist destination, with around 860,000 arrivals per month (March 2008) of which around 210,000 is from outside the African continent. In 2012 South Africa received 9.2 million international arrivals. In August 2017 3.5 million travelers came to South Africa. According to the World Travel & Tourism Council, travel and tourism directly contributed ZAR102 billion to South African GDP in 2012 and supports 10.3% of jobs in the country. Among the main attractions are the diverse and picturesque landscape, the game reserves and the highly regarded local wines.

Financial services

Johannesburg

South Africa has a sophisticated financial structure with the JSE Securities Exchange, a large and active stock exchange that ranks 18th in the world in terms of total market capitalization of $1.2 Trillion as of March 2018.

The banking industry, overseen by the South African Reserve Bank, is dominated by four local players: Nedbank, ABSA, Standard Bank and First Rand. These banks provide both retail and investment banking services as the sector has become highly competitive with the re-entry of many experienced foreign banks, which returned to the market in the mid-1990s, having left in the late 1980s. Banks operating in South Africa, when left short of liquidity, need to borrow from the SARB at a fluctuating repo rate, which in turn allows the central bank to monitor liquidity positions.

Informal sector

South Africa's informal sector contributes 8% of the country's GDP and supports 27% of all working people. The South African Local Economic Development Network values the informal economy at 28% of SA's GDP. Given the relevance of this input, there is a constant interest in developing actions on an inclusive urban planning for the working poor.

Trade and investment

Principal international trading partners of South Africa—besides other African countries—include Germany, the United States, China, Japan, the United Kingdom and Spain. Chief exports include corn, diamonds, fruits, gold, metals and minerals, sugar, and wool. Machinery and transportation equipment make up more than one-third of the value of the country's imports. Other imports include chemicals, manufactured goods, and petroleum.

As a result of a November 1993 bilateral agreement, the Overseas Private Investment Corporation (OPIC) can assist US investors in the South African market with services such as political risk insurance and loans and loan guarantees. In July 1996, the US and South Africa signed an investment fund protocol for a $120 million OPIC fund to make equity investments in South and Southern Africa. OPIC is establishing an additional fund – the Sub-Saharan Africa Infrastructure Fund, capitalized at $350 million – to investment in infrastructure projects. The Trade and Development Agency also has been actively involved in funding feasibility studies and identifying investment opportunities in South Africa for U.S. businesses.

Despite the numerous positive economic achievements since 1994, South Africa has struggled to attract significant foreign direct investment. The situation may have started to change however, with 2005 seeing the largest single FDI into South Africa when Barclays bought a majority share in local bank Absa Group Limited. Deals between the British-based Vodafone and South Africa's Vodacom have taken place in 2006. In 2010, two multibillion-dollar deals, one by HSBC to acquire Nedbank and one by Walmart to acquire Massmart Holdings, fell through. (Walmart did buy Massmart in 2011)

Land reform and property rights

Nationalization of mines debate

South Africa has been riven by arguments over whether the state should take over mineral resources. A study commissioned by the African National Congress recommended against the policy, saying nationalization would be an "economic disaster." However, the ANC Youth Employment supporters disagree and state that it will give the government direct control over the mining sector which is also in alignment with the Freedom Charter signed in 1995.

Land redistribution

The government aimed to transfer 30% of the 82 million hectares presumed to be in the hands of white farmers by Gugile Nkwinti, Minister of Rural Development and Land Reform, amounting to 24.5 million hectares, to black farmers by 2014. 6.7 million hectares had been transferred by early 2012 via redistribution and restitution.

The land reform program has been criticized both by farmers' groups and by landless workers, the latter alleging that the pace of change has not been fast enough, and the former alleging anti-white racist treatment with threats of genocide, voiced openly on multiple occasions by the ANC, including the former president Zuma, and expressing concerns that a similar situation to Zimbabwe's land reform policy may develop, a fear exacerbated by comments made by former deputy president Phumzile Mlambo-Ngcuka.

Labour market

South Africa has an extreme and persistent high unemployment rate of over 25%, which interacts with other socioeconomic problems such as: inadequate education, poor health and high levels of crime. The poorest have limited access to economic opportunities and basic services. According to a 2013 Goldman Sachs report, that number increases to 35% when including people who have given up looking for work. A quarter of South Africans live on less than US$1.25 a day.

South Africa's mass unemployment dates back to the 1970s, and continued to rise throughout the 1980s and 1990s. Unemployment has increased substantially since the African National Congress came to power in 1994, increasing from 15.6% in 1995 to 30.3% in 2001. In the second quarter of 2010, the jobless rate increased to 25.3%, and the number of people with work fell by 61,000 to 12,700,000. The biggest decline in employment was recorded in the manufacturing industry, which lost 53,000 jobs. Agriculture lost 32,000 jobs, employment in the construction industry fell by 15,000. In the third quarter of 2010, 29.80% of Blacks were recorded as unemployed, compared with 22.30% of Coloureds, 8.60 of Asians and 5.10% of Whites.

The official unemployment rate, though very high by international standards, understates its magnitude because it includes only adults who are actively looking for work. Only 41% of the population of working age have any kind of job (formal or informal). This rate is 30% points lower than that of China, and about 25% lower than that of Brazil or Indonesia. The relatively generous social grants reduces the political cost of unemployment. There is some evidence that households view paid employment and social grants as substitutes at the margin: households that lose a pension-eligible member subsequently report increased labour force participation.

The unemployment problem is characterised by its lengthy duration. In the mid-1990s, nearly two-thirds of unemployed people had never worked for a salary. The 2005 Labour Force Survey found that 40% of unemployed individuals have been unemployed for more than three years, while 59% had never had a job at all. The unemployment rate has fueled crime, inequality and social unrest. The global economic downturn made the problem worse, wiping out more than one million jobs. In September 2010, over one-third of South Africa's workforce were out of work, and so were more than half of Blacks aged 15–34, three times the level than Whites.

Some experts contend that higher wages negotiated by politically powerful trade unions have suppressed job growth. According to a study by Dani Rodrik, the shrinkage of the non-mineral tradable sector since the early-1990s and the weakness of the export-oriented manufacturing were more to blame for the low level of employment.

Knowledge

There has been a large degree of human capital flight from South Africa in recent years. South Africa's Bureau of Statistics estimates that between 1 million and 1.6 million people in skilled, professional, and managerial occupations have emigrated overseas since 1994 and that, for every emigrant, 10 unskilled people lose their jobs. There are a range of causes cited for the migration of skilled South Africans.

In mid-1998, the Southern African Migration Project (SAMP) undertook a study to examine and assess the range of factors that contribute to skilled South Africans' desire to leave the country: over two-thirds of the sample said that they had given the idea of emigration some thought while 38% said they had given it a "great deal of thought". Among the reasons cited for wishing to leave the country was the declining quality of life and high levels of crime. Furthermore, the government's affirmative action policy was identified as another factor influencing the emigration of skilled White South Africans. The results of the survey indicate that skilled Whites are strongly opposed to this policy and the arguments advanced in support of it, due to the negative impact it has had on South Africa.

However, flight of human capital in South Africa should not be attributed solely to regional factors. For example, the demand for skilled laborers in the UK, US, Canada, New Zealand, and Australia has led to active recruitment programs by those countries in South Africa. These countries accounted for 75% (by volume) of recent skilled emigration with the UK receiving approximately half of annual skilled South African emigration from 1990-96. It has been suggested that the role of domestic socio-political variables may be negligible. The health sector has been hit particularly hard.

A widespread skills drain in South Africa and in the developing world in general is generally considered to be a cause for concern.

For the medical sector, the loss of returns from investment for all doctors emigrating is $1.41bn for South Africa. The benefit to destination countries is huge: $2.7bn for the United Kingdom alone.

In a case of reverse brain drain a net 359,000 high-skilled South Africans have returned to South Africa from foreign work assignments over a five-year period from 2008 to 2013. This was catalyzed by the global financial crisis of 2007-8 and perceptions of higher quality of life in South Africa relative to the countries from which they first emigrated to. It is estimated that around 37% of those returning are professionals such as lawyers, doctors, engineers and accountants.

Illegal immigration

Immigration to South Africa and Xenophobia in South Africa

Refugees from poorer neighbouring countries include many immigrants from the Democratic Republic of the Congo, Mozambique, and Zimbabwe, Malawi and others, representing a large portion of the informal sector. With high unemployment levels amongst poorer South Africans, xenophobia is prevalent and many South Africans feel resentful of immigrants who are seen to be depriving the native population of jobs, a feeling which has been given credibility by the fact that many South African employers have employed migrants from other countries for lower pay than South African citizens, especially in the construction, tourism, agriculture and domestic service industries. Illegal immigrants are also heavily involved in informal trading. However, many immigrants to South Africa continue to live in poor conditions, and the South African immigration policy has become increasingly restrictive since 1994.

Trade unions

Since 2007 the South African unions representing public sector workers recurrently went on strike, demanding pay rises significantly above inflation, in a practice that some experts argue is suppressing job growth, harming millions of South Africans who are out of a job.

In August and September 2010, South African unions organized a crippling four-week national strike involving 1.3 million public sector workers, demanding an 8.6% wage increase. The strike ended after the government had raised its 5.2% wage increase to 7.5%. The deal swelled state spending by about 1%.

Protesters sought to block hospitals, and South African media have reported numerous acts of violence against health and education staff who insisted on going to work. Volunteers and army medics were called in to help at hospitals, and some patients were moved to private medical facilities.

There is a persistent wage differential between unionized and non-unionized workers in South Africa, suggesting that unions are keeping wages higher for their members, thereby posing additional challenges to the unemployment problem.

In July 2014, amidst a national strike by 220,000 metalworkers, General Motors temporarily shut down its vehicle assembly plant, frustrating its plans to build 50,000 cars a year in the country. "The ongoing labour disruptions are harming the South African economy and are affecting the country's image around the globe," the company said in a statement at the time.

Black Economic Empowerment

The demise of apartheid in 1994 left a skewed racial economic hierarchy that placed Whites firmly at the top, followed by Indians, Coloureds, and then Blacks. Since then, the African National Congress government has made Black Economic Empowerment (BEE) a policy centre-piece, but by the party's own admission it has failed to improve the lot of the vast majority of Black South Africans and has taken much opportunity from the White minority, who are mainly a skilled minority. As of 2014 roughly ten percent of the Top 100 companies on the Johannesburg Stock Exchange were directly held by black investors though Black Economic Empowerment schemes. Black Economic Empowerment policies have been credited with creating a class of Black South Africans with a level of wealth on the same order of magnitude as very rich White South Africans.

Black Economic Empowerment—its purpose the "economic empowerment of all black people, including women, workers, youth, people with disabilities and people living in rural areas"—requires the Minister of Trade and Industry to develop and publish Codes of Good Practice, aimed at setting guidelines for the process of BEE in the whole economy. A scorecard is used by the Department to measure compliance with the BEE requirements, and is used for public procurement, public-private partnerships, sale of state-owned enterprises, when licenses are applied for, and for any other relevant economic activity.

The government's Black Economic Empowerment policies have drawn criticism from the Development Bank of Southern Africa for focusing "almost exclusively on promoting individual ownership by black people (which) does little to address broader economic disparities, though the rich may become more diverse." The System has also been criticized for placing lesser educated people in more important positions in the workplace and their failure to perform to the standards required has had an immense impact on the economy. Another criticism also includes that the system goes against the constitution's preaching of equality by having preference over people, not on merit, but for their skin Colour and is considered the opposite of what many people fought for during the Apartheid era. Official affirmative action policies have seen a rise in black economic wealth and an emerging black middle class. An increasing number of black candidates who are supposed to be beneficiaries of affirmative action are dissociating themselves from it, largely because of the perception that the appointments are not based on merit. The policy has also been criticized for having a negative impact on employment levels as it is viewed as being more of an additional burden for employees than as a transformative agent for the unemployed, particularly in an economy where a major cause of inequality has been a growing disparity of income within the majority black population divided along lines of employment.

Gender Equality

South Africans in general, regardless of race, hold what would be considered "traditional" stances on gender roles for men and women. The majority of the workforce is composed of males, while the majority of women do not participate. This viewpoint on males as "breadwinners" is very much in line with traditional African values across the continent. Additionally, females face a problem in terms of earnings, with 77% of women earning the same as their male counterparts. However, more women are becoming part of the agricultural workforce (55%) as of 2012, marking a move towards modernization for women's participation in the economy. South African legislation is strongly geared to promoting gender equality in the workplace. This is characterised by several comprehensive government programs and organisations that provide resources and services to females, both adult and adolescent. Such initiatives include the Employment Equity Act, No. 55 of 1988 (aimed at promoting women's participation in mainly private sector jobs). UNFPA South Africa is one such promoter of these policies and programs. Internally, the South African government has founded the Commission for Gender Equality. The commission's main focus is on securing adequate education and job training for women who are disenfranchised or otherwise at a disadvantage when attempting to enter the workforce.

Not uncommon in Africa, gender equality seems to be a very cogent problem in the South African workforce. According to Bain & Company, around 31% of companies have no form of female leadership, either in management or executive positions. 22% of board directors are women, however, only 7% were designated as "executives", lower than the global average of 12%. Additionally, the ENPE (Employee Net Promoter Score) for women is a net negative (- 4) as compared to men (8), according to a survey conducted of 1000 participants. This indicated a low level of actual economic promotion for women, despite public and international initiative towards the contrary.

Infrastructure

Energy

After years of sub-standard maintenance and the South African government's inability to manage strategic resources, the state-owned power supplier Eskom started experiencing deficiency in capacity in the electrical generating and reticulation infrastructure in 2007. Such lack led to inability to meet the routine demands of industry and consumers, resulting in countrywide rolling blackouts. Initially, the lack of capacity was triggered by a failure at Koeberg nuclear power station, but a general lack of capacity due to increased demand and lack of government planning soon came to light. The supplier and the South African government has been widely criticized for failing to adequately plan for and construct sufficient electrical generating capacity, although ultimately the government has admitted that it was at fault for refusing to approve funding for investment in infrastructure.

The crisis was resolved within a few months, but the margin between national demand and available capacity is still low (particularly in peak hours), and power stations are under strain, such that another phase of rolling blackouts is probable if parts of the supply are halted for whatever reason. The government and Eskom are currently planning new power stations, at cost to the South African consumer. The power utility plans to have 20,000 megawatts of nuclear power in its grid by 2025.

Water

Some predictions show surface water supply could decrease by 60% by the year 2070 in parts of the Western Cape.

The South African government planned to spend R69 billion on water infrastructure between 2008 and 2015. This involves building new dams and ancillary infrastructure, and repairing existing infrastructure. South Africa has an estimated total water capacity of 38 billion cubic metres, but will need 65 billion by 2025 if the economy is to keep on growing. The massive urban migration has placed further strain on the country's ageing water infrastructure and created a large backlog.

Developments and Maintenance

As part of an international attempt to modernize infrastructure, South Africa has faced increasing pressure to invest government funds into its water and electricity sectors. At current, these sectors are underfunded by approximately US$464 billion (This is according to the G20 GI Hub).

Income levels

Annual per capita personal income by race group relative to white levels

Year	*White*	*Coloureds*	*Asian*	*Black*
1917	100	22.0	22.1	9.1
1924	100	20.0	19.4	7.9
1936	100	15.6	23.1	7.6
1946	100	16.3	23.0	8.9
1956	100	16.9	21.9	8.6
1960	100	15.9	17.1	8.1
1970	100	17.3	20.2	6.8
1975	100	19.4	25.4	8.6
1980	100	19.1	25.5	8.5
1987	100	20.9	30.2	8.5
1993	100	19.3	42.0	10.9
1995	100	20.0	48.4	13.5
2000	100	23.0	41.0	15.9
2008	100	22.0	60.0	13.0

Gini coefficient by race in 2004

	White	*Coloureds*	*Asian*	*Black*	*Total*
Rural	0.37	0.38	–	0.43	0.51
Urban	0.36	0.45	0.43	0.53	0.56
Overall	0.36	0.47	0.43	0.51	0.59

South Africa has extreme differences in incomes and wealth. The good level of economic growth in the post-apartheid period has led to a measurable decline in income poverty, but inequality has increased. The high level of overall income inequality has further accentuated: the country's Gini coefficient increased by four percentage points, from 0.66 to 0.70, between 1993 and 2008, and income has become increasingly concentrated in the top decile. Inequality between urban and rural areas is changing: while rural poverty rates remain substantially higher than those in urban areas, urban poverty rates are rising and rural rates seem to be falling.

While between-race inequality is slowly falling, an increase in intra-race inequality is preventing the aggregate measures from declining. Despite that, between-race inequality remains a central issue: real incomes have been rising for all groups, but many blacks in the country still live in poverty. At any poverty line, blacks are very much poorer than coloreds, who are very much poorer than Indians, who are poorer than whites. In 2002, according to one estimate, 62% of Black Africans, 29% of Coloreds, 11% of Asians, and 4% of Whites lived in poverty.

The mean per-capita income has risen from R10, 741 in 1993 to R24, 409 in 2008, but these figures hide large differences in household welfare, both within and across population groups: the average Black income increased from ₹ 6, 018 in 1993 to ₹ 9, 718 in 2008; for Colored households, the increase was from ₹ 7,498 to ₹ 25, 269; for Whites, the increase was from ₹ 29, 372 to ₹ 110, 195. While mean income rose about 130% from 1993 to 2008, the median income rose just 15% over the same period, from ₹ 4,444 to ₹ 5,096, indicating that the increases are being driven by a small number of very large incomes, especially for Whites.

In 2000 the average white household was earning six times more than the average black household. In 2004, 29.8% of all households had an income (at constant 2001 prices) of less than R9, 600 per annum, while 10.3% of all households enjoyed an annual income (at constant 2001 prices) of more than ₹ 153,601 per annum.

One study using calculations based on National Income Dynamics Study (NIDS) data suggests that 47% of South Africans live below the poverty line: 56% of blacks live in poverty compared to 2% of whites, using an arbitrary income poverty line of R502 per capita. Although, it should also be noted that black South Africans make up the majority of the population at 79.2% while white South Africans make up only 8.9% of the population according to the Statistics South Africa census released in 2011. The United Nations Development Program's Human Development Index (HDI) ranked South Africa 110 out of 169 countries in 2010. The report notes, however, that the region's assessment has improved slowly since 1980. The HDI includes a Human Poverty Index (HPI-1), which ranked South Africa 85 out of 135 countries.

The number of South Africans living below the poverty line, identified according to Apartheid-era social categories, was calculated in one study as 56% "black", 27% "colored", 9% "Indian", and 2% "white". In the past inequality in South Africa was largely defined along race lines, but it has become increasingly defined by inequality within population groups as the gap between rich and poor within each group has increased substantially.

The Organization HYPERLINK "https://en.wikipedia.org/wiki/Organisation_for_Economic_Co-operation_and_Development" for Economic Co-operation and Development proposals for addressing income inequality included: encouraging more saving and investment; a liberalization of product-market regulation; easier access to credit for small businesses; greater co-ordination in wage bargaining; and measures to tackle the high level of youth unemployment. Some proposals have included wage subsidies for people being trained, a minimum wage differentiated by age, and extended periods of probation for young workers.

A 2011 study published by the University of Cape Town about the richest 10% found that nearly 40% are black, where this group had once been almost exclusively white. While only 29% of the absolute wealthiest South Africans are black, this jumps to 50% among the "entry-level" rich (defined as earning more than $4,000 per month). Factors that were found to be common among those in the entry-level rich group include being young, entrepreneurial and having some post-secondary education.

According to one estimate, 10.4% of South Africans belonged to the "higher middle class" in 2004, defined as having a per capita income of over R40,000 (in 2000 Rand).

Taxes and transfers

Taxation

Main article: Taxation in South Africa

The top rate of personal income tax rate in South Africa is 45%; the corporate tax rate is 28%. Other taxes include a value-added tax and a capital gains tax, with the overall tax burden amounting to 23.4% of total domestic income.

Social benefits

South Africa has about three times as many recipients of social benefits as it has income tax-payers, an extremely high ratio by international standards. After 1994 resources have been rapidly reallocated to black households: while approximately 40% of aggregate social spending was directed to whites and 43% to blacks in the mid-1980s, by the late 1990s fully 80% of total social spending was assigned to blacks and less than 10% to whites.

The Unemployment Insurance Fund is financed out of premiums, contributions and benefits depend on earnings, and focuses on insuring workers against the risk of income loss.

Social assistance grants

Social assistance grants are non-contributory, income-tested benefits provided by the state to the poor, and are financed out of general tax revenues without any links between contributions and benefits. They are provided in the form of: grants for older persons; disability grants; war veterans grants; care dependency grants; foster child grants; child support grants; grant-in-aid; social relief of distress.

The state old age pension, received by over 80% of the elderly, is a non-contributory pension and pays more than twice median per capita Black income, thus representing an important source of income for a third of all Black households in the country. It pays a maximum of ₹ 1,780 (as of July 2019) to people who reach pension age without access to private pensions.

The child support grant provides ₹ 420 per month, per child (as of July 2019) for every child in the household younger than 18, and benefited 9.1 million children by April 2009.

The war veterans grant is provided to former soldiers who fought in the Second World War or the Korean War, and pays a maximum amount of ₹ 1,800 per month (as of July 2019).

Comparison with other emerging markets

According to a December 2010 article by the South African Government Communication and Information System's now-defunct BuaNews news service, South Africa was said to compare well to other emerging markets on affordability and availability of capital, financial market sophistication, business tax rates and infrastructure, but to fare poorly on the cost and availability of labour, education, and the use of technology and innovation.

Released in early December 2010 and no longer available online, the survey by Brazil's National Confederation of Industry, "Competitividade Brazil 2010: Comparaçao com Paises Selecionados", (Competition Brazil: A comparison with selected countries), found South Africa to have the second most sophisticated financial market and the second-lowest effective business tax rate (business taxes as a percentage of company profits), out of 14 surveyed countries. The country was also ranked fourth for ease of accessing capital, fourth for cost of capital, sixth for its transport infrastructure (at the time considered better than that of China, India, Mexico, Brazil and Poland, but behind that of Korea and Chile), and seventh for foreign direct investment as a percentage of GDP: in 2008 it was over 3% of the GDP.

Nevertheless, South Africa is falling behind other emerging markets, such as India and China, owing to several factors: the country is relatively small, without the advantage of a huge domestic customer base; it has had for decades an unusually low rate of saving and investment, partly because of low disposable income; an inadequate education system results in an acute shortage of skilled manpower; a strong and volatile currency deters investors and makes its exports less competitive; the infrastructure, though far better than in the rest of Africa, suffers from severe bottlenecks, including scheduled power shortages, and urgently needs upgrading.

In 2011, after a year of observer status, South Africa officially joined the BRICS group of now-five emerging-market nations at the summit held in Sanya, Hainan, China.

Critical Observations of present status of the economy of South Africa

(1) The formal economy of South Africa (SA) has its beginning of Dutch Settlers in 1652. As the colony expanded in size, with the arrival of French and German citizens, some colonists were set free to pursue commercial farming, leading to the dominance of agriculture in economy.

(2) At the end of 19th century, the Britishers annexed the colony to its empire. This led to the Great Trek.

(3) In 1870, diamonds were discovered. In 1986, world's largest gold deposits were discovered quickly transforming the economy into a resource-dominated one. The British annexed the area as a result of the Boer War which witnessed the placement of Boer woman and children in British-built concentration camps. Country also entered industralisation leading to organization of SA in trade Unions.

(4) SA colony got independence in 1948. The country was putting laws of distinguishing between different races. After independence, SA conducted National Party election in 1948 and started implementing an ever stricter race-based policy named apartheid effectively dividing the economy into a privileged white one and an impoverished black one. The policy was widely criticized and led to crippling sanctions being placed against the country in 1980s.

(5) SA held first multiracial election in 1994, leaving newly African Congress (ANC) government the daunting task of trying to restore order to an economy harmed by sanctions while integrating the previously disadvantaged segment of population into it. 1994 government inherited economy wracked by long years of conflicts and external sanctions.

(6) Inflation brought down, public finances were stabilized and foreign capital was attracted. In 2002, President Mbeki vowed to promote economic growth and foreign investment by relaxing restrictive labour laws, and stepping up the pace of privatization, raising general spending, and cutting interest rates sharply from 1998 levels led to strong opposition from the organized labour. From 2004, economic growth picked up significantly. Employment and capital formation increased GDP. Foreign reserves increased from $3 billion to $50 billion during 2011-19. SA is only African country who is the member of G-20. The banking sector was in the strongest position Challenges with economy were, however, weak on account of (1) inefficient government bureaucracy, (2) restrictive labour laws, (3) shortage of skilled workers, (4) political instability and (5) corruption.

(7) Tourism is a popular destination with round 86000 arrivals per month (March 2008) out of which 210000are from outside African Continent. In 2012, South Africa received 9.2 million international arrivals. In August 2012, 3.5 million travelers came to SA contributed ZAR 102 billion to SA GDP and supported 10.3% of jobs in 2012.

(8) SA and particularly the Cape Town region has established itself as a successful Call Centre and business processing outsourcing destination, large overseas firms like Lufthansa, Amazon, Carphone, Warehouse and Delta Airlines.

(9) The domestic telecommunications infrastructure provides modern and efficient service to urban area.

(10) The manufacturing industry's contribution to the economy is relatively small providing just 13.3% of jobs and 15% of GDP.

(11) The agricultural industry contributes about 5% of formal employment, lower than other parts of Africa. Casual Laborers contributed around 2.8% of GDP. Due to the aridity of land, only 13.5% land can be utilized for crop production, with increased foreign competition and crime being two major challenges to the industry.

(12) Mining has been the main driving force behind development of Africa's most advanced economy. Large scale and profitable mining started with recovery of a diamond on the banks of Organge River in 1867. Subsequent discovery and exploitation of Kimberley pipes. Gold mines were subsequently discovered. In 1886, Gold rush and subsequent rapid development of the gold fields were found. SA is one of the world's leading mining and minerals processing countries. Its contribution to GDP is falling from 21% to 6% in 2011. But it represents 60% of its exports. Mining accounts for 9% of value added.

(13) Refugees from poorer neighbouring countries include immigrates from the Democratic Republic of Congo, Mozambique, Zimbabwe, Malawi, and others representing large portion of the informal section. With the high unemployment levels among the poor African countries. Many South Africans feel resentful of immigrates who are seen to be depriving the native population of jobs. Many South African employers have employed migrates from other countries for lower pay than South African citizens in the construction, tourism, agriculture and domestic services.

(14) There is 25% unemployment in SA. S 1 million skilled workers personnel and managerial occupation have migrated overseas in UK, Germany and other European countries. There is thus drain from SA to other European countries.

(15) Stock Market was established in Johannesburg. Capitalization was $1.2 trillion in March 2018. South African Reserve Bank oversees banking activities. Banking industry is dominated by Nedbank, ABSA, Standard Bank and First Rand. Banks provide retail and investment banking services. The banking has become highly Competative with the re-entry of many experienced foreign banks. Central Bank monitors liquidity position. Banks borrow from SARB at fluctuating repo rate.

(16) Personal income tax is 34% and Corporate tax 28%.In addition, there are value-added and capital gains tax.

(17) 40% Social pending was directed to Whites while 43% to Blacks in the mid - 1980s. 80% of total spending was assigned to Blacks and less than 10% on the whites by late 1990s.

(18) University of Cape Town observed in 2011 that out of 10% richest, nearly 40% riches were Blacks when previously this group was exclusively Whites.

(19) South Africa's currency is South Africa Rand (ZAR)

Financial year is 1 April to 31 March (government) and 1 March-28/29 February (Corporate & Private)

(20) South Africa is Developing/Emerging Country. It is Upper-middle income country.

(21) GDP was $385 billion and GDP per capita $6550 in 2019.

(22) Population is 5.877 crores with Labour Force is 2.31 crores which is 40% employment rate. Population below poverty level is 55.5% which is very high and needs to be reduced to 30%.

(23) Unemployment rate is 29.8% and youth unemployment rate is 59.1% which are very high and dangerous which needs to be curtailed to 5%-7%.

(24) Unemployment is high because of racial inequality status or apartheid. Whites are earning 6 times more than blacks. 57% of blacks are unemployed. International sanctions on South Africa has resulted in changing its outlook for apartheid and reduced the racial non- equalities.

(25) Public debt is 53% of GDP and Gross external debt is 44% of GDP. Should be 40% of GDP.

(26) Imports are $81.9 billion and exports $108 billion. There is trade Surplus.

(27) Fiscal deficit is $16 billion which is 4.15% of GDP. $92 billion in 2017 and needs to be reduced to curtail inflation.

(28) The Rulers are administrating their own country and do not dominate and show their supremacy to other countries by installing military base in other country. They have not allowed other country to install military base in their country and are aloof from Communism or Socialism and are not dominated by China, Russia or USA.

(29) The country should treat all its citizens on equality basis and racial differences should be eliminated to avoid economic sanctions from the countries like USA.

(30) Income tax rate for individuals is 45% which is very high and needs to be reduced substantially to 30 and the corporate tax @ 28% is reasonable.

(31) USA, China and USSR are trying to establish their presence in the South Africa by building/installing military Base there or building roads under one Belt One Road principle by China and other countries. But these countries are not succeeded in their efforts. In fact, South Africa can make its progress with the assistance of any country. On the other hand, it will created conflict of interest. South Africa should therefore keep aloof from Communism and Capitalized country like China, USSR and USA.

(32) In April 2017, political tensions in the country arose over the sacking of nine cabinet members including Minister of Finance Pravin Gordhan by the President Jacob Zuma. The finance Minister was seen as central to efforts to restore the confidence in South Africa. As a result of the tensions, S & P Global cut South Africa's credit rating to junk status on Monday 3 April2017. Fitch Ratings followed suit on Friday 7 April 2017 and cut the country's credit status to the sub-investment grade of BBB-. The South African rand lost more than 11% in the week following the cabinet reshuffling.

13

Economy of Afghanistan

The economy of Afghanistan and India suffered from the same enemy i.e. extremists. Afghanistan is attacked often by Taliban and Jai-se group attacks India on Kashmir Border. Jai-se group is terrorist group in Pakistan known as independent warriors fighting for independence of Kashmir Valley. Previously Taliban were rulers of Afghanistan. Recently India has fought with terrorists group in Pakistan which is instigated by Pakistani army. These groups are giving training on how to attack India in Kashmir and Pakistan provides funds to them which resulted in Pakistan becoming a very poor country. It is reported that Pakistan has no money to fight recent Corona Virus and there is no medical treatment for those 500 suffering from this disease. India fought and almost finished terrorism in India.

Unlike India, Afghanistan was protected by American troops against Taliban. Taliban were first defeated by U.S. against Russia in 1990s with the help of Pakistani Army. Russians withdrew their military forces from Afghanistan. India has been investing funds in Afghanistan to improve the conditions of Afghan people in the field of education, industry building etc. which Taliban and Pakistan protested.

Recently there is an Agreement between Taliban and US. According to that Agreement there will be cease-fire and Americans will withdraw the troops from Afghanistan. But Taliban still attacks Afghanistan in which solders from Afghanistan and US both are killed heavily. Recent Cease-fire Agreement is therefore not properly implemented and may be dropped in future if aggressive activities of Taliban are not stopped.

The economy of Afghanistan has improved significantly in the last decade due to the infusion of billions of dollars in international assistance and remittances from Afghan expatriates. The assistance that came from expatriates and outside investors saw this increase when there was more political reliability after the fall of the Taliban regime. The nation's GDP stands at about $70 billion with an exchange rate of $20 billion (2017), and the GDP per capita is about $2,000. It imports over $6 billion worth of goods but exports nearly $1 billion only, mainly fruits and nuts.

Despite holding over $1 trillion in proven untapped mineral deposits, Afghanistan remains one of the least developed countries in the world. Its unemployment rate is 23.9% and about 54.5% of its population lives below the poverty line. Many of the unemployed men join the foreign-funded militant groups or the world of crime, particularly as smugglers. The Afghan government has long been pleading for foreign investment in order to improve Afghanistan's economy.

Economic history

In the early modern period under the rule of kings Abdur Rahman Khan (1880–1901) and Habibullah Khan (1901–1919), a great deal of Afghan commerce was centrally controlled by the Afghan government. The Afghan monarchs were eager to develop the stature of government and the country's military capability, and so attempted to raise money by the imposition of state monopolies on the sale of commodities and high taxes. This slowed the long-term development of Afghanistan during that period. Western technologies and manufacturing methods were slowly introduced during these eras at the command of the Afghan ruler, but in general only according to the logistical requirements of the growing army. An emphasis was placed on the manufacture of weapons and other military material. This process was in the hands of a small number of western experts invited to Kabul by the Afghan kings. Otherwise, it was not possible for outsiders, particularly westerners, to set up large-scale enterprises in Afghanistan during that period.

The first prominent plan to develop Afghanistan's economy in modern times was the Helmand Valley Authority project of 1952, modeled on the Tennessee Valley Authority in the United States, which was expected to be of primary economic importance The country began facing severe economic hardships during the 1970s when neighboring Pakistan, under Zulfikar Ali Bhutto, began closing the Pakistan-Afghanistan border crossings. This move resulted in Afghanistan increasing political and economic ties with its northern neighbor, the powerful Soviet Union of that time.

The 1979 Soviet invasion and ensuing civil war destroyed much of the country's limited infrastructure, and disrupted normal patterns of economic activity. Eventually, Afghanistan went from a traditional economy to a centrally planned economy up until 2002 when it was replaced by a free market economy. Gross domestic product has fallen substantially since the 1980s due to disruption of trade and transport as well as loss of labor and capital. Continuing internal strife severely hampered domestic efforts to rebuild the nation or provide ways for the international community to help.

According to the International Monetary Fund, the Afghan economy grew 20% in the fiscal year ending in March 2004, after expanding 30% in the previous 12 months. The growth is attributed to international aid and to the end of droughts. An estimated $100 billion of aid entered the nation from 2002 to 2017. A GDP of $4 billion in fiscal year 2003 was recalculated by the IMF to $6.1 billion, after adding proceeds from opium products. Mean graduate pay was $0.56 per man-hour in 2010.

Agriculture and livestock

Afghan grapes

Afghanistan currently produces roughly 1.5 million tons of fresh fruits annually, which could be increased significantly. It is known for producing some of the finest fruits, especially apples, apricots, cherries, figs, grapes, melons, sweet mulberries, peaches, and pomegranates. Building and using greenhouses is a fast-growing industry in the country.

The northern Afghan provinces are famous for pistachio cultivation. In recent years, farmers in the southern and western provinces have also began cultivating pistachios. Provinces in the east of the country are famous for pine nuts. The northern and central provinces are also famous for almonds and walnuts. The Bamyan Province in central Afghanistan is known for growing superior quality potatoes, and on an average produces 140,000 to 170,000 tonnes. Nangarhar Province is known for oranges, olives, peanuts, and dates. Cultivation of these fruits are now spreading to other provinces in the south of the country.

Wheat and cereal production is Afghanistan's traditional agricultural mainstay. National wheat production in 2015 was 5 million tons Afghanistan is nearing self-sufficiency in grain production. It requires an additional 1 million ton of wheat to become self-sufficient, which is predicted to be accomplished in 2020.The overall agricultural production sometimes declines following droughts.

Livestock in Afghanistan mainly include cattle, sheep, and goats. Building and using modern poultry farms is also a fast-growing industry. The availability of land suitable for grazing has traditionally made animal husbandry an important part of the economy. There are two main types of animal husbandry: sedentary, practiced by farmers who raise both animals and crops; and nomadic, practiced by animal herders known as Kochis. Natural pastures cover some 7,500,000 acres (30,000 km^2) but are being overgrazed. The northern regions around Mazar-i-Sharif and Maymana were the home range for about six million karakul sheep in the late 1990s. Most flocks move to the highlands in the summer to pastures in the north.

Arable land in Afghanistan is around 8 million hectares. Wheat production stands at about 5 million tonnes, nurseries hold 119,000 hectares of land, and grape production is at 615,000 tonnes. Almond production has jumped to 56,000 tons and cotton to 45,000 tonnes. It was reported in 2019 that about 10,000 acres of land in Afghanistan is used to cultivate saffron.

According to the World Bank's report published in April 2019, Afghanistan's economy suffered from the consequences of a severe drought that affected the agriculture production in 2018. While the wheat production declined by 24%, milk production declined by 30%.

Fishing

The country has plenty of reservoirs, rivers and streams, which make it a suitable climate for fish farming. Fishing takes place in the lakes and rivers, particularly in Nangarhar Province and in the Helmand River in southern Afghanistan. Fish constitute a smaller part of the Afghan diet today because fish farmers are unable to produce enough fish to keep up with the demands of customers. Most fish and seafood are imported from neighboring Pakistan, Iran, and the United Arab Emirates. There are hundreds of fish farms throughout the country and the largest one is at the Qargha, which supplies fish eggs to the other fish farms. Fish farming has also been launched in the Salma Dam.

Forestry

Afghanistan's timber has been greatly depleted, and since the mid-1980s, only about 3% of the land area has been forested, mainly in the east. Significant stands of trees have been destroyed by the ravages of the war in the late 20th century. Exploitation has been hampered by insecurity and access roads. Moreover, the distribution of the forest is uneven, and most of the remaining woodland is only found in the Kunar, Nuristan and the Paktia regions in the east of the country. Some steps have been taken in recent years in planting trees across Afghanistan. Even the Taliban leaders have recently called for planting more trees.

The natural forests in Afghanistan are mainly of two types: dense forests of oak trees, walnut trees, and many other species of nuts that grow in the southeast, and on the northern and northeastern slopes of the Sulaiman ranges; and sparsely distributed short trees and shrubs on all other slopes of the Hindu Kush. The dense forests of the southeast cover only 2.7% of the country. Roundwood production in 2003 was 3,148,000 cubic metres, with 44% used for fuel.

The destruction of the forests to create agricultural land, logging, forest fires, plant diseases, and insect pests are all causes of the reduction in forest coverage. Illegal logging and clear-cutting by timber smugglers have exacerbated this destructive process. There is currently a ban on cutting new timber in Afghanistan. Prior to 2001 and under Taliban rule, massive deforestation of the country side was permitted and Afghans moved large quantities of logs into storage centers for profit, where the trees wait for processing on an individual tree by tree request.

Trade and industry

A proportional representation of Afghan exports, 2009

Officials of Afghanistan, Georgia, Turkey, Azerbaijan and Turkmenistan signing the Lapis Lazuli Route agreement in 2016, which will create a new trade route from Afghanistan to the Caucusus and Turkey

Afghanistan's trade with other countries is steadily increasing. Afghan handwoven rugs are one of the most popular products for exportation. Other products include hand crafted antique replicas as well as leather and furs. Afghanistan is the third largest exporter of cashmere.

Afghanistan is endowed with a wealth of natural resources, including extensive deposits of natural gas, petroleum, coal, marble, gold, copper, chromite, talc, barites, sulfur, lead, zinc, iron ore, salt, precious and semi-precious stones, and many rare earth elements. In 2006, a U.S. Geological Survey estimated that Afghanistan has as much as 36 trillion cubic feet (1.0×10^{12} m^3) of natural gas, 3.6 billion barrels (570×10^{6} m^3) of oil and condensate reserves. According to a 2007 assessment, Afghanistan has significant amounts of undiscovered non-fuel mineral resources. Geologists also found indications of abundant deposits of colored stones and gemstones, including emerald, ruby, sapphire, garnet, lapis, kunzite, spinel, tourmaline and period.

In 2010, U.S. Pentagon officials along with American geologists have revealed the discovery of nearly $1 trillion in untapped mineral deposits in Afghanistan. A memo from the Pentagon stated that Afghanistan could become the "Saudi Arabia of lithium". Some believe, including former Afghan President Hamid Karzai, that the untapped minerals are worth up to $3 trillion.

Another US Geological Survey estimate from September 2011 showed that the Khanashin carbonatites in the Helmand Province of the country have an estimated 1 million metric tonnes of rare earth elements. Regina Dubey, Acting Director for the Department of Defence *Task Force for Business and Stability Operations (TFBSO)* stated that "this is just one more piece of evidence that Afghanistan's mineral sector has a bright future."

Afghanistan signed a copper deal with China (Metallurgical Corp. of China Ltd.) in 2008, which is to a large-scale project that involves the investment of $2.8 billion by China and an annual income of about $400 million to the Afghan government. The country's Ainak copper mine, located in Logar province, is one of the biggest in the world and is expected to provide jobs to 20,000 Afghans. It is estimated to hold at least 11 million tonnes or US$33 billion worth of copper.

Trucks on the road in Afghanistan

Experts believe that the production of copper could begin within two to three years and the iron ore in five to seven years as of 2010. The country's other recently announced treasure is the Hajigak iron ore mine, located 130 miles west of Kabul and is believed to hold an estimated 1.8 billion to 2 billion metric tons of the mineral used to make steel. AFISCO, an Indian consortium of seven companies, led by the Steel Authority of India Limited (SAIL), and Canada's Kilo Goldmines Ltd are expected to jointly invest $14.6 billion in developing the Hajigak iron mine. The country has several coal mines but need to be modernized.

Afghanistan's important resource in the past has been natural gas, which was first tapped in 1967. During the 1980s, gas sales accounted for $300 million a year in export revenues (56% of the total). 90% of these exports went to the Soviet Union to pay for imports and debts. However, during the withdrawal of Soviet troops in 1989, Afghanistan's natural gas fields were capped to prevent sabotage by the Mujahideen. Gas production has dropped from a high of 8.2 million cubic metres (2.9×10^8 cu ft) per day in the 1980s to a low of about 600,000 cubic meters (2.2×10^7 cu ft) in 2001. After the formation of the Karzai administration, production of natural gas was once again restored.

A locally owned company, Azizi Hotak General Trading Group, is currently the main supplier of diesel fuel, gasoline, jet fuel and LPG in Afghanistan. In December 2011, Afghanistan signed an oil exploration contract with China National Petroleum Corporation (CNPC) for the development of three oil fields along the Amu Darya River. The state will have its first oil refineries within the next three years, after which it will receive very little of the profits from the sale of the oil and natural gas. CNPC began Afghan oil production in late October 2012, with extracting 1.5 million barrels of oil annually.

Trade in goods smuggled into Pakistan once constituted a major source of revenue for Afghanistan. Many of the goods that were smuggled into Pakistan have originally entered Afghanistan from Pakistan, where they fell under the 1965 Afghanistan–Pakistan Transit Trade Agreement. This permitted goods bound for Afghanistan to transit through Pakistani seaports free of duty. Once in Afghanistan, the goods were often immediately smuggled back into Pakistan over the porous border that the two countries share, often with the help of corrupt officials. Additionally, items declared as Afghanistan-bound were often prematurely offloaded from trucks and smuggled into Pakistani markets without paying requisite duty fees This resulted in the creation of a thriving black market, with much of the illegal trading occurring openly, as was common in Peshawar's bustling Karkhano Market, which was widely regarded as a smuggler's bazaar.

In 2010, Afghanistan and Pakistan signed into law a new Afghanistan–Pakistan Transit Trade Agreement (APTTA), which allows their shipping trucks to transit goods within both nations. This revised US-sponsored APTTA agreement also allows Afghan trucks to transport exports to India via Pakistan up to the Wagah crossing point. Afghanistan's main land ports are Shir Khan Bandar, Hairatan, Islam Qala, Towraghondi, Torkham, Wesh–Chaman, and Zaranj. Many Afghan traders use the Pakistani ports of Karachi and Port Qasim.

Economic development and recovery

From left to right: Indian Prime Minister Narendra Modi, Iranian President Hassan Rouhani, and Afghan President Ashraf Ghani, during the signing of the Chabahar Port transit agreement in May 2016

Afghanistan embarked on a modest economic development program in the 1930s. The government founded banks; introduced paper money; established a university; expanded primary, secondary, and technical schools; and sent students abroad for education. In 1952 it created the Helmand Valley Authority to manage the economic development of the Helmand

and Arghandab valleys through irrigation and land development, a scheme which remains one of the country's most important capital resources.

In 1956, the government promulgated the first in a long series of ambitious development plans. By the late 1970s, these had achieved only mixed results due to flaws in the planning process as well as inadequate funding and a shortage of the skilled managers and technicians needed for implementation.

Afghan United Bank

Da Afghanistan Bank serves as the central bank of the nation. The "Afghani" (AFN) is the national currency, which has an exchange rate of nearly 70 Afghanis to 1 US dollar. There are over 16 different banks operating in the country, including Afghanistan International Bank, Kabul Bank, Azizi Bank, Pashtany Bank, Standard Chartered Bank, and First Micro Finance Bank. Cash is still widely used for most transactions. A new law on private investment provides three to seven-year tax holidays to eligible companies and a four-year exemption from exports tariffs and duties. According to a UN report in 2007, Afghanistan has received over $3.3 billion from its expatriate community in 2006. UN officials familiar with the issue said remittances to Afghanistan could have been more if the banking regulations are more convenient. Additionally, improvements to the business-enabling environment have resulted in more than $1.5 billion in telecom investment and created more than 100,000 jobs since 2003.

Afghanistan is a member of World Trade Organization, SAARC, ECO, OIC, and has an observer status in the SCO. It seeks to complete the so-called *New Silk Road* trade project, which is aimed to connecting South Asia with Central Asia and the Middle East. This way Afghanistan will be able to collect large fees from trade passing through the country, including from the Trans-Afghanistan Pipeline. Foreign Minister Zalmai Rassoul has stated that the "goal is to achieve an Afghan economy whose growth is based on trade, private enterprise and investment". Experts believe that this will revolutionize the economy of the region.

Shopping district in the Khair Khana neighborhood of Kabul

As part of an attempt to modernize the city and boost the economy, a number of new high rise buildings are under construction by various developers. Some of the national development projects include the $35 bn New Kabul City next to the capital, the Aino Mena in Kandahar, and the Ghazi Amanullah Khan City east of Jalalabad. Similar development projects are also found in Herat in the west, Mazar-e-Sharif in the north and in other cities.

As a competitor of the Coca-Cola Company, the Pepsi-Cola Company is said to be establishing itself in Afghanistan. This not only promotes foreign investment but also makes the country less dependent on imports from neighboring countries and helps provide employment opportunity to many Afghans. Watan Group is a company based in Afghanistan that provides telecommunications, logistics and security services.

In February 2019, it was reported that the World Bank granted $235 million to the government of Afghanistan for the country's development and growth. The acting Minister of Finance Humayon Qayoumi said that out of the total amount granted, $75 million will finance "the Tackling Afghanistan's Government HRM (Human Resource Management) and Institutional Reforms (TAGHIR) project, which will strengthen the capacity of selected line ministries. The grant also includes 25 million U.S. dollars from IDA (International Development Association) and 50 million U.S. dollars from ARTF (Afghanistan Reconstruction Trust Fund)."

Afghanistan's economy grew by only 1% in 2018, which has been the slowest growth rate since 2001, the World Bank 2019 report stated. However, the economy is expected to recover by 2.5% in 2019.

Tourism

Tourism in Afghanistan was at its peak in 1977. Many tourists from around the world came to visit Afghanistan, including from as far away as Europe and North America. All of that ended with the start of the April 1978 Saur Revolution. However, it is again gradually increasing despite the insecurity. Each year about 20,000 foreign tourists visit Afghanistan. Tourists should avoid areas where armed criminals operate in the name of Taliban. As a policy, the Taliban are known not to harm tourists. Distinguishing the two groups is very difficult.

The country has four international airports, including the Hamid Karzai International Airport, Mazar-e-Sharif International Airport, Kandahar International Airport and Herat International Airport. It also has several smaller airports throughout the country. The city of Kabul has many guest houses and hotels, including the Serena Hotel, the Hotel Inter-Continental Kabul, and the Safi Landmark Hotel. Guest houses and hotels can also be found in the other cities, including in Bamyan.

Critical Observations of present status of economy of Afghanistan

(1) After Soviet Union withdrew its troops in 1989, the country was looking to build infrastructure in the country with strong military troops. Among the other countries, India assisted the country with

financial funds to erect education institutions and also to find out coal mines and iron in Afghanistan.

(2) Afghanistan is expected to build up its refineries within next three years.

(3) In 1979, Soviet Union invasion and ensuing civil war destroyed much of the country's limited infrastructure and disrupted normal pattern of economic activities. Soviet Union withdrew its troops in 1989.

(4) Illicit trade in opium was destroyed by Afghanistan with great efforts. There was strong opposition in destroying such trade as it was given lot of money and funds to the various illegal tribes.

(5) Country began facing several economic hardships during the 1970s when Pakistan President Bhutto began closing Pakistan Afghanistan border crossings. This resulted in Afghanistan increasing political and economic ties with its northern neighbors. The powerful Soviet Union of that time. This resulted in Pakistan and US relationship and military ties were built up between Pakistan and US. US give largest economic Aid to Pakistan ($1.3 Billion yearly) which were used by Pakistan to fund in building terrorists tribes. Since India was in the Russian Group, US Secretary ignored this activity but this resulted in the terrorists attacking India on Kashmir issue as the Independence solider to free Kashmir from Indian administration.

(6) In order to dig and extract estimated copper worth $33billion, China invested $ 2.8 billion and Canada and SAIL in India invested $14.6 billion to tap iron from the mines. Afghanistan is expected to have untapped natural resources in the country which valued at $3 trillion including Rare earth minerals estimated at 1 million metric tonnes.

(7) Due to the international aid to end droughts, $100 billion entered the nation from 2002-2017.

(8) Building and using greenhouses is fast growing industry.

(9) Country is self - sufficient in foodgrains except it has to import 1 million ton of wheat from the neighbouring countries.

(10) Currency Afghani 70 =$1

(11) Fiscal year 21 December- 20 December

(12) GDP $ 18.734 billion Nominal, $ 76.486 billion PPP

(13) GDP Growth by Sector: Agriculture 2.7%, Industry 21.1% Services 55.9% 2016

(14) Inflation 4.3%

(15) Population 3.65 crores

(16) Population below poverty line:54.5%

(17) Labour Force 1.44 crores

(18) Labour Force by occupation: Agriculture 44.3%, Industry 18.1% Service 37.6%

(19) Unemployment 23.9% Mean graduate pay was $0.56 per man hour. Unemployment Very high and Per man hour salary very low

(20) Main Industries: Small scale production of textiles, Soap, furniture, shoes, fertilizers, apparel, food products, non-alcoholic beverages, mineral water, cement, handwoven carpet, fruits, copper, coal, natural gas.

(21) Exports $784 million (not included illicit exports)

(22) Exports: Fruits, nuts, Afghan rags, wool, hides, gemstones, medical herbs

(23) Main exports India 56%

(24) Import: $ 7.616 billion. Trade Deficit $6.832 38.88% of GDP. Exports should be increased or imports should be substantially reduced.

(25) Import Goods: Machinery and other capital goods, fuel, textiles, petroleum products

(26) Import Partners China 21% & India 20.5%

(27) Current Account: $1.014 billion - 2017

(28) Gross external debts: $1.014 billion

(29) Public debts: $2.84 billion

(30) Revenue $2.276 Billion

(31) Expenses $5.328 billion Fiscal deficit $3.052 billion 15.1% of GDP very high.

(32) Foreign Reserves $7.8 billion. Comfortable.

(33) It is observed that Afghanistan is planning to build up a strong military force to fight against Taliban. The country is not trying to interfere in the affairs of any other country but to self defence, it is building the army which is very much appreciated. It has very rich potential of untapped minerals of $3 trillion and 1 million metric tonnes of rare earth minerals. China is investing $ 2.8 billion in tapping copper mines expecting $33 billion worth copper. Afghanistan should not take financial assistance from China

which is the dominating country. SAIL of India and Canadian firm have invested $ 14.6 billion to extract iron from mines. If these minerals are discovered, Afghanistan will be a very rich country.

(34) Chabahar port in Iran has been built recently to facilitate trade between Afghanistan, Iran and India. India took the leading part. The transit agreement was signed between Iran President Rohani, Afghan President Ashraf Ghani and Indian Prime Minister Mr. Narendra Modi signed Chabahar Port Transit Agreement in May 2016.

14

Economy of Italy

Presently as at 21st March 2020, Italy is known to the world for widespread and dangerous spreading of the Corona virus in the country. More than 4K died and 30000 people are Corona patients in Italy.

The economy of Italy is the 3rd-largest national economy in the Eurozone, the 8th-largest by nominal GDP in the world, and the 12th-largest by GDP (PPP). Italy has a major advanced economy, and is a founding member of the European Union, the Eurozone, the OECD, the G7 and the G20. Italy is the eighth largest exporter in the world with $514 billion exported in 2016. Its closest trade ties are with the other countries of the European Union, with whom it conducts about 59% of its total trade. The largest trading partners, in order of market share, are Germany (12.6%), France (11.1%), the United States (6.8%), Switzerland (5.7%), the United Kingdom (4.7%), and Spain (4.4%)

In the post-World War II period, Italy was transformed from an agricultural based economy which had been severely affected by the consequences of the World Wars, into one of the world's most advanced nations and a leading country in world trade and exports. According to the Human Development Index, the country enjoys a very high standard of living, and has the world's 8th highest quality of life according to *The Economist*. Italy owns the world's third-largest gold reserve, and is the third net contributor to the budget of the European Union. Furthermore, the advanced country private wealth is one of the largest in the world.

Italy is a large manufacturer (overall the second in EU behind Germany) and exporter of a significant variety of products including machinery, vehicles, pharmaceuticals, furniture, food, clothing, and robots. Italy has therefore a significant trade surplus. The country is also well known for its influential and innovative business economic sector, an industrious and competitive agricultural sector (Italy is the world's largest wine producer), and for its creative and high-quality automobile, naval, industrial, appliance and fashion design. Italy is the largest hub for luxury goods in Europe and the third luxury hub globally.

Despite these important achievements, the country's economy today suffers from structural and non-structural problems. Annual growth rates have often been below the EU average with Italy being hit particularly hard by the late-2000s recession. Massive government spending from the 1980s onwards has produced a severe rise in public debt. In addition, Italian living standards have a considerable North–South divide: the average GDP per capita in Northern and Central Italy significantly exceeds the EU average, while some regions and provinces in Southern Italy are dramatically below. In recent years, Italy's GDP per capita growth slowly caught-up with the Eurozone average while its employment rate still lags behind; however, economists dispute the official figures because of the large number of informal jobs (estimated between 10% and 20% of the labour force) that lift the inactivity or unemployment rates.

History

The economic history of Italy can be divided in three main phases: an initial period of struggle after the unification of the country, characterised by high emigration and stagnant growth; a central period of robust catch-up from the 1890s to the 1980s, interrupted by the Great Depression of the 1930s and the two world wars; and a final period of sluggish growth that has been exacerbated by a double-dip recession following the 2008 global financial crush, and from which the country is slowly reemerging only in recent years.

Age of Industrialization

Terni steel mills in 1912.

Prior to unification, the economy of the many Italian satellites was overwhelmingly agrarian; however, the agricultural surplus produced what historians call a "pre-industrial" transformation in North-western Italy starting from the 1820s, that led to a diffuse, if mostly artisanal, concentration of manufacturing activities, especially in Piedmont-Sardinia under the liberal rule of the Count of Cavour.

After the birth of the unified Kingdom of Italy in 1861, there was a deep consciousness in the ruling class of the new country's backwardness, given that the per capita GDP expressed in PPS terms was roughly half of that of Britain and about 25% less than that of France and Germany. During the 1860s and 1870s, the manufacturing activity was backward and small-scale, while the oversized agrarian sector was the backbone of the national economy. The country lacked large coal and iron deposits and the population was largely illiterate. In the 1880s, a severe farm crisis led to the introduction of more modern farming techniques in the Po valley, while from 1878 to 1887 protectionist policies were introduced with the aim to establish a heavy industry base. Some large steel and iron works soon clustered around areas of high hydropower potential, notably the Alpine foothills and Umbria in central Italy, while Turin and Milan led a textile, chemical, engineering and banking boom and Genoa captured civil and military shipbuilding.

However, the diffusion of industrialization that characterised the northwestern area of the country largely excluded Venetia and, especially, the South. The resulting Italian diaspora concerned up to 26 million Italians, the most part in the years between 1880–1914; by many scholars it is considered the biggest mass migration of contemporary times. During the Great War, the still frail Italian state successfully fought a modern war, being able of arming and training some 5 million recruits. But this result came at a terrible cost: by the end of the war, Italy had lost 700,000 soldiers and had a ballooning sovereign debt amounting to billions of lira.

Fascist regime

Italy emerged from World War I in a poor and weakened condition. The National Fascist Party of Benito Mussolini came to power in 1922, at the end of a period of social unrest. However, once Mussolini acquired a firmer hold of power, laissez-faire and free trade were progressively abandoned in favour of government intervention and protectionism.

In 1929, Italy was hit hard by the Great Depression. Trying to handle the crisis, the Fascist government nationalized the holdings of large banks which had accrued significant industrial securities, establishing the Istituto per la Ricostruzione Industriale. A number of mixed entities were formed, whose purpose was to bring together representatives of the government and of the major businesses. These representatives discussed economic policy and manipulated prices and wages so as to satisfy both the wishes of the government and the wishes of business.

This economic model based on a partnership between government and business was soon extended to the political sphere, in what came to be known as corporatism. At the same time, the aggressive foreign policy of Mussolini led to an increasing military expenditure. After the invasion of Ethiopia, Italy intervened to support Franco's nationalists in the Spanish

Civil War. By 1939, Italy had the highest percentage of state-owned enterprises after the Soviet Union.

Italy's involvement in World War II as a member of the Axis powers required the establishment of a war economy. The Allied invasion of Italy in 1943 eventually caused the Italian political structure – and the economy – to rapidly collapse. The Allies, on the one hand, and the Germans on the other, took over the administration of the areas of Italy under their control. By the end of the war, Italian per capita income was at its lowest point since the beginning of the 20th century.

Post-war economic miracle

The Fiat 500, launched in 1957, is considered a symbol of Italy's postwar economic miracle.

After the end of World War II, Italy was in rubble and occupied by foreign armies, a condition that worsened the chronic development gap towards the more advanced European economies. However, the new geopolitical logic of the Cold War made possible that the former enemy Italy, a hinge-country between Western Europe and the Mediterranean, and now a new, fragile democracy threatened by the NATO occupation forces, the proximity of the Iron Curtain and the presence of a strong Communist party, was considered by the United States as an important ally for the Free World, and received under the Marshall Plan over US$1.2 billion from 1947-51.

The end of aid through the Plan could have stopped the recovery but it coincided with a crucial point in the Korean War whose demand for metal and manufactured products was a further stimulus of Italian industrial production. In addition, the creation in 1957 of the European Common Market, with Italy as a founding member, provided more investment and eased exports.

These favorable developments, combined with the presence of a large labour force, laid the foundation for spectacular economic growth that lasted almost uninterrupted until the "Hot Autumn's" massive strikes and social unrest of 1969–70, which then combined with the later 1973 oil crisis and put an abrupt end to the prolonged boom. It has been calculated that the Italian economy experienced an average rate of growth of GDP of 5.8% per year between 1951–63, and 5% per year between 1964–73. Italian rates of growth were second only, but very close, to the German rates, in Europe, and among the OEEC countries only Japan had been doing better.

The 1970s were a period of economic, political turmoil and social unrest in Italy, known as Years of Lead. Unemployment rose sharply, especially among the young, and by 1977 there were one million unemployed people under age 24. Inflation continued, aggravated by the increases in the price of oil in 1973 and 1979. The budget deficit became permanent and intractable, averaging about 10 percent of the Gross Domestic Product (GDP), higher than any other industrial country. The lira fell steadily, from 560 lira to the U.S. dollar in 1973 to 1,400 lira in 1982.

The economic recession went on into the mid-1980s until a set of reforms led to the independence of the Bank of Italy and a big reduction of the indexation of wages that strongly reduced inflation rates, from 20.6% in 1980 to 4.7% in 1987. The new macroeconomic and political stability resulted in a second, export-led "economic miracle", based on small and medium-sized enterprises, producing clothing, leather products, shoes, furniture, textiles, jewelry, and machine tools. As a result of this rapid expansion, in 1987 Italy overtook the British economy (an event known as *IL sorpasso*), becoming the sixth in the world. The Milan stock exchange increased its market capitalization more than fivefold in the space of a few years.

However, the Italian economy of the 1980s presented a problem: it was booming, thanks to increased productivity and surging exports, but unsustainable fiscal deficits drove the growth. In the 1990s, the new Maastricht criteria boosted the urge to curb the public debt, already at 104% of GDP in 1992. The consequent restrictive economic policies worsened the impact of the global recession already underway. After a brief recover at the end of the 1990s, high tax rates and red tape caused the country to stagnate between 2000 and 2008.

Great Recession

GDP per capita of Italy, France, Germany and Britain from 1970 to 2008.

Italy was among the countries hit hardest by the Great Recession of 2008-2009 and the subsequent European debt crisis. The national economy shrunk by 6.76% during the whole period, totaling seven-quarters of recession. In November 2011 the Italian bond yield was 6.74 percent for 10-year bonds, nearing a 7 percent level where Italy is thought to lose access to financial markets. According to Eurostat, in 2015 the Italian government debt stood at 128% of GDP, ranking as the second biggest debt ratio after Greece (with 175%). However, the biggest chunk of Italian public debt is owned by Italian nationals and relatively high levels of private savings and low levels of private indebtedness are seen as making it the safest among Europe's struggling economies. As a shock therapy to avoid the debt crisis and kick-start growth, the National unity government led by the famous economist Mario Monti launched a program of massive austerity measures, that have brought down the deficit but precipitated the country in a double-dip recession in 2012 and 2013, receiving widespread criticism from numerous economists.

Economic recovery

The Ferrari Portofino represents the synergy of "Made in Italy" brands that strengthens the Italian economy.

In spite of a very high public debt and political instability (Italy has had five governments since 2011), the Italian economy since 2014 has returned to growth (an event known as "la ripresa") and is expected to grow by 1.5% or more in 2017, mainly thanks to a rise in exports and the reform of the banking system.

Overview

Data

The following table shows the main economic indicators in 1980–2018. Inflation under 2% is in green.

Year	*GDP (in bn. Euro)*	*GDP per capita (in Euro)*	*GDP growth (real)*	*Inflation rate (in Percent)*	*Unemploy-ment (in Percent)*	*Government debt (in % of GDP)*
1986	▲497.5	▲8,790	▲2.9 %	▲5.8 %	▲8.9 %	n/a
1990	▲722.8	▲12,749	▲2.1 %	▲6.4 %	▼8.9 %	▲98.8 %
1995	▲985.0	▲17,328	▲2.3 %	▲5.4 %	▲11.1 %	▼116.9 %
2000	▲1,239.3	▲21,771	▲3.7 %	▲2.6 %	▼10.1 %	▼105.1 %
2005	▲1,489.7	▲25,656	▲1.0 %	▲2.2 %	▼7.7 %	▲101.9 %
2010	▲1,604.5	▲26,873	▲1.7 %	▲1.6 %	▲8.3 %	▲115.4 %
2018[78]	▲1,757.0	▲29,049	▲0.9 %	▲1.2 %	▼10.6 %	▲132.2 %

Companies

Ferrari is the world's most powerful brand according to the Global 500 annual study published by Brand Finance in 2014.

The labour productivity level of Italy. OECD, 2015

Of the world's 500 largest stock-market-listed companies measured by revenue in 2016, the Fortune Global 500, nine are headquartered in Italy. The country's major companies by sector are: Fiat Chrysler Automobiles, CNH Industrial, Ducati, Piaggio (motor vehicles); Pirelli (tyre manufacturing); Enel, Edison, A2A, Terna (energy); Eni (petrochemicals); Candy, Indesit, De'Longhi (home appliances); Leonardo that has absorbed its subsidiary companies Alenia Aermacchi, AgustaWestland and Oto Melara (defence); Avio, Telespazio (space); Beretta, Benelli (firearms); Armani, Versace, Dolce HYPERLINK "https://en.wikipedia.org/wiki/Dolce_%26_Gabbana"&HYPERLINK "https://en.wikipedia.org/wiki/Dolce_%26_Gabbana" Gabbana, Gucci, Benetton, Diesel, Prada, Luxottica, YOOX (fashion); Ferrero, Barilla, Autogrill, Lavazza, Perfetti Van Melle, Campari, Parmalat (food&beverages); Techint, Lucchini, Gruppo Riva, Danieli (steel); Prysmian, Salini Impregilo, Italcementi, Buzzi Unicem, Astaldi (construction); STMicroelectronics (electronics); Telecom Italia, Mediaset (communications); Assicurazioni Generali, Unipol (insurance); UniCredit, Intesa Sanpaolo (banking); Ferrari, Maserati, Lamborghini (luxury vehicles); Fincantieri, Ferretti, Azimut (shipbuilding).

Rank (World)	*Rank (Italy)*	*Company*	*Headquarters*	*Revenue (€bn)*	*Profit (€bn)*	*Employees (World)*	*Main sector*
19	1	Fiat	Turin	152.6	0.83	225,587	Automotive
49	2	Generali Group	Trieste	102.6	2.25	74,000	Insurance
65	3	Eni	Rome	93.0	1.33[83]	80,911	Petroleum
78	4	Enel	Rome	83.9	2.44	62,080	Electric utility
224	5	Intesa Sanpaolo	Turin	42.2	3.04	90,807	Banking
300	6	UniCredit	Milan	34.6	1.88	117,659	Banking
305	7	Poste italiane	Rome	34.1	0.61	142,268	Postal services
404	8	Telecom Italia	Milan	26.6	0.44[84]	66,025	Telecommunications
491	9	Unipol	Bologna	21.5	0.30	14,223	Insurance

Figures are for 2016. Figures in italic = Q3 2017

Wealth

Italy has over 1.4 million people with a net wealth greater than $1 million, a total national wealth of $11.857 trillion, and represents the 5th largest cumulative net wealth globally (it accounts for 4.92% of the net wealth in the world). According to the Credit Suisse's Global Wealth Data book 2013, the median wealth per adult is $138,653 (5th in the world), while according

Rank (World)	*Rank (Italy)*	*Name*	*Net Worth ($bn)*	*Main source*	*Main sector*
29	1	Maria Franca Fissolo Ferrero & family	25.2	Ferrero SpA	Food
50	2	Leonardo Del Vecchio	17.9	Luxottica	Eyewear
80	3	Stefano Pessina	13.9	Walgreens Boots	Pharmaceutical retail
133	4	Massimiliana Landini Aleotti	9.5	Menarini	Pharmaceutical
199	5	Silvio Berlusconi	7.0	Fininvest	Financial services
215	6	Giorgio Armani	6.6	Armani	Fashion
250	7	Augusto & Giorgio Perfetti	5.8	Perfetti Van Melle	Confectionery
385	8	Paolo & Gianfelice Rocca	3.4	Techint	Conglomerate
474	9	Giuseppe De' Longhi	3.8	De'Longhi	Small appliance
603	10	Patrizio Bertelli	3.3	Prada	Apparels

to the Allianz's Global Wealth Report 2013, the net financial wealth per capita is €45,770 (13th in the world).

The following top 10 list of Italian billionaires is based on an annual assessment of wealth and assets compiled and published by Forbes in 2017.

North–South divide

Since the unification HYPERLINK "https://en.wikipedia.org/wiki/Unification_of_Italy"of Italy in 1861, a wide and increasing economic divide has been growing between the Northern provinces and the southern half of the Italian state. This gap was mainly induced by the region-specific policies selected by the Piedmontese elite, who dominated the first post-unitary governments, and that more heavily penalized the regions farther away from the rulers' fiercer enemies, as recently confirmed by Guilherme de Oliveira and Carmine Guerriero. To illustrate, the 1887 protectionist reform, instead of safeguarding the arboriculture sectors crushed by 1880s fall in prices, shielded the Po Valley wheat breeding and those Northern textile and manufacturing industries that had survived the liberal years thanks to state intervention. While indeed the former dominated the allocation of military clothing contracts, the latter monopolized both coal mining permits and public contracts. A similar logic guided the assignment of monopoly rights in the steamboat construction and navigation sectors and, above all, the public spending in the railway sector, which represented 53% of the 1861-1911 total. To make things worse, the resources necessary to finance this public spending effort were obtained through highly unbalanced land property taxes, which affected the key source of savings available for investment in the growth sectors absent a developed banking system. To elaborate, the 1864 reform fixed a 125 million target revenue to be raised from 9 districts resembling the pre-unitary states. Given the inability of the government to estimate the land profitability, especially because of the huge differences among the regional cadasters, this policy irreparably induced large regional discrepancies. To illustrate, the ex-Papal State (central Italy) took on the 10%, the ex-Kingdom of Two Sicilies (Southern Italy) the 40%, and the rest of the state (ex-Kingdom of Sardinia, Northern Italy) the 21%.To weigh this burden down, a 20% surcharge was added by 1868.

The 1886 cadastral reform opened the way to more egalitarian policies and, after the First World War, to the harmonization of the tax-rates, but the impact of extraction on the economies of the two blocks was at that point irreversible. While indeed a flourishing manufacturing sector was established in the North, the mix of low public spending and heavy taxation squeezed the Southern investment to the point that the local industry and export-oriented farming were wiped out. Moreover, extraction destroyed the relationship between the central state and the Southern population by unchaining first a civil war called Brigandage, which brought about 20,000 victims by 1864 and the militarization of the area, and then favoring emigration, especially from 1892 to 1921. To elaborate, extractive policies induced a dramatic fall in the accumulation of both social and human capital in the Southern regions and favored the rise of organized crime.

After the rise of Benito Mussolini, the "Iron Prefect" Cesare Mori tried to defeat the already powerful criminal organizations flourishing in the South with some degree of success. Fascist policy aimed at the creation of an Italian empire and Southern Italian ports were strategic for all commerce towards the colonies. With the invasion of Southern Italy, the Allies restored the authority of the mafia families, lost during the Fascist period, and used their influence to maintain public order.

In the 1950s the Cassa per il Mezzogiorno was set up as a huge public master plan to help industrialize the South, aiming to do this in two ways: through land reforms creating 120,000 new smallholdings, and through the "Growth Pole Strategy" whereby 60% of all government investment would go to the South, thus boosting the Southern economy by attracting new capital, stimulating local firms, and providing employment. However, the objectives were largely missed, and as a result the South became increasingly subsidized and state dependent, incapable of generating private growth itself.

Even at present, huge regional disparities persist. Problems in Southern Italy still include widespread political corruption, pervasive organized crime, and very high unemployment rates. In 2007, it was estimated that about 80% of the businesses in the Sicilian cities of Catania and Palermo paid protection money; thanks to grassroots movement like Addiopizzo, the mafia racket is slowly but constantly losing its verve. The Italian Ministry of Interior reported that organized crime generated an estimated annual profit of €13 billion.

Economic Sectors

Primary

According to the last national agricultural census, there were 1.6 million farms in 2010 (-32.4% since 2000) covering 12.7 million hectares (63% of which are located in Southern Italy). The vast majority (99%) are family-operated and small, averaging only 8 hectares in size. Of the total surface area in agricultural use (forestry excluded), grain fields take up 31%, olive tree orchards 8.2%, vineyards 5.4%, citrus orchards 3.8%, sugar beets 1.7%, and horticulture 2.4%. The remainder is primarily dedicated to pastures (25.9%) and feed grains (11.6%). The northern part of Italy produces primarily maize corn, rice, sugar beets, soybeans, meat, fruits and dairy products, while the South specializes in wheat and citrus fruits. Livestock includes 6 million head of cattle, 8.6 million head of swine, 6.8 million head of sheep, and 0.9 million head of goats. The total annual production of the fishing industry in Italy from capture and aquaculture, including crustaceans and molluscs, is around 480,000 tons.

Italy is the largest producer of wine in the world, and one of the leading producers of olive oil, fruits (apples, olives, grapes, oranges, lemons, pears, apricots, hazelnuts, peaches, cherries, plums, strawberries and kiwifruits), and vegetables (especially artichokes and tomatoes). The most famous Italian wines are probably the Tuscan Chianti and the Piedmontese Barolo. Other famous wines are Barbaresco, Barbera d'Asti, Brunello di Montalcino, Frascati, Montepulciano d'Abruzzo, Morellino di Scansano, Amarone della Valpolicella DOCG and the sparkling wines Franciacorta and Prosecco. Quality goods in which Italy specializes, particularly the already mentioned wines and regional cheeses, are often protected under the quality assurance labels DOC/DOP. This geographical indication certificate, which is attributed by the European Union, is considered important in order to avoid confusion with low-quality mass-produced ersatz products.

Secondary

Italy has a smaller number of global multinational corporations than other economies of comparable size, but there is a large number of small and medium-sized enterprises, many of them grouped in clusters, which are the backbone of the Italian industry. This has produced a manufacturing sector often focused on the export of niche market and luxury products, that on one side is less capable of competing on quantity, but on the other side is more capable of facing the competition from emerging economies based on lower labor costs, with higher quality products. The industrial districts are regionalized: in the Northwest there is a large modern group of industries, as in the so-called "Industrial Triangle" (Milan-Turin-Genoa), where there is an area of intense machinery, automotive, aerospace and naval production; in the Northeast and the Center, previously rural areas that experienced social and economic development around family-based firms, there are small enterprises of low technology but high craftsmanship, specialized in clothing, leather products, footwear, furniture, textiles, machine tools, spare parts, appliances, and jewellery; finally, in the less-developed South, the two forms exist side by side.

Tertiary

The origins of modern banking can be traced to medieval and early Renaissance Italy, to the rich cities like Florence, Lucca, Siena, Venice and Genoa. The Bardi and Peruzzi families dominated banking in 14th-century Florence, establishing branches in many other parts of Europe. One of the most famous Italian banks was the Medici Bank, set up by Giovanni di Bicci de' Medici in 1397. The earliest known state deposit bank, the Bank of Saint George, was founded in 1407 in Genoa, while Banca Monte dei Paschi di Siena, founded in 1472, is the oldest surviving bank in the world. Today, among the financial services companies, UniCredit is one of the largest bank in Europe by capitalization and Assicurazioni Generali is second largest insurance group in the world by revenue after AXA.

The following is a list of the main Italian banks and insurance groups ranked by total assets and gross premiums written.

Infrastructure

Energy in Italy

The early 1970s Italy was a major producer of pyrites (from the Tuscan Maremma), asbestos (from the Balangero mines), fluorite (found in Sicily), and salt. At the same time, it was self-sufficient in aluminum (from Gargano), sulphur (from Sicily), lead, and zinc (from Sardinia). By the beginning of the 1990s, however, it had lost all its world-ranking positions and was no longer self-sufficient in those resources. There are no substantial deposits of iron, coal, or oil. Moderate natural gas reserves, mainly in the Po Valley and offshore Adriatic Sea, have been discovered in recent years and constitute the country's most important mineral resource. Italy is one of the world's leading producers of pumice, pozzolana, and feldspar. Another mineral resource for which Italy is well-known is marble, especially the world-famous white Carrara marble from the Massa and Carrara quarries in Tuscany. Most raw materials needed for manufacturing and more than 80% of the country's energy sources are imported (99.7% of the solid fuels demand, 92.5% of oil, 91.2% of natural gas and 13% of electricity). Due to its reliance on imports, Italians pay approximately 45% more than the EU average for electricity. Italy has managed four nuclear reactors until the 1980s, but in 1987, after the Chernobyl disaster, a large majority of Italians passed a referendum opting for phasing out nuclear power in Italy. The government responded by closing existing nuclear power plants and stopping work on projects underway, continuing to work to the nuclear energy program abroad. The national power company Enel operates seven nuclear reactors in Spain (through Endesa) and four in Slovakia (through Slovenské elektrárne), and in 2005 made an agreement with Électricité de France for a nuclear reactor in France. With these agreements, Italy has managed to access nuclear power and direct involvement in design, construction, and operation of the plants without placing reactors on Italian territory. In the last decade, Italy has become one of the world's largest producers of renewable energy, ranking as the second largest producer in the European Union after Germany and the ninth in the world. The country is also the world's fifth largest producer of energy from solar power. Renewable sources account for the 27.5% of all electricity produced in Italy, with hydro alone reaching 12.6%, followed by solar at 5.7%, wind at 4.1%, bioenergy at 3.5%, and geothermal at 1.6%. The rest of the national demand is covered by fossil fuels (38.2% natural gas, 13% coal, 8.4% oil) and by imports.

Transport

Rome Fiumicino Airport in 2014 was the eighth-busiest airport in Europe. Italy was the first country in the world to build motorways, the so-called "autostrade", reserved for motor vehicles. The Milano-Laghi motorway, connecting Milan to Varese and now parts of the A8 and A9 motorways, was devised by Piero Puricelli, a civil engineer and entrepreneur. He received the first authorization to build a public-utility fast road in 1921, and completed the construction between 1924 and 1926. By the end of the 1930s, over 400 kilometers of multi- and dual-single-lane motorways were constructed throughout Italy, linking cities and rural towns. Today there are 668,721 km of serviceable roads in Italy, including 6,661 km of motorways (mostly toll roads, national and local roads), state-owned but privately operated mainly by Atlantia company. The railway network is also extensive, especially in the north, totalizing 16,862 km of which 69% are electrified and on which 4,937 locomotives and railcars circulate. It is the 12th largest in the world, and is operated by state-owned Ferrovie dello Stato, while the rail tracks and infrastructure are managed by Rete Ferroviaria Italiana. While a number of private railroads exist and provide mostly commuter-type services, the national railway also provides sophisticated high-speed rail service that joins the major cities. The Florence–Rome high-speed railway was the first high-speed line opened in Europe when more than half of it opened in 1977. In 1991 the TAV was created for the planning and construction of high-speed rail lines along Italy's most important and saturated transport routes (Milan-Rome-Naples and Turin-Milan-Venice). High-speed trains include ETR-class trains, with the Frecciarossa 1000 reaching 400 km/h. There are approximately 130 airports in Italy, of which 99 have paved runways (including the two hubs of Leonardo Da Vinci International in Rome and Malpensa International in Milan), and 43 major seaports including the Port of Genoa, the country's largest and the third busiest by cargo HYPERLINK "https://en.wikipedia.org/wiki/List_of_busiest_ports_in_Europe" tonnage in the Mediterranean Sea. The national inland waterway network comprises 1,477 km of navigable rivers and channels. In 2007 Italy maintained a civilian air fleet of about 389,000 units and a merchant fleet of 581 ships.

Poverty

In 2015, poverty in Italy hit the highest levels in the previous 10 years. The level of absolute poverty for a two-person family was €1050.95/month. The poverty line per capita changed by region from €552.39/month to €819.13/month. The numbers of those in absolute poverty rose nearly an entire percent in 2015, from 6.8% in 2014, to 7.6% in 2015. In the south of Italy the numbers are even higher, with 10% living in absolute poverty, up from 9 percent in 2014. The north is better off at 6.7%, but this is still an increase from 5.7% in 2014. The national statistics reporting agency, ISTAT, defines absolute poverty as those who cannot buy goods and services which they need to survive. In 2015, the proportion of poor households in relative poverty also increased to 13.7 from 12.9 in 2014. ISTAT defines relative poverty as people whose disposable income is less than around half the national average. The unemployment rate in February 2016 remained at 11.7%, which has been the same for almost a year, but even having a job does not guarantee freedom from poverty. Those who have at least one family member employed still suffer from 6.1% to 11.7% poverty, the higher number being for those who have factory jobs. The numbers are even higher for the younger generations because their unemployment rate is over 40%. Also, children are hit hard. In 2014, 32% of those aged 0–17 are at risk of poverty or social exclusion, which is one child out of three. In the last ISTAT report, poverty is in decline.

Critical Observations of the present status of the economy of Italy

(1) Italian currency is Euro as Italy is the founder member of European Union and Eurozone.

(2) Financial year is the calendar year.

(3) Country Group Developed/Advanced. High income economy.

(4) Population 6.03 crores

(5) GDP $ 1.989 trillion Nominal and $ 2.44 trillion PPP

(6) GDP growth 1.7% In 2017and 0.5% In 2020

(7) GDP per capita $32947 Nominal and $40470 PPP

(8) Population below poverty lines 5.7%

(9) Labour Force 2.34 crores

(10) Labour force by occupation Agriculture 3.9%, Industry 28.3% and services 67.8%

(11) Average gross salary euro 2595 monthly

(12) Main Industries Tourism, Machinery, Iron & Steel, chemicals, food processing, textiles, motor vechicles, clothing and footwear

(13) Exports $496.3 billion. Largest in European countries

(14) Export goods engineering products, textiles, clothing, production machinery, motor vehicles, transport equipments, chemicals, foodstuff, beverage, tobacco

(15) Imports $432.9 billion. Trade Surplus $ 63.4 billion. Good performance.

(16) Import Goods engineering products, chemicals, transport equipments, energy products, textile & clothing

(17) Current Account $ 53.42 billion

(18) External debt $2.324 trillion is high because of high spending on public expenditure and military buildup. 5 million army was built up out of which 7 lacs died in World War. This made country's economy vulnerable and per capita GDP was half of per capita GDP of UK.

(19) External debt was 134.43% of GDP. Very high. It should be 40%-50% of GDP at the maximum

(20) Budget/ Fiscal Deficit is 2.2 of GDP with Revenue 46.2% and Expenses 46.4%. It is comfortable

(21) International Credit Agencies Rating : S & P BBB Outlook Stable, Moody Baa2, Scope BBB+, Outlook Stable

(22) In the Post World War II period, Italy transformed from agricultural based economy into the most advanced nations' economy and a leading country in the world trade and exports.

(23) Today, Country's economy suffers from structural and non-structural problems. Italy was hit by the late 2000s recession.

(24) Massive government spending from 1980s onwards produced a severe rise in public debt and hyperinflation.

(25) There was significantly wide differences between Northern and Central Italy and Southern Italy in per capita income.

(26) Population was largely illiterate. Benito Mussolini's Fascist regime started in 1922. In order to improve economy, Mussolini abandoned laissez faire and free trade were abandoned in favour of government intervention and protectionism.

(27) Mussolini fought against France and Ethiopia and supported Nazi aggressive policy in World War II which resulted in imposing various restrictions on Italy and it was administered by the winning countries. Tremendous war expenditure resulted in falling growth of the Italian economy. 700000 soldiers were killed, 5 million army was built up and there were economic crisis after the War.

(28) After the end of the war, Italy was occupied by foreign armies that worsened the chronic development gap. In 1973, oil crisis abrupt end to slow economic boom.

(29) When the country diversifies its attention from the good administration and Ruler shows his power to the world as Mussolini, the country suffers and economic crisis occurs. To avoid this, Ruler should always concentrate on the country's progress and should not support wrong aggressive Nazi Party as Mussolini did and led to the economic crisis of his country after World War II. This occurs often as it is now happening to Iran and other countries who are showing their mighty strength to superpower USA and is under Economic Sanctions of USA. Iranian economy suffers heavily from this sanctions. In future, Italy should take lessons from Fascist Rule and should concentrate only on the growth of its economy.

15

Economy of Greece

Country is at present in light due to the Country's clashes with Turkey. Recep Erdogan, Turkey's President had accepted refugees from other countries on the basis of agreement with EU on terms that EU will provide financial assistance as a compensation to Turkey. Turkey has dispute recently with Syrian President Assad on Syrian Army supporting Kurdish tribes in Iraq against Turkey's fight with Kurdish tribes. In this dispute, Turkey's soldiers are killed substantially. Erdogan has therefore asked for military assistance of European countries to support this dispute in Syria which European countries refused. Erdogan thereafter threatened the European countries that he will release the Turkey's boarder and will send thousands of refugees in Turkey to the European countries which these countries will have to accept them as emigrates. This was the unilateral act of Turkey's President Mr. Recep Erdogan which EU never agreed. Erdogan then released Turkey's Boarder with Greece and thousands of refugees started entering the Greece Boarder. Greece ruthlessly banned them to enter its boarder by applying military force which Erdogan wrongly criticized. This issue has not been resolved and Greece has kept military on its Boarder to prevent the refugees from Turkey to enter its Borders. There are stone throwing and other violent acts of refugees to forcefully enter Greece boarder but they are unable to succeed.

The economy of Greece is the 51st largest in the world with a nominal Gross Domestic Product (GDP) of $218.032 billion per annum. In terms of purchasing power parity, Greece is the world's 55th largest economy, at $317.455 billion per annum. As of 2018, Greece is the seventeenth-largest economy in the 28-member European Union. According to IMF figures for 2018, Greece's GDP per capita was $20,317 at nominal value and $29,072 at purchasing power parity.

Greece is a developed country with an economy based on the service (80%) and industrial sectors (16%), with the agricultural sector contributing an estimated 4% of national economic output in 2017. Important Greek industries include tourism and shipping. With 18 million international tourists in 2013, Greece was the 7th most visited country in the European Union and 16th in the world. The Greek Merchant Navy is the largest in the world, with Greek-owned vessel accounting for 15% of global deadweight tonnage as of 2013. The increased demand for international maritime transportation between Greece and Asia has resulted in unprecedented investment in the shipping industry.

The country is a significant agricultural producer within the EU. Greece has the largest economy in the Balkans and is as an important regional investor. Greece was the largest foreign investor in Albania in 2013, the third in Bulgaria, in the top-three in Romania and Serbia and the most important trading partner and largest foreign investor in North Macedonia. The Greek telecommunications company OTE has become a strong investor in certain former Yugoslav and other Balkan countries.

Greece is classified as an advanced, high-income economy, and was a founding member of the OrganizationHYPERLINK "https://en.wikipedia.org/wiki/Organisation_for_Economic_Co-operation_and_Development" for Economic Co-operation and Development (OECD) and of the Organization of the Black Sea Economic Cooperation (BSEC). The country joined what is now the European Union in 1981. In 2001 Greece adopted the euro as its currency, replacing the Greek drachma at an exchange rate of 340.75 drachmae per euro. Greece is a member of the International Monetary Fund and of the World Trade Organization, and ranked 34th on Ernst & Young's Globalization Index 2011.

World War II (1939-1945) devastated the country's economy, but the high levels of economic growth that followed from 1950 to 1980 have been called the Greek economic miracle. From 2000 Greece saw high levels of GDP growth above the Eurozone average, peaking at 5.8% in 2003 and 5.7% in 2006. The subsequent Great Recession and Greek government-debt crisis, a central focus of the wider European debt crisis, plunged the economy into a sharp downturn, with real GDP growth rates of "0.3% in 2008, "4.3% in 2009, "5.5% in 2010, "9.1% in 2011, "7.3% in 2012 and "3.2% in 2013. In 2011, the country's public debt reached €356 billion (172% of nominal GDP). After negotiating the biggest debt restructuring in history with the private sector, a loss of 100 billion for bonds private investors, Greece reduced its sovereign debt burden to €280 billion (137% of GDP) in the first quarter of 2012. Greece achieved a real GDP growth rate of 0.7% in 2014—after 6 years of economic decline—but contracted by 0.4% in 2015 and by 0.2% in 2016. The country returned to modest growth of 1.5% in 2017 and 1.9% in 2018.

History

The evolution of the Greek economy during the 19th century (a period that transformed a large part of the world because of the Industrial Revolution) has been little researched. Recent research from 2006 examines the gradual development of industry and further development of shipping in a predominantly agricultural economy, calculating an average rate of per capita GDP growth between 1833 and 1911 that was only slightly lower than that of the other Western European nations. Industrial activity, (including heavy industry like shipbuilding) was evident, mainly in Ermoupolis and Piraeus. Nonetheless, Greece faced economic hardships and defaulted on its external loans in 1826, 1843, 1860 and 1893.

Other studies support the above view on the general trends in the economy, providing comparative measures of standard of living. The per capita income (in purchasing power terms) of Greece was 65% that of France in 1850, 56% in 1890, 62% in 1938, 75% in 1980, 90% in 2007, 96.4% in 2008 and 97.9% in 2009.

The country's post-World War II development has largely been connected with the Greek economic miracle. During that period, Greece saw growth rates second only to those of Japan, while ranking first in Europe in the of GDP growth. It is indicative that between 1960 and 1973 the Greek economy grew by an average of 7.7%, in contrast to 4.7% for the EU15 and 4.9% for the OECD. Also during that period, exports grew by an average annual rate of 12.6%.

Strengths and weaknesses

Greece enjoys a high standard of living and very high Human Development Index, ranking 32nd in the world in 2018. However, the severe recession of recent years saw GDP per capita fall from 94% of the EU average in 2009 to 67% in 2017, with a slight improvement to 68% in 2018. Actual Individual Consumption (AIC) per capita fell from 104% of the EU average to 76% between 2009 and 2017, before rising slightly to 77% in 2018.

Greece's main industries are tourism, shipping, industrial products, food and tobacco processing, textiles, chemicals, metal products, mining and petroleum. Greece's GDP growth has also, as an average, since the early 1990s been higher than the EU average. However, the Greek economy continues to face significant problems, including high unemployment levels, an inefficient public sector bureaucracy, tax evasion, corruption and low global competitiveness.

Greece is ranked 60th in the world on the Corruption Perceptions Index, above Croatia, Romania, Hungary and Bulgaria among EU member states.

It has the EU's lowest Index of Economic Freedom and second lowest Global Competitiveness Index, ranking 106th and 59th in the world respectively.

After fourteen consecutive years of economic growth, Greece went into recession in 2008. By the end of 2009, the Greek economy faced the highest budget deficit and government debt-to-GDP ratio in the EU. After several upward revisions, the 2009 budget deficit is now estimated at 15.7% of GDP. This, combined with rapidly rising debt levels (127.9% of GDP in 2009) led to a precipitous increase in borrowing costs, effectively shutting Greece out of the global financial markets and resulting in a severe economic crisis.

Greece was accused of trying to cover up the extent of its massive budget deficit in the wake of the global financial crisis. The allegation was prompted by the massive revision of the 2009 budget deficit forecast by the new PASOK government elected in October 2009, from "6–8%" (estimated by the previous New Democracy government) to 12.7% (later revised to 15.7%). However, the accuracy of the revised figures has also been questioned, and in February 2012 the Hellenic Parliament voted in favor of an official investigation following accusations by a former member of the Hellenic Statistical Authority that the deficit had been artificially inflated in order to justify harsher austerity measures.

The Greek labor force, which amount around 5 million workers, average 2,032 hours of work per worker annually in 2011, is ranked fourth among OECD countries, after Mexico, South Korea and Chile. The Groningen Growth HYPERLINK "https://en.wikipedia.org/wiki/University_of_Groningen" &HYPERLINK "https://en.wikipedia.org/wiki/University_of_Groningen" Development Centre has published a poll revealing that between 1995 and 2005, Greece was the country whose workers have the most hours/year work among European nations; Greeks worked an average of 1,900 hours per year, followed by Spaniards (average of 1,800 hours/year).

As a result of the ongoing economic crisis, industrial production in the country went down by 8% between March 2010 and March 2011.The volume of building activity saw a reduction of 73% in 2010. Additionally, the turnover in retail sales saw a decline of 9% between February 2010 and February 2011.

Between 2008 and 2013 unemployment skyrocketed, from a generational low of 7.2% in the second and third quarters of 2008 to a high of 27.9% in June 2013, leaving over a million jobless. Youth unemployment peaked at 64.9% in May 2013. Unemployment figures have steadily improved in recent years, with the overall rate falling to 16.8% and youth unemployment dropping to 32.4% in September 2019.

Eurozone entry

Greece entered the Eurozone in 2001

Greece was accepted into the Economic and Monetary Union of the European Union by the European Council on 19 June 2000, based on a number of criteria (inflation rate, budget deficit, public debt, long-term interest rates, exchange rate) using 1999 as the reference year. After an audit commissioned by the incoming New Democracy government in 2004, Eurostat revealed that the statistics for the budget deficit had been under-reported.

Most of the differences in the revised budget deficit numbers were due to a temporary change of accounting practices by the new government, i.e., recording expenses when military material was ordered rather than received. However, it was the retroactive application of ESA95 methodology (applied since 2000) by Eurostat, which finally raised the reference year (1999) budget deficit to 3.38% of GDP, thus exceeding the 3% limit. This led to claims that Greece (similar claims have been made about other European countries like Italy) had not actually met all five accession criteria, and the common perception that Greece entered the Eurozone through "falsified" deficit numbers.

In the 2005 OECD report for Greece, it was clearly stated that "the impact of new accounting rules on the fiscal figures for the years 1997 to 1999 ranged from 0.7 to 1 percentage point of GDP; this retroactive change of methodology was responsible for the revised deficit exceeding 3% in 1999, the year of [Greece's] EMU membership qualification". The above led the Greek minister of finance to clarify that the 1999 budget deficit was below the prescribed 3% limit when calculated with the ESA79 methodology in force at the time of Greece's application, and thus the criteria had been met.

The original accounting practice for military expenses was later restored in line with Eurostat recommendations, theoretically lowering even the ESA95-calculated 1999 Greek budget deficit to below 3% (an official Eurostat calculation is still pending for 1999).

An error sometimes made is the confusion of discussion regarding Greece's Eurozone entry with the controversy regarding usage of derivatives' deals with U.S. Banks by Greece and other Eurozone countries to artificially reduce their reported budget deficits. A currency swap arranged with

Goldman Sachs allowed Greece to "hide" 2.8 billion Euros of debt, however, this affected deficit values after 2001 (when Greece had already been admitted into the Eurozone) and is not related to Greece's Eurozone entry.

A study of the period 1999–2009 by forensic accountants has found that data submitted to Eurostat by Greece, among other countries, had a statistical distribution indicative of manipulation; "Greece with a mean value of 17.74, shows the largest deviation from Benford's law among the members of the Eurozone, followed by Belgium with a value of 17.21 and Austria with a value of 15.25". 2010–2018 government debt crisis.

Previous situation

Greece, like other European nations, had faced debt crises in the 19th century, as well as a similar crisis in 1932 during the Great Depression. In general, however, during the 20th century it enjoyed one of the highest GDP growth rates on the planet (for a quarter century from the early 1950s to mid-1970s, second in the world after Japan). Average Greek government debt-to-GDP for the entire century before the crisis (1909-2008) was lower than that for the UK, Canada, or France (see table), while for the 30-year period (1952-1981) until entrance into the European Economic Community, the Greek government debt-to-GDP ratio averaged only 19.8%.

Between 1981 and 1993 it steadily rose, surpassing the average of what is today the Eurozone in the mid-1980s (see chart below). For the next 15 years, from 1993 to 2007 (i.e., before the Financial crisis of 2007–2008), Greece's government debt-to-GDP ratio remained roughly unchanged (the value was not affected by the 2004 Athens Olympics), averaging 102% - a value lower than that for Italy (107%) and Belgium (110%) during the same 15-year period, and comparable to that for the U.S. or the OECD average in 2017.

During the latter period, the country's annual budget deficit usually exceeded 3% of GDP, but its effect on the debt-to-GDP ratio was counterbalanced by high GDP growth rates. The debt-to-GDP values for 2006 and 2007 (about 105%) were established after audits resulted in corrections according to Eurostat methodology, of up to 10 percentage points for the particular years (as well as similar corrections for the years 2008 and 2009). These corrections, although altering the debt level by a maximum of about 10%, resulted in a popular notion that "Greece was previously hiding its debt".

Evolution of the debt crisis

The Greek crisis was triggered by the turmoil of the Great Recession, which lead the budget deficits of several Western nations to reach or exceed 10%

of GDP. What was exceptional for Greece, was that the high budget deficit (which, after several corrections, was revealed that it had been allowed to reach 10.2% and 15.1% of GDP in 2008 and 2009, respectively) was simultaneously coupled with a high public debt to GDP ratio (which, until then, was relatively stable for several years, at just above 100% of GDP - as calculated after all corrections. Thus, the country appeared to lose control of its public debt to GDP ratio, which already reached 127% of GDP in 2009. In addition, being a member of the Eurozone, the country had essentially no autonomous monetary policy flexibility. Finally, there was an effect of controversies about Greek statistics (due the aforementioned drastic budget deficit revisions which lead to an increase in the calculated value of the Greek public debt by about 10%, i.e., a public debt to GDP of about 100% until 2007), while there have been arguments about a possible effect of media reports. Consequently, Greece was "punished" by the markets which increased borrowing rates, making impossible for the country to finance its debt since early 2010.

Thus, the Greek economy faced its most-severe crisis since the restoration of democracy in 1974 as the Greek government revised its deficit forecasts from 3.7% in early 2009 and 6% in September 2009, to 12.7% of gross domestic product (GDP) in October 2009.

The aforementioned budget deficit and debt revisions were connected with findings that, through the assistance of Goldman Sachs, JP Morgan Chase and numerous other banks, financial products were developed which enabled the governments of Greece, Italy and many other European countries to hide parts of their borrowing. Dozens of similar agreements were concluded across Europe whereby banks supplied cash in advance in exchange for future payments by the governments involved; in turn, the liabilities of the involved countries were "kept off the books".

According to *Der Spiegel*, credits given to European governments were disguised as "swaps" and consequently did not get registered as debt because Eurostat at the time ignored statistics involving financial derivatives. A German derivatives dealer had commented to *Der Spiegel* that "The Maastricht rules can be circumvented quite legally through swaps," and "In previous years, Italy used a similar trick to mask its true debt with the help of a different US bank." These conditions had enabled Greek as well as many other European governments to spend beyond their means, while meeting the deficit targets of the European Union and the monetary union guidelines. In May 2010, the Greek government deficit was again revised and estimated to be 13.6% which was among the highest relative to GDP, with Iceland in first place at 15.7% and the United Kingdom third with 12.6%. Public debt was forecast, according to some estimates, to hit 120%

of GDP during 2010. As a consequence, there was a crisis in international confidence in Greece's ability to repay its sovereign debt, as reflected by the rise of the country's borrowing rates (although their slow rise – the 10-year government bond yield only exceeded 7% in April 2010 – coinciding with a large number of negative articles, has led to arguments about the role of international news media in the evolution of the crisis). In order to avert a default (as high borrowing rates effectively prohibited access to the markets), in May 2010 the other Eurozone countries, and the IMF, agreed to a "rescue package" which involved giving Greece an immediate €45 billion in bail-out loans, with more funds to follow, totaling €110 billion. In order to secure the funding, Greece was required to adopt harsh austerity measures to bring its deficit under control. Their implementation was to be monitored and evaluated by the European Commission, the European Central Bank and the IMF.

The financial crisis – particularly the austerity package put forth by the EU and the IMF – has been met with anger by the Greek public, leading to riots and social unrest, while there have been theories about the effect of international media. Despite - others say because of - the long range of austerity measures, the government deficit has not been reduced accordingly, mainly, according to many economists, because of the subsequent recession.

Public sector workers have come out on strike in order to resist job cuts and reductions to salaries as the government promises that a large scale privatization programme will be accelerated. Immigrants are sometimes treated as scapegoats for economic problems by far-right extremists.

In 2013, Greece became the first developed market to be reclassified as an emerging market by financial services companies MSCI and S&P Dow Jones Indices.

By July 2014 there were still anger and protests about the austerity measures, with a 24-hour strike among government workers timed to coincide with an audit by inspectors from the International Monetary Fund, the European Union and European Central Bank in advance of a decision on a second bailout of one billion euros ($1.36 billion), due in late July.

Greece exited its six-year recession in the second quarter of 2014, but the challenges of securing political stability and debt sustainability remain.

A third bailout was agreed in July, 2015, after a confrontation with the newly elected leftist government of Alexis Tsipras. In June 2017, news reports indicated that the "crushing debt burden" had not been alleviated and that Greece was at the risk of defaulting on some payments. The International Monetary Fund stated that the country should be able to borrow again "in due course". At the time, the Euro zone gave Greece another credit of $9.5-billion, $8.5 billion of loans and brief details of a possible debt relief with the assistance of the IMF. On 13 July, the Greek government sent a letter of intent to the IMF with 21 commitments it promised to meet by June 2018. They included changes in labour laws, a plan to cap public sector work contracts, to transform temporary contracts into permanent agreements and to recalculate pension payments to reduce spending on social security.

Greece's bailouts successfully ended (as declared) on August 20, 2018.

Effects of the bailout programmes on the debt crisis

There was a 25% drop in Greece's GDP, connected with the bailout programmes. This had a critical effect: the Debt-to-GDP ratio, the key factor defining the severity of the crisis, would jump from its 2009 level of 127% to about 170%, solely due to the GDP drop (i.e., for the same Debt). Such a level is considered unsustainable. In a 2013 report, the IMF admitted that it had underestimated the effects of so extensive tax hikes and budget cuts on the country's GDP and issued an informal apology

Data

Primary sector

In 2010, Greece was the European Union's largest producer of cotton (183,800 tons) and pistachios (8,000 tons) and ranked second in the production of rice (229,500 tons) and olives (147,500 tons), third in the production of figs (11,000 tons) and almonds (44,000 tons), tomatoes (1,400,000 tons) and watermelons (578,400 tons) and fourth in the production of tobacco (22,000 tons). Agriculture contributes 3.8% of the country's GDP and employs 12.4% of the country's labor force

Greece is a major beneficiary of the Common Agricultural Policy of the European Union. As a result of the country's entry to the European Community, much of its agricultural infrastructure has been upgraded and agricultural output increased. Between 2000 and 2007 organic farming in Greece increased by 885%, the highest change percentage in the EU.

In 2007, Greece accounted for 19% of the EU's fishing haul in the Mediterranean Sea, ranked third with 85,493 tons, and ranked first in the number of fishing vessels in the Mediterranean between European Union members. Additionally, the country ranked 11th in the EU in total quantity of fish caught, with 87,461 tons.

Secondary sector

Between 2005 and 2011, Greece has had the highest percentage increase in industrial output compared to 2005 levels out of all European Union members, with an increase of 6%. Eurostat statistics show that the industrial sector was hit by the Greek financial crisis throughout 2009 and 2010 with domestic output decreasing by 5.8% and industrial production in general by 13.4%. Currently, Greece is ranked third in the European Union in the production of marble (over 920,000 tons), after Italy and Spain.

Between 1999 and 2008, the volume of retail trade in Greece increased by an average of 4.4% per year (a total increase of 44%), while it decreased by 11.3% in 2009. The only sector that did not see negative growth in 2009 was administration and services, with a marginal growth of 2.0%.

In 2009, Greece's labor productivity was 98% that of the EU average, but it's productivity-per-hour-worked was 74% that the Eurozone average. The largest industrial employer in the country (in 2007) was the manufacturing industry (407,000 people), followed by the construction industry (305,000) and mining (14,000).

Greece has a significant shipbuilding and ship maintenance industry. The six shipyards around the port of Piraeus are among the largest in Europe. In recent years, Greece has become a leader in the construction and maintenance of luxury yachts. Mining

Tertiary sector

Between 1949 and the 1980s, telephone communications in Greece were a state monopoly by the Hellenic Telecommunications Organization, better known by its acronym, OTE. Despite the liberalization of telephone communications in the country in the 1980s, OTE still dominates the Greek market in its field and has emerged as one of the largest telecommunications companies in Southeast Europe. Since 2011, the company's major shareholder is Deutsche Telekom with a 40% stake, while the Greek state continues to own 10% of the company's shares. OTE owns several subsidiaries across the Balkans, including Cosmote, Greece's top mobile telecommunications provider, Cosmote Romania and Albanian Mobile Communications.

Other mobile telecommunications companies active in Greece are Wind Hellas and Vodafone Greece. The total number of active cellular phone accounts in the country in 2009 based on statistics from the country's mobile phone providers was over 20 million, a penetration of 180%. Additionally, there are 5.745 million active landlines in the country.

Greece has tended to lag behind its European Union partners in terms of Internet use, with the gap closing rapidly in recent years. The percentage of households with Internet access more than doubled between 2006 and 2013, from 23% to 56% respectively (compared with an EU average of 49% and 79%). At the same time, there was a massive increase in the proportion of households with a broadband connection, from 4% in 2006 to 55% in 2013 (compared with an EU average of 30% and 76%). By 2019, the percentage of Greek households with Internet access and a broadband connection had reached 78.5% and 78.1% respectively.

Tourism

Tourism in the modern sense has only started to flourish in Greece in the years post-1950, although tourism in ancient times is also documented in relation to religious or sports festivals such as the Olympic Games. Since the 1950s, the tourism sector saw an unprecedented boost as arrivals went from 33,000 in 1950 to 11.4 million in 1994.

Greece attracts more than 16 million tourists each year, thus contributing 18.2% to the nation's GDP in 2008 according to an OECD report. The same survey showed that the average tourist expenditure while in Greece was $1,073, ranking Greece 10th in the world. The number of jobs directly or indirectly related to the tourism sector were 840,000 in 2008 and represented 19% of the country's total labor force. In 2009, Greece welcomed over 19.3 million tourists, a major increase from the 17.7 million tourists the country welcomed in 2008.

Among the member states of the European Union, Greece was the most popular destination for residents of Cyprus and Sweden in 2011.

The ministry responsible for tourism is the Ministry of Culture and Tourism, while Greece also owns the Greek National Tourism Organization which aims in promoting tourism in Greece.

In recent years a number of well-known tourism-related organizations have placed Greek destinations in the top of their lists. In 2009 Lonely Planet ranked Thessaloniki, the country's second-largest city, the world's fifth best "Ultimate Party Town", alongside cities such as Montreal and Dubai, while in 2011 the island of Santorini was voted as the best island in the world by Travel + Leisure. The neighbouring island of Mykonos was ranked as the 5th best island Europe. Thessaloniki was the European Youth Capital in 2014.

Trade and investment

Foreign investment

Since the fall of communism, Greece has invested heavily in neighbouring Balkan countries. Between 1997 and 2009, 12.11% of foreign direct investment capital in North Macedonia was Greek, ranking fourth. In 2009 alone, Greeks invested €380 million in the country, with companies such as Hellenic Petroleum having made important strategic investments.

Greece invested €1.38 billion in Bulgaria between 2005 and 2007 and many important companies (including Bulgarian Postbank, United Bulgarian Bank Coca-Cola Bulgaria) are owned by Greek financial groups. In Serbia, 250 Greek companies are active with a total investment of over €2 billion. Romanian statistics from 2016 show that Greek investment in the country exceeded €4 billion, ranking Greece fifth or sixth among foreign investors. Greece has been the largest investor in Albania since the fall of communism with 25% of foreign investments in 2016 coming from Greece, in addition business relations between both are extremely strong and continuously rising.

Trade

Since the start of the debt crisis, Greece's negative balance of trade has decreased significantly from €44.3 billion in 2008 to €21.7 billion in 2019. In 2019, exports increased by 1% and imports rose by 2.6%.

Greece is also the largest import partner of Cyprus (18.0%) and the largest export partner of Palau (82.4%).

Transport

As of 2012, Greece had a total of 82 airports, of which 67 were paved and six had runways longer than 3,047 meters. Of these airports, two are classified as "international" by the Hellenic Civil Aviation Authority, but 15 offer international services. Additionally Greece has 9 heliports. Greece does not have a flag carrier, but the country's airline industry is dominated by Aegean Airlines and its subsidiary Olympic Air.

Between 1975 and 2009, Olympic Airways (known after 2003 as Olympic Airlines) was the country's state-owned flag carrier, but financial problems led to its privatization and relaunch as Olympic Air in 2009. Both Aegean Airlines and Olympic Air have won awards for their services; in 2009 and 2011, Aegean Airlines was awarded the "Best regional airline in Europe" award by Skytrax, and also has two gold and one silver awards by the ERA, while Olympic Air holds one silver ERA award for "Airline of the Year" as well as a *"Condé Nast Traveller 2011 Readers Choice Awards: Top Domestic Airline"* award.

The Greek road network is made up of 116,986 km of roads, of which 1863 km are highways, ranking 24th worldwide, as of 2016. Since the entry of Greece to the European Community (now the European Union), a number of important projects (such as the Egnatia Odos and the Attiki Odos) have been co-funded by the organization, helping to upgrade the country's road network. In 2007, Greece ranked 8th in the European Union in goods transported by road at almost 500 million tons.

Greece's rail network is estimated to be at 2,548 km. Rail transport in Greece is operated by Train OSE, a current subsidiary of the Ferrovie dello Stato Italiane after the Hellenic Railways HYPERLINK "https://en.wikipedia.org/wiki/Hellenic_Railways_Organisation" Organization had sold its 100% stake on the operator. Most of the country's network is standard gauge (1,565 km), while the country also has 983 km of narrow gauge. A total of 764 km of rail are electrified. Greece has rail connections with Bulgaria, North Macedonia and Turkey. A total of three suburban railway systems (Proastiakos) are in operation (in Athens, Thessaloniki and Patras), while one metro system, the Athens Metro, is operational in Athens with another, the Thessaloniki Metro, under construction.

According to Eurostat, Greece's largest port by tons of goods transported in 2010 is the port of Aghioi Theodoroi, with 17.38 million tons. The Port of Thessaloniki comes second with 15.8 million tons, followed by the Port of Piraeus, with 13.2 million tons, and the port of Eleusis, with 12.37 million tons. The total number of goods transported through Greece in 2010 amounted to 124.38 million tons, a considerable drop from the 164.3 million tons transported through the country in 2007. Since then, Piraeus has grown to become the Mediterranean's third-largest port thanks to heavy investment by Chinese logistics giant COSCO. In 2013, Piraeus was declared the fastest-growing port in the world.

In 2010 Piraeus handled 513,319 TEUs, followed by Thessaloniki, which handled 273,282 TEUs. In the same year, 83.9 million people passed through Greece's ports, 12.7 million through the port of Paloukia in Salamis, another 12.7 through the port of Perama, 9.5 million through Piraeus and 2.7 million through Igoumenitsa. In 2013, Piraeus handled a record 3.16 million TEUs, the third-largest figure in the Mediterranean, of which 2.52 million were transported through Pier II, owned by COSCO and 644,000 were transported through Pier I, owned by the Greek state.

Energy

Energy production in Greece is dominated by the Public Power Corporation (known mostly by its acronym ÄÅÇ, or in English DEI). In 2009 DEI supplied for 85.6% of all energy demand in Greece, while the number fell to 77.3% in 2010. Almost half (48%) of DEI's power output is generated using lignite, a drop from the 51.6% in 2009. Another 12% comes from hydroelectric power plants and another 20% from natural gas. Between

2009 and 2010, independent companies' energy production increased by 56%, from 2,709 Gigawatt hour in 2009 to 4,232 GWh in 2010.

In 2008 renewable energy accounted for 8% of the country's total energy consumption, a rise from the 7.2% it accounted for in 2006, but still below the EU average of 10% in 2008. 10% of the country's renewable energy comes from solar power, while most comes from biomass and waste recycling. In line with the European Commission's Directive on Renewable Energy, Greece aims to get 18% of its energy from renewable sources by 2020. In 2013 and for several months, Greece produced more than 20% of its electricity from renewable energy sources and hydroelectric power plants. Greece currently does not have any nuclear power plants in operation, however in 2009 the Academy of Athens suggested that research in the possibility of Greek nuclear power plants begin.

Greece had 10 million barrels of proven oil reserves as of 1 January 2012. Hellenic Petroleum is the country's largest oil company, followed by Motor Oil Hellas. Greece's oil production stands at 1,751 barrels per day (bbl/d), ranked 95th worldwide, while it exports 19,960 bbl/d, ranked 53rd, and imports 355,600 bbl/d, ranked 25th.

In 2011 the Greek government approved the start of oil exploration and drilling in three locations within Greece, with an estimated output of 250 to 300 million barrels over the next 15 to 20 years. The estimated output in euros of the three deposits is €25 billion over a 15-year period, of which €13–€14 billion will enter state coffers. Greece's dispute with Turkey over the Aegean poses substantial obstacles to oil exploration in the Aegean Sea.

In addition to the above, Greece is also to start oil and gas exploration in other locations in the Ionian Sea, as well as the Libyan Sea, within the Greek exclusive economic zone, south of Crete. The Ministry of the Environment, Energy and Climate Change announced that there was interest from various countries (including Norway and the United States) in exploration, and the first results regarding the amount of oil and gas in these locations were expected in the summer of 2012. In November 2012, a report published by Deutsche Bank estimated the value of natural gas reserves south of Crete at €427 billion.

A number of oil and gas pipelines are currently under construction or under planning in the country. Such projects include the *Interconnector Turkey-Greece-Italy* (ITGI) and *South Stream* gas pipelines.

Euro Asia Interconnector will electrically connect Attica and Crete in Greece with Cyprus and Israel with 2000 MW HVDC undersea power cable. EuroAsia Interconnector is especially important for isolated systems, like

Cyprus and Crete. Crete is energetically isolated from mainland Greece and Hellenic Republic covers for Crete electricity costs difference of around €300 million per year.

Taxation and tax evasion

Greece has a tiered tax system based on progressive taxation. Greek law recognizes six categories of taxable income: immovable property, movable property (investment), income from agriculture, business, employment, and income from professional activities. Greece's personal income tax rate, until recently, ranged from 0% for annual incomes below €12,000 to 45% for annual incomes over €100,000.Under the new 2010 tax reform, tax exemptions have been abolished.

Also under the new austerity measures and among other changes, the personal income tax-free ceiling has been reduced to €5,000 per annum while further future changes, for example abolition of this ceiling, are already being planned.

Greece's corporate tax dropped from 40% in 2000 to 20% in 2010. For 2011 only, corporate tax will be at 24%. Value added tax (VAT) has gone up in 2010 compared to 2009: 23% as opposed to 19%.

The lowest VAT possible is 6.5% (previously 4.5%) for newspapers, periodicals and cultural event tickets, while a tax rate of 13% (from 9%) applies to certain service sector professions. Additionally, both employers and employees have to pay social contribution taxes, which apply at a rate of 16% for white collar jobs and 19.5% for blue collar jobs, and are used for insurance now (2017) the VAT tax rate is 24% with minor exceptions, 13% Reduced for some basic foodstuffs which will be soon abolished and everything, as it seems, will soon go to 24% in order to fight the phantom of tax evasion.

The Ministry of Finance expected tax revenues for 2012 to be €52.7 billion (€23.6 billion in direct taxes and €29.1 billion in indirect taxes), an increase of 5.8% from 2011. In 2012, the government was expected to have considerably higher tax revenues than in 2011 on a number of sectors, primarily housing (an increase of 217.5% from 2011).

Tax evasion

Greece suffers from very high levels of tax evasion. In the last quarter of 2005, tax evasion reached 49%, while in January 2006 it fell to 41.6%. It is worth noting that the newspaper Ethnos which published these figures went bankrupt; it is no longer published and some sources suggest that the information it had published was highly debatable. A study by researchers from the University of Chicago concluded that tax evasion in 2009 by self-employed professionals alone in Greece (accountants, dentists, lawyers, doctors, personal tutors and independent financial advisers) was €28 billion or 31% of the budget deficit that year.

Greece's "shadow economy" was estimated at 24.3% of GDP in 2012, compared with 28.6% for Estonia, 26.5% for Latvia, 21.6% for Italy, 17.1% for Belgium, 14.7% for Sweden, 13.7% for Finland, and 13.5% for Germany, and is certainly related to the fact that the percentage of Greeks that are self-employed is more than double the EU average (2013 est.).

The Tax Justice Network estimated in 2011 that there were over 20 billion euros in Swiss bank accounts held by Greeks. The former Finance Minister of Greece, Evangelos Venizelos, was quoted as saying, "Around 15,000 individuals and companies owe the taxman 37 billion euros". Additionally, the TJN put the number of Greek-owned off-shore companies at over 10,000.

In 2012, Swiss estimates suggested that Greeks had some 20 billion euros in Switzerland of which only one percent had been declared as taxable in Greece. Estimates in 2015 were even more dramatic. They indicated that the amount due to the government of Greece from Greeks' accounts in Swiss banks totaled around 80 billion euros.

A mid-2017 report indicated Greeks have been "taxed to the hilt" and many believed that the risk of penalties for tax evasion were less serious than the risk of bankruptcy. One method of evasion is the so-called black market, grey economy or shadow economy: work is done for cash payment which is not declared as income; as well, VAT is not collected and remitted. A January 2017 report by the DiaNEOsis think-tank indicated that unpaid taxes in Greece at the time totaled approximately 95 billion euros, up from 76 billion euros in 2015, much of it was expected to be uncollectable. Another early 2017 study estimated that the loss to the government as a result of tax evasion was between 6% and 9% of the country's GDP, or roughly between 11 billion and 16 billion euros per annum.

The shortfall in the collection of VAT (sales tax) is also significant. In 2014, the government collected 28% less than was owed to it; this shortfall was about double the average for the EU. The uncollected amount that year was about 4.9 billion euros. The DiaNEOsis study estimated that 3.5% of GDP is lost due to VAT fraud, while losses due to smuggling of alcohol, tobacco and petrol amounted to approximately another 0.5% of the country's GDP.

Planned solutions

Following similar actions by the United Kingdom and Germany, the Greek government was in talks with Switzerland in 2011, attempting to force Swiss banks to reveal information on the back accounts of Greek citizens. The Ministry of Finance stated that Greeks with Swiss bank accounts would either be required to pay a tax or reveal information such as the identity of the bank account holder to the Greek internal revenue services. The Greek and Swiss governments were to reach a deal on the matter by the end of 2011.

The solution demanded by Greece still had not been effected as of 2015. That year, estimates indicated that the amount of evaded taxes stored in Swiss banks was around 80 billion euros. By then, however, a tax treaty to address this issue was under serious negotiation between the Greek and Swiss governments. An agreement was finally ratified by Switzerland on 1 March 2016 creating a new tax transparency law that would allow for a more effective battle against tax evasion. Starting in 2018, banks in both Greece and Switzerland will exchange information about the bank accounts of citizens of the other country to minimize the possibility of hiding untaxed income.

In 2016 and 2017, the government was encouraging the use of credit cards or debit cards to pay for goods and services in order to reduce cash only payments. By January 2017, taxpayers were only granted tax-allowances or deductions when payments were made electronically, with a "paper trail" of the transactions that the government could easily audit. This was expected to reduce the problem of businesses taking payments but not issuing an invoice; that tactic had been used by various companies to avoid payment of VAT (sales) tax as well as income tax.

By 28 July 2017, numerous businesses were required by law to install a point of sale device to enable them to accept payment by credit or debit card. Failure to comply with the electronic payment facility can lead to fines of up to 1,500 euros. The requirement applied to around 400,000 firms or individuals in 85 professions. The greater use of cards was one of the factors that had already achieved significant increases in VAT collection in 2016.

Wealth and standards of living

National and regional GDP

Greece's most economically important regions are Attica, which contributed €87.378 billion to the economy in 2018, and Central Macedonia, which contributed €25.558 billion. The smallest regional economies were those of the North Aegean (€2.549 billion) and Ionian Islands (€3.257 billion).

In terms of GDP per capita, Attica (€23,300) far outranks any other Greek region. The poorest regions in 2018 were the North Aegean (€11,800), Eastern Macedonia and Thrace (€11,900) and Epirus (€12,200). At the national level, GDP per capita in 2018 was €17,200.

Welfare state

Greece is a welfare state which provides a number of social services such as quasi-universal health care and pensions. In the 2012 budget, expenses for the welfare state (excluding education) stand at an estimated €22.487 billion (€6.577 billion for pensions and €15.910 billion for social security and health care expenses), or 31.9% of the all state expenses.

Largest companies by revenue 2017

According to the 2018 Forbes Global 2000 index, Greece's largest publicly traded companies are:

Labour force

Working hours

In 2011, 53.3 percent of employed persons worked more than 40 to 49 hours a week and 24.8 percent worked more than 50 hours a week, totaling up to 78.1 percent of employed persons working 40 or more hours a week. When accounting for varying age groups, the percentage of employees working 40 to 49 hours a week peaked in the 25 to 29 age range. As workers got older, they gradually decreased in percentage working 40 to 49 hours, but increased in working 50+ hours, suggesting a correlation that as employees grow older, they work more hours. Of different occupation groups, skilled agricultural, forestry, and fishery workers and managers were the most likely to work 50+ hours; however, they do not take up a significant portion of the labor force, only 14.3 percent. In 2014, the average number of working hours for Greek employees was 2124 hours, ranking as the third highest among OECD countries and the highest in the Eurozone.

Recent trends in employment indicate that the number of workings hours will decrease in the future due to the rise of part-time work. Since 2011, average workings hours have decreased. In 1998, Greece passed legislation introducing part-time employment in public services with the goal of reducing unemployment, increasing the total, but decreasing the average number of hours worked per employee. Whether the legislation was successful in increasing public-sector part-time work, labor market trends show that part-time employment has increased from 7.7 percent in 2007 to 11 percent in 2016 of total employment. Both men and women have had the part-time share of employment increase over this period. While women still constitute a majority of part-time workers, recently men have been taking a larger share of part-time employment.

Currency

Between 1832 and 2002 the currency of Greece was the drachma. After signing the Maastricht Treaty, Greece applied to join the eurozone. The two main convergence criteria were a maximum budget deficit of 3% of GDP and a declining public debt if it stood above 60% of GDP. Greece met the criteria as shown in its 1999 annual public account. On 1 January 2001, Greece joined the eurozone, with the adoption of the euro at the fixed exchange rate 340.75 to €1. However, in 2001 the euro only existed electronically, so the physical exchange from drachma to euro only took place on 1 January 2002. This was followed by a ten-year period for eligible exchange of drachma to euro, which ended on 1 March 2012.

Prior to the adoption of the euro, 64% of Greek citizens viewed the new currency positively, but in February 2005 this figure fell to 26% and by June 2005 it fell further to 20%. Since 2010 the figure has risen again, and a survey in September 2011 showed that 63% of Greek citizens viewed of the euro positively.

Unemployment rate

IMF's forecast said that Greece's unemployment rate would hit the highest 14.8 percent in 2012 and decrease to 14.1 in 2014. But in fact, the Greek economy suffered a prolonged high unemployment. The unemployment figure was between 9 per cent and 11 per cent in 2009, and it soared to 28 per cent in 2013. In 2018, Greece's jobless rate was around 20.1 per cent. It is thought that Greece's potential output has been eroded by this prolonged massive unemployment due to the associated hysteresis effects.

Poverty

Greece has suffered from recession, massive public debt, and poverty has increased. Those living in extreme poverty rose to 15% in 2015, up from 8.9% in 2011, and a huge increase from 2009 when it was not more than 2.2%. Those people at risk for poverty or social exclusion are at 35.7%. The rate among children 0-17 is 17.6% and for young people 18-29 the rate is 24.4%. With unemployment on the rise, those without jobs are at the highest risk at 70-75%, up from less than 50% in 2011. With jobs harder and harder to come by, a quarter of the population is out of work, and for people under 25 the rate is 50%. In some harder hit areas of western Greece, the younger generation unemployment rate is more than 60%. When people are out of work for more than two years, they lose their health insurance, further increasing the problems of those in poverty. When younger people are out of work, they rely on the older generations of their families to provide for them to get them through the hard times. However, long term unemployment across the country causes pension funds to decrease because they are getting less money from the working population, so those older generations are getting less money to provide for the younger generations and their entire families, putting more of them in poverty. Many aspects of the economic problems add to the problem. The Greek people have continued job loss and wage cuts, as well as deep cuts in workers compensation and social welfare benefits. For those who are working, their wages have dropped. From 2008 to 2013, Greeks have become 40% poorer on average, and in 2014 saw their disposable household income drop below 2003 levels. The Economic Survey of Greece 2016 shows optimism in a stronger recovery in 2017 by using things like the reforms in place and outside investment in jobs to help change the course of the high levels of poverty.

Critical Observation of Present Status of Economy of Greece

(1) Greece is a developed country with an economy based on the services (80%) and industrial sector (16%) and agriculture sector contributing 4% of national economic output in 2017.

(2) Important Greek Industries are tourism and shipping. 18 million international tourists visited Greece. Greece is the 7th most visited country in the EU and 16th in the world.

(3) Greece Merchant Navy is the largest in the world, with Greek owned vessels accounting for 15% of global deadweight tonnage as of 2013. On account of increased demand for international maritime, transport between Greece and Asia has resulted in unprecedent investment in the shipping industry.

(4) The country is also significant agriculture producer within EU. Greece has largest economy in the Balkans. The Greek telecommunications company OTE has become a strong investor in certain former Yugoslav and Balkan countries.

(5) Greece is classified as an advanced, high income economy and founding member of the OECD and Organization of the Black Sea Economic Corporation (OBSEC).

(6) Country joined with EU in 1981. Greece adopted the Euro as its currency replacing Greek drachma at an exchange rate of 340.75 drachma per Euro in 2001.

(7) Greece is a member of the IMF and WTO.

(8) Greece was accepted into the Economic and Monetary Union of the EU by the European Council in June 2000 based on number of criteria such as inflation rate, budget deficit, public debt, long term interest rate, exchange rate using 1999 as the reference year. But it was observed in 2004 that this criteria was not complied with by Greece while admitting it as member of EMC. Budget deficit was under reported.

(9) Economic crisis resulting from huge public debt and fiscal deficit and increased borrowing rate made it impossible for the country to finance its debt since early 2010. In order to avert a default, in 2010 the European Countries and IMF agreed to a "rescue package" which involved giving Greece an immediate Euro 45 billion bail-out loan, with more funds to follow, totaling Euro 110 billion. In order to secure the funding, Greece was required to adopt hard austerity measures to bring its deficit under control. Austerity measures implementation was to be monitored and evaluated by the European Commission, European Central Bank and IMF.

(10) Austerity package met with anger by Greek public leading to riots and social unrest. There were labour strikes in the industry on account of unemployment, reduced wages etc. Austerity measures did not reduce the government deficit because of subsequent recessions.

(11) Second bail-out package was given in 2014 for $1.36 billion and third bail-out package was given in 2017 with Credit $9.5 billion and $ 8.5 billion loan. Bail-out resulted in 25% drop in GDP. This increased debt to GDP ratio.

(12) Unemployment rate was14.8% in 2012. Poverty was 15% in 2015 from 8.9% in 2011.Unempolyment of young labour force was 60% and for others it was under 25%.

(13) High spending on Budget coupled with recession and debt crisis resulted in the economic crisis.

(14) Greek labour force worked an average of 1900 hours per year followed by Spaniards 1800 hours per year.

(15) On account of persistent economic crisis, industrial production in the country went down by 8% between 2010 and 2011. Building construction activity was reduced by 73% in 2010. Turnover in retail sales saw a decline of 9% between 2010 and 2011. Unemployment skyrocketed from 7.2% in late 2008 to high of 27.9% in June 2013 leaving one million jobless. Young unemployment was up 64% in 2013 Unemployment figure are steadily improved in recent year.

(16) Greece faced economic crisis in 1826, 1843, 1860 and 1893.

(17) Corruption and tax evasion also added fuel to the fire of economic crisis.

(18) Currency : Euro

(19) Fiscal year: Calendar year

(20) Trade Organizations: EU, WTO, OEDC, BIS,

(21) Country Group: Developed/Advanced, High Income Country

(22) Population: 1.07 Crore

(23) GDP: $214.012 billion Nominal & $324.128 billion PPP

(24) GDP Growth: 1.3% in 2017, 1.9% in 2018, 1.9% in 2019 and 2.2% in 2020 Forecast

(25) GDP per capita $19974 Nominal & $30252 PPP

(26) GDP per capita: Agriculture 4.1%, Industry 16.9% and Services 79.1% - 2017

(27) Inflation 0.9% in 2020 (forecast), 0.6% in 2019, 0.08 % in 2018

(28) Population below poverty level: 31.8% - 2018

(29) Labour Force: 46.56 lacs

(30) Labour Force by Occupation: agriculture 12.6%, Industry 15% and Services 72.4% -2013

(31) Unemployment : 16.3% in 2019 39.5% in 2018

(32) Average Gross Salary: euro17512 in 2018,

(33) Average net salary; euro 9034 in 2018

(34) Median net salary: euro 7863 in 2018

(35) Main Industries: Shipping and shipbuilding, tourism, food and tobacco processing, textiles, chemicals, metal products, mining and petroleum

(36) Exports : euro 33.800 billion

(37) Export goods: petroleum 38.88%, aluminum and articles 4.38%, electrical, electrical equipment 3.75%, pharmaceutical products

3.48%, plastic and articles 3.32%, vegetables, fruits 3.1% and iron& steel products 3%

(38) Imports: euro 55.521 billion.

(39) Import goods: crude petroleum, electricals, pharmaceutical products, machinery, ships, boats, plastic articles, cars, car parts

(40) Trade deficit euro 21.721 billion Trade Deficit is 13.9% of GDP which is very high.

(41) FDI stock: $65.12 billion. - 2017

(42) Current Account -$1.596 billion

(43) Gross external debt: euro 436. 71 billion 222.30% of GDP

(44) Public debt euro 334.261 billion 178.21 % of GDP

(45) Budget Balance euro 1.836 billion

(46) Revenue 48.0% of GDP

(47) Expenses 47% of GDP

(48) Foreign Reserves $7.807 billion

(49) Credit Rating DBRs BB Trade Positive, Fitch BB, Outlook Positive, Moody's B1 Outlook Stable S & P BB T & C AAA T&C BB Outlook Positive Scope BB Outlook Positive

(50) If you observe how many times the economy of Greece was in crisis, we are surprised how International Credit Agencies have awarded credit rating to Greece as BBB and Outlook as Stable or positive. The Credit rating may be given at high level on the consideration that though the country is spending high, trade deficit and Sovereign loans are high, loan costs are high, many bail out packages have been granted to the country, tax evasion and corruption are high and recession is adding fuel to the fire, the country is developed, advanced country with high income and low population.

16

Economy of Iran

The economy of Iran depends upon the American sanctions. After the Iran Revolution in 1979, the US ended its economic and diplomatic ties with Iran, banned Iranian oil imports and froze approximately $11 billion of its assets.

In 1986, the US government passed the Iran & Libya Sanctions Act (ISSA) which prohibits US (and non US) companies from investing and trading with Iran in amounts of more than $20 million annually, Since 2000, exceptions to this restrictions have been made for pharmaceuticals and medical equipment.

Iran's nuclear program has been subject of contraction with the West. Since 2006, over suspicious of its intentions, the UN Security Council imposed sanctions against select companies linked to the nuclear program, thus furthering the country's economic isolation. The economic effects of sanctions were severe. Sanctions notably banned nuclear missiles and many military exports to Iran and target investment in oil, gas and petrochemicals, exports of refined petroleum products as well as the Islamic Revolutionary Guard Corps, bank, insurance, financial transactions and shipping. In 2012, EU tightened its own sanctions by joining the three decade-old US oil embargo against Iran.

In 2015, Iran and P5+1 reached a deal on nuclear program that will remove the main sanctions by early 2016. US was party to this settlement. US therefore withdrew the main sanctions. This was the golden period of Iran who was in isolation since 1979. But this golden period lasted only for three year. In 2018, US withdrew from Nuclear Settlement of 2015 unitarily on the ground that Iran was not complying with terms and conditions of Nuclear Settlement, 2015. US re-imposed its sanctions on Iran's oil sales, petrochemicals, shipping, metal trading and banking transactions. Concessions given to the countries like India to import oil from Iran were withdrawn in early 2020. On 02-03-2020, India announced that its imports from Iran in January 2020 diminished by 97% compared to January 2019.

In January 2019, Iran President Hassan Rouhani blamed the US for Iran's declining economy. Following the US pullout from an international nuclear deal with Iran and re-imposed sanctions, Ian faced toughest economic situation in 40 years.

Iran had never cordial relations With the US and Israel. Iranian Supreme religious and de facto supreme leader Ayatoliah Ali Khamenei always treated the US and Israel as his enemies. This has worsened the political situation between Iran and US. Kasem Sulemani who was the chief Military Commander and Military Head of Kurdish forces in Iraq was killed with this assistant Muhandees in the car bombing near Baghdad Airport. Kasem Sulemani was the most favorite Military Commander of Supreme de fact Leader of Iran Khamenei which resulted in heavy blows to Iran. It therefore vowed to retaliate and take revenge on US for this killing. Iran tried to drop missiles on the military bases of US in Baghdad but their very negligible losses to US. US, however, dropped missiles in Baghdad military Bases of Iran which killed 26 Extremists of Iran.

Iran fought war with Iraq during the period 1980-88 and in which its 300000 soldiers were killed and 500000 soldiers were injured. Iran spent $500 billion in the War with Iraq.

On 15-11-2019, Iran raised the oil prices by 50% and imposed a strict rationing system. Price per liter gasoline rose to 15000 riyals, 60 liters were permitted to private cars for a month. Oil purchase beyond the limit will cause 30000 royals per liter. Policy changes came in effect to the US sanctions, and caused protests across the country. Protesters began to demand the ousting of President Hassan Rouhani. The protests began to grow violent, where people began setting fire to public property. On 17-11-2019, the Iranian Supreme Leader Ayatollah Ali Khamenei called these protesters "thug" amidst the talks with clerics. He signaled a potential crackdown in which hundreds of protesters were reported killed while internet access was also shut down for the entire nation.

Iranian Prime Ministers administered its country very well with the goal of distribution of the available resources among all citizens of the country equally to promote maximum comforts and happiness to all. The country adopted Five Year Plans to implement these goal successfully. Iran has oil as a natural resource for export. But Iran diversified in the field of construction, agriculture, tele-communication, information Technology, Banking and Stock Market. It also built up large foreign exchange reserves $ 120 billion as at 31-12-2017 to fight against sanctions and recession in oil prices.

Iranian Supreme leader Khamenei's attitude to treat the US the enemy of Iran costed very heavily. Iran also wanted to expel Israel from the heart of the Arab country in the Gulf. Iran started air bombing and missile attacks on Israel but Israel retaliated heavily by bombing and missile attacks on Iranian military bases in Iran, Syria, Iraq and other countries destroyed the storage of weapons and ammunitions which resulted in disaster and tremendous financial loss and destruction of military equipments. Continuous Economic sanctions by the US also added fuel to the fire. Iran also unnecessarily involved itself in the affairs of other countries such as Syria, Libya and Yemen and air attacked Saudi Arabia in military assistance to Hothi soldiers of Haftar in Yemen to destroy/damage Saudi Arabia's biggest oil tankers and refineries. Saudi had to stop oil export for few days to redress the damages before restarting export of oil to the countries.

In order to avoid the clashes with various country and especially with the USA, the country should start building good relationship with all countries and avoid isolation. The country should fully concentrate in the economic and political affairs of its own to achieve its goal of welfare state which is the ultimate goal of the entire mankind.

Critical Observations of present status of Economy of Iran

(1) The economy of Iran is a mixed and transition (leading to market) economy with a large public sector. 60% of the Iran's economy is centrally planned. It is dominated by oil and gas production, although over 40 industries are directly involved in the Tehran Stock Market with 10% of the world's proven reserves and 15% of its gas reserves. Iran is considered an "energy superpower.

(2) Iran's economy has been hit hard since US sanctions which came into effect in mid-2018 and a result nearly half of its import and exports estimated at 600000 bbd of oil being slashed.

(3) Iran's economy has the presence of large religious foundations called Bonyad. Whose combined budgets represent more than 30% of central government spending.

(4) Price controls and subsidies on food and energy burden the economy. Contraband, administrative controls, widespread corruption and other restrictive factors undermine private sector growth. In 2009, subsidy reforms plan was passed in legislature.

(5) 80% of Iranian public revenue is contributed by exports of oil and gas in 2012. Iran was able to create $135 billion in foreign exchange reserves on account of oil revenue exports as at December 2016.

(6) Iran made significant growth in science in 2011 and has one of the fastest rates of development in telecommunication globally.

(7) Iran was initially able to avoid recession in the aftermath of 2008 global financial crisis due to its relative isolation from global financial markets. However, expansion of international sanctions, related to Iran's nuclear program, the Iranian riyal fell to a record low of 23900 to the US dollar in September 2012.

(8) Export aided self-sufficiency and domestic investment, Iran's educated population, high human development, constrained economy and insufficient foreign and domestic investment prompted an increasing number of Iranians to seek overseas employment resulting in a significant "brain drain".

(9) In 2015, Iran reached a deal on the nuclear program with P5+1 which removed sanctions. After removal of most sanctions in 2016, inflation decreased and employment was reduced. Iranian tourism industry was significantly improved.

(10) Rising fuel prices in 2019 led to a grave economic crisis and widespread protest, which the government ruthlessly crushed resulting in hundreds of death.

(11) During the accident time in 546 B.C. Persians adopted gold as main metal for their coins.

(12) Modern agriculture in Iran dates back in 1820 when Amir Kabir undergone a number of changes to the traditional agricultural system. Changes included improved modified seeds and signing collaboration contracts with other countries.

(13) Bank was passed into the hands of the Iranian government by contract with Russia in 1920. Activities were made until 1933 as the Bank of Iran. New bank founded named Keshavarzi bank thereafter.

(14) The Imperial Bank of Persia established in 1885 with offices at all major cities of Persia. Raza Shah and Pahlavi (1925-41) improved the country's overall infrastructure, implemented educational reform, campaigned reformed the legal system, and introduced modern industries. During this time, Iran experienced a period of social change, economic development, and relatively political stability.

(15) Reza Shah Pahlavi was abdicated in 1941 and his son succeeded him named Mohammed Reza Shah Pahlavi (1941-74). No fundamental change occurred during the Second World War (1939-45) and immediate years thereafter. Rapid increase in oil revenues and sustained foreign aid during 1954-60 led to greater

investment and fast-faced economic growth in the government sector. Subsequently inflation increased, the value of the national currency riyal depleted, and a foreign trade deficit developed. Economic policy implementation to combat these problems led to declines in the rates of nominal economic growth and per capita income by 1961.

(16) Prior to 1979, Iran developed rapidly traditionally, agricultural. By the 1970 the country has undergone significant industrialization and modernization. The pace slowed by the 1978 as capital flight reached \$30 to \$40 billion 1980- US dollars just before the revolution.

(17) Following nationalization in 1979 and outbreak of Iran- Iraq War, over 80% of the economy came under government controls. The eight year war claimed 300000 Iranians lives and more than 500000 injured. The cost of the war was \$500 billion.

(18) After hostilities ceased in 1988, the government tried to develop the country's communications, transport, manufacturing, health care, education and energy sectors (including nuclear power facilities) and began integrating its communication and transport systems with those of neighbouring states.

(19) The government's long term objectives were stated as economic independence, full employment and comfortable standard of living but Iran's population increased more than double between 1980 and 2000 and its maiden age declined by two third population (74 million) was less than 30 years age. Though many Iranians are farmers, agricultural production has constantly fallen since 1960. By 1990, Iran imported much of its food. Economic hardship forced many people moving cities.

(20) Net primary school enrolment is almost 100% suggesting a secondary "demographic boom". Iran's national science budget in 2005 was \$900 million, roughly equivalent to the 1990 figure. By early 2000, Iran allocated annual 0.4% of its GDP to research and development. In 2009, it reached 0.89% for research. Iran ranked 1st in scientific growth in the world in 2011, and 17th in science production in 2012.

(21) Iran has a braved and diversified industrial base. Iran is producing \$23 billion of industrial products in 2008 and stood 39th rank in a list of industrial nations. Annual industrial production growth increased in 2009.

(22) Service sector was largest in early 21st century followed by industry, mining and agriculture. In 2008, GDP was estimated at $382.3 billion or $5470 per capita.

(23) In 2012-2016, international sanctions have damaged the economy by reducing oil exports by half before recovering it in 2016.

(24) Political policy and currency stability are regarded as the most problematic factors in doing business in Iran. Accessing financing for small and medium enterprises was a major concern. Iran's financial sources are mostly engaged at trading, smuggling and speculation instead of production and manufacturing.

(25) Expansion of public healthcare and international relations are other major objectives of the plan which includes subsidy reforms, banking, recapitalization, currency, taxation customs construction, employment, nationwide goods and services distribution, social justice and productivity. To make the country self-sufficient by 2015 and replace the payment of $100 billion in subsidies annually with targeted social assistance.

(26) Iran's budget is designed by the Management of Planning Organization of Iran and proposed by the government to the Parliament for approval. After approval by the parliament, Central Bank presents a detailed monetary and credit policy to the Money and Credit Council for approval. Thereafter major elements of the policy are incorporated in five-year economic development plan. Planning commenced from 1991 and first plan was introduced in 1991. The fifth development plan for 2011-15 is designed to delegate powers to the people and to develop a knowledge economy. In sixth plan, priority is given for the development of a resilient economy.

(27) Since the 1979 revolution, government spending has averaged 55% on social policies, 17% on economic matters, 15% on national defence and 13% on general affairs. Payments averaged 39% on education, health and social security, 20% in other social programs, 3% on agriculture, 16% on water, power, and gas, 5% on manufacturing and mining, 12% on roads and transportation, 5% on other economic affairs. Iran's investment was 27.7% of GDP in 2009. Around 55% of government revenue earned came from oil and natural gas, 31% from taxes and fees. Millions of people virtually do not plan taxes.

If the rules of the budget will be observed, government could save 30% -35% of its expenses. Central Bank interest rate was

21% p.a., inflation 22%. 10% higher than 2011. There was no alignment between fiscal and monetary policy. Gap between rich and poor narrowed because of subsidies but trend could reverse if high inflation persists.

(28) Iran had $110 billion in foreign reserves in 2011 and its balances in external payments by pricing oil at appropriately $75 per barrel. As of 2011, only $30million to $50 billion of these reserves are accessible on account of current sanctions.

(29) Following the hostilities with Iraq, government declared its intention to privatize must industries and to liberalize and decentralize the economy. Sale of state-owned companies proceed slowly, due to the opposition by nationalist majority in the parliament. In 2006, most industries, some 70% of the economy remain state owned. The majority of heavy industries including steel, petrochemicals, copper, automobiles and machine tools remain in the public sector. Most light industries were privately owned. As per Article 44 of the constitution of Iran, the country's economy should consists of state, co-operative and private based sectors. The state sector includes all large-scale industries, foreign trade, major minerals, banking, insurance, power generation, dams and large-scale irrigation network, radio and television, post, telegraph and telephone services, aviation, shipping, roads, railways and the like. There are publicly owned and administered by the state co-operative companies and enterprises concerned with production and distribution in urban and rural areas form the basis of the co-operation sector and operated according with Sharia law. Co-operatives employed 128396 in 2012, 6million members. Private sector operates in construction, agriculture, animal husbandry, industry, trade and services. Article 44 was never seriously enforced. Private sector has played a large role. Islamic Revolutionary guard Corps (IRGC) control the third of Iran's economy through subsidies and trusts.

(30) Labour force had lack of education. After the revolution, the government established a national education system that improved literacy rates. In 2008, 85% of the population was literate.

(31) Around economic growth of about 5% is necessary to absorb 750000 new labour force entrants each year.

(32) Although Iranian workers have a theoretical right to form labour unions, there is no union system in the country. Ostensibly, worker representation is provided by the Workers House.

(33) Agriculture contributes 10% of GDP and employs 16% of the labour force. About 9% of Iran's land area is arable. Main area is located in the Caspian region and in northeastern valleys. Under fertilized soil, poor seed and water scanty are principal obstacles to increased population. 1/3 of the total cultivated land is irrigated. Construction of multipurpose dams and reservoirs have increased the amount of water available for irrigation. Agricultural production is increasing as a result of modernization, mechanization, improvement to crops and livestock as well as land redistribution program. Wheat is grown in the west and northwest. Rice is in the Caspian region. Iran is 90% self-sufficient in agriculture. By 1997, gross value reached $25 billion. Limited rice production leads to substantial imports. It is sometime net exporter of wheat.

(34) Large scale factory manufacturing began in the 1920. Iran is "semi-developed" manufacturing economy. It has diversified and has broad industrial base. During Iran-Iraq war, Iraq bombed many of Iran's petrochemicals plants, damaging the large oil refinery at Abadan bring production to a halt. Reconstruction began in 1988 and production resumed in 1993. In spite of the war, many small factories sprang up to produce import-substituted goods and materials needed by the military. Iran's major manufacturing products are petrochemicals, steel and copper products, automobiles, home and electric appliances, telecommunication equipment, cement & industrial machinery.

(35) 13 Public Sector and Private Sector owned automakers within Iran in 2001.

(36) Iran's defence budget was $7.31 billion in 2007i.e. 2.7% of GDP or $102 per capita. Since 1992, Defence Industries Organization (DIO) has produced its own tanks, armed personnel carriers, guided missiles destroyer, military vessels, radar system, submarines and fighting planes. Iran exported weapons to 57 countries in 2006 including NATO members and export reached $100 million. It is also developing a sophisticated mobile air defence system dubbed as Bavar 373.

(37) The construction industry revived in mid-1980s. Banks gave loans upto $10 billion to construction firms to construct residential buildings. Construction is one of most important sectors accounting for 20.50% of the total private investment in urban areas. Annual turnover amounted to $38.4 billion in 2005 and 32.8 billion in

2011. Because of poor construction quality, many buildings needed seismic reinforcement or renovation.

(38) Mineral production contributed to 0.6% of the GDP in 2011. Figure reached to 4% when mining relating industries are included. Although the petroleum industry provides the majority of revenues, there are other minerals like coal, iron ore, copper lead, zinc, aluminum, salt, gypsum, uranium and gold.

(39) Estimates of service sector spending in Iran are regularly more than 2/5 of GDP. This includes military expenditure, government salaries, social security disbursement.

(40) Iran plans to generate 23000MW of electricity through nuclear technology by 2025 to meet its increasing demand for energy. Iran generates electricity 85.6% from fossil fuel, 12.4% from hydro 1.2% from nuclear and 0.8% from others in 2012.

(41) Oil production was 3.3 million bbl/d and exports 1.04 million in 2013.Imports were 874440bbl/d. Natural gas production was 174.5 km in 2014 and consumption 170.2 km in 2014. Iran is the world's second largest reservoir of natural gas after Russia. In 2010, Iran completed its first nuclear power plant with Russian assistance.

(42) On 15-11-2019, Iran raised the oil prices by 50% and imposed a strict rationing system. Prices per barrel gasoline rose to 15000 riyals, where only 60 liters were permitted to private cars per month. Oil purchase beyond this limit will cause 30000 riyals per liter. The policy changes came in effect to the US sanctions, and caused protests across the country. Protesters began to demand the ousting of President Hassan Rouhani. The protest began to grow violent, where people began setting fire to public property. On 17-11-2019, the Iranian Supreme Leader Ayatollah Ali Khamenei called these protesters "thug" amidst the talks with clerics. He signaled a potential crackdown killing hundreds of protesters, while the internet access was also shut down for the entire nation.

(43) Tourism declined significantly during the war with Iraq. It has subsequently recovered. About 1.659 million foreign tourists visited in 2004 and 2.3 million in 2009 mostly from Asian countries, including the Republics of Central Asia. While about 10% came from the EU and North America.

(44) Government loans and credits are available to industrial and agricultural projects through banks. Iran's unit of currency is

riyal. Exchange rate of riyal is 9326 riyals per US$. Government nationalized private banks. The restructured banking system replaced interest on loan with the handling fees, in accordance with Islamic law. This system was implemented in mid 1980s. Banking system consists of Central Bank which issues currency and overseas all state and private banks. Several commercial banks have branches throughout the country. Two development banks exist and housing bank specializes in home mortgages. The government began to privatize banking sector in 2001 and Licences issued to two nearly privately own banks.

Foreign transactions with Iran amounted to $150-$200 billion of major contracts between 2000 and 2007.

As of 2010, Tehran Stock Market traded in shares of more than 330 registered companies. Listed companies were valued at $100 billion in 2011. Insurance premium accounted for just 1% of GDP in 2008. Five state owned insurance firms dominate the market, four of which are active in commercial insurance. The leading player is the Iran Insurance Company, followed by Asia, Alborz and Daria Insurance. In 2002-2003, third party insurance accounted for 46% of premium, followed by health insurance (13%), fire insurance (10%) and life insurance (9.91).

(45) Iran has an extensive paved road system linking most towns and all cities. Country's major port of entry is Bandar-Abbas on the Strait of Hormuz. Imported goods are distributed by tracks and freight trains.

(46) After the Iranian Revolution in 1979, the US ended its economic and diplomatic ties with Iran, banned Iranian oil imports and froze approximately $11 billion of its assets.

In 1996, the US government passed the Iran and Libya sanctions Act (ILSA) which prohibits US (and non US) companies from investing and trading with Iran in amounts of more than $20 million annually. Since 2000, exceptions to this restrictions have been made for items including pharmaceuticals and medical equipment.

Iran's nuclear program has been subject of contention with the West since 2006 over suspicions of its intentions. The U.N. Security Council imposed sanctions against select companies linked to the nuclear program, then furthering the company's economic isolation. The economic effects of sanctions have been severe. Sanctions notably bar nuclear missile and other military exports to Iran and target investment in oil, gas, and petrochemicals, export of refined petroleum products as well as the Islamic Revolutionary Guard Corps, bank, insurance, financial transactions and shipping. In 2012, EU tightened its own sanctions by joining the three decade old US oil embargo against Iran. In 2015, Iran and the P5+1 reached a deal on nuclear program that will remove the main sanctions by EU and US in early 2016. Even Iran can trade in its own currency. Some problems subsist mainly due to the fact that it cannot transact in US dollar freely. Given its large reserves of oil and gas, the Iranian riyal could became a world reserve currency if parity is established with oil and gas. In 2018, the US government unilaterally withdrew from the JCVPOA agreement and re-imposed its sanctions on Iran's oil sales, petrochemicals, shipping, metals trading and banking transactions. On 02-03-2020, India announced that its imports from Iran in January 2020 diminished by 97% comparing to January 2019. This came after US refused to continue exceptions for customers Iran's oil.

(47) Iran may be using as much as $60billion annually in energy investment. Sanctions are making imports 24% more costly on average. Latest round of sanctions could cost Iran annually $50 billion in lost oil revenues. Iran is increasingly used the barter trade because its access to the international dollar payment system has be denied.

IEA estimated that Iran export fell to a record of 860000 bpd in September 2012 from 2.2 million bpd at the end of 2011. This fall led to a drop in revenues and clashes on the street of Teheran when the local currency, the riyal, collapsed. Iran had the lowest output in September 2012 since 1988.

The US Energy Department has warned that imposing oil embargoes on Iran would increase world oil [prices by widening supply and demand. According to US, Iran could reduce the world oil prices by widening the gap between supply and demand. According to the US, Iran could reduce the world price of crude petroleum by 10%, saving the US annually $ 76 billion.

According to NIAC, sanctions cost the US over $175 billion in lost trade and 279000 lost job opportunities. Between 2010 and 2012, sanction cost the EU states more than double as much as US in terms of lost trade revenues. Germany was hit the hardest, losing between $23.1 billion and $73 billion between 2010-2012 with Italy and France following at $13.6 billion to 42.8 billion and $10.9 billion to $34.2 billion respectively.

GDP growth turned negative in 2013 (-5%). The unofficial unemployment rate was 20% by 2012. Oil export dropped to 1.4 million bpd in 2014 from 2.5 million bpd in 2011. By 2013, Iran had $80 billion in foreign exchange reserves frozen overseas. Automobile production declined 40% between 2011 and 2013. In 2015, Iran's economy has reached a point where it is "fundamentally incapable of recovery" with a nuclear accommodation with the West.

The tentative rapprochement between Iran and the US which began in the second half of 2013, has potential to become world changing development, and unleash tremendous geopolitical and economic opportunities, if it is sustained. Iran and U, S. were to achieve a diplomatic breakthrough, geopolitical tensions in the Middle East could decline sharply and Iran could come to be perceived as promising emerging market in its own right.

In January 2019, Iran's President Hassan Rouhani blamed the US for Iran's declining economy. Following the US pullout from the international nuclear deal with Iran and re-imposed sanctions, Iran faced toughest economic situation in last 40 years.

(48) Currency: Iranian Riyal

(49) Fiscal year: 21 March-20 March

(50) Trade Organizations: ECO, OPEC, WTO, GFCF

(51) Country Group: Developing/emerging Upper Middle income economy.

(52) Population: 8.18 crores

(53) GDP: $458.50 billion Nominal $1.471 trillion PPP in 2019

(54) GDP Growth: 3.8% in 2017, -4.9% in 2018 -8.7% in 2018 & 0% in 2020 forecast

(55) GDP per capita $ 5506 Nominal & $17663 PPP in 2019

(56) GDP by Sector: Agriculture 9.1%, Industries 35.9% and services 55% in 2017

(57) Inflation: 31%

(58) Population below poverty line: 20% living in poverty (2018), 11.6% on less than $5.50 day in 2016

(59) Labour Force: 2.74 crores

(60) Unemployment: 12.10% in March 2019

(61) Average Salary: Urban Household IRR 17 million monthly .Rural IRR 10 million monthly in 2017

(62) Main Industries: Petroleum, Petrochemicals, fertilizers, Caustic soda, car manufacturing parts, pharmaceuticals, home appliances, electronics, telecom, construction, ferrous & non-ferrous metals.

(63) Exports: $107.43 billion in 2018

(64) Export goods: Petroleum, chemicals and petrochemicals, automobiles, fruits and nuts, carpets

(65) Imports: $54.46 billion in 2018Trade Surplus: 62.97 billion

(66) Import Goods: Industrial raw materials & intermediate goods, capital goods, foodstuffs and other consumer goods

(67) Gross external debts: $7.995 billion in December 2017

(68) Public debt: 39.5% of GDP in 2017

(69) Budget balance: -2.3% of GDP in 2017

(70) Revenue: $74.4 billion

(71) Expenses: $ 84.45 billion Fiscal Deficit $ 10 billion in 2017

(72) Foreign Reserves:$ 120.6 billion in December 2017

(73) Credit Rating: Economic Intelligence Unit : CCC (Sovereign risk) CCC (Currency risk), CC (Banking Sector risk), CC (Political Risk), BB (economic Structure Risk) CC (country Risk) Iran is continuously under financial sanctions from US and EU since 1979except for 2015, 2016 and 2017 where the Nuclear Agreement was signed in 2015 which withdrew main sanctions on Iran by US. This is a golden period for Iran's economy. Sanctions were again imposed by US in 2018 when it withdraws unilaterally from the Nuclear Agreement in 2018. Under constant sanctions, Iran economy became vulnerable. It has therefore potential Sovereign risk, currency risk and Country risk. Economic structure is sound as its oil exports earned revenues of $50 billion and it has $120.6 billion as foreign reserves. It is in conflict with Israel, Saudi Arabia, Iraq and UAE. Only it has Qatar as its friend in Arabian Gulf. In order to establish its supremacy on other countries, it interferes in the political affairs of Syria, Yemen, Iraq and Libya. Clashes in these country results in losing amenities and military weapons stored in its military Bases in these countries. In Iran-Iraq War in 1980-88, it lost 300000 soldiers, another 500000 were injured and cost of the war was $500 billion. Political risk is therefore potential.

17

Economy of Libya

Libya Civil started in 2011. There is war between ruling party Saraj and General Haftar. It has become very acute and United Nations have directed both parties to negotiate and settle their dispute. But both of them are in fighting mood and there seems to be no compromise in near future.

UN has imposed sanctions on Libya and has instructed all nations not to interfere in the dispute and affairs of Libya. In spite of clear instructions, Turkey, Egypt, UAE, Russia, and Saudi Arabia are supporting two rivals in Libya. These countries are responsible for unrest and continuous conflict in Libya.

Turkey is supporting Saraj government by providing them military equipments to fight with General Haftar soldiers in spite of UN prohibiting all countries to interfere in the Libyan conflict. Last month, Italy captured Lebanese ship with full of military weapons to Saraj Government in the Middle Sea. It has been found that Turkey has sent these weapons on the Ship for Saraj government. In retaliation, Egypt and UAE are giving military training to the soldiers of General Haftar to fight marine war. The training is imparted by special Commando of Egypt and UAE Military. With some countries supporting Saraj and some supporting Haftar, the civil war is becoming acute and there is no possibility that there will be peace in Syria in near future.

Various international sanctions were imposed during the Gaddafi regime. As at 13-03-2011, Libya oil holdings had held its euro 38 million stake in Irish explorations firm Circle Oil frozen on foot of a European Union Order that it has been put in place to pressure on the Gaddafi regime.

The economy of Libya depends primarily on revenues from the petroleum sector, which represents over 95% of export earnings and

60% of GDP. These oil revenues and a small population have given Libya one of the highest nominal per capita GDP in Africa.

After 2000, Libya recorded favourable growth rates with an estimated 10.6% growth of GDP in 2010. This development was interrupted by the Libyan Civil War, which resulted in contraction of the economy by 62.1% in 2011. After the war the economy rebounded by 104.5% in 2012, but then crashed again following the Second Libyan Civil War. As of 2017, Libya's per capita PPP GDP stands at 60% of its pre-wars level.

Macro-economic trend

Libya had seen fantastic growth rate, however these proved unsustainable in the face of global oil recession and international sanctions. Consequently, the GDP per capita shrank by 40% in the 1980s. Successful diversification and integration into the international community helped current GDP per capita to cut further deterioration to just 3.2% in the 1990s.

Libyan GDP per capita was about $40 in the early 1920s and it rose to $1,018 by 1967. In 1947 alone, per capita GDP rose by 42 percent.

Notes:

1. for purchasing power parity comparisons, the US Dollar is exchanged at 0.77 Libyan Dinars only.

   Mean wages were $9.51 per man-hour in 2009 (amounts to a compensation of $1598 for 21 working days of 8 hours).

Oil sector

Libya is an OPEC member and holds the largest proven oil reserves in Africa (followed by Nigeria and Algeria), 41.5 Gbbl (6.60×10 m) as of January 2007, up from 39.1 Gbbl (6.22×10 m) in 2006. About 80% of Libya's proven oil reserves are located in the Sirte Basin, which is responsible for 90% of the country's oil output. The state-owned National Oil Corporation (NOC) dominates Libya's oil industry, along with smaller subsidiaries, which combined account for around 50% of the country's oil output. Among NOC's subsidiaries, the largest oil producer is the Waha Oil Company (WOC), followed by the Agoco, Zueitina Oil Company (ZOC), and Sirte Oil Company (SOC). Oil resources, which account for approximately 95% of export earnings, 75% of government receipts, and over 50% of GDP. Oil revenues constitute the principal foreign exchange source. Reflecting the heritage of the command economy, three quarters of employment is in the public sector, and private investment remains small at around 2% of GDP.

Falling world oil prices in the early 1980s and economic sanctions caused a serious decline in economic activity, eventually leading to a slow private sector rehabilitation. At 2.6% per year on average, real GDP growth was modest and volatile during the 1990s. Libya's GDP grew in 2001 due to high oil prices, the end of a long cyclical drought, and increased foreign direct investment following the suspension of UN sanctions in 1999. Real GDP growth has been boosted by high oil revenues, reaching 4.6% in 2004 and 3.5% in 2005. Despite efforts to diversify the economy and encourage private sector participation, extensive controls of prices, credit, trade, and foreign exchange constrain growth.

Although UN sanctions were suspended in 1999, foreign investment in the Libyan gas and oil sectors were severely curtailed due to the U.S. Iran and Libya Sanctions Act (ILSA), which capped the amount foreign companies can invest in Libya yearly at $20 million (lowered from $40 million in 2001). As of May 2006, the U.S. has removed Libya from its list of states that sponsor terrorism and has normalized ties and removed sanctions. This clears the road for U.S. oil companies to exploit Libyan oil and is expected to have a positive impact on the Libyan economy.

The NOC hopes to raise oil production from 1.80 million bpd in 2006 to 2 million bpd by 2008. FDI into the oil sector is likely, which is attractive due to its low cost of oil recovery, high oil quality, and proximity to European markets. Most Libyan oil is sold on a term basis, including to the country's Oilinvest marketing network in Europe; to companies like Agip, OMV, Repsol YPF, Tupras, CEPSA, and Total; and small volumes to Asian and South African companies.

Field Development and Exploration

In November 2005, Repsol YPF discovered a significant oil deposit of light, sweet crude in the Murzuq Basin. Industry experts believe the discovery to be one of the biggest made in Libya for several years. Repsol YPF is joined by a consortium of partners including OMV, Total and Norsk Hydro. Also located in Murzuq Basin is Eni's Elephant field. In October 1997, a consortium led by British company Lasmo, along with Eni and a group of five South Korean companies, announced that it had discovered large recoverable crude reserves about 800 kilometres (500 mi) south of Tripoli. Lasmo estimated field production would cost around $1 per barrel. Elephant began production in February 2004.

WOC's Waha fields currently produce around 350,000 bbl/d (56,000 m/d). In 2005, ConocoPhillips and co-ventures reached an agreement with NOC to return to its operations in Libya and extend the Waha concession

25 years. ConocoPhillips operates the Waha fields with a 16.33% share in the project. NOC has the largest share of the Waha concession, and additional partners include Marathon and Amerada Hess.

Refining and Downstream

Libya has five domestic refineries:

Diversification

Oil wealth has enabled Libya to pursue extravagant projects such as agriculture and the Great Manmade River in the Sahara Desert.

In 2007, mining and hydrocarbon industries accounted for well over 95 percent of the Libyan economy. Diversification of the economy into manufacturing industries remain a long-term issue.

Although agriculture is the second-largest sector in the economy, Libya depends on imports in most foods. Climatic conditions and poor soils severely limit farm output, and domestic food production meets only about 25% of demand. Domestic conditions limit output, while higher incomes and a growing population have caused food consumption to rise. Because of low rainfall levels in Libya, agricultural projects such as the Kufra oasis rely on underground water sources. Libya's primary agricultural water source remains the Great Manmade River (GMMR), but significant resources are being invested in desalinization research to meet growing demand. Libyan agricultural projects and policies are overseen by a General Inspector; there is no Ministry of Agriculture, *per se.*

Labor market

Libya posted a 3.3% rate of population growth during 1960-2003. In 2003, 86% of the population was urban, compared to 45% in 1970. Although no reliable estimates are available, unemployment is reportedly acute: over 50% of the population under the age of 20. Moreover, despite the bias of labor market regulations favoring Libyan workers, the mismatch of the educational system with market demand has produced a large pool of expatriate workers, with typically better-suited education and higher productivity. However, because of shortages for manual labor, Libya has also attracted important numbers of less skilled immigrants. Expatriate workers represent an estimated fifth of the labor force.

Although significant, the proportion of expatriate workers is still below oil producing countries in the Persian Gulf. Foreign workers mainly come from the Maghreb, Egypt, Turkey, India, the Philippines, Malaysia, Thailand, Vietnam, Poland, Chad, Sudan, and Bosnia and Herzegovina. They tend to earn relatively high wages, taking either skilled or hard manual jobs. Census data for 2000 show the share of expatriates earning over LD 300 (US$230) per month was 20%, compared to 12% for Libyan nationals. A campaign encouraging conversion of qualified civil servants to entrepreneurs, in the face of public sector over employment and declining productivity, does not seem to be producing the desired results thus far.

External trade and finance

The Government is in the process of preparing a financial sector reform program. Recent legislation setting corporate governance standards for financial institutions makes progress towards better management and greater operational independence of public banks. However, Libyan public banks still lack management structures supported by skills in critical areas like credit, investment, risk management, and information and control systems.

The new banking law reinforces the independence of the Central Bank of Libya (CBL) and offers a legal framework for regulating banking activities, even if some provisions call for improvement. Despite progress brought by the new banking Law that specifies and limits its duties and responsibilities, the CBL remains the owner of the public banks, with the associated potential conflict of interest between ownership and regulation.

Financial sector reform has also progressed with partial interest rate liberalization. Interest rates have been liberalized on deposits, while a lending rate ceiling has been set above the discount rate. The Libyan Stock Exchange, established in 2007, is the first exchange of its kind in the country.

As of 13 March 2011, Libya Oil Holdings has had its €38m stake in Irish exploration firm Circle Oil frozen on foot of a European Union order that's been put in place to put pressure on the Gaddafi regime.

International rankings

Critical Observations of the present status of Economy of Libya

(1) This articles does not give any information of Gaddafi regime which was very oppressive and that resulted in international sanctions from UN and US during his regime. Libya's economy is small with population of just 6.7 million and large revenues through exports of crude oils.

(2) The economy of Libya depends primarily on revenues from the petroleum sector, which represents 95% of export earnings and 60% of GDP. These oil revenues and a small population

have given Libya one of the highest per capita GDP Nominal in Africa.

(3) After 2000, Libya recorded favourable growth rates with an estimated 10.6% growth of GDP in 2010. This development was interrupted by the Libyan Civil War when Gaddafi was the dictator in Libya which resulted in contraction of economy by 621% in 2011. After the war, economy rebounded by 1045%in 2012, but again crashed following the Second Civil War. As of 2017, Libya per capita PPP GDP stands at 60% of its pre-wars level.

(4) Libyan economy does not give the war information in details in this Article. It is therefore assumed that Saraj-Haftar conflict continues from 2011 to date.

(5) Since the oil is the main export, Libya's fantastic growth rate proved unsustainable in the face of global oil recession and international sanctions. Consequently the GDP per capita shrank by 40% in the 1980s. Successful diversification and integration into the international commodities helped current GDP per capita to cut further deterioration to just 3.2% in the 1990s.

(6) Libyan GDP per capita was $40 in the early 1920s but it rose to $1018 by 1967. In 1947 alone, per capita GDP rose by 42%.

(7) It is to be noted that GDP PPP per capita was $27894 in 1980 and came down to $9986 in 2017. This is much volatile. Inflation rate also was above 14.4% in 1980 which rose to 28% in 2017. Budget deficit was 12.5% in 2010 which rose to 28% in 2017. This is also widely fluctuating. Fiscal deficit was 12.5% in 2010 which rose dangerously to 43.2% of GDP. In 2017. Budget deficit should not be more than 4% of GDP.

(8) One Libyan dinar equals to $0.77 and mean wages were & 9.51 per hour in 2009.

(9) Libya is an OPEC member and holds the largest proven oil reserves in Africa, 41.5 gbbl as of January 2007. About 80% of Libya's proven oil reserves are located in Sirte Basin, which is responsible for 90% of the country's oil output. The state-owned National Oil Corporation (NOC) dominates Libya's oil industry.

(10) Although UN sanctions were suspended in 1999, foreign investment in the Libyan gas and oil sectors were severally curtailed due to the US. Iran and Libya sanction Act capped the amount foreign companies can invest in Libya yearly at

$20 million (reduced from previous $40 million in 2001). As of May 2006, US has removed Libya from the list of state that sponsor terrorism and has normalized ties and removed sanctions. This clears the road for US oil companies to exploit Libyan oil and is expected to have a passive impact on the Libyan economy.

(11) Production of oil raised from 1.80 million bpd in 2006 to 2 million bpd by 2008.

(12) In November 2003, Libya discovered a significant oil deposit of light, sweet crude in the Murzuq Basin.

(13) Oil Wealth has enable Libya to pursue extravagant projects such as agriculture and the Great Manmade River in the Sahara desert.

(14) In 2007, mining and hydrocarbon industries accounted for well over 95% of the Libyan economy. Diversification of the economy into manufacturing industries remain a large term issue.

(15) Although agriculture is the second largest sector in the economy, Libya depends on import in most food. Climatic conditions and poor soil severally limit farm output. Higher incomes and a growing population have caused food consumption to rise but low rainfall levels in Libya, agricultural projects rely upon underground water source. Libya's primary agricultural water source depends mostly on Great Man Made River, but significant resources are being invested in desalinization research to meet growing demand. Libyan agricultural projects and policies are overseen by a General Inspector.

(16) Libya posted a 3.3% rate of population growth during 1960-2003. In 2003, 86% of the population was urban compared to 45% in 1970. Unemployment is reportedly acute. 50% of the population is under the age of 20 years. Labour Market regulations favour Libyan workers. Mismatch of the educational system with the market demand has produced a large pool of expatriate workers, with typically better-suited education and high productivity. However, because of shortage for manual labour, Libya has attracted important number of less skilled expatriate workers which represents an estimated fifth of the labour force. The proportion of expatriate workers is below oil producing countries in the Persian Gulf. Foreign workers came from Egypt, Turkey, Sudan and Bosnia. Share of expatriates is LD 300 ($230) per month. This was 20% compared to 12% for Libyan workers.

(17) The government is in the process of preparing a financial sector reform program. Libyan public banks still lack management

structures supported by skills in critical areas like credit, investment, risk management, information and control systems.

(18) Central Bank of Libya is independent. It regulates banking activities and makes provisions for improvement. It is owner of the public banks, with associated potential conflict of interest between ownership and regulations.

(19) Financial sector reforms also progressed with partial interest rate liberalization. Interest rates have been liberalized on deposits, with a lending rate ceiling set up above the discount rate. Libyan Stock Market established in 2007, is the first exchange of its kind in the country.

(20) As of 31-03-2011, Libya Oil Holdings has had its euro 38 million stake in Irish exploration firm Circle Oil frozen on foot of a European Union order that has been put in place to pressure on Gaddafi regime.

(21) Currency: Libyan Dinar

(22) Financial year: Calendar year

(23) Trade Organization: OPEC, COMESA, CEN, SAD, AMU

(24) Country Group: Developing/emerging. Upper-middle income economy

(25) Population: 66.79 lacs

(26) GDP: $40.951 billion Nominal $74.717 billion PPP in 2018

(27) GDP growth: 26.7% in 2017, 7.9% in 2018, 5.5% in 2019 & -0.6% in 2020 forecast. Growth is fluctuating and volatile.

(28) GDP per Capita : $6288 Nominal $ 11473 PPP in 2018

(29) GDP by Sector: Agriculture 1.3%, industry 63.8% and Services 34.9%

(30) Inflation: 9.293% in 2018

(31) Labour Force: 25.53 lacs

(32) Labour force by occupation: agriculture 17%, industries 24% and Services 59%

(33) Unemployment: 30% On account of education does not match with jobs

(34) Main Industries: Petroleum, steel, iron, food processing, textiles & cement.

(35) Exports: $18.38 billion

(36) Export goods: Crude oil, refined petroleum products, natural gas, chemicals

(37) Imports: $11.36 billion Trade Surplus: $ 7.02 billion

(38) Import goods: Machinery, Transport equipment, semi-finished goods, food, consumer goods

(39) FDI stock: $20.21 billion

(40) Economic Aid: $9 million in 2010, $642 million in 2011 $87 million in 2012

(41) Foreign Trade $ 74.71 billion on 31-03-2017

(42) Current Account $2.574 billion

(43) Gross external debt: $3.02 billion

(44) Public debt: 4.7% of GDP

(45) Fiscal Deficit : -25.1% too high

(46) Revenues: $15.78 billion

(47) Expenses: $23.46 billion

(48) Fiscal deficit: $ 7.68 billion

Conclusion

Gaddafi ruled the country for a long time. Gaddafi was a cruel Monarch who ruled the country ruthlessly. He had clashes with many countries like US, EU and UN. Therefore there were international sanctions on Libya by UN, US and EU. This resulted in economy of Libya making vulnerable as GDP and national growth crippled. GDP was the most volatile and widely fluctuating.

There was total unrest in Libya after Gaddafi. Saraj rule was challenged by General Haftar and Civil War commenced which is still not ended. In spite of UN instructing all countries not to interfere with this conflict, Turkey is assisting Saraj government by providing it with military weapons. A ship full of military weapons provided by Turkey was caught by Italians in Middle Sea. Since Turkey is supporting Saraj government, UAE and Egypt Commando started training Haftar troops in naval field recently. UN has instructed both parties in Libya to negotiate and settle their issues amicably but they refused to do so. Turkey's support to Saraj government militarily and UAE and Egypt support to Haftar troops in military and naval training has added fuel to the fire and no settlement in Libya is at sight.

Country's main resource of revenue is oil. Country's economy therefore depends upon oil prices. Country has not diversified in other areas. But it has large foreign reserves and with small population, Libya can survive without any financial assistance from IMF or the World Bank in time of recession in oil prices.

18

Economy of Syria

Syrian Civil War started in 2011 when Assad was the President of Syria. The economy of Syria has deteriorated considerably since the beginning of the war. Syria has limited production of crude oil and agriculture. Main export of Syria are crude oil and agricultural products which accounts for 50% of its exports. Assad government introduced many reforms in agriculture but water and irrigation were two serious problems. Agitators in Civil war wanted Assad to oust but Assad strongly refused to oust. It is reported that US wanted Assad to oust but Russia wanted to oppose US as usual on this issue. There were Sanctions from US, Arab Countries, European Union, Australia, Canada and other countries which badly affected the economy of Syria. There was aggression by Israel on Syrian occupied Gaza Strip, West Sea and Palestine which were captured by Israel but never returned to Syria after the war as per the war rules. Israel is therefore permanent enemy of Syria. During the civil war, there were invasion in Syria from Al Qaeda. USSR intervened and sent troops to Syria along with US. Iran and Turkey. Al Qaeda was completely defeated by these troops but Russia, US, Iran also established their Military bases in Syria. Iran is a big enemy of Israel and many times Israel makes air attacks on Iran's Military Base in Syria and destroys storages of ammunition. Constant wars and bomb dropping on the Syrian territory has created fear in the minds of Syrian public. It is also reported that Assad government ruthlessly used chemical bombs and weapons to abolish the protesters. Though US want Assad to oust, it is not able to achieve its plan opposed by Russia, Iran and China. Out of fear, Syrians have left their country and have taken asylum in European countries as refugees. EU have prescribed quota for each European country to accommodate these Syrian refugees. There is economic crisis in Syria but Assad is adamant and not leaving his position as the political head of the country. This has further aggravated the political and economic conditions of the country and the country has become vulnerable. Now Assad has declared Election in Syria on the advice of Russia but because of Coronavirus, the election in May has been postponed. In fact, as a good administrator, Assad should have resigned from the Head of the State in the interest of the Syrian citizens and Syrian country.

The economy of Syria has deteriorated considerably since the beginning of the Syrian Civil War. Moreover, Syria's economic history has been turbulent. In 1963, the Arab Socialist Ba'ath Party came to power, and instituted socialist policies of nationalization and land reform. In 1970, General Hafiz al-Assad took power. The restrictions on private enterprise were relaxed, but a substantial part of the economy was still under government control. By the 1980s, Syria found itself politically and economically isolated, and in the midst of a deep economic crisis. Real per capita GDP fell 22 percent between 1982 and 1989. In 1990, the Assad government instituted a series of economic reforms, although the economy remained highly regulated. The Syrian economy experienced strong growth throughout the 1990s, and into the 2000s. Syria's per capita GDP was 4,058 US dollars in 2010. There is no authoritative GDP data available after 2012, due to Syria's civil war.

Before the civil war the two main pillars of the Syrian economy were agriculture and oil, which together accounted for about one-half of GDP. Agriculture, for instance, accounted for about 26% of GDP and employed 25% of the total labor force. However, poor climatic conditions and severe drought badly affected the agricultural sector, thus reducing its share in the economy to about 17% of 2008 GDP, down from 20.4% in 2007, according to preliminary data from the Central Bureau of Statistics. On the other hand, higher crude oil prices countered declining oil production and led to higher budgetary and export receipts.

Since the outbreak of the Syrian civil war, the Syrian economy has been hit by massive economic sanctions restricting trade with the Arab League, Australia, Canada, the European Union, (as well as the European countries of Albania, Iceland, Liechtenstein, Moldova, Montenegro, North Macedonia, Norway, Serbia, and Switzerland) Georgia, Japan, South Korea, Taiwan, Turkey, and the United States.

The sanctions, destruction and dislocation associated with the Civil War have devastated Syria's economy. By the end of 2013, the UN estimated total economic damage of the Syrian civil war at $143 billion. The total economic loss from the Syrian Civil War will reach $237 billion by the end of 2015, according to the United Nations Economic and Social Commission for Western Asia, with the Syrian opposition's capture of Nasib border crossing costing the government a further $500–$700 million a year on top of this. In 2018, the World Bank estimated that about one-third of Syria's housing stock and one half of its health and education facilities had been destroyed by the conflict. According to the World Bank, a cumulative total of $226 billion in GDP was lost due to the conflict from 2011 to 2016.

The Syrian economy suffered from conflict-related hyperinflation. The Syrian annual inflation rate is one of the highest in the world.

Basic information

During the 1960s, along socialist lines, the government nationalized most major enterprises and adopted economic policies designed to address regional and class disparities. Economic reform has been incremental and gradual. In 2001, Syria legalized private banking. In 2004, four private banks began operations. In August 2004, a committee was formed to supervise the establishment of a stock market. Beyond the financial sector, the Syrian Government has enacted major changes to rental and tax laws, and is reportedly considering similar changes to the commercial code and to other laws, which impact property rights. (Ohachq) Syria has produced heavy-grade oil from fields inside in the northeast since the late 1960s. In the early 1980s, light-grade, low-sulphur oil was discovered near Deir ez-Zor in eastern Syria. This discovery relieved Syria of the need to import light oil to mix with domestic heavy crude in refineries. Recently, Syrian oil production has been about 379,000 barrels per day (bpd).[1] Syria's oil reserves are being gradually depleted and reached 2.5 billion barrels in January 2009. Experts generally agree that Syria will become a net importer of petroleum by the end of the next decade. Recent developments have helped revitalize the energy sector, including new discoveries and the successful development of its hydrocarbon reserves. According to the 2009 Syria Report of the Oxford Business Group, the oil sector accounted for 23% of government revenues, 20% of exports, and 22% of GDP in 2008. Syria exported roughly 150,000 bpd in 2008, and oil accounted for a majority of the country's export income.

Ad hoc economic liberalization continues to add wealth inequality, impoverishing the average population while enriching a few people in Syria's private sector. In 1990, the government established an official parallel exchange rate to provide incentives for remittances and exports through official channels. This action improved the supply of basic commodities and contained inflation by removing risk premiums on smuggled commodities.

Foreign aid to Syria in 1997 totaled an estimated US$199 million. The World Bank reported that in July 2004 that it had committed a total of US$661 million for 20 operations in Syria. One investment project remained active at that time.

External trade and investment

Syrian exports in 2006

Despite the mitigation of the severe drought that plagued the region in the late 1990s and the recovery of energy export revenues, Syria's economy faces serious challenges. With almost 60% of its population under the age of 20, unemployment higher than the current 9% is a real possibility unless sustained and strong economic growth takes off.

Commerce has always been important to the Syrian economy, which benefited from the country's strategic location along major east-west trade routes. Syrian cities boast both traditional industries such as weaving and dried-fruit packing and modern heavy industry. Given the policies adopted from the 1960s through the late 1980s, Syria refused to join the "global economy". In late 2001, however, Syria submitted a request to the World Trade Organization (WTO) to begin the accession process. Syria had been an original contracting party of the former General Agreement on Tariffs and Trade but withdrew in 1951 because of Israel's joining. Major elements of current Syrian trade rules would have to change in order to be consistent with the WTO. In March 2007, Syria signed an Association Agreement with the European Union that would encourage both sides to negotiate a free trade agreement before 2010.

The bulk of Syrian imports have been raw materials essential for industry, agriculture, equipment, and machinery. Major exports include crude oil, refined products, raw cotton, clothing, fruits, and cereal grains.

Over time, the government has increased the number of transactions to which the more favorable neighboring country exchange rate applies. The government also introduced a quasi-rate for non-commercial transactions in 2001 broadly in line with prevailing black market rates.

Given the poor development of its own capital markets and Syria's lack of access to international money and capital markets, monetary policy remains captive to the need to cover the fiscal deficit. Although in 2003 Syria lowered interest rates for the first time in 22 years and again in 2004, rates remain fixed by law.

Debt

Under Syrian President Bashar al-Assad, national debt in relation to GDP went from 152.09% 2000 down to 30.02% in 2010. Syria has made progress in easing its heavy foreign debt burden through bilateral rescheduling deals with virtually all of its key creditors in Europe. In December 2004, Syria and Poland reached an agreement by which Syria would pay $27 million out of the total $261.7 million debt. In January 2005, Russia and Syria signed a deal that wrote off nearly 80% of Syria's debt to Russia, approximately €10.5 billion ($13 billion). The agreement left Syria with less than €3 billion (just over $3.6 billion) owed to Moscow. Half of it would be repaid over the next 10 years, while the rest would be paid into Russian accounts in Syrian banks and could be used for Russian investment projects in Syria and for buying Syrian products. This agreement was part of a weapons deal between Russia and Syria. And later that year Syria reached an agreement with Slovakia, and the Czech Republic to settle debt estimated at $1.6 billion. Again Syria was forgiven the bulk of its debt, in exchange for a onetime payment of $150 million.

Agriculture

Agriculture is a high priority in Syria's economic development plans, as the government seeks to achieve food self-sufficiency, increase export earnings, and halt rural out-migration. Thanks to sustained capital investment, infrastructure development, subsidies of inputs, and price supports, Syria has gone from a net importer of many agricultural products to an exporter of cotton, fruits, vegetables, and other foodstuffs. One of the prime reasons for this turnaround has been the government's investment in huge irrigation systems in northern and northeastern Syria. The agriculture sector, as of 2009, employs about 17% of the labor force and generates about 21% of the gross domestic product, of which livestock accounted for 16% and fruit and grains for more than 40%.

In 2015, Syria's main exports included spice seeds ($83.2 million), apples and pears ($53.2 million).

Most land is privately owned, a crucial factor behind the sector's success. Of Syria's 196,000 km (72,000 square miles), about 28% of it is cultivated, and 21% of that total is irrigated. Most irrigated land is designated "strategic", meaning that it encounters significant state intervention in terms of pricing, subsidies, and marketing controls. "Strategic" products such as wheat, barley, and sugar beets, must be sold to state marketing boards at fixed prices, often above world prices in order to support farmers, but at a significant cost to the state budget. The most widely grown arable crop is wheat, but the most important cash crop is cotton; cotton was the largest single export before the development of the oil sector. Nevertheless, the total area planted with cotton has declined because of an increasing problem of water shortage coupled with old and inefficient irrigation techniques. The output of grains like wheat is often underutilized because of poor storage facilities.

Water and energy are among the most pervasive issues facing the agriculture sector. Another difficulty suffered by the agricultural sector is the government's decision to liberalize prices of fertilizers, which have increased between 100% and 400%. Drought was an alarming problem in 2008; however, the drought situation slightly improved in 2009. Wheat and barley production about doubled in 2009 compared to 2008. In spite of that, the livelihoods of up to 1 million agricultural workers have been threatened. In response, the UN launched an emergency appeal for $20.2 million. Wheat has been one of the crops most affected, and for the first time in 2 decades Syria has moved from being a net exporter of wheat to a net importer. During the civil war which began in 2011, the Syrian government was forced to put out a tender for 100,000 metric tonnes of wheat, one of the few trade products not subject to economic sanctions.

Less than 2.7% of Syria's land area is forested, and only a portion of that is commercially useful. Limited forestry activity is centered in the higher elevations of the mountains just inland from the coast, where rainfall is more abundant.

Energy and mineral resources

Mining

Phosphates are the major minerals exploited in Syria. According to estimates Syria has around 1,700 million tons of phosphate reserves. Production dropped sharply in the early 1990s when world demand and prices fell, but output has since increased to more than 2.4 million tons. Syria produced about 1.9% of the world's phosphate rock output and was the world's ninth ranked producer of phosphate rock in 2009. Other major minerals produced in Syria include cement, gypsum, industrial sand (silica), marble, natural crude asphalt, nitrogen fertilizer, phosphate fertilizer, salt, steel, and volcanic tuff, which generally are not produced for export.

Oil and natural gas

Syria is a relatively small oil producer, accounting for just 0.5% of global production in 2010. Although Syria is not a major oil exporter by Middle Eastern standards, oil is a major pillar of the economy. According to the International Monetary Fund, oil sales for 2010 were projected to generate $3.2 billion for the Syrian government and account for 25.1% of the state's revenue.

Electrical generation

In 2001 Syria reportedly produced 23.3 billion kilowatt hours (kWh) of electricity and consumed 21.6 billion kWh. As of January 2002, Syria's total installed electric generating capacity was 7.6 gigawatts (GW), with fuel oil and natural gas serving as the primary energy sources and 1.5 GW generated by hydroelectric power. A network totaling 45 GW linking the electric power grids of Syria, Egypt, and Jordan was completed in March 2001. Syria's electric supply capacity is an important national priority, and the government hopes to add 3,000 megawatts of power generating capacity by 2010 at a probable cost of US$2 billion, but progress has been slowed by a lack of investment capital. Power plants in Syria are undergoing intensive maintenance, and four new generating plants have been built. The power distribution network has serious problems, with transmission losses estimated as high as 25 percent of total generated capacity as a result of poor quality wires and transformer stations. A project for the expansion and upgrading of the power transmission network is scheduled for completion in 2005.

As of May 2009 it was reported that the Islamic Development Bank and the Syrian government signed an agreement stating that the bank would provide a €100 million loan for the expansion of Deir Ali power station in Syria.

Nuclear energy

Syria abandoned its plans to build a VVER-440 reactor after the Chernobyl accident. The plans for a nuclear program were revived at the beginning of the 2000s when Syria negotiated with Russia to build a nuclear facility that would include a nuclear power plant and a seawater atomic desalination plant.

Industry and manufacturing

The industrial sector, which includes mining, manufacturing, construction, and petroleum, accounted for 27.3 percent of Gross Domestic Product (GDP) in 2010 and employed about 16 percent of the labor force. The main industrial products are petroleum, textiles, food processing, beverages, tobacco, phosphate rock mining, cement, oil seeds crushing, and car assembly. Syria's manufacturing sector was largely state dominated until the 1990s, when economic reforms allowed greater local and foreign private-sector participation. Private participation remains constrained, however, by the lack of investment funds, input/output pricing limits, cumbersome customs and foreign exchange regulations, and poor marketing.

Because land prices are not controlled by the state, real estate is one of the few domestic avenues for investment with realistic and safe returns. Activity in the construction sector tends to mirror changes in the economy. Investment Law No. 10 of 1991, which opened the country to foreign investment in some areas, marked the beginning of a strong revival, with growth in real terms increasing over 2001 and 2002.

Services

Services accounted for 60.4% of Gross Domestic Product (GDP) in 2017 and employed 67% of the labor force, including government, in 2008. As of May 2009, it was reported that Damascus office prices are skyrocketing.

Banking and finance

Since the start of the Syrian Civil War in 2011, there has been a capital flight to nearby countries. Syria has been subject to sanctions by US, Canada, EU, Arab League and Turkey because of the civil war. The currency of Syria is the Syrian pound (SYP). The pound's exchange rate has deteriorated significantly, falling from 47 SYP for US$1 in March 2011 to 515 SYP for US$1 in July 2017.

The Central Bank of Syria began operations in 1959. It controls all foreign exchange and trade transactions and gives priority to lending to the public sector. The Central Bank has been subject to US sanctions since May 2004, which has accused the Bank of money laundering. These US sanctions may have increased the role of Lebanese and European banks because a ban on transactions between U.S. financial institutions and the Central Bank of Syria created an increase in demand for intermediary sources for US$ transfers. The US, EU, Arab league and Turkey all also imposed sanctions on the Central Bank because of the Civil War.

The six specialized state-owned banks — the Central Bank of Syria, Commercial Bank of Syria, Agricultural Co-Operative Bank, Industrial Bank, Popular Credit Bank, and Real Estate Bank — are major financial operators. They each extend funds to, and take deposits from, a particular sector. The Industrial Bank also is directed more toward the public sector, although it is under-capitalized. As a result, the private sector often is forced to bank abroad, a process that is more expensive and therefore a poor solution to industrial financing needs. Many business people travel abroad to deposit or borrow funds. It is estimated that Syrians have deposited US$6 billion in Lebanese banks.

In the 2000s, Syria started reforms in the financial sector, including the introduction of private banks and the opening of the Damascus Securities Exchange in March 2009. In 2001, Syria legalized private banks and the sector, while still nascent, has been growing. Foreign banks were given licenses in December 2002, under Law 28 March 2001 which allows the establishment of private and joint-venture banks. Foreigners are allowed up to 49% ownership of a bank, but may not hold a controlling stake. As of January 2010, 13 private banks had opened, including two Islamic banks.

Syria has taken gradual steps to loosen controls over foreign exchange. In 2003, the government canceled a law that criminalized private sector use of foreign currencies, and in 2005 it allowed licensed private banks to sell specific amounts of foreign currency to Syrian citizens under certain circumstances and to the private sector to finance imports. In October 2009, Syria further loosened its restrictions on currency transfers by allowing Syrians travelling abroad to withdraw the equivalent of up to US$10,000 from their Syrian pound accounts. In practice, the decision allows local banks to open accounts of a maximum of US$10,000 that their clients can use for their international payment cards. The holders of these accounts will be able to withdraw up to US$10,000 per month while travelling abroad.

To attract investment and to ease access to credit, the government allowed investors in 2007 to receive loans and other credit instruments from foreign banks, and to repay the loans and any accrued interest through local banks using project proceeds. In February 2008, the government permitted investors to receive loans in foreign currencies from local private banks to finance capital investments. Syria's exchange rate is fixed, and the government maintains two official rates—one rate on which the budget and the value of imports, customs, and other official transactions are based, and a second set by the Central Bank on a daily basis that covers all other financial transactions. The government passed a law in 2006 which permits the operation of private money exchange companies. However, there is still a small black market for foreign currency.

Tourism

Non-Arab visitors to Syria reached 1.1 million in 2002, which includes all visitors to the country, not just tourists. The total number of Arab visitors in 2002 was 3.2 million, most from Lebanon, Jordan, Saudi Arabia, and Iraq. Many Iraqi businesspeople set up ventures in Syrian ports to run import operations for Iraq, causing an increased number of Iraqis visiting Syria in 2003–4. Tourism is a potentially large foreign exchange earner and a source of economic growth. Tourism generated more than 6 percent of Syria's gross domestic product in 2000, and more reforms were discussed to increase tourism revenues. As a result of projects derived from Investment Law No. 10 of 1991, hotel bed numbers had increased 51 percent by 1999 and increased further in 2001. A plan was announced in 2002 to develop ecological tourism with visits to desert and nature preserves. Two luxury hotels opened in Damascus at the end of 2004. Since March 2011 tourism in Syria has fallen due to the ongoing civil war.

Labour

Syria has a population of approximately 21 million people, and Syrian government figures place the population growth rate at 2.37%, with 65% of the population under the age of 35 and more than 40% under the age of 15. Each year more than 200,000 new job seekers enter the Syrian job market, but the economy has not been able to absorb them. In 2017, the Syrian labor force was estimated to total about 3.767 million people. An estimated 67 percent worked in the services sector including government, 17 percent in agriculture, and 16 percent in industry in 2008. Government and public sector employees constitute about 30% of the total labor force and are paid very low salaries and wages.

According to Syrian Government statistics, the unemployment rate in 2009 was 12.6%; however, more accurate independent sources place it closer to 20%. About 70 percent of Syria's workforce earns less than US$100 per month. Anecdotal evidence suggests that many more Syrians are seeking work over the border in Lebanon than official numbers indicate. In 2002 the Unemployment Commission (UC) was established, tasked with creating several hundred thousand jobs over a five-year period. As of June 2009 it was reported that some 700,000 households in Syria - about 3.5 million people - have no income. Government officials acknowledge that the economy is not growing at a pace sufficient to create enough new jobs annually to match population growth. The UN Development Program announced in 2005 that 30% of the Syrian population lives in poverty and 11.4% live below the subsistence level.

Opportunity Cost of Conflict

A report by Strategic Foresight Group, an India-based think tank, calculated the opportunity cost of conflict for the Middle East for 1991—2010 at US$12 trillion in 2006 dollars. Syria's share in this was US$152 billion, more than four times the projected 2010 GDP of US$36 billion.

The Syrian Center for Policy Research stated in March 2015 that, by then, nearly three million Syrians had lost their jobs because of the civil war, causing the loss of the primary source of income of more than 12 million people; unemployment levels "surged" from 14.9 percent in 2011 to 57.7 percent at the end of 2014. As a result, 4 in 5 Syrians were by then living in poverty, with 30 percent of the population living in "abject poverty" and frequently unable to meet basic household food needs.

Critical Observations of present status of economy of Syria

(1) The economy of Syria has deteriorated considerably since the beginning of Syrian Civil War. Moreover, Syria's history has been

turbulent. In 1963, the Arab Socialist Ba'ath Party came to power and instituted socialist policies of nationalization and land reforms.

(2) In 1970, General Hafiz al Assad took power. The restrictions on private enterprise were relaxed, but the substantial part of the economy was still under the government control. By the 1980s, Syria founded itself politically and economically isolated, and in the midst of a deep economic crisis. Real per capita GDP fell 20% between 1982 and 1989. In 1990, the Assad government instituted a series of economic reforms, though economy remain highly regulated.

(3) The Syrian government experienced strong growth throughout the 1990s and into the 2000s. Syria per capita income was $4058 in 2010. There is no authoritative GDP data available after 2012, due to Syria's Civil War.

(4) Before the Civil War, agriculture and oil were two pillars of the Syrian economy accounting for more than 50% of the GDP. However poor climatic conditions and severe drought badly affected the agriculture, thus reducing its share in the economy to about 17% of 2008 GDP from 20.4% in 2007. On the other hand, higher crude prices countered declining oil production and led to higher budgetary and export receipts.

(5) Since the outbreak of the Syrian Civil War in 2011, The economy has been hit and scattered by the massive economic sanctions restricting trade with the Arab League, Australia, Canada, The EU (as well as the European countries of Albania, Iceland, Moldova, North Macedonia, Norway, Serbia and Switzerland), Georgia, Japan, South Korea, Taiwan, Turkey and US. The Sanctions, destruction and dislocation associated with the Civil War have divested Syria's economy.

(6) By the end of 2013, the UN estimated total economic damage of the Syrian Civil War at $143 billion. This will reach $237 billion by the end of 2015 with the Syrian opposition's capture of Nasib Border crossing costing the government a further $500-$700 million per year on top of this. In 2018, The World Bank estimated that about one-third of Syria's housing stock and one half of its health and education facilities had been destroyed by the conflict. According to the World Bank, a cumulative total of $ 226 billion in GDP was lost due the conflict between 2011 and 2016.

(7) Syrian economy suffered from conflict-related hyperinflation. The Syrian annual inflation rate 30% is one of the highest in the world.

(8) In 1960, government nationalized most major enterprises and adopted economic policies designated to address regional and cross disparities. Economic reform has been incremented and gradual. In 2001, Syria legalized private banking. In 2004, four private banks began operations. In 2004, a committee was formed to supervise the establishment of a stock market. It also enacted major changes to the rental and tax laws.

(9) Syria had provided heavy-grade oil from the fields inside in the northeast since the late 1960s. In the early 1980s. Light grade, low Sulphur oil was discovered in eastern Syria. This needed Syria to import light oil to mix with domestic heavy crude in refineries. Syria's oil production is 379000 barrels per dy. Oil reserves are 2.5 billion barrels in 2009. By end of the next decade, Syria will become importer of petroleum.

(10) With liberalization, government established an official parallel exchange rate to provide incentives for remittances and exports through official channels. This action improved the supply of basic commodities and contained inflation by removing risk premiums on smuggling commodities.

(11) Foreign aid was $199 million in 1997> World Bank committed $661 million for 20 operations in Syria in 2004.

(12) Agriculture and oil were main exports earning $1 billion.

(13) Syria had been original contracting party of the formal GATT but withdrew in 1951 because of Israel's joining the membership of GATT. Syria has signed an Associate Agreement with the EU that would encourage both sides to negotiate a free trade agreement before 2010.

(14) Bulk of Syrian import have been raw materials essential for industry, agriculture equipment and machinery, Major exports are crude oil, refined products, raw cotton clothing, fruits and cereal grain.

(15) Poor development of Capital Markets and lack of access to international money and capital markets, monetary policy remains captive to the needs to cover fiscal deficit. In 2003, Syria lower interest rates for the first time in 22 years and again in 2004, rates remain fix by law.

(16) Under Syrian President Bashar al-Assad, national debt in relation to GDP went from 152% in 2002 to 30.02% in 2010. Syria has made progress in easing its heavy foreign debt burden through bilateral re-scheduling deals with virtually all of its key creditors in Europe. In 2004, Syria & Poland reached an agreement by which Syria would pay $27 million out of the total of $261.7 million debt. In January 2005, Russia and Syria signed a deal that wrote off nearly 80% of the Syria's debt to Russia approximately euro 10.5 billion ($13billion). The agreement left Syria with less than euro 3billion ($3.6 billion) owed to Moscow. Half of it will be repaid over next 10 years. In 2006, Syria reached agreement with Slovakia and Czech Republic to settle debt estimated at $1.6 billion. Syria was forgiven the bulk of its debt, in exchange for one-time payment of $150 million.

(17) In agriculture, most of the land is privately owned, a crucial factor behind the sector's success. Of Syria's 196000 km (122500 Miles). 28% of its cultivated and 21% of that total is irrigated. Most irrigated land is designated "strategic". It encounters sufficient state intervention in terms of pricing, subsidies and market control. 'Strategic' products such as wheat, barley and sugar beets must be sold to the State Marketing Boards at fixed prices, often above the world prices in order to support farmers; but at a significant cost to the State Budget. Most widely grown arable crop is wheat, but most important cash crop is cotton. Cotton was the largest single export. Total area planted for cotton has declined because of an increasing problem of water shortages and inefficient irrigation techniques. Water and energy are two most pervasive issues facing agriculture sector. Less than 2.7% of Syria's land is forest, part of which is used for fuel.

(18) Phosphates are main minerals exploited in Syria. Syria has around 1700 million tons of phosphates reserves. Production dropped sharply in early 1990 when world demand and prices fell but output increased more than 24 million tons. Syria produced 1.9 of the world's phosphate rock output and was world's ninth ranked producer of phosphate rock in 2009. Other major minerals are cement, gypsum, sand, fertilizers, marble and steel.

(19) Syria is relatively small oil producer. It is not a major exporter by Middle East standards but the pillar of the Syrian economy. Oil projected to generate $3.2 billion according IMF which is 25% of the state revenue.

(20) In 2001, Syria produced 23.3 billion kilowatt hours of electricity and consumed 21.6 billion kWh. In 2002, total installed electric generating capacity was 7.6 gigawatts. In May 2009, Islamic Development Bank and Syrian Government signed an agreement stating that bank will provide euro 100 million loan for expansion and upgrading of power transmission Station in Syria.

(21) Syria abandoned its plans to build VVER 440 reactor after the Chernobyl accident. The plans for nuclear program were revived at the beginning of 2000s when Syria negotiated with Russia to build a nuclear facility that would include a nuclear power plant and a sea water atomic desalination plant.

(22) The industrial sector includes mining, manufacturing, construction, petroleum, accounting for 27.3% in 2010 and employed 16% of the labour force. Main industrial products are petroleum, textiles, food processing, beverages, tobacco, phosphate rock mining, cement, oil seeds crushing and car assembly.

(23) Services account for 60.4% of GDP in 2017 and employed 67% of Labour force including government in 2008. As of 2009, it was reported that Damascus offer prices are skyrocketing.

(24) Since the start of Syrian Civil War in 2011, there has been a capital flight to nearby countries. Syria has been subjected to international sanctions by US, Canada, EU, Arab League and Turkey because of Civil War. Syrian Pound devalued from 47 Syrian Pound =US$1 in 2011 to 515 Syrian pounds =US$1in July 2017.

Central Bank of Syria began operations in 1959. It controls all foreign exchange and trade transactions and gives priority to lending to the public sector. The Central Bank has been subject to US sanctions since May 2004 which has been accused the Bank of money laundering. US sanctions may have increased the role of Lebanese and European banks because of ban on transaction between US Financial Institutions and Central Bank of Syria. This created increase in demand for intermediate sources for US$ transfer. US, EU, Arab League and Turkey also imposed sanctions on the Central Bank of Syria on account of Civil War in Syria.

Six specialized state-owned banks are major financial and banking operations. Syrians have to operate through banks abroad. They travelled abroad to deposit or borrow funds. Syrians have deposited $6 billion in Lebanese banks.

(25) Non-Arab visitors to Syria reached 1.1 million in 2002 which includes all visitors to the country, not just tourists. Total number of Arab visitors in 2002 was 3.2 million, most of them from Lebanon, Jordon, Saudi Arabia and Iraq. Tourism generated more than 6% of GDP in 2000s.

(26) Syria has population of approximately 21 million. Population growth rate was 2.33%. 655 of population is under the age of 15. 200000 new job seekers enter Syrian job market each year. But economy has not been able to absorb them. In 2017, labour force was 3.767. 67% were in Service sector, 17% in agriculture and 16% in industry. 70% of workforce earns less than $100 per month.

(27) Opportunity cost of conflict for Middle East 1991-2010 was $12 trillion as per 2006 US$ value. Syria's share was $152 billion. 3 million Syrians lost job in Civil war, 14.9% in 2011 and 57% in 2019. 4 out of 5 are living in poverty. 30% of population living in "abject poverty" and frequently unable to meet basic household food needs.

(28) Currency: Syrian Pounds

(29) Fiscal year : Calendar year

(30) Trade Organization: CAEU

(31) Country Group: Developing/Emerging with Low Income economy

(32) Population 1.69 crore

(33) GDP: $24.6 billion Nominal, $ 50.28 billion PPP in 2005 & 2014 respectively

(34) GDP growth: -30.9% in 2013, -36.5% in 2015.

(35) GDP per capita : $ 1455 Nominal & $ 2900 PPP

(36) GDP by sector : Agriculture 20%, Industry 19.55% & Services 60.5% in 2017

(37) Inflation 30% in 2017 Very high

(38) Population below Poverty lines: 82.5% Low economy

(39) Labour Force: 47.97 lacs

(40) Unemployment : 50% Very poor performance

(41) Labour force by Occupation: agriculture 17%, industry 16% and services 67%

(42) Main Industries: Petroleum, textiles, food processing, beverages, tobacco, phosphate rock mining, cement, oilseed crushing, meat, live animals and car assembly

(43) Exports: $1.85 billion in 2017

(44) Exports Goods: crude oil, minerals, petroleum products, fruits & vegetables, cotton fibre, clothing meat, live animals and wheat

(45) Imports: $6.279 billion Trade Deficit $4.429 billion 185 of GDP very high

(46) Import Products: machinery and transportation equipment, electric power machinery, food & live Stock, metal & metal products, chemical production, plastic and paper, yarn

(47) Gross external debt: $5.1 billion in 2017

(48) Public debt: 60% of GDP

(49) Revenue: $1.033 billion, Expenses: 10 Billion in 2017

(50) Fiscal deficit: $8.997 billion #6.45% of GDP

(51) Economic and recipient : $200 billion in 2012

(52) Foreign Aid: $2 billion in 2014

Conclusion

(1) Bashar al-Assad became President of Syria in 2010. Syrian economy was performing satisfactory upto 2012 and petroleum and agriculture were two pillars of Syrian economy.

(2) Civil War commenced in Syria in 12011. US wanted Assad to oust from his post as President of Syria but Assad who was supported by Russia refused to resign.

(3) Civil war coupled with International Sanctions by US, EU, Iran, Turkey, European countries made the economic conditions of Syria vulnerable.

(4) Protesters in Civil war were against Assad and wanted him to oust but Assad was adamant and refused to resign. He did not agree for any of the Protesters demand including election of the President.

(5) Syria was attacked by Al Qaeda. In order to abolish and defeat them, US, Russia, Iran and Turkey sent their troops and set up Military Bases in Syria. Al Qaeda was completely defeated and Al Qaeda soldiers. Few soldiers who remained alive run away from battle field. But Military Bases of US, Russia, Iran and Turkey remained in Syria and no country withdraw its military Base in Syria.

(6) Assad ruthlessly tried to finish the civil war. It is reported that Assad government used chemical weapons and chemical bombs to finish citizens who took part in Civil War. There were continuous

air attacks and missile attacks on Military Bases of Iran which resulted creating fear in the minds of citizens. Hundreds of thousand left the country and tried to settle in European countries as refuges. They took asylum in other countries. Because of his adamant attitude, Assad scattered the economy. In the interest of Economy, he should have resigned. This worsened the living conditions of Syrians very miserable.

(7) Now, in consultation with Russia, Assad declared that fresh election will be taken in May 2020. But Coronavirus has resulted in postponing the lections at a later date.

19

Economy of Iraq

The economy of Iraq is dominated by oil sector. Production costs of oil are relatively low. However four wars were fought in Iraq. (1) Iraq-Iran War in 1980-88, (2) Gulf War where Kuwait was conquered by Iraq in August 1990 (3) International Sanctions (1991) (4) US Invasion in 2003 and end of Saddam Hussein and Civil War with Kurdistan which has rich oil resources.

In May 2003, US waged war against President of Iraq Mr. Saddam Hussein on the ground that Iraq has chemical weapons including bombs which he is using against his opponents. He killed thousands of his rivals ruthlessly. These serious charges proved false ultimately but after the war, US arrested Saddam Hussein and killed him. There are various rival tribes in Iraq and to administer these various tribes was difficult task but President Saddam Hussein was doing well in controlling them. It was proved after the war. After the war, managing these tribes became difficult as oil rich Kurdish was de facto Independent State. US war expenses were about $500 billion in 2003. During Iraq-Iran war, Iraq lost $80 billion. Under the international sanctions, Iraq was prohibited to export oil in 1991 which led Iraq to financial crisis. International Oil for food was introduced in 1997 in which food to the extent of 90% was imported by Iraq.

US is always opposed to Assad rule in Syria. Kurdish tribes along with US army in Syria were used by US to fight against Assad soldiers. US army was brought into Syria to fight against terrorists Al Qaeda. Turkeys and Russia have also sent its troops in Syria to fight against terrorists which had sometimes clashes with Kurdish soldiers. US defended Kurdish tribes and soldiers against Turkey. But recently, US abandoned Kurdish tribes fighting against Assad forces in Syria, Russian forces and Turkish forces as US has withdrawn its military from Syria.

US has established military Base in Iraq. There are military Bases of Iran in Iraq. There are clashes between Iran and USA. On 03-01-2020, two motor cars started from Baghdad airport in Iraq. In one car, Head of

Kurdish forces Mr. Kasem Sulemani and Iraqis supported Iran army's head MR. Muhandees were travelling. US initiated air attacks on these cars and these two strong Iran military personnel were killed. This was a great shock to President of Iran Mr. Hasan Rohani and Supreme religious leader Mr. Khamenei. Iran has declared that the country will militarily attack USA by Ballistic missiles. Iran attacked US Base in Iraq but there was no much loss to US. On other hand, US attacked Iran's military base in Baghdad and destroyed its storage of artilleries. On account of continuous air attacks between Iran and US Baes, Iraq has instructed to US to withdraw its Military Base in Iraq. US is not prepared to withdraw its Base in Baghdad unless the Iraq will give financial compensation to US for withdrawing its military Base.

Iran's economy is fully based on oil exports. Iraq has not diversified its economy for other industries. In fact, Iraq should save 25%of its export income each year to face any financial calamities resulting from crisis of oil prices in any year. Sabotage by Islamic State and UN international sanctions on oil exports from 1990-2003 has resulted in collapsing economy of Iraq. Iraq-Iran War (1980-1988), Gulf war, International Sanctions, US military attack by US on Saddam Hussein in 2003 and Civil War with de facto Independence of Kurdish Government and others have shattered the Iraqi economy.

The economy of Iraq is dominated by the oil sector, which has provided about 99.7% of foreign exchange earnings in modern times. Iraq's hitherto agrarian economy underwent rapid development following the 14 July Revolution overthrowing the Hashemite Iraqi monarchy, becoming the third-largest economy in the Middle East by 1980. This occurred in part because of the Iraqi government's successful industrialization and infrastructure development initiatives in the 1970's, which included irrigation projects, railway and highway construction, and rural electrification.

In the 1980s, financial problems caused by massive expenditures in the Iran-Iraq War and damage to oil export facilities by Iran led the Ba'athist government to implement austerity measures, borrow heavily, and later reschedule foreign debt payments; Iraq suffered economic losses of at least $80 billion from the war. After the end of hostilities, in 1988, oil exports gradually increased with the construction of new pipelines and restoration of damaged facilities, but again underwent a sharp decline after the Persian Gulf War, dropping to one-fourth of its 1980 gross domestic product and continuing to decline under postwar international sanctions until receiving aid from the U.N. Oil-for-Food Programme in 1997.

Despite the efforts of the Coalition Provisional Authority to modernize Iraq's economy after the 2003 U.S.-led invasion through privatization and reducing its foreign debt, its economy continued to decline due to continued violence, economic mismanagement, and oil shortages caused by outdated technology. Since mid-2009, oil export earnings have returned to levels seen before Operation New Dawn and government revenues have rebounded, along with global oil prices. In 2011 Baghdad probably will increase oil exports above the current level of 1,900,000 bbl (300,000 m) per day as a result of new contracts with international oil companies, but is likely to fall short of the 2,400,000 barrels (380,000 m) per day it is forecasting in its budget. Iraq's recent contracts with major oil companies have the potential to greatly expand oil revenues, but Iraq will need to upgrade its oil processing, pipeline, and export infrastructure to enable these deals to reach their potential.

An improved security environment and an initial wave of foreign investment are helping to spur economic activity, particularly in the energy, construction, and retail sectors. Broader economic improvement, long-term fiscal health, and sustained increases in the standard of living still depend on the government passing major policy reforms and on continued development of Iraq's massive oil reserves. Although foreign investors viewed Iraq with increasing interest in 2010, most are still hampered by difficulties in acquiring land for projects and by other regulatory impediments.

Inflation has decreased consistently since 2006 as the security situation has improved. However, Iraqi leaders remain hard pressed to translate macroeconomic gains into improved lives for ordinary Iraqis. Unemployment remains a problem throughout the country.

Recent history

Nominal GDP grew by 213% in the 1960s, 1325% in the 1970s, 2% in the 1980s, "47% in the 1990s, and 317% in 2000s.

Real GDP per capita (measured in 1990 $) increased significantly during the 1950s, 60s and 70s, which can be explained by both higher oil production levels as well as oil prices, which famously peaked in the 1970s due to the OPEC's oil embargo, causing the 1973 oil crisis. In following two decades however, GDP per capita in Iraq dropped substantially because of multiple wars, namely the 1980-88 war with Iran, the 1990-1991 Gulf War.

Iran-Iraq War

Prior to the outbreak of the war with Iran in September 1980, Iraq's economic prospects were bright. Oil production had reached a level of 560,000 m (3.5 million barrels) per day in 1979, and oil revenues were 21 billion dollars in 1979 and 27 billion in 1980 due to record oil prices. At the outbreak of the war, Iraq had amassed an estimated 35 billion in foreign exchange reserves.

The Iran–Iraq War and the 1980s oil glut depleted Iraq's foreign exchange reserves, devastated its economy, and left the country saddled with a foreign debt of more than $40 billion. After the initial destruction of the war, oil exports gradually increased with the construction of new pipelines and the restoration of damaged facilities.

Sanctions

Iraq's seizure of Kuwait in August 1990, subsequent international economic sanctions on Iraq, and damage from military action by an international coalition beginning in January 1991, drastically reduced economic activity. The regime exacerbated shortages by supporting large military and internal security forces and by allocating reduces to key supporters of the Ba'ath Party. The implementation of the UN's Oil for Food program in December 1996 helped improve economic conditions. For the first six-month phases of the program, Iraq was allowed to export increasing amounts of oil in exchange for food, medicine, and other humanitarian goods. In December 1999, the UN Security Council authorized Iraq to export as much oil as required to meet humanitarian needs. Per capita food imports increased substantially, while medical supplies and health care services steadily improved, though per capita economic production and living standards were still well below their prewar level.

Iraq changed its oil reserve currency from the U.S. dollar to the euro in 2000. However, 28% of Iraq's export revenues under the program were deducted to meet UN Compensation Fund and UN administrative expenses. The drop in GDP in 2001 was largely the result of the global economic slowdown and lower oil prices.

After the fall of Saddam Hussein

The removal of sanctions on 24 May 2003 and rising oil prices in the mid-to-late 2000s led to a doubling in oil production from a low of 1.3 mbpd during the turbulence of 2003 to a high of 2.6 mbpd in 2011. Furthermore, reduced inflation and violence since 2007 have translated to real increases in living standards for Iraqis.

One of the key economic challenges was Iraq's immense foreign debt, estimated at $125 billion. Although some of this debt was derived from normal export contracts that Iraq had failed to pay for, some was a result of military and financial support during Iraq's war with Iran.

The Jubilee Iraq campaign argued that much of these debts were odious (illegitimate). However, as the concept of odious debt is not accepted trying to deal with the debt on those terms would have embroiled Iraq in legal disputes for years. Iraq decided to deal with its debt more pragmatically and approached the Paris Club of official creditors.

In a December 2006 *Newsweek International* article, a study by Global Insight in London was reported to show "that Civil war or not, Iraq has an economy, and—mother of all surprises—it's doing remarkably well. Real estate is booming. Construction, retail and wholesale trade sectors are healthy, too, according to [the report]. The U.S. Chamber of Commerce reports 34,000 registered companies in Iraq, up from 8,000 three years ago. Sales of secondhand cars, televisions and mobile phones have all risen sharply. Estimates vary, but one from Global Insight puts GDP growth at 17 percent last year and projects 13 percent for 2006. The World Bank has it lower: at 4 percent this year. But, given all the attention paid to deteriorating security, the startling fact is that Iraq is growing at all.

Industry

Traditionally, most of Iraq's manufacturing activity has been closely connected to the oil industry. The major industries in that category have been petroleum refining and the manufacture of chemicals and fertilizers. Before 2003, diversification was hindered by limitations on privatization and the effects of the international sanctions of the 1990s. Since 2003, security problems have blocked efforts to establish new enterprises. The construction industry is an exception; in 2000 cement was the only major industrial product not based on hydrocarbons. The construction industry has profited from the need to rebuild after Iraq's several wars. In the 1990s, the industry benefited from government funding of extensive infrastructure and housing projects and elaborate palace complexes.

Primary sectors

Agriculture

Agriculture contributes just 3.3% to the gross national product and employs a fifth of the labor.

Historically, 50 to 60 percent of Iraq's arable land has been under cultivation. Because of ethnic politics, valuable farm in Kurdish territory has not contributed to the national economy, and inconsistent agricultural policies under Saddam Hussein discouraged domestic market production. Despite its abundant land and water resources, Iraq is a net food importer. Under the UN Oil for Food program, Iraq imported large quantities of grains, meat, poultry, and dairy products. The government abolished its farm collectivization program in 1981, allowing a greater role for private enterprise in agriculture.

Iraqi agriculture suffered substantial physical disruption from the Gulf War, and economic disruption from sanctions imposed by the United Nations (August 1990). Sanctions curtailed imports by cutting off Iraq's petroleum exports, and embargoing those agricultural production inputs deemed to have potential military applications. The Iraqi government responded by monopolizing grain and oilseed marketing, imposing production quotas, and instituting a Public Distribution System for basic foodstuffs. By mid-1991 the government supplied a "basket" of foodstuffs that provided about one-third of the caloric daily requirement, and cost consumers about five percent of its market value. With subsidies for agricultural inputs diminished, the prices that the government paid to farmers failed to cover their costs. The implicit tax on agricultural production was estimated to reach 20 to 35 percent by the mid-1990s. In October 1991 the Baghdad regime had withdrawn personnel from the northern region controlled by two Kurdish parties. Kurdistan Region was described as "... a market economy essentially left alone by a very weak governing structure, but heavily influenced by substantial international humanitarian aid flows."

Under an "Oil for Food Program" negotiated with the United Nations, in December 1996 Iraq started exporting petroleum, and used the proceeds to start importing foodstuffs three months later. Grain imports averaged $828 million in the years 1997-2001, an increase of over 180 percent from the previous five-year period. Due to foreign competition, Iraqi production declined (29 percent for wheat, 31 percent for barley, and 52 percent for maize). Because the government had generally neglected the production of forage crops, fruits, vegetables, and livestock other than poultry, those sectors had remained more traditional and market-based, and less buffeted by international affairs. Nevertheless, severe drought, an outbreak of screwworm, and an epizootic of foot-and-mouth disease devastated production during this period. As the Oil for Food Program expanded to cover more agricultural inputs and machinery, the productivity of Iraqi agriculture stabilized around 2002.

Following the invasion led by the United States in March 2003, with incomes of many Iraqis devastated, the market for foodstuffs shrunk. Seeking to re-orient Iraq's economy toward private ownership and international competitiveness, the United States saw the dismantling of the Public Distribution System as essential for a market-driven agriculture. Because of the great reliance of most Iraqis on government-subsidized food, this goal was never realized. Increased productivity became the focus of much of the US-funded agricultural reconstruction program. Many of these projects were undertaken by the Agricultural Reconstruction and Development Iraq (ARDI) program run by Development Alternatives, Inc. (DAI) of Bethesda, Maryland, under a contract with USAID signed on 15 October 2003. While ARDI participated in limited ways, the restoration of Iraq's irrigation systems was mostly funded under USAID's contract with Bechtel International.

ARDI conducted demonstration trials of improved practices and varieties of many crops: winter cereals (wheat and barley), summer cereals (rice, maize, and sorghum), potatoes, and tomatoes. Feed supplements and veterinary treatments were demonstrated to increase ovulation, conception, and birth weights of livestock. Surveys were conducted of poultry growers and apple farmers. Nurseries were established for date palms and grapes. College buildings and farm tractors were rebuilt. ARDI had projects promoting trade associations and producers' co-ops, but also supported extension as an appropriate governmental function. The contract eventually cost over $100 million and lasted through December 2006. Under its Community Action Program, USAID also funded an analysis of markets for sheep and wool. It awarded a contract to the University of Hawaii to revitalize higher education in agriculture. It awarded a contract for $120 million to the Louis Berger Group to promote Iraq's private sector, including agriculture.

Starting in 2006, agricultural reconstruction was also conducted by Provincial Reconstruction Teams within the occupying military forces. Intended to promote goodwill and sap the insurgency, "PRTs" allowed military commanders to identify local needs and, with few bureaucratic hurdles, to dispense up to $500,000. Civilians from many agencies within the U.S. Department of Agriculture, as well as USAID, served tours on PRTs. Some participants criticized the absence of a national agricultural strategy, or clear direction on the design of projects. Others complained that projects emphasized "American-style, 21st-century agricultural technologies and methodologies..." that were inappropriate for Iraq.

Agricultural production has not rebounded noticeably from the reconstruction program. According to the Food and Agriculture Organization (FAO), between 2002 and 2013, production of wheat increased 11 percent and milled rice 8 percent, but barley had decreased 13 percent and maize 40 percent. Scaled in "international dollars" (2004-2006 base equaling 100) Iraq's per capita food production was 135 in 2002, 96 in 2007, and 94 in 2012. The agricultural sector shed workers. In those same years, production per worker was 117, 106, and 130, respectively.

The international Oil-for-Food program (1997–2003) further reduced farm production by supplying artificially priced foreign foodstuffs. The military action of 2003 did little damage to Iraqi agriculture; because of favorable weather conditions, in that year grain production was 22 percent higher than in 2002. Although growth continued in 2004, experts predicted that Iraq will be an importer of agricultural products for the foreseeable future. Long-term plans call for investment in agricultural machinery and materials and more prolific crop varieties—improvements that did not reach Iraq's farmers under the Hussein regime. In 2004 the main agricultural crops were wheat, barley, corn, rice, vegetables, dates, and cotton, and the main livestock outputs were cattle and sheep.

The Agricultural Cooperative Bank, capitalized at nearly 1 G$ - by 1984, targets its low-interest, low-collateral loans to private farmers for mechanization, poultry projects, and orchard development. Large modern cattle, dairy, and poultry farms are under construction. Obstacles to agricultural development include labour shortages, inadequate management and maintenance, salinization, urban migration, and dislocations resulting from previous land reform and collectivization programs.

In 2011, an agricultural adviser to the Iraqi government, Layth Mahdi, summarized the forced United States agricultural reconstruction:

Prior to 2003, Iraq had imported about 30 percent of its food needs annually. The decline in agricultural production after this period, created the need for importing 90 percent of the food at a cost estimated at more than $12 billion annually. Due to the sudden shift in the agricultural policy from subsidized assistance to an immediate shift to a free market policy, the outcomes led to a decline in production. The observed outcome resulted in many farmers abandoning the land and agriculture. The impact on natural resources results in an exploited and degraded environment leaving the land destitute and the people impoverished, unemployed [and] experiencing a sense of losing their human dignity.

Importation of foreign workers and increased entry of women into traditionally male labour roles have helped compensate for agricultural and industrial labour shortages exacerbated by the war. A disastrous attempt to drain the southern marshes and introduce irrigated farming to this region merely destroyed a natural food producing area, while concentration of salts and minerals in the soil due to the draining left the land unsuitable for agriculture.

In the Mada'in Qada region east of Baghdad, hundreds of small farmers united to form the Green Mada'in Association for Agricultural Development, an agricultural cooperative that provides its members with drip irrigation and greenhouses as well as access to credit.

Forestry, fishing, and mining

Throughout the twentieth century, human exploration, shifting agriculture, forest fires, and uncontrolled grazing denuded large areas of Iraq's natural forests, which in 2005 were almost exclusively confined to the northeastern highlands. Most of the trees found in that region are not suitable for lumbering. In 2002 a total of 112,000 cubic meters of wood were harvested, nearly half of which was used as fuel.

Despite its many rivers, Iraq's fishing industry has remained relatively small and based largely on marine species in the Persian Gulf. In 2001 the catch was 22,800 tons.

Aside from hydrocarbons, Iraq's mining industry has been confined to extraction of relatively small amounts of phosphates (at Akashat), salt, and sulfur (near Mosul). Since a productive period in the 1970s, the mining industry has been hampered by the Iran–Iraq War (1980–88), the sanctions of the 1990s, and the economic collapse of 2003.

Energy

Iraq is one of the most oil-rich countries in the world. The country holding the fifth largest proven crude oil reserves, totaling 147.22 billion barrels at the end of 2017. Most of this oil—4 million barrels per day out of 4.3 million barrels produced daily—is exported, making Iraq the third-largest exporter of oil. Despite its ongoing civil war, Iraq was able to increase oil production during 2015 and 2016, with production dipping by 3.5 percent in 2017 due to conflict with the Kurdistan Regional Government and OPEC production limits. By world standards, production costs for Iraqi oil are relatively low. However, four wars—the 1980–1988 Iraq-Iran War, 1991 Gulf War, the 2003-2011 War in Iraq, and the civil war—and the 1991–2003 UN sanctions have left the industry's infrastructure in poor condition, and the de facto independence of oil-rich Kurdistan Region have limited production.

In the 1970s, Iraq produced over 3.5 million barrels of oil per day. Production began to fall during the Iran-Iraq War, before plummeting 85 percent after the 1991 invasion of Kuwait. UN sanctions prevented the export of oil until 1996, and then allowed exports only in exchange for humanitarian aid in the Oil-for-Food Programme.

The 2003 lifting of sanctions enabled production—and exports—to restart. Production has since recovered to pre-Gulf War levels, and most of Iraq's oil infrastructure has been repaired, in spite of persistent sabotage by the Islamic State (ISIL) and others. In 2004 Iraq had eight oil refineries, the largest of which were at Baiji, Basra, and Daura.

Despite its oil wealth, sabotage and technical problems at refineries have forced Iraq to import petroleum, other refined oil products, and electricity from neighboring countries, especially Iran. In 2004, for example, Iraq spent $60 million per month for imported gasoline. Sabotage In late 2004 and early 2005, regular sabotage of plants and pipelines reduced export and domestic distribution of oil, particularly to Baghdad. Nationwide fuel shortages and power outages resulted. Persistent ISIL sabotage of pipelines, power plants and power lines, and theft of oil and electricity have also contributed to the July 2018 protests in southern Iraq.

In 2004 plans called for increased domestic utilization of natural gas to replace oil and for use in the petrochemical industry. However, because most of Iraq's gas output is associated with oil, output growth depends on developments in the oil industry.

Half of Iraq's power plants were destroyed in the Persian Gulf War of 1991, and full recovery never occurred. In mid-2004, Iraq had an estimated 5,000 megawatts of power-generating capacity, compared with 7,500 megawatts of demand. At that time, the transmission system included 17,700 kilometers of line. In 2004 plans called for construction of two new power plants and restoration of existing plants and transmission lines to ease the blackouts and economic hardship caused by this shortfall, but sabotage and looting kept capacity below 6,000 megawatts. The ongoing civil war, sabotage of transmission lines, and government corruption caused the electricity shortage to worsen: by 2010 demand outstripped supply by 6000 megawatts.

Oil continues to dominate Iraq's economy. As of 2018, oil is responsible for over 65 percent of GDP, 90 percent of government revenue. Petroleum constitutes 94% of Iraq's exports with a value of $59.73 billion in 2017. The central government hopes to diversify the economy away from oil, and has had some success: non-oil GDP growth, which was below the regional average from 2014-2016, pushed above the average in 2017. Despite this, the percent of government spending going to non-oil investment has continued to decline since 2013 and now stands at only 34 percent.

2009 oil services contracts

Between June 2009 and February 2010 the Iraqi Oil Ministry tendered for the award of Service Contracts to develop Iraq's existing oil fields. The results of the tender, which were broadcast live on Iraqi television, are as follows for all major fields awarded but excluding the Kurdistan Region where Production Sharing Contracts have been awarded that are currently being disputed by the Baghdad government. All contracts are awaiting final ratification of the awards by the Iraqi government.

Company shares are subject to change as a result of commercial negotiations between parties.

Notes: 1. Field shares are as a % of the total. The Iraq state retains a 25% share in all fields for which Service Contracts have been awarded. 2. Production Increase Share is the millions bbls per day that will attract the Service Fee for the company. 3. Gross revenue at plateau is the total payment each company will receive upon reaching their declared target plateau production rate (in between 5 and 8 years depending on field), before deduction of any operating costs but in addition to recovery of all development costs as billions of US$ per annum. The total gross revenue for all companies, after recovery of capital costs, is at plateau production of an additional 9.4 mb/d, 4.34 bn US per annum at a $70 bbl oil price. The 2010 Iraq govt budget is $60 billion. $300 billion is approximately $10,000 per annum for each Iraqi citizen.

In summary the shares by region in the increased production are:

Services

Finance

Iraq's financial services have been the subject of post-Hussein reforms. The 17 private banks established during the 1990s were limited to domestic transactions and attracted few private depositors. Those banks and two main state banks were badly damaged by the international embargo of the 1990s. To further privatize and expand the system, in 2003 the Coalition Provisional Authority removed restrictions on international bank transactions and freed the Central Bank of Iraq (CBI) from government control. In its first year of independent operation, the CBI received credit for limiting Iraq's inflation. In 2004 three foreign banks received licenses to do business in Iraq.

Private security

Because of the danger posed by Iraq's ongoing insurgency, the security industry has been a uniquely prosperous part of the services sector. Often run by former US military personnel, in 2005 at least 26 companies offered personal and institutional protection, surveillance, and other forms of security.

Retail

In the early post-Hussein period, a freewheeling retail trade in all types of commodities straddled the line between legitimate and illegitimate commerce, taking advantage of the lack of income tax and import controls.

Tourism

The Iraq tourism industry, which in peaceful times has profited from Iraq's many places of cultural interest (earning US$14 million in 2001), has been dormant since 2003. Despite conditions, in 2005 the Iraqi Tourism Board maintained a staff of 2,500 and 14 regional offices. Between 2009 and 2010, 165 tourists from 16 different countries entered Iraq to visit historic sites; as of January 2011, a U.S. State Department grant provided $2 million to help preserve Babylon, supporting the re-opening of one of the site's two museums.

Telecommunications

During 2003-8, mobile phone subscriptions had expanded over hundred-fold to 10 million nationwide, according to the Brookings Institution.

Labor force

In 2002 Iraq's labor force was estimated at 6.8 million people.

In 1996 some 66.4 percent of the labor force worked in services, 17.5 percent in industry, and 16.1 percent in agriculture. 2004 estimates of Iraq's unemployment ranged from 30 percent to 60 percent.

The CPA has referred to a 25% unemployment rate, the Iraqi Ministry of Planning mentioned a 30% unemployment rate, whereas the Iraqi Ministry of Social Affairs claims it to be 48%. Other sources are claiming a 20% unemployment rate and a probably 60% under-employment rate. The actual figure is problematic because of high participation in black-market activities and poor security conditions in many populous areas. In central Iraq, security concerns discouraged the hiring of new workers and the resumption of regular work schedules. At the same time, the return of Iraqis from other countries increased the number of job seekers. In late 2004, most legitimate jobs were in the government, the army, the oil industry, and security-related enterprises. Under Saddam Hussein, many of the highest-paid workers were employed by the greatly overstaffed government, whose overthrow disrupted the input of these people to the economy. In 2004 the U.S. Agency for International Development committed US$1 billion for a worker-training program. In early 2004, the minimum wage was US$72 per month.

External trade

Iraq is a founding member of OPEC. Petroleum constitutes 99.7% of Iraq's exports with a value of $43.8 billion in 2016.

From the 1990s until 2003, the international trade embargo restricted Iraq's export activity almost exclusively to oil. In 2003 oil accounted for about US$7.4 billion of Iraq's total US$7.6 billion of export value, and statistics for earlier years showed similar proportions. After the end of the trade embargo in 2003 expanded the range of exports, oil continued to occupy the dominant position: in 2004 Iraq's export income doubled (to US$16.5 billion), but oil accounted for all but US$340 million (2 percent) of the total. In late 2004, sabotage significantly reduced oil output, and experts forecast that output, hence exports, would be below capacity in 2005 as well. In 2004 the chief export markets were the United States (which accounted for nearly half), Italy, France, Jordan, Canada, and the Netherlands. In 2004 the value of Iraq's imports was US$21.7 billion, incurring a trade deficit of about US$5.2 billion. In 2003 the main sources of Iraq's imports were Turkey, Jordan, Vietnam, the United States, Germany, and Britain. Because of Iraq's inactive manufacturing sector, the range of imports was quite large, including food, fuels, medicines, and manufactured goods. By 2010, exports rose to US$50.8 billion and imports rose to US$45.2 billion. Chief 2009 export partners were: U.S., India, Italy, South Korea, Taiwan, China, Netherlands, and Japan. Chief 2009 import partners were: Turkey, Syria, U.S., China, Jordan, Italy, and Germany.

Critical Observations of present status of economy of Iraq

(1) Economic sector of Iraq is dominated by oil sector which has provided 99.7% of exports earnings to Iraq. Iraq has, however, not diversified its economy to other industries/ other fields.

(2) In the 1980s, Iraq faced financial problems on account of massive expenditure $80 billion in the Iraq-Iran War (1980-88).

(3) Iraq's agrarian economy underwent rapid development following the 14th July revolution overthrowing Hashemite Iraqi monarchy. Iraq became third largest economy in the Middle Eat by 1980.

(4) Iraq was successful in industralisation and infrastructure development of industries in 1970 which included irrigation projects, railways and highway constructions and rural electrification.

(5) In the 1980s, massive expenditure of Iraq- Iran War and damages to oil exports facilities by Iran and UN International Sanctions as well as sabotage by the Islamic State damaging refineries, pipes and infrastructure led government to austerity measures which include borrowing heavily and later rescheduling foreign debt payments.

(6) In 1988, oil exports gradually increased with construction of new pipelines and restoration of damages facilities.

(7) Gulf War in 1990 resulted in conquering Kuwait which was wrong decision. This resulted in UN international Sanctions on export of oil from 1990to 2003. This was slightly relaxed in 1997 by export for food programme facility given by UN.

(8) US invaded Iraq in 2003 and defeated Saddam Hussein which costed heavily to US as the unemployment in various IT companies spread dangerously.

(9) Post Hussein efforts were made to modernize economy through privatization and reducing in foreign exchange debt. Economy continued to decline due to continuance violence, economic mismanagement and oil shortage caused by outdated technology.

(10) In 2011, Iraq increased oil exports above the current level of 19 million bbl. per day as a result of new contracts with international oil companies. But forecast of 24 billion bbl. per day has not been achieved.

Foreign investors viewed Iraq with increasing interest in 2010, most are still hampered by difficulties in acquiring land for project and by other regulatory impediments.

(11) Inflation has decreased consistently since 2006 as the security has improved. Iraqi leaders are pressurized to translate macroeconomic gain into improved lives to ordinary Iraqi. Unemployment remained a problem throughout the country.

(12) GDP growth was very volatile and fluctuating. It grew by 253% in the 1960s, 1325% in 1970s, 2% in 1980s, -47% in the 1990s and again rebounded to 317% in 2000s. Iraq has amassed $35billion foreign exchanges reserves at the outbreak of Iran-Iraq War in September 1980.

(13) After the initial destruction of the war, oil exports gradually increased with the construction of new pipelines and restoration of damage facilities.

(14) Iraq's seizure of Kuwait in August 1990, consequent international economic sanctions on Iraq, and damage from military action by international coalition beginning in January 1991, drastically reduced economic activity. The regime exacerbated shortages by exporting large military and internal security forces and by allocating reduces to key supporters of Ba'ath party. The implementation of the UN's oil for food program in December 1996 helped improve economic conditions. For the first six-month phases of the program; Iraq was allowed to export increasing

amount of oil in exchange for food, medicine and other humanitarian needs. In December 1999, the UN Security Council authorized Iraq to export as much as oil as required to meet humanitarian needs.

(15) Iraq changed its oil reserve currency from US dollar to euro in 2000. However, 28% of Iraq's export revenues under the program were deducted to meet UN Compensation fund and UN administration expenses. GDP supported in 2001 on account of fall of oil prices and global economic slowdown.

(16) One of the key economic challenges was Iraq's immense foreign debt, estimated $125 billion. Although some of this debt was derived from normal export contracts that Iraq had failed to pay for, some was a result of military and financial support during the Iraq's war with Iran.

(17) Most of Iraq's manufacturing activity has been closely connected to the oil industry. The major industries in that category have been petroleum refining and manufacture of chemicals and fertilizers. Before 2003, diversification was hindered by limitations on privatization and the effects of international sanctions of 1990s. Since 2003, security problems have blocked efforts to establish new enterprises, Construction industry is exception. The construction industry has profited from the need to rebuild after Iraq's several wars. In the 1990s, the industry benefited from government funding of extensive infrastructure and housing projects and elaborate palace complexes.

(18) Agriculture contributed just 3.3% of GDP and employs 20% of the labour force. 50%-60% of Iraq's arable land has been under cultivation. Because of ethnic politics, valuable farm in Kurdish territory has not contributed to the national economy. Inconsistent agricultural policies under Saddam Hussein discouraged domestic market production. Despite its abundant land and water resources, Iraq is a net importer. Under the Oil to Food Program, Iraq imported large quantities of grain, meat, poultry and daily products. The Government abolished to form cultivation programs in 1981 allowing greater role for private enterprises in agriculture.

(19) Iraq's agriculture suffered substantial physical disruption from the Gulf war, and economic disruption from Sanctions imposed by UN in August 1990. Sanctions curtailed imports by cutting off Iraq's petroleum exports and embargoing those agriculture production. Inputs deemed to have potentially military applications.

The Iraq Government responded by monopolizing grain and oil seeds marketing, imposing production quotas, and instituting a public Distribution System for basic foodstuffs.

(20) Under an Oil for Food Program, Iraq started exporting petroleum and importing food three months later. Grain imports averaged $828 million in the years 1997-2001, 180% from the previous five year period.

(21) For Market driven economy, US found after invasion of Iraq in 2003, that Public Distribution Policy needs to be abolished. Because of great reliance of most of the Iraqis on government subsidized food, this goal was never achieved. Increased productivity became the focus of much of the US –funded agricultural reconstruction program. Agricultural production has not rebounded noticeably from the reconstruction program. During 2002-2003, production of wheat increased 11%, milled rise 8% but barley had decreased by 13% and maize 40%. Iraq's per capita food production was 135 in 2002, 96 in 2007 and 94 in 2012. Production per worker was 117,106 and 130 respectively.

Sudden shift in the agricultural policy from subsidized assistance to an immediate shift to a free market policy led to the decline in production. Many farmers abandoned the land and agriculture. Importation of foreign workers and increased entry of women into traditionally male labour roles have helped compensate for agricultural and industrial labour shortage exacerbated by the war.

(22) Iraq's human exploration, shifting agriculture, forest fires and uncontrolled grazing denuded large areas of natural forest were almost exclusively confined to the northeastern region are not suitable for lumbering. In 2002, total of 112000 cubic metres of wood were harvested, nearly half of which was used as fuel. Iraq's fishing industry has remained negatively small based largely on marine species in the Persian Gulf. In 2001, that catch was 22800 tons.

(23) Besides hydrocarbons, Iraq's mining industry has been confined to extraction of relatively small amounts of phosphates, salt, sulfur. Mining industry has been hampered by the Iraq-Iran War (1980-88), the sanctions of 1990s and the economic collapse of 2003.

(24) Iraq has holdings of proven crude oil reserves totaling 147.22 billion barrels at the end of 2017. Iraq extracts 4 million out of 4.3 million barrels are exported. Despite production was damaged

by Sabotage by the Islamic Country and various wars commencing from 1980, Iraq was able to increase oil production during 2015 and 2016. Production dipped by 3.5% in 2017 on account of conflict with Kurdistan Regional Government and OPEC production limits. Production costs of Iraq oil are relatively low by World Standards. In spite of persistent Sabotage by Islamic State and others, Iraq was able to restart export of oil in 2003. Most of the infrastructure damaged by Sabotage has been repaired.

(25) 17 banks were established during 1990s were limited to domestic transactions and attracted few private depositors. These banks were badly damaged by the international embargo of the 1990s. Post Hussein reforms enabled restrictions on international bank to abolish/remove and freed Central Bank of Iraq (CBI) from government control. In 2004 (1st year of Independence), CBI received credit for limiting Iraq's inflation. In 2004, three foreign banks received Licences to do business in Iraq.

(26) The danger posed by the Iraq's ongoing insurgency resulted in the security industry a uniquely prosperous part of the services sector often run by the former US military personnel in 2005. At least 26 companies offered personal and institutional protection, surveillance and other form of security.

(27) In the early post-Hussein period, freewheeling retail trade in all types of commodities straddled the line between legitimate and illegitimate commerce, taking advantage of the lack of income tax and import controls.

(28) Iraq tourism earned $14 million in 2001. Since 2003, it has been dormant. In 2005, Iraq Tourism Board maintained a staff of 2500 and 14 regional offices. US funded $2 million to help preserve Babylon, supporting the reopening of one of state's four museums.

(29) Movable phone subscriptions have expanded over hundred times to 10 million nationwide during 2003-2008 according to the Brooking Institution.

(30) Iraq is the founding member of OPEC and 99.7% of Iraq export i.e. 43.8 billion accounts in 2016.

(31) Currency: Iraqi dinar

(32) Trade Organisations: OPEC

(33) Country Group: Developing/emerging

(34) Upper–middle income economy

(35) Population: 3.84 crores

(36) GDP: $224.228 billion Nominal & $ 669.906 billion PPP in 2018

(37) GDP growth: -2.5% in 2017, -0.6% in 2018, 4.8$ in 2019 & 5% in 2020 Forecast

(38) GDP per Capita $ 5882 Nominal $17572 PPP in 2018

(39) Labour Force: 1.0378 crore

(40) Labour Force by Occupation: Agriculture 21.8%, Industry 18.7% and services 59.5 in 2008

(41) Unemployment 13% high

(42) Main Industries: Petroleum, chemicals, textiles, construction materials, food processing, fertilizers, crude oil

(43) Exports: $63.31 billion

(44) Export goods: crude oil, food, live animals

(45) Imports: $39.47 Billion Trade Surplus $23. 84 billion

(46) Import goods: foodgrains

(47) FDOI Stock: $26.63 billion in 2015 abroad $2.109 Billion

(48) Current account: $4.344 billion

(49) External debt: $ 73.02 billion

(50) Public debt: $59.7 billion

(51) Budget deficit: -4.2% of GDP

(52) Revenues: $60.71 billion

(53) Expenses: $76.82 billion

(54) Economic Aide: $700 million in 2017

(55) Foreign reserves: $41.38 billion

(56) Credit Rating: B- - S & Ps

Conclusion

Country has faced Iran-Iraq War for 8 Years which costed $80 billion. Gulf War resulted in winning Kuwait which was very costly as UN imposed sanctions on Iraq from 1990-2003. Country's only income was from export of crude oil. Since country was prohibited from exporting crude oil, there was economic crisis

Invasion of Iraq by US in 2003 further deteriorated the economy. There was civil war. There are many militant tribes which fought with each other. Kurdish has its own independent, de facto, state. Kurdish do not obey President's orders. Sabotage is done on petroleum pipe lines and infrastructure which resulted in difficulties to export crude oil.

Crude petrol is the only resource of income of Iraq. But it has not diveratified its economy in other fields. Country has to depend on imports for foodgrains from other countries.

At Present, Iran and the US have military bases in Iraq. There are clashes between two countries which results in air attacks including missiles. Recently on 03-01-2020, on Baghdad airport, Sulemani, highest military head on whom Iran's religious Guru Mr. Khamenei was dependent was killed in Motor by air attack by US. This has resulted in Iran attacking US with ballistic missiles in the military Base in Baghdad.

Iran is not able to control various tribes in its country. Only to some extent, President Saddam Hussein was controlling these tribes and ruling the country. But US attacked, attested him and killed him.

Future rulers of Iraq should concentrate in growth and welfare of the economy as well as establishing a tight security to control sabotage of the Islamic country and various tribes in Iraq including Kurdish. But no war or interference in any country's economic or political affairs to show personal supremacy of the ruler at the cost of the Iraq's economic and political interest and promotion of the Iraq as a Welfare State.

20

Economy of Turkey

The State of Turkey is always on lime light on the policies announced by Turkey President Erdogan. Presently, Erdogan announced that the soldiers support him in Syria conflict and in order to protect them, EU and US should militarily assist Turkey but neither EU nor U.S. helped it and Turkey's soldiers were killed in attack by Syrian soldiers. Erdogan therefore released its Border with EU and especially with Greece and Bulgaria. This resulted in thousands of refugees trying to enter Greece border. Greece, however, has kept army on the boarder and prohibited refugees to enter the Greece border as Greece will not accommodate these refugees. In fact, under the Agreement of EU and Turkey, Turkey agreed to accommodate these refugees with the financial assistance to Turkey by EU for these refugees accommodation. Sudden unilaterally change in the Turkey's attitude is not approved/accepted by EU and this clashes occurred for which Turkey alone is responsible. On 18-03-2020, Turkey have closed its Boarder with Greece and Bulgaria on account of Coronavirus spread which results in further worsening the situation on Greece Border. Greece is, of course, very firm on not allowing refugees in its country and it is prohibiting strongly these refugees from entering into its country. Erdogan compared this action of Greece with Nazi which is of course wrong.

By refusing to obey the UN's directives, Turkey is assisting Saraj government in the Libya and providing military weapons to the soldiers of Saraj government to fight against Haftar terrorists. This Turkey's military aid is intervened and stopped by the UN.

Presently, in order to hold dominating position over Pakistan and Muslim countries, Turkey President Mr. Recep Erdogan has not agreed to approve India's action on removal of Article 370 on Kashmir and NCR and CAA which both amendments were passed by the Indian Parliament. This created clash between India and Turkey but Erdogan was adamant in not rethinking on this decision. Whimsical and wrong decision costs high to its Country. Erdogan is interfering with the political affairs in Syria, Libya and Yemen instead of improving economic conditions of turkey and downgrading of its international credit rating. It is spending very high and has very high deficit financing as well as international borrowings. Servicing of debt is a critical issue which Erdogan should solve instead of inferring in the political affairs of these country to show his dominated position which is false prestige but leads to economic crisis of Turkey as it has happened in Turkey in 2018 in respect of currency and debt crisis. Turkey should work for Welfare State to improve standard of living of its citizens. Recently US has imposed economic sanctions against turkey which has further deteriorated its economy.

The economy of Turkey is an emerging market economy as defined by the International Monetary Fund. Turkey is among the world's developed countries according to the CIA World Face book. Turkey is also defined by economists and political scientists as one of the world's newly industrialized countries. Turkey has the world's 19th-largest nominal GDP, and 13th-largest GDP by PPP. The country is among the world's leading producers of agricultural products; textiles; motor vehicles, transportation equipment; construction materials; consumer electronics and home appliances (see the related chapters below).

In 2018, Turkey went through a currency and debt crisis, characterised by the Turkish lira (TRY) plunging in value, high inflation, rising borrowing costs, and correspondingly rising loan defaults. The crisis was caused by the Turkish economy's excessive current account deficit and foreign-currency debt, in combination with the ruling Justice and Development Party's increasing authoritarianism and President Erdogan's unorthodox ideas about interest rate policy.

Macroeconomic trends

The country is a founding member of the OECD (1961) and the G-20 major economies (1999). Since 1995, Turkey is a party to the European Union–Turkey Customs Union. The CIA classifies Turkey as a developed country. Turkey is often classified as a newly industrialized country by economists and political scientists; while Merrill Lynch, the World Bank, and *The Economist* describe Turkey as an emerging market economy. The World Bank classifies Turkey as an upper-middle income country in terms of the country's per capita GDP in 2007. Mean graduate pay was $10.02 per man-hour in 2010. Turkey's labour force participation rate of 56.1% is by far the lowest of the OECD states which have a median rate of 74%. According to a 2014 survey by Forbes magazine, Istanbul, Turkey's financial capital, had a total of 37 billionaires in 2013, ranking 5th in the world. 2017 was the second consecutive year that saw more than 5.000 high net-worth individuals (HNWIs, defined as holding net assets of at least $1 million) leaving Turkey, reasons given as government crackdown on the media deterring investment, and loss of currency value against the U.S. dollar.

A longstanding characteristic of the economy of Turkey is a low savings rate. Since under the government of Recep Tayyip Erdogan an, Turkey has been running huge and growing current account deficits, reaching $7.1 billion by January 2018, while the rolling 12-month deficit rose to $51.6 billion, one of the largest current account deficits in the world. The economy has relied on capital inflows to fund private-sector excess, with Turkey's banks and big firms borrowing heavily, often in foreign currency. Under these conditions, Turkey must find about $200 billion a year to fund its wide current account deficit and maturing debt, always at risk of inflows drying up, having gross foreign currency reserves of just $85 billion.

Turkey has been meeting the "60 percent EU Maastricht criteria" for public debt stock since 2004. Similarly, from 2002 to 2011, the budget deficit decreased from more than 10 percent to less than 3 percent, which is one of the EU Maastricht criteria for the budget balance. In January 2010, International credit rating agency Moody's Investors Service upgraded Turkey's rating one notch. In 2012, credit ratings agency Fitch upgraded Turkey's credit rating to investment grade after an 18-year gap, followed by a ratings upgrade by credit ratings agency Moody's Investors Service in May 2013, as the service lifted Turkey's government bond ratings to the lowest investment grade, Moody's first investment-grade rating for Turkey in two decades and the service stated in its official statement that the nation's "recent and expected future improvements in key economic and public finance metrics" was the basis for the ratings boost. In March 2018, Moody's downgraded Turkey's sovereign debt into junk status, warning of an erosion of checks and balances under Recep Tayyip Erdogan. In May 2018, credit ratings agency Standard HYPERLINK "https://en.wikipedia.org/wiki/Standard_%26_Poor%27s"&HYPERLINK "https://en.wikipedia.org/wiki/Standard_%26_Poor%27s" Poor's cut Turkey's debt rating further into junk territory, citing widening concern about the outlook for inflation amid a sell-off in the Turkish lira currency.

Share prices in Turkey nearly doubled over the course of 2009. On May 10, 2017, the Borsa Istanbul (BIST) 100 Index, the benchmark index of Turkey's stock market, set a new record high at 95,735 points. As of January 5, 2018, the Index reached 116,638 points. However, in the course of the 2018 Turkish currency and debt crisis, the index dipped back below

100.000 in May. In early June, the BIST-100 dropped to the lowest level in dollar terms since the global financial crisis in 2008.

In 2017, the OECD expected Turkey to be one of the fastest growing economies among OECD members during 2015-2025, with an annual average growth rate of 4.9 percent. In May 2018, Moody's Investors Service lowered its estimate for growth of the Turkish economy in 2018 from 4 percent to 2.5 percent and in 2019 from 3.5 percent to 2 percent.

According to a 2013 *Financial Times* Special Report on Turkey, Turkish business executives and government officials believed the quickest route to achieving export growth lies outside of traditional western markets. While the European Union used to account for more than half of all Turkey's exports, by 2013 the figure was heading down toward not much more than a third. However, by 2018 the share of exports going to the EU was back above fifty percent. Turkish companies' foreign direct investment outflow has increased by 10 times over the past 15 years, according to the 2017 Foreign Investment Index.

With policies of Recep Tayyip Erdogan fueling the construction sector, where many of his business allies are active, Turkey as of May 2018 had around 2 million unsold houses, a backlog worth three times average annual new housing sales. The 2018 Turkish currency and debt crisis ended a period of growth under Erdogan-led governments since 2003, built largely on a construction boom fueled by easy credit and government spending.

On August 10, 2018, Turkish currency lira nosedived following Trump's tweet about doubling tariffs on Turkish steel and aluminum that day. The currency weakened 17% that day and has lost nearly 40% of its value against the dollar till that time. The crash of the lira has sent ripples through global markets, putting more pressure on the euro and increasing investors' risk aversion to emerging-market currencies across the board. On Aug. 13, South Africa's rand slumped nearly 10%, the biggest daily drop since June 2016. Lira crisis spotlighted deeper concerns about the Turkish economy that have long signaled turmoil long ago.

By the end of 2018, Turkey went into recession. The Turkish Statistical Institute claimed that the Turkish economy declined by 2.4% in the last quarter of 2018 as compared to the previous quarter. This followed a 1.6% drop the previous quarter. Lira shrank down to 30% against the US dollar in 2018.

In May 2019, European Bank for Reconstruction and Development (EBRD) released an economic outlook in which it is reported that Turkey's economy will probably see a gradual recovery of growth to around 2.5 percent in 2020.

Main economic sectors

Agricultural sector

Atatürk Dam is the largest of the 22 dams in the Southeastern Anatolia Project. The program includes 22 dams, 19 hydraulic power plants, and the irrigation of 1.82 million hectares of land. The total cost of the project is estimated at $32 billion. The total installed capacity of power plants is 7476 MW and projected annual energy production reaches 27 TWh.

As of 2016, Turkey is the world's largest producer of hazelnuts, cherries, figs, apricots, and pomegranates; the second-largest producer of quinces and watermelons; the third-largest producer of cucumbers, green peppers, lentils and pistachios; the fourth-largest producer of apples, tomatoes, eggplants, and olives; the fifth-largest producer of tea, chickpeas and sugar beet; the sixth-largest producer of almonds and onions; the seventh-largest producer of lemons, grapefruit, and cotton; and the eighth-largest producer of barley. Turkey has been self-sufficient in food production since the 1980s. In the year 1989, the total production of wheat was 16.2 million tonnes, and barley 3.44 million tonnes. The agricultural output has been growing at a respectable rate. However, since the 1980s, agriculture has been in a state of decline in terms of its share in the total economy. Turkish agriculture emits greenhouse gases and suffers from climate change in Turkey.

The country's large agricultural sector accounted for 29.5% of the employment in 2009. Historically, Turkey's farmers have been fairly fragmented. According to the 1990 census, "85% of agricultural holdings were under 10 hectares and 57% of these were fragmented into four or more non-contiguous plots. Many old agricultural attitudes remain widespread. Turkey is dismantling the incentive system. Fertilizer and pesticide subsidies have been curtailed and remaining price supports have been gradually converted to floor prices. The government has also initiated many planned projects, such as the Southeastern Anatolia Project (G.A.P project). The program includes 22 dams, 19 hydraulic power plants, and the irrigation of 1.82 million hectares of land. The total cost of the project is estimated at $32 billion. The total installed capacity of power plants is 7476 MW and projected annual energy production reaches 27 billion kWh. The physical realization of G.A.P. was 72.6% as of 2010.

The livestock industry, compared to the initial years of the Republic, showed little improvement in productivity, and the later years of the decade saw stagnation. However, livestock products, including meat, milk, wool, and eggs, contributed to more than one third of the value of agricultural output. Fishing is another important part of the economy; in 2005 Turkish fisheries harvested 545,673 tons of fish and aquaculture.

The EU imported fruit and vegetables from Turkey worth €738.4 million up to September 2016, an increase of 21% compared to the same period in 2015, according to Eurostat data processed by FEPEX (Federación Española de Asociaciones de Productores). Turkey is the EU's fourth largest non-EU vegetable supplier and the seventh largest fruit supplier. The European Commission had already started the formal process for extending the Customs Union Agreement to agricultural products, before European Union–Turkey relations deteriorated and efforts to extend and modernize the Customs Union Agreement came to a halt in 2018.

Olive production

Olio Officine Globe reported 2016 olive statistics for Turkey: There are 180 million trees covering 700,000 hectares (1,700,000 acres) with a production of 500,000 tonnes (490,000 long tons; 550,000 short tons) of table olives and 300,000 tonnes (300,000 long tons; 330,000 short tons) of olive oil. Exports are 70,000 tonnes (69,000 long tons; 77,000 short tons) of table olives and 60,000 tonnes (59,000 long tons; 66,000 short tons) of olive oil a year. *Edremit* (Ayval1k) is the main variety in northern Turkey and *Memecik* in the south. Gemlik is a black table olive and other varieties are *Büyük Topak*, *Ulak*, *Çakır*, *Çekişte*, *Çelebi*, *Çilli*, *Domat*, *Edincik Su*, *Eğriburun*, *Erkence*, *Halhalı*, *Ýzmir Sofralýk*, *Kalembezi*, *Kan Çelebi*, *Karamürsel Su*, *Kilis Yaðlýk*, *Kiraz*, *Manzanilla*, *Memeli*, *Nizip Yaðlýk*, *Samanlý*, *Sarý Haþebi*, *Sarý Ulak*, *Saurani*, *Taþan Yüreði*, *Uslu*, and *Yað Celebi*.

Industrial sector

Turkish brands like Beko and Vestel are among the largest producers of consumer electronics and home appliances in Europe.

Turkey's Vestel is the largest TV producer in Europe, accounting for a quarter of all TV sets manufactured and sold on the continent in 2006. By January 2005, Vestel and its rival Turkish electronics and white goods brand Beko accounted for more than half of all TV sets manufactured in Europe. Another Turkish electronics brand, Porfolio, was Europe's third-largest TV producer in 2005. EU market share of Turkish companies in consumer electronics has increased significantly following the Customs Union agreement signed between the EU and Turkey: in color TVs from 5% in 1995 to more than 50% in 2005, in digital devices from 3% to 15%, and in white goods from 3% to 18%.

Textiles and clothing

Turkish companies made clothing exports worth $13.98 billion in 2006; more than $10.67 billion of which (76.33%) were made to the EU member states.

Motor vehicles and automotive products

Turkish automotive companies like TEMSA, OTOKAR and BMC are among the world's largest van, bus and truck manufacturers.

In 2008 Turkey produced 1,225,400 motor vehicles, ranking as the fifth-largest producer in Europe (behind the United Kingdom and above Italy) and the twelfth-largest producer in the world.

The automotive industry is an important part of the economy since the late 1960s. The companies that operate in the sector are mainly located in the Marmara Region. With a cluster of car-makers and parts suppliers, the Turkish automotive sector has become an integral part of the global network of production bases, exporting over $22.94 billion worth of motor vehicles and components in 2008.

Turkey's annual auto exports, including trucks and buses, surpassed 1 million units for the first time in 2016 as foreign automakers' investment in new models and a recovery in its mainstay European market lifted shipments. According to industry group the Automotive Manufacturers Association, or OSD, Turkey exported 1.14 million units in 2016, up 15% from the year before. Auto exports hit a record high for the fourth straight year. Production grew 9% year on year in 2016 to 1.48 million units, setting a new record for the second consecutive year. Nearly 80% of vehicles produced in Turkey were exported.

Multiple unit trains, locomotives and wagons

TÜLOMSAS (1894), TÜVASAS (1951) and EUROTEM (2006) are among the major producers of multiple unit trains, locomotives and wagons in Turkey, including high-speed EMU and DMU models.

Defense industry

SOM cruise missile developed by TÜB0 TAK SAGE and Roketsan for the Turkish Air Force

Turkey has many modern armament manufacturers. Annual exports reached $1.6 billion in 2014. MKEK, TAI, Aselsan, Roketsan, FNSS, Nurol HYPERLINK "https://en.wikipedia.org/wiki/Nurol_Makina"Makina, Otokar, and Havelsan are major manufacturers. On July 11, 2002, Turkey became a Level 3 partner of the F-35 Joint Strike Fighter (JSF) development program. TAI builds various aircraft types and models, such as the F-16 Fighting Falcon for the Turkish Air Force. Turkey has recently launched domestically built new military/intelligence satellites including a 0.8m resolution reconnaissance satellite (Project Göktürk-1) for use by the Turkish Armed Forces and a 2m resolution reconnaissance satellite (Project

Göktürk-2) for use by the Turkish National Intelligence Organization. Other important products include the Altay main battle tank, A400M, TAI TFX, TF-2000 class AAW frigate, Milgem class corvette, TAI Anka UAV, Aselsan izci UGV, T-155 Firtina self-propelled howitzer, J-600T missile, T-129 attack helicopter, Roketsan UMTAS anti-tank missile, Roketsan Cirit laser-guided rocket, Panter Howitzer, ACV-300, Otokar Cobra and Akrep, BMC - Kirpi, FNSS Pars 6x6 and 8x8 APC, Nurol Ejder 6×6 APC, TOROS artillery rocket system, Bayraktar Mini UAV, ASELPOD, and SOM cruise missile.

Steel-Iron industry

Turkey ranks 8th in the list of countries by steel production. In 2013, total steel production was 29 million tonnes. Turkey's crude steel production reached a record high of 34.1 million tons in 2011. Notable producers (above 2 million tonnes) and their ranks among top steel producing companies.

- Erdemir (7.1 million tonnes) (47th) (Only Erdemir-Turkey; Erdemir-Romania is not included)
- Habas (4.4 million tonnes) (72nd)
- Içdas (3.6 million tonnes) (76th)
- Diler (2.3 million tonnes) (108th)
- Çolakoglu (2.1 million tonnes) (110th)

Science and technology

TÜBITAK is the leading agency for developing science, technology and innovation policies in Turkey. TÜBA is an autonomous scholarly society acting to promote scientific activities in Turkey. TAEK is the official nuclear energy institution of Turkey. Its objectives include academic research in nuclear energy, and the development and implementation of peaceful nuclear tools.

Turkish government companies for research and development in military technologies include Turkish Aerospace Industries, Aselsan, Havelsan, Roketsan, MKE, among others. Turkish Satellite Assembly, Integration and Test Center is a spacecraft production and testing facility owned by the Ministry of National Defence and operated by the Turkish Aerospace Industries. The Turkish Space Launch System is a project to develop the satellite launch capability of Turkey. It consists of the construction of a spaceport, the development of satellite launch vehicles as well as the establishment of remote earth stations.

Construction and contracting sector

The Turkish construction and contracting industry is made up of a large number of businesses, the largest of which was ranked 40th in the world by size. In 2016 a total of 39 Turkish construction/contracting companies were listed in the Top 250 International Contractors List prepared by the Engineering News-Record.

Over half of Turkey's building stock contravenes housing regulations. An amnesty program to register illegal constructed buildings brought in $3.1billion, but the safety issues largely remain. In mid-February 2019, an 8-story building that was registered in the amnesty collapsed killing 21 people. As Turkey is prone to strong earthquakes, poor building quality is even more concerning.

Service sector

Transport

Turkish Airlines, flag carrier of Turkey, has been selected by Skytrax as Europe's best airline for five years in a row (2011–2015). With destinations in 126 countries worldwide, Turkish Airlines is the largest carrier in the world by number of countries served as of 2016.

In 2013 there were ninety-eight airports in Turkey, including 22 international airports. As of 2015, Istanbul Atatürk Airport is the 11th busiest airport in the world, serving 31,833,324 passengers between January and July 2014, according to Airports Council International. The new (third) international HYPERLINK "https://en.wikipedia.org/wiki/%C4% Bstanbul_New_Airport"airport of Istanbul is planned to be the largest airport in the world, with a capacity to serve 150 million passengers per annum. Turkish Airlines, flag carrier of Turkey since 1933, was selected by Skytrax as Europe's best airline for five consecutive years from 2011 and 2015. With 435 destinations (51 domestic and 384 international) in 126 countries worldwide, Turkish Airlines is the largest carrier in the world by number of countries served as of 2016.

A TCDD HT80000 high-speed train of the Turkish State Railways

The total length of the rail network was 10,991 km in 2008, ranking 22nd in the world, including 2,133 km of electrified track. The Turkish State Railways started building high-speed rail lines in 2003. The first line, which has a length of 533 km from Istanbul (Turkey's largest metropolis) via Eskisehir to Ankara (the capital) is under construction and will reduce the travelling time from 6–7 hours to 3 hours and 10 minutes. The Ankara-Eskisehir section of the line, which has a length of 245 km and a projected travel time of 65 minutes, is completed. Trials began on April 23, 2007, and revenue earning service began on March 13, 2009. The Eskisehir-Istanbul section of the line is scheduled to be completed by 2012, and includes the Marmaray tunnel which will enter service in 2012 and establish the first direct railway connection between Europe and Anatolia. Second high-speed rail line, which has length of 212 km between Ankara and Konya become operational in 2011.

As of 2010, the country had a roadway network of 426,951 km, including 2,080 km of expressways and 16,784 km of divided highways.

As of 2010, the Turkish merchant marine included 1,199 ships (604 registered at home), ranking 7th in the world. Turkey's coastline has 1,200 km of navigable waterways.

In 2008, 7,555 kilometres (4,694 mi) of natural gas pipelines and 3,636 kilometres (2,259 mi) of petroleum pipelines spanned the country's territory.

Communications

Türksat operates the Türksat series of communications satellites. Göktürk-1 and Göktürk-2 are Turkey's earth observation satellites for reconnaissance, operated by the Turkish Ministry of National Defence. BILSAT-1 and RASAT are the scientific earth observation satellites operated by the TÜBITAK Space Technologies Research Institute.

As of 2008, there were 17,502,000 operational landline telephones in Turkey, which ranked 18th in the world; while there were 65,824,000 registered mobile phones in the country, which ranked 15th in the world during the same year. The largest landline telephone operator is Türk Telekom, which also owns TTNET, the largest internet service provider in Turkey. The largest mobile phone operators in the country are Turkcell, Vodafone Turkey, Avea and TTNET Mobil.

The telecommunications liberalization process started in 2004 after the creation of the Telecommunication Authority, and is still ongoing. Private sector companies operate in mobile telephony, long distance telephony and Internet access. Additional digital exchanges are permitting a rapid increase in subscribers; the construction of a network of technologically advanced intercity trunk lines, using both fiber-optic cable and digital microwave radio relay, is facilitating communication between urban centers. The remote areas of the country are reached by a domestic satellite system, while the number of subscribers to mobile-cellular telephone service is growing rapidly.

The main line international telephone service is provided by the SEA-ME-WE 3 submarine communications cable and by submarine fiber-optic cables in the Mediterranean Sea and Black Sea that link Turkey with Italy, Greece, Israel, Bulgaria, Romania, and Russia. In 2002, there were

12 Intelsat satellite earth stations; and 328 mobile satellite terminals in the Inmarsat and Eutelsat systems.

Türksat A.S. is the primary communications satellite operator of Turkey, controlling the Turksat series of satellites. TÜBITAK and Turkish Aerospace Industries have developed scientific observation satellites and reconnaissance satellites like the RASAT, Göktürk-1 and Göktürk-2.

As of 2001, there were 16 AM, 107 FM, and 6 shortwave radio stations in the country.

As of 2015, there were 42,275,017 internet users in Turkey, which ranked 15th in the world; while as of 2012, there were 7,093,000 internet hosts in the country, which ranked 16th in the world.

Tourism sector

Ölüdeniz on the Turquoise Coast of Turkey, which is famous for its shades of turquoise and aquamarine, while its beach is an official Blue Flag beach, frequently rated among the top 5 beaches in the world by travelers and tourism journals alike.

Tourism is one of the most dynamic and fastest developing sectors in Turkey. According to travel agencies TUI AG and Thomas Cook, 11 of the 100 best hotels of the world are located in Turkey. In 2005, there were 24,124,501 visitors to the country, who contributed $18.2 billion to Turkey's revenues, with an average expenditure of $679 per tourist. In 2008, the number of visitors rose to 30,929,192, who contributed $21.9 billion to Turkey's revenues. For 2011, the World Tourism Organization (UNWTO) reported 34,654,000 arrivals and US$25 billion in receipts for Turkey. According to the World Travel & Tourism Council, in 2012 travel and tourism made a total contribution of 10.9% to Turkish GDP and supported 8.3% of all jobs in the country. Over the years, Turkey has emerged as a popular tourist destination for many Europeans, competing with Greece, Italy and Spain. Resorts in provinces such as Antalya and Mugla (which are located on the Turkish Riviera) have become very popular among tourists.

Financial sector

Bankalar Caddesi was Istanbul's financial center during the Ottoman period. Completed in 1892, the Ottoman Central Bank headquarters is the first building at right.

The Central Bank of the Republic of Turkey (*Türkiye Cumhuriyet Merkez Bankasý*) was founded in 1930, as a privileged joint-stock company. It possesses the sole right to issue notes. It also has the obligation to provide for the monetary requirements of the state agricultural and commercial enterprises. All foreign exchange transfers are exclusively handled by the central bank.

Originally established as the Ottoman Stock Exchange (*Dersaadet Tahvilat Borsasý*) in 1866, and reorganized to its current structure at the beginning of 1986, the Istanbul Stock Exchange (ISE) is the sole securities market of Turkey. During the 19th and early 20th centuries, Bankalar Caddesi (Banks Street) in Istanbul was the financial center of the Ottoman Empire, where the headquarters of the Ottoman Central Bank (established as the *Bank-i Osmanî* in 1856, and later reorganized as the *Bank-i Osmanî-i Sahane* in 1863) and the Ottoman Stock Exchange (1866) were located. Bankalar Caddesi continued to be Istanbul's main financial district until the 1990s, when most Turkish banks began moving their headquarters to the modern central business districts of Levent and Maslak. In 1995, the Istanbul Stock Exchange moved to its current building in the Istinye quarter. The Istanbul Gold Exchange was also established in 1995. The stock market capitalisation of listed companies in Turkey was valued at $161,537,000,000 in 2005 by the World Bank.

Until 1991, establishing a private sector bank in Turkey was subject to strict government controls and regulations. On 10 October 1991 (ten days before the general elections of 20 October 1991) the ANAP government of Prime Minister Mesut Yilmaz gave special permissions to five prominent businessmen (who had close links to the government) to establish their own small-scale private banks. These were *Kentbank* (owned by Süzer); *Park Yatirim Bankasi* (owned by Karamehmet); *Toprakbank* (owned by Toprak); *Bank Ekspres* (owned by Betil); and *Alternatif Bank* (owned by Doðan.) They were followed by other small-scale private banks established between 1994 and 1995, during the DYP government of Prime Minister Tansu Çiller, who introduced drastic changes to the banking laws and regulations; which made it very easy to establish a bank in Turkey, but also opened many loopholes in the system. In 1998, there were 72 banks in Turkey; most of which were owned by construction companies that used them as financial assets for siphoning money into their other operations. As a result, in 1999 and 2001, the DSP government of Prime Minister Bülent Ecevit had to face two major economic crises that were caused mostly by the weak and loosely regulated banking sector; the growing trade deficit; and the devastating Izmit earthquake of 17 August 1999. The Turkish lira, which was pegged to the U.S. dollar prior to the crisis of 2001, had to be floated, and lost an important amount of its value. This financial breakdown reduced the number of banks to 31. Prime Minister Bülent Ecevit had to call the renowned economist Kemal Dervis to tidy up the economy and especially the weak banking system so that a similar economic crisis would not happen again.

At present, the Turkish banking sector is among the strongest and most expansive in East Europe, the Middle East and Central Asia. During the past decade since 2001, the Turkish lira has also gained a considerable amount of value and maintained its stability, becoming an internationally exchangeable currency once again (in line with the inflation that dropped to single-digit figures since 2003.) The economy grew at an average rate of 7.8% between 2002 and 2005. Fiscal deficit is benefiting (though in a small amount) from large industrial privatizations. Banking came under stress beginning in October 2008 as Turkish banking authorities warned state-run banks against the pullback of loans from the larger financial sectors. More than 34% of the assets in the Turkish banking sector are concentrated in the Agricultural Bank (*Ziraat Bankasi*), Housing Bank (*Yapi Kredi Bankasi*), Isbank (*Türkiye is Bankasi*) and Akbank. The five big state-owned banks were restructured in 2001. Political involvement was minimized and loaning policies were changed. There are also numerous international banks, which have branches in Turkey. A number of Arabian trading banks, which practice an Islamic banking, are also present in the country.

Government regulations passed in 1929 required all insurance companies to reinsure 30% of each policy with the *Millî Reasürans T.A.S.* (National Reinsurance Corporation) which was founded on February 26, 1929. In 1954, life insurance was exempted from this requirement. The insurance market is officially regulated through the Ministry of Commerce.

After years of low levels of foreign direct investment (FDI), in 2007 Turkey succeeded in attracting $21.9 billion in FDI and is expected to attract a higher figure in following years. A series of large privatizations, the stability fostered by the start of Turkey's EU accession negotiations, strong and stable growth, and structural changes in the banking, retail, and telecommunications sectors have all contributed to the rise in foreign investment.

In recent years, the chronically high inflation has been brought under control and this has led to the launch of a new currency, the "New Turkish lira", on January 1, 2005, to cement the acquisition of the economic reforms and erase the vestiges of an unstable economy. On January 1, 2009, the New Turkish lira was renamed once again as the "Turkish lira", with the introduction of new banknotes and coins.

Largest companies

In 2014, 12 Turkish companies were listed in the Forbes Global 2000 list - an annual ranking of the top 2000 public companies in the world by Forbes magazine. Banking industry leads with 5 companies in the list followed by telecommunication industry which has 2 companies in the list. There are also 2 conglomerates followed by transportation and beverages industries with 1 companies each. As of 2014, listed companies were:

External trade and investment

As of 2016, the main trading partners of Turkey are Germany, Russia and the United Kingdom, UAE, Iraq, Italy and China, many being top in both export as well as import. Turkey has taken advantage of a customs union with the European Union, signed in 1995, to increase industrial production for exports, while benefiting from EU-origin foreign investment into the country. In addition to Customs Union, Turkey has free-trade agreements with 22 countries.

A very large aspect of Turkey trade revolves around the automotive industry, where its top exports are cars, accounting for $13.2 billion. Other top exports from the country are gold, delivery trucks, vehicle parts and jewelry, which are respectively, $6.96 billion, $5.04 billion, $4.64 billion, and $3.39 billion. These values are calculated using the 1992 revision of the Harmonized System classification. Comparatively, it imports many of the same industries, such as, gold valued at $17.1 billion, refined petroleum at $9.8 billion, cars at $8.78 billion, vehicle parts at $6.34 billion and scrap iron at $5.84 billion.

Turkey is also a source of foreign direct investment in central and Eastern Europe and the CIS, with more than $1.5 billion invested. 32% has been invested in Russia, primarily in the natural resources and construction sector, and 46% in Turkey's Black Sea neighbors, Bulgaria and Romania. Turkish companies also have sizable FDI stocks in Poland, at about $100 million.

The construction and contracting companies have been significant players, such as Enka, Tekfen, Gama, and Üçgen Ýnþaat, as well as the three industrial groups, Anadolu Efes Group, ÞiþeCam Group and Vestel Group.

Natural resources

Energy

The energy sector is the main source of greenhouse gas emissions by Turkey and contributes to climate change in Turkey, which is in turn affecting the economy by increasing droughts, which reduce agriculture and hydropower in Turkey.

Petroleum and natural gas

Turkey is an oil and natural gas producer, but the level of production by the state-owned TPAO is not enough to make the country self-sufficient, which makes Turkey a net importer of both oil and gas.

The pipeline network in Turkey included 1,738 kilometres (1,080 mi) for crude oil, 2,321 kilometres (1,442 mi) for petroleum products, and 708 kilometres (440 mi) for natural gas in 1999. The Baku–Tbilisi–Ceyhan pipeline, the second-longest oil pipeline in the world, was inaugurated on May 10, 2005. The pipeline delivers crude oil from the Caspian Sea basin to the port of Ceyhan on Turkey's Mediterranean coast, from where it is distributed with oil tankers to the world's markets. The planned Nabucco Pipeline will also pass from Turkey and provide the European Union member states with natural gas from the Caspian Sea basin. The Blue Stream, a major trans-Black Sea gas pipeline, is operational since November 17, 2005, and delivers natural gas from Russia to Turkey. The Tabriz–Ankara pipeline is a 2,577-kilometre-long (1,601-mile) natural gas pipeline, which runs from Tabriz in northwestern Iran to Ankara in Turkey. The pipeline was commissioned on July 26, 2001. In Erzurum, the South Caucasus Pipeline, which was commissioned on May 21, 2006, is linked to the Iran-Turkey pipeline. In the future, these two pipelines will be among the main supply routes for the planned Nabucco Pipeline from Turkey to Europe.

Nuclear energy

To cover the increasing energy needs of its population and ensure the continued raising of its living standards, Turkey plans to build several nuclear power plants. Following the construction of experimental reactors, proposals to build large scale nuclear power plants were presented as early as in the 1950s by Turkish Atomic Energy Authority, but plans were repeatedly canceled even after bids were made by interested manufacturers because of high costs and safety concerns. Turkey has always chosen CANDU reactors because they burn natural uranium which is cheap and available locally and because they can be refueled online. Turkey's first nuclear power plants are expected to be built in Mersin's Akkuyu district on the Mediterranean coast; in Sinop's Inceburun district on the Black Sea coast; and in Kirklareli's Igneada district on the Black Sea coast.

Geothermal energy

Turkey has the fifth-highest direct utilization and capacity of geothermal power in the world.

Energy security

Turkey is a partner country of the EU INOGATE energy programme, which has four key topics: enhancing energy security, convergence of member state energy markets on the basis of EU internal energy market principles, supporting sustainable energy development, and attracting investment for energy projects of common and regional interest.

The proportion of renewable energy in Turkey is twice the EU average, at around 25–26%. Turkey plans to raise this to 30% by 2023.

The share of renewable energy, which serves as one of the most important pillars of the National Energy and Mine Policy and led by hydro, wind and solar energy, reached 32 percent in the third quarter of 2017, surpassing the target of 30 percent that was set for 2023.

Turkey led the way in Europe with an increase of 1.79 GW in solar capacity making the country one of the most promising markets in terms of solar business.

Minerals

Turkey is the tenth-ranked producer of minerals in the world in terms of diversity. Around 60 different minerals are currently produced in Turkey. The richest mineral deposits in the country are boron salts, Turkey's reserves amount to 72% of the world's total. According to the CIA World Factbook, other natural resources include coal, iron ore, copper, chromium, uranium, antimony, mercury, gold, barite, borate, celestine (strontium), emery, feldspar, limestone, magnesite, marble, perlite, pumice, pyrites (sulfur), clay, arable land, hydropower, and geothermal power.

Environment

With the establishment of the Turkish Environment Ministry on August 9, 1991 (currently the Ministry of Environment and Urban Planning), Turkey began to make significant progress addressing some of its most important environmental problems. The most dramatic improvements were significant reductions of air pollution in Istanbul and Ankara. The most urgent needs are for water treatment plants, waste water treatment facilities, solid waste management and the conservation of biodiversity.

Regional disparities

The country's wealth is mainly concentrated in the northwest and west, while the east and southeast suffer from poverty, lower economic production and higher levels of unemployment. However, in line with the continuous economic growth in Turkey during the recent decade, parts of Anatolia began reaching a higher economic standard. These cities are known as the Anatolian Tigers

Critical Observations of present status of Economy of Turkey

(1) The economy of Turkey is an emerging market economy as defined by IMF. Turkey is among the world's developed countries according to CAI world Facebook.

(2) Turkey is defined as one of the World's new industrial country.

(3) The country is among the world's leading producers of agricultural products, textiles, motor vehicles, transportation equipment, construction materials, consumer electronics and home appliances.

(4) In 2018, Turkey went through a currency and debt crisis, characterized by the Turkish Lira plunging in value, high inflation, rising borrowing cost and correspondingly rising loan defaults. This crisis was caused by the Turkish economy's excessive current account deficit and foreign currency debt, in combination with the ruling Justice & Development Party's increasing authoritarianism and President Erdogan's unorthodox ideas about interest rate policy.

(5) Turkey is the founding member of OECD (1961) AND G-7 major economies (1999). Turkey is a party to the European Union – Turkey Customs Union. Mean graduate pay was $10.02 per man hour in 2010. Turkey's labour participation of 56.1% is the lowest of OECD states which have rate 74%.

(6) Turkey's financial capital Istanbul, had a total of 37 billionaires in 2003, ranking 5th in the world.

(7) Turkey's Savings rate is low. Under the government of Recep Erdogan, Turkey has been running huge and growing current account deficit reaching $7.1 billion by January 2008. While the rolling twelve month deficit rose to $51.6 billion which is the largest current account deficit in the world.

(8) The economy has relied on capital inflows to fund private sector excess, with Turkey's Banks and big firms borrowing heavily, often in foreign currency. Turkey must find about $200 billion a year to fund its wide current account deficit and maturing debt, always risk of inflows drying ups having foreign currency reserves of just $85 billion.

(9) Turkey has been complying with 60% criteria public debt stock since 2004, the budget deficit decreased from more than 10% to less than 3% during 2002 to 2011.

(10) International Credit rating Agency Moody's Investors Services upgraded Turkey's rating one notch. In 2012, Credit rating of Finch upgraded Turkey's credit rating to investment grade after 18 year gap. Moody's investment Service in 2013, lifted Turkey's government bond rating to lowest investment grade. In 2018, Moody's downgraded Turkey's sovereign debt into junk status. In May 2018, S & Ps cut Turkey's debt rating further into junk territory, citing widening concern about the outlook for inflation amid a self-off in the Turkish lira currency.

(11) In May 2018, Moody's Investors Services lowered its estimate for growth of Turkey's economy in 2018 from 4% to 2.5% and 3.5% to 2% in 2019.

(12) With policy of Recep Erdogan fueling the construction sector, where many of his business allies are active, Turkey as of May 2018 had around 2 million unused houses, blocking worth three times average annual new housing sales.

(13) In 2018, Turkish currency and debt crisis ended a period of growth under Erdogan led government since 2003, built largely on a construction boom fueled by easy credit and government spending.

(14) On 10-08-2018, Turkish lira nosedived following Trump's tweet about doubling tariffs on Turkish steel and aluminum that day. Currency weakened 17% and has lost nearly 40% of its value against $ till that time. The crash of Lira has sent ripples-through global markets, putting more pressures on the euro and increasing investors' risk aversion to emerging market currencies across the board. On August 13, South African rand slumped nearly 10%. Lira crisis spotlighted deeper concerns about the Turkey's economy that have long signaled turmoil long along. By end of 2018, Turkey went in recession. Turkish economy reduced by 2.4% in the last quarter of 2018. Lira shrunk down to 30% against US dollar in 2018.

(15) Turkey constructed 22 dams. Ataturk dam is the largest in the southeastern Anatolia project. Out of 22 projects, 19 are hydraulic power plants, and make provision of irrigation of 1.82 hectares of land. Total cost of the project is estimated at $32 billion. Total installed capacity of power plants is 7476 MW and projected annual energy production reaches 27 TWH.

(16) Turkish is the largest producer of cherries, apricots, figs and promenades. Turkey is the self-sufficient in food production since

1980s. In 1989 total production of wheat was 16.2 million tonnes and barley 3.44 million tonnes. Since 1980, agriculture has been in a state of decline in terms of its share in the total economy. Turkish agriculture emits green-house gas and suffers from climate change in Turkey.

(17) Agriculture sector accounted for 29.5% of employees in 2009. 85% of agriculture holdings were under 10 hectares and 57% of these were fragmented into four or more non-contiguous plots. Many old agricultural attitudes remain widespread.

(18) The livestock industry showed little improvement in productivity. Livestock products include meat, milk, wool and eggs contributed to more than 1/3 of the value of agricultural output. Fishing is another important part of the economy. In 2005 Turkish fisheries harvested 545,673 tons of fish and aquaculture.

(19) EU imported fruit and vegetables from Turkey worth euro 738.4 million in September 2016.

(20) There are 180 million trees covering 700,000 hectares with a production of 500000 tons of table olives and 300000 tonnes of olive oil. Exports are 70000 tonnes of table olive and 60000 tons of olive oil a year.

(21) Turkish brands are like Bako and Vessel are among the largest products of consumer electronics and home appliances in Europe.

(22) Turkish companies made clothing exports worth $13.98 billion in 2006.

(23) Turkish automobiles companies like TEMSA, BMC are among the world's largest vans, bus, and truck manufacturers. In 2008, Turkey produced 1225400 motor vechicles. Exports were over $22.94 billion of vehicles and components in 2008.

(24) Turkey's annual auto exports, including trucks and buses surpassed 1 million units in 2016. Turkey exported 1.14 million units in 2016. 80% production was exported.

(25) Turkey has many modern armament manufacturers. Annual exports reached $ 1.6 billion in 2014. Turkey recently launched domestically built new military/intelligence satellites including a 0.8 m resolution reconnaissance satellite for use by Turkish armed forces.

(26) Total production of steel was 29 million tonnes. Turkey's crude steel production reached 34.1 million tons in 2011.

(27) Tuba is an autonomous scholarly society for developing science, technology and innovation policies in Turkey. TAEK is official nuclear energy institution of Turkey. Its objective includes academic research in nuclear energy and the development and implementation of peaceful nuclear industries, satellite assembly, owned by Ministry of National Defence and operated by Turkish aerospace industries.

(28) Turkish construction and contracting industry is made up of a large number of business. Over half of Turkey's building stock contravenes housing regulations. An amnesty program to register illegal constructed buildings bought in \$3.1 billion but safety issues largely remain. In mid-February 2019, an eight store building collapsed killing 21 people. Turkey is prone to strong earthquake.

(29) There are 98 airports in Turkey out of which 22 airports are international. Total length of the rail network was 10991 km in 2008. 2133 km were electrified tracks. Turkish State Railways started building high-speed rail-lines in 2003.

As of 2010, Turkish Merchant Marine included 1199 ships. Turkey's coastline has 1200 km of navigable waterways.

(30) As of 2008, there were 17,502,000 operational landline telephones in Turkey. 65,824,000 mobiles registered.

(31) Tourism is one of the most dynamic and fastest sector in Turkey. There were 24,124,501 visitors to the country who contributed \$18.2 billion to Turkey's revenues. With an average expenditure of \$679 per tourist. Tourists rose to 30 million in 2008. World Tourism Organization reported 36.654 million arrivals and \$25 billion in receipts in 2012. Total contribution works out 10.9% GDP and supporting 8.3% of workforce.

(32) The Central Bank of the Republic of turkey founded in 1930. Stock Market Capitalization of listed companies in Turkey was \$ 161.537 billion in 2005. First private sector bank was established in Turkey in 1991. Five eminent businessmen were given permission to open private sector bank. Turkish banking is the strongest and the most expensive in East Europe, Middle East and Central Asia.

(33) In 2007, FDI was \$219 billion. As of 2016, main trading partners of Turkey are Germany, Russia, UK, UAE, Iraq, Italy and China. Investment in Europe was \$1.5 billion out of which 32% in Russia.

(34) Turkey is the producer of minerals. About 60 different minerals are produced.

(35) The country's wealth is mainly concentrated in the north east and west, while east and Southeast suffer from poverty, lower economic production and high level of unemployment. But economic growth gradually began reaching a higher economic standard. These cities are known as Anatolian Tigers.

(36) Turkish currency: Turkish lira

(37) Financial year: Calendar year

(38) Trade Organization: G20, OECD, EC Customers, WTO, ECO, BSEC, ABB, EU

(39) Country Group: Developing/Emerging, Upper-middle Class income

(40) Population: 8.20 crores

(41) GDP: $743.708 billion Nominal, $2.347 trillion PPP in 2019

(42) GDP Growth: 7.5% in 2017, 2.8% in 2018, 0.0% in 2019 3% in 2020 forecast

(43) GDP per capita: $8958 Nominal $28264 PPP

(44) GDP by Sector: Agriculture 8.6%, Industry 27.1% and Services 64.3% in 2016

(45) Inflation: 12.6% high on account of increased borrowing of foreign currency debts and high spending. Austerity measures required.

(46) Population below poverty line: 41.3%

(47) Labour Force: 3.3 crores (40.24% of population. Very low)

(48) Labour Force by Occupation: Agriculture 17.7%, Industries 29% Services 53.3%

(49) Unemployment 13.3% in 2019 27.4% youth unemployment in 2019 too high. May be causing unrest in the country. President Erdogan to look into this issue.

(50) Average gross salary: $573 monthly and $ 412 net in 2018

(51) Exports: $180.2 billion

(52) Export Goods: Apparel, food stuffs, textiles, metal manufacturing, transport equipment

(53) Import goods: machinery, chemicals, semi finish goods, transport equipment

(54) FDI $180.3 billion in 2017Abroad: 47.44 billion

(55) Current Account -27.6 billion

(56) Gross external debt: $452.4 billion in 2017 FDI investment abroad: $47.44 billion. External 60% of GDP.

(57) Public debt: 26.5% of GDP

(58) Budget balance -1.5% of GDP Revenue: $172.8 billion and Expenses: $185.8 billion

(59) Foreign Reserves: $104.8 billion

(60) Credit Rating: S& Ps B+, Moody Ba, Fitch BB, SCOPE BB-

Conclusion

Turkey has 8 crore population and Turkey is developing/emerging and middle income economy. There was currency and debt crisis in Turkey in 2018. Turkey President should effectively manage Turkey's economy.

Turkey President Mr. Recep Erdogan is however very aggressive in nature and he wants to control the political policy of the other countries. He is a dominated personality and interfere with the affairs of some countries.

Erdogan sent his military to Syria for attack on terrorists thereby spent lot of energy and financial resources which result in economic crisis in that country.

Turkey is a member of European Union. As per the Agreement between EU and turkey in 2016, Turkey agreed to accommodate refugees from other countries in consideration of the financial assistance given to it by EU. Recently, he unilaterally gave ultimatum to the EU that if EU countries will not give military assistance to Turkey in its attack on Syria, he will release this Borders with European countries to send refugees to their countries in hundreds of thousand refugees and European countries will have to accommodate them. European countries did not agree to this proposal of military assistance to Turkey in its fight with Syria. Erdogan is a very hot temper man who released Turkey's Boarder with Greece. Thousands of refugees started attacking Greece Border to take entry into Greece. Greece army ruthlessly prevented them from entering in Greece. Attacks were made by refugees with arms, through water. But refugees are not successful in their entry in Greece. Erdogan's plan is completely failed as EU strongly stand in favour of Greece.

There is no reason for Erdogan to offer military help to Saraj Government to fight against Haftar military. This is prohibited by UN. In-spite of this Erdogan interferes in this affairs but country like Egypt and UAE are strongly opposing to Turkey's aggressive policy and will stand in opposition to Erdogan in this fight and military attack.

Erdogan is trying to have good relationship with Russia on Syrian issue and with USA on military assistance issue. But he is not successful. Erdogan took AS400 advanced fighters from Russia. USA strongly opposed to this movement. In spite of that Erdogan was firm on his agreement with Russia. USA imposed financial sanctions on Turkey. Turkey's economy was vulnerable in 2018 on currency and debt crisis. USA Sanctions fueled fire to this economic situation and country's economic position has become more vulnerable.

In order to show his authority and control over Islamic countries like Pakistan, Iran and others, Erdogan took Pakistan side on abolition of Article 370 in Kashmir by the Government of India. Secondly, Citizen Amendment Act and NRR were also opposed by Erdogan and has conflict with India on political issues. Erdogan has no right to interfere with India's matter. He has spoiled relation with India on these India's internal issue unnecessarily.

Erdogan should concentrate on his country's internal matters instead of interfering in the internal matters of other countries and should make his country financially strong.

21

Economy of Israel

Until 1948, Jews have to continuously fight for their existence. Jews were settled mainly in the Arab gulf. Arab had hatred towards Jews and did not want to give them independent state for settlement. Brave leaders of Jews continuously fight with Arab Empire in Palestine and Jordon. Most of the times, Jews have to work as slaves of Arab. In the Second World War, Jews were kept in the Dark Custody in the Jail by Nazis and Hitler killed thousands of Jews in the Jail ruthlessly. In Arab-Jews War in 1948, Jews won the battle and set up a separate independent. Jews settled in the other countries were invited in Israel. Jews were very educated and research minded and they made great progress in the agriculture. Except imports of some foodgrains from other countries, Israel is self-sufficient in agriculture. Textiles is the another source of Jews in addition to jewel cutting and polishing. American Jews are very wealthy and they were financing the US economy. Relation of Israel with West Bank, Gaza Strip and Palestine including Jerusalem are generally normal except the suicide bomb attacks on Israel by Palestinian Fatah and Hamas. Palestinian economy is completely dependent on Israeli. When Israel imposes restrictions on jobs by the Palestine people in Israel, the economy of Palestine scatters. Israeli economy also depends on Palestine economy. There are various Compromise and Peace negotiations between Israeli Prime Minister and Palestinian Prime Minister Mr. Abbas but no compromise has reached. Recently, US President unilaterally declared Jerusalem as the Capital of Israel and establish its diplomatic office in Jerusalem. But this was strongly opposed by Palestinian government, EU, UN, Russia, China and all other countries. President Trump has also taken initiative for compromise between Israel and Palestine by giving a proposal of offering $4 billion aid to Palestine on the condition that Palestine should agree that Jerusalem is the Capital of Israel. But Palestine refused to do so rightly on the ground that the issue is not economical but political. As per 2007 Accord, Palestine declarers the Eastern Jerusalem is and will be the Capital of Palestine and there will be no compromise on recognizing Jerusalem as the capital of Israel on account of issue of protecting rights of refugees there. Israel has unilaterally and illegally constructed buildings in Gaza Strip for accommodating Jews refugees there by forcibly removing Palestinians from these territories. Under the US Blind support to Israel, Israel is becoming more and more aggressive and the possibility of materializing the Peace Accord between Palestine and Israel is very bleak.

The economy of Israel is a highly advanced free-market, primarily knowledge-based economy. Israel ranks 22 on the latest report of the UN's Human Development Index, which places it in the category of "Very Highly Developed", allowing the country to enjoy a higher standard of living than many other Western countries. The prosperity of Israel's advanced economy allows the country to have a sophisticated welfare state, a modern infrastructure, and a high-technology sector competitively on par with Silicon Valley. Israel has the second-largest number of startup companies in the world after the United States, and the third-largest number of NASDAQ-listed companies after the U.S. and China. Intel, Microsoft, and Apple built their first overseas research and development facilities in Israel, and other high-tech multi-national corporations, such as IBM, Google, HP, Cisco Systems, Facebook and Motorola have opened R&D centres in the country.

The country's major economic sectors are high-technology and industrial manufacturing; the Israeli diamond industry is one of the world's centers for diamond cutting and polishing, amounting to 23.2% of all exports Relatively poor in natural resources, Israel depends on imports of petroleum, raw materials, wheat, motor vehicles, uncut diamonds and production inputs, though the country's nearly total reliance on energy imports may change in the future with recent discoveries of natural gas reserves off its coast on the one hand and the leading role of the Israeli solar energy industry on the other.

Israel's quality university education and the establishment of a highly motivated and educated populace is largely responsible for ushering in the country's high technology boom and rapid economic development. With its strong educational infrastructure and high quality incubation system for new cutting edge ideas to create value driven goods and services has allowed the country to create a high concentration of high-tech companies across the country financially backed by a strong venture capital industry. Its central high technology hub "Silicon Wadi" is considered second in importance only to its Californian counterpart. Numerous Israeli companies have been acquired by global corporations for their reliable and quality corporate personnel.

With such an impressive track record for creating profit driven technologies, Israel has become the first choice for many of world's leading entrepreneurs, investors, and industry giants. The economic dynamism of Israel has attracted attention from international business leaders such as Microsoft founder Bill Gates, investor Warren Buffett, real estate developer and U.S. President Donald Trump and telecommunications giant Carlos Slim. Each entrepreneur has praised Israel's economy and invested heavily across numerous Israeli industries beyond their traditional business activities and investments back in their home nations. In 2007, American investor Warren Buffett's holding company Berkshire Hathaway bought an Israeli company, Iscar, its first acquisition outside the United States, for $4 billion. The country was also the destination for Berkshire Hathaway's first investment outside the United States when it acquired ISCAR Metalworking.

In September 2010, Israel was invited to join the OECD. Israel has also signed free trade agreements with the European Union, the United States, the European Free Trade Association, Turkey, Mexico, Canada, Ukraine, Jordan, Egypt, and on 18 December 2007, became the first non-Latin-American country to sign a free trade agreement with the Mercosur trade bloc. Israel is also a major tourist destination, with 3.6 million foreign tourists visiting it in 2017.

History

The British Mandate of Palestine that came into effect in 1920 aimed at restricting land purchases by Jewish immigrants. For this reason the Jewish population was initially more urban and had a higher share in industrial occupations. This particular development resulted economically in one of the few growth miracles of the region whereby the structure of firms was determined mainly by private entrepreneurs rather than by the government. The first survey of the Dead Sea in 1911, by the Russian Jewish engineer Moshe Novomeysky, led to the establishment of Palestine Potash Ltd. in 1930, later renamed the Dead Sea Works. In 1923, Pinhas Rutenberg was granted an exclusive concession for the production and distribution of electric power. He founded the Palestine Electric Company, later the Israel Electric Corporation between 1920 and 1924. From 1924, trade fairs were held in Tel Aviv. The Levant Fair was inaugurated in 1932.

After independence

After statehood, Israel faced a deep economic crisis. As well as having to recover from the devastating effects of the 1948 Arab–Israeli War, it also had to absorb hundreds of thousands of Jewish refugees from Europe and almost a million from the Arab world. Israel was financially overwhelmed and faced a deep economic crisis, which led to a policy of austerity from 1949 to 1959. Unemployment was high, and foreign currency reserves were scarce.

In 1952, Israel and West Germany signed an agreement stipulating that West Germany was to pay Israel for the persecution of Jews during the Holocaust, and compensate for Jewish property stolen by the Nazis. Over the next 14 years, West Germany paid Israel 3 billion marks (equivalent to US$111.5bn in modern currency). The reparations became a decisive part of Israel's income, comprising as high as 87.5% of Israel's income in 1956. In 1950, the Israeli government launched Israel Bonds for American and Canadian Jews to buy. In 1951, the final results of the bonds program exceeded $52 million. Additionally, many American Jews made private donations to Israel, which in 1956 were thought to amount to $100 million a year. In 1957, bond sales amounted to 35% of Israel's special development budget. Later in the century Israel became significantly reliant on economic aid from the United States, a country which also became Israel's most important source of political support internationally.

The proceeds from these sources was invested in industrial and agricultural development projects, which allowed Israel to become economically self-sufficient. Among the projects made possible by the aid was the Hadera power plant, the Dead Sea Works, the National Water Carrier, port development in Haifa, Ashdod, and Eilat, desalination plants, and national infrastructure projects.

After statehood, priority was given to establishing industries in areas slated for development, among them Lachish, Ashkelon, the Negev and Galilee. The expansion of Israel's textile industry was a consequence of the development of cotton growing as a profitable agricultural branch. By the late 1960s, textiles were one of the largest industrial branches in Israel, second only to the foodstuff industry. Textiles constituted about 12% of industrial exports, becoming the second-largest export branch after polished diamonds. In the 1990s, cheap East Asian labor decreased the profitability of the sector. Much of the work was subcontracted to 400 Israeli Arab sewing shops. As these closed down, Israeli firms, among them Delta, Polgat, Argeman and Kitan, began doing their sewing work in Jordan and Egypt, usually under the QIZ arrangement. In the early 2000s, Israeli companies had 30 plants in Jordan. Israeli exports reached $370 million a year, supplying such retailers and designers as Marks & Spencer, The Gap, Victoria's Secret, Walmart, Sears, Ralph Lauren, Calvin Klein, and Donna Karan.

In its first two decades of existence, Israel's strong commitment to development led to economic growth rates that exceeded 10% annually.

Between 1950 and 1963, the expenditure among wage-earner's families rose 97% in real terms. Between 1955 and 1966, per capita consumption rose by 221%. The years after the 1973 Yom Kippur War were a lost decade economically, as growth stalled, inflation soared and government expenditures rose significantly. Also worthy of mention is the 1983 Bank stock crisis. By 1984, the economic situation became almost catastrophic with inflation reaching an annual rate close to 450% and projected to reach over 1000% by the end of the following year. However, the successful economic stabilization plan implemented in 1985 and the subsequent introduction of market-oriented structural reforms reinvigorated the economy and paved the way for its rapid growth in the 1990s and became a model for other countries facing similar economic crises.

Two developments have helped to transform Israel's economy since the beginning of the 1990s. The first is waves of Jewish immigration, predominantly from the countries of the former USSR, that has brought over one million new citizens to Israel. These new Soviet Jewish immigrants, many of them highly educated, had a wellspring of scientific and technical expertise to help spur Israel's burgeoning technology sector, now constitute some 15% of Israel's population. The second development benefiting the Israeli economy is the peace process begun at the Madrid conference of October 1991, which led to the signing of accords and later to a peace treaty between Israel and Jordan (1994).

In the early 2000s, the Israel economy went into a downturn due to the crashing of the global dot-com bubble which bankrupted many startups established during the height of the bubble. The Second Intifada, which cost Israel billions of dollars in security costs, and a decline in investment and tourism, sent unemployment in Israel to the double digits, growth in one quarter of 2000 was 10%. In 2002 the Israeli economy declined in one quarter about 4%. Afterwards Israel managed to create a remarkable recovery by opening up new markets to Israeli exporters farther afield, such as in the rapidly growing countries of East Asia. As well as a rebound in the tech sector with the gradual bottoming out of the dotcom crash and global increase in internet usage worldwide which created a demand for software, and a demand post-9/11 in Security and defense products. Both of which Israel was ready to provide due to early investment in those fields, allowed for a gradual easing of the unemployment situation within the country.

In the past few years there has been an unprecedented inflow of foreign investment in Israel, as companies that formerly shunned the Israeli market now see its potential contribution to their global strategies. In 2006, foreign investment in Israel totaled $13 billion, according to the Manufacturers

Association of Israel. The *Financial Times* said that 'bombs drop, yet Israel's economy grows'. Moreover, while Israel's total gross external debt is US$95 billion, or approximately 41.6% of GDP, since 2001 it has become a net lender nation in terms of net external debt (the total value of assets vs. liabilities in debt instruments owed abroad), which as of June 2012 stood at a significant surplus of US$60 billion. The country also maintains a current account surplus in an amount equivalent to about 3% of its grossed.

Bank of Israel

The Israeli economy withstood the late-2000s recession, registering positive GDP growth in 2009 and ending the decade with an unemployment rate lower than that of many western countries. There are several reasons behind this economic resilience, for example, the fact, as stated above, that the country is a net lender rather than a borrower nation and the government and the Bank of Israel's generally conservative macro-economic policies. Two policies in particular can be cited, one is the refusal of the government to succumb to pressure by the banks to appropriate large sums of public money to aid them early in the crisis, thus limiting their risky behavior. The second is the implementation of the recommendations of the Bach'ar commission in the early to mid-2000s which recommended decoupling the banks' depository- and Investment banking activities, contrary to the then-opposite trend, particularly in the United States, of easing such restrictions which had the effect of encouraging more risk-taking in the financial systems of those countries.

OECD membership

In May 2007, Israel was invited to open accession discussions with the OECD. In May 2010, the OECD voted unanimously to invite Israel to join, despite Palestinian objections. It became a full member on 7 September 2010. The OECD praised Israel's scientific and technological progress and described it as having "produced outstanding outcomes on a world scale."

Challenges

Despite economic prosperity, the Israeli economy faces many challenges, some are short term and some are long term challenges. On the short term its inability to duplicate its success in the telecommunication industry into other growing industries hampers its economic outlooks. Its inability to foster large multinational companies in the last decade also calls into question its ability to employ large numbers of people in advanced industries. On the long term, Israel is facing challenges of high dependency of the growing number of Ultra-Orthodox Jews who have a low level of official labor force participation amongst men, and this situation could lead to a materially lower employment-to-population ratio and a higher dependency ratio in the future. The governor of the Bank of Israel, Stanley Fischer, stated that the growing poverty amongst the Ultra-Orthodox is hurting the Israeli economy. According to the data published by Ian Fursman, 60% of the poor households in Israel are of the Haredi Jews and the Israeli Arabs. Both groups together represent 25–28% of the Israeli population. Organizations such as The Kemach Foundation, Gvahim, Jerusalem Village and The Jerusalem Business Networking Forum are addressing these challenges with job placement services and networking events.

Sectors

Agriculture

In 2017, 2.3% of the country's GDP is derived from agriculture. Of a total labor force of 2.7 million, 2.6% are employed in agricultural production while 6.3% in services for agriculture. While Israel imports substantial quantities of grain (approximately 80% of local consumption), it is largely self-sufficient in other agricultural products and food stuffs. For centuries, farmers of the region have grown varieties of citrus fruits, such as grapefruit, oranges and lemons. Citrus fruits are still Israel's major agricultural export. In addition, Israel is one of the world's leading greenhouse-food-exporting countries. The country exports more than $1.3 billion worth of agricultural products every year, including farm produce as well as $1.2 billion worth of agricultural inputs and technology.

Financial services

Israel has over 100 active venture capital funds operating throughout the country with US$10 billion under management. In 2008, venture capital investment in Israel, rose 19 percent to $1.9 billion.

"Between 1991 and 2000, Israel's annual venture-capital outlays, nearly all private, rose nearly 60-fold, from $58 million to $3.3 billion; companies launched by Israeli venture funds rose from 100 to 800; and Israel's information-technology revenues rose from $1.6 billion to $12.5 billion. By 1999, Israel ranked second only to the United States in invested private-equity capital as a share of GDP. Israel led the world in the share of its growth attributable to high-tech ventures: 70 percent."

Israel's thriving venture capital industry has played an important role in funding the country's booming high-technology sector. The country is now teeming with hundreds of prosperous Israeli private equity and venture capital firms looking to invest in the next potential million or billion dollar business startup. The financial crisis of 2007–08 also affected the availability of venture capital locally. In 2009, there were 63 mergers and acquisitions in the Israeli market worth a total of $2.54 billion; 7% below 2008 levels ($2.74 billion), when 82 Israeli companies were merged or acquired, and 33% lower than 2007 proceeds ($3.79 billion) when 87 Israeli companies were merged or acquired. Numerous Israeli high tech companies have been acquired by global corporations for its reliable corporate management and quality personnel.

Israel also has a small but fast growing hedge fund industry. Within five years between 2007 and 2012, the number of active hedge funds have doubled to 60 while the total asset values that the funds control have quadrupled in the same period. Israel based hedge funds have registered an increase of 162% since 2006 and currently manage a total of $2 billion (₪8 billion) as well as employing about 300 people.

High technology

Weizmann Institute of Science, Rehovot

Science and technology in Israel is one of the country's most highly developed and industrialized sectors. The modern Israeli ecosystem of high technology is highly optimized making up a significant bulk of Israeli economy. The percentage of Israelis engaged in scientific and technological inquiry, and the amount spent on research and development (R&D) in relation to gross domestic product (GDP), is among the highest in the world. Israel ranks fourth in the world in scientific activity, as measured by the number of scientific publications per million citizens. Israeli scientists, engineers, and technicians have contributed to the modern advancement of the natural sciences, agricultural sciences, computer sciences, electronics, genetics, medicine, optics, solar energy and various fields of engineering. Israel is home to major corporate players in the high-tech industry and has one of the world's technologically most literate populations. In 1998, Tel Aviv was named by *Newsweek* as one of the ten technologically most influential cities in the world.

As a result of the country's highly renowned and creative start-up culture, Israel is often referred to as the Start-up Nation (adapted from the book Start-Up Nation, by Dan Senor and Saul Singer) and the "Silicon Valley of the Middle East".

Energy

Coal consumption rose steadily since 1980 when it was negligible. Natural gas consumption was nearly zero in 2003 and has risen steadily since.

Historically, Israel relied on external imports for meeting most of its energy needs, spending an amount equivalent to over 5% of its GDP per year in 2009 on imports of energy products. The transportation sector relies mainly on gasoline and diesel fuel, while the majority of electricity production is generated using imported coal. As of 2013, Israel was importing about 100 million barrels of oil per year. The country possesses negligible reserves of crude oil but does have domestic natural gas resources which were discovered in more significant quantities starting in 2009, after many decades of previously unsuccessful exploration.

Natural gas

Until the early 2000s, natural gas use in Israel was minimal. In the late 1990s, the government of Israel decided to encourage the usage of natural gas because of environmental, cost, and resource diversification reasons. At the time however, there were no domestic sources of natural gas and the expectation was that gas would be supplied from overseas in the form of LNG and by a future pipeline from Egypt (which eventually became the Arish–Ashkelon pipeline). Plans were made for the Israel Electric Corporation to construct several natural gas-driven power plants, for erecting a national gas distribution grid, and for an LNG import terminal.

Recent discoveries

In 2000, a modest discovery was made when a 33-billion-cubic-metre (BCM), or 1,200-billion-cubic-foot, natural-gas field was located offshore Ashkelon, with commercial production starting in 2004. As of 2014 however, this field is nearly depleted—earlier than expected due to increased pumping to partially compensate for the loss of imported Egyptian gas in the wake of unrest associated with the fall of the Mubarak regime in 2011. In 2009, a significant gas find named Tamar, with proven reserves of 223 BCM or 7.9×10^{12} cu ft (307 BCM total proven + probable) was located in deep water approximately 90 km (60 mi) west of Haifa, as well as a smaller 15 BCM (530×10^{9} cu ft) field situated nearer the coastline. Furthermore, results of 3D seismic surveys and test drilling conducted since 2010 have confirmed that an estimated 621 BCM (21.9×10^{12} cu ft) natural-gas deposit named Leviathan exists in a large underwater geological formation nearby the large gas field already discovered in 2009.

The Tamar field began commercial production on 30 March 2013 after four years of development. The supply of gas from Tamar was expected to aid the Israeli economy, which had suffered losses of more than ₪20 billion between 2011 and 2013 resulting from the disruption of gas supplies from neighboring Egypt (and which are not expected to resume due to Egypt's decision to indefinitely suspend its gas supply agreement to Israel). As a result, Israel, as well as its other neighbor Jordan, which also suffered from disruption of gas deliveries from Egypt, had to resort to importing significantly more expensive and polluting liquid heavy fuels as substitute sources of energy. The ensuing energy crisis in Israel was lifted once the Tamar field came online in 2013, while Jordan committed to a US$10 billion, 15-year gas supply deal totaling 45 BCM from the Israeli Leviathan field which is scheduled to come online in late 2019. The agreement is estimated to save Jordan US$600 million per year in energy costs. In 2018, the owners of the Tamar and Leviathan fields announced that they are negotiating an agreement with a consortium of Egyptian firms for the supply of up to 64 BCM of gas over 10 years valued at up to US$15 billion. In early 2012 the Israeli cabinet announced plans to set up a sovereign wealth fund (called "the Israeli Citizens' Fund").

Electricity

Since the founding of the state through the mid-2010s decade, the state-owned utility, Israel Electric Corporation (IEC) had an effective monopoly on power generation in the country. In 2010 the company sold 52,037 GWh of electricity. Until the mid-2010s the country also faced a persistently low operating reserve, which is mostly the result of Israel being an "electricity island". Most countries have the capability of relying on power drawn from producers in adjacent countries in the event of a power shortage. Israel's grid however, is unconnected to those of neighboring countries. This is mostly due to political reasons but also to the considerably less-developed nature of the power systems of Jordan and Egypt, whose systems constantly struggle to meet domestic demand and whose per-capita electric generation is less than one fifth that of Israel's. Nevertheless, while operating reserves in Israel were low, the country possessed sufficient generation and transmission capacity to meet domestic electricity needs and unlike in the countries surrounding it, rolling blackouts have historically been quite rare, even at periods of extreme demand.

Facing increasing demand for electricity and concerned about the low reserve situation, the government of Israel began taking steps to increase the supply of electricity and operating reserve, as well to reduce the monopoly position of the IEC and increase competition in the electricity market starting in second half of the 2000s decade. It instructed the IEC to construct several new power stations and encouraged private investment in the generation sector. By 2015, the IEC's share of total nationwide installed electric generation capacity had fallen to about 75%, with the company then possessing an installed generation capacity of about 13.6 gigawatts (GW). Since 2010, Independent Power Producers have constructed three new gas-fired combined cycle power stations with a total generation capacity of about 2.2 GW, while various industrial concerns constructed on-premises cogeneration facilities with a total electricity output of about 1 GW, and which are licensed by the electric authority to sell surplus electricity to the national grid at competitive rates. Also under construction is a 300 MW pumped storage facility, with two more in planning, plus several solar-powered plants.

In addition to the above steps, Israel and Cyprus are considering implementing the proposed EuroAsia Interconnector project. This consists of laying a 2000MW HVDC undersea power cable between them and between Cyprus and Greece, thus connecting Israel to the greater European power grid. If carried out, this will allow to further increase the country's operating reserve as well as sell surplus electricity abroad.

In 2016, total nationwide electricity production was 67.2 GWh, of which 55.2% was generated using natural gas and 43.8% using coal — the first time the share of electricity production using natural gas exceeded that generated using coal.

Solar power

The Negev Desert is home to the Israeli solar research industry, in particular the National Solar Energy Center and the Arava Valley, which is the sunniest area of Israel.

Solar power in Israel and the Israeli solar energy industry has a history that dates to the founding of the country. In the 1950s, Levi Yissar developed a solar water heater to help assuage an energy shortage in the new country. By 1967 around one in twenty households heated their water with the sun and 50,000 solar heaters had been sold. With the 1970s oil crisis, Harry Zvi Tabor, the father of Israel's solar industry, developed the prototype solar water heater that is now used in over 90% of Israeli homes. Israeli engineers are on the cutting edge of solar energy technology, and its solar companies work on projects around the world.

Industrial manufacturing

Israel has a large industrial capacity with a well-developed chemical industry with many of its products aimed at the export market. Most of the chemical plants are located in Ramat Hovav, the Haifa Bay area and near the Dead Sea. Israel Chemicals is one of largest fertilizer and chemical companies in Israel and its subsidiary, the Dead Sea Works in Sdom is the world's fourth largest producer and supplier of potash products. The company also produces other products such as magnesium chloride, industrial salts, de-icers, bath salts, table salt, and raw materials for the cosmetic industry. One of the country's largest employers is Israel Aerospace Industries which produces mainly aviation, space, and defense products. In 2017 the company had an order backlog of 11.4 billion US dollars. Another large employer is Teva Pharmaceutical Industries, one of the world's largest pharmaceutical companies, employing 40,000 people as of 2011. It specializes in generic and proprietary pharmaceuticals and active pharmaceutical ingredients. It is the largest generic drug manufacturer in the world and one of the 15 largest pharmaceutical companies worldwide. Industrial production of metals, electrical equipment, construction materials, consumer goods, and textiles, as well as food processing also form a significant part of the manufacturing sector.

Diamond industry

Israel is one of the world's three major centers for polished diamonds, alongside Belgium and India. Israel's net polished diamond exports slid 22.8 percent in 2012 as polished diamond exports fell to \$5.56 billion from \$7.2 billion in 2011. Net exports of rough diamonds dropped 20.1 percent to \$2.8 billion and net exports of polished diamonds slipped 24.9 percent to \$4.3 billion, while net rough diamond imports dropped 12.9 percent to \$3.8 billion. Net exports and imports have dropped due to the ongoing Global financial crisis, particularly within the Eurozone and the United States. The United States is the largest market accounting for 36% of overall export market for polished diamonds while Hong Kong remains at second with 28 percent and Belgium at 8 percent coming in third. As of 2016, cut diamonds were Israel's largest export product, comprising 23.2% of all exports.

Defense contracting

Israel is one of the world's major exporters of military equipment, accounting for 10% of the world total in 2007. Three Israeli companies were listed on the 2010 Stockholm International Peace Research Institute index of the world's top 100 arms-producing and military service companies: Elbit Systems, Israel Aerospace Industries and RAFAEL. The Defense industry in Israel is a strategically important sector and a large employer within the country. It is also a major player in the global arms market and is the

11th largest arms exporter in the world as of 2012. Total arms transfer agreements topped 12.9 billion between 2004 and 2011. There are over 150 active defense companies based in the country with combined revenues of more than US$3.5 billion annually. Israeli defense equipment exports have reached 7 billion U.S. dollars in 2012, making it a 20 percent increase from the amount of defense-related exports in 2011. Much of the exports are sold to the United States and Europe. Other major regions that purchase Israeli defense equipment include Southeast Asia and Latin America. India is also major country for Israeli arms exports and has remained Israel's largest arms market in the world. Israel is considered to be the leading UAV exporter in the world. According to the Stockholm International Peace Research Institute, Israeli defense companies were behind 41% of all drones exported in 2001–2011.

Tourism

Tourism is one of Israel's major sources of income in the country, attracting 3.6 million foreign tourists in 2017, yielding a 25 percent growth since 2016 and contributed ₪20 billion to the Israeli economy making it an all-time record. The most popular paid site is Masada.

External trade

In 2016, Israeli goods exports totaled US$55.8 billion. It imported US$61.9 billion worth of goods in the same year. In 2017 total exports (goods and services) amounted to US$102.3 billion, while imports totaled $96.7 billion. Israel usually posts a modest trade deficit in goods. Its main goods imports consist of raw materials, crude oil, production inputs and finished consumer goods. Most of its exports are high-value-added items such as electronic components and other high-technology equipment, tools, and machinery, cut diamonds, refined petrochemicals, and pharmaceuticals. It normally posts a substantial trade surplus in services thanks to tourism and service industries such as software development, engineering services, and biomedical and scientific research and development. Therefore, overall external trade is positive, contributing to a significant current account surplus which as of 2017 stood at 4.7% of GDP,

The United States is Israel's largest trading partner, and Israel is the United States' 26th-largest trading partner; two-way trade totaled some $24.5 billion in 2010, up from $12.7 billion in 1997. The principal U.S. exports to Israel include computers, integrated circuits, aircraft parts and other defense equipment, wheat, and automobiles. Israel's chief exports to the U.S. include cut diamonds, jewelry, integrated circuits, printing machinery, and telecommunications equipment. The two countries signed a free trade agreement (FTA) in 1985 that progressively eliminated tariffs on most goods traded between the two countries over the following ten years. An agricultural trade accord was signed in November 1996, which addressed the remaining goods not covered in the FTA. Some non-tariff barriers and tariffs on goods remain, however. Israel also has trade and cooperation agreements in place with the European Union and Canada, and is seeking to conclude such agreements with a number of other countries, including Turkey, Jordan and several countries in Eastern Europe.

In regional terms, the European Union is the top destination for Israeli exports. In the four-month period between October 2011 and January 2012, Israel exported goods totaling $5 billion to the EU – amounting to 35% of Israel's overall exports. During the same period, Israeli exports to East Asia and the Far East totaled some $3.1 billion.

Until 1995, Israel's trade with the Arab world was minimal due to the Arab League boycott, which was begun against the Jewish community of Palestine in 1945. Arab nations not only refused to have direct trade with Israel (the primary boycott), but they also refused to do business with any corporation that operated in Israel (secondary boycott), or any corporation that did business with a corporation that did business with Israel (tertiary boycott).

Critical Observations of Present Status of Economy of Israel

(1) Economy of Israel is a highly advance free market primarily knowledge-based economy. It ranks 22nd on the latest report of the UN's Human Development Index, which places it in the category of very high developed economy. It is the sophisticated welfare state with its small population of 90.53 lacs. It has a modern infrastructure, a high technology competitively on par with Silicon Valley.

(2) Israel has the second largest number of Start-up companies in the world after US.

(3) Israel's quality university education and the establishment of a high motivated and educated populace is largely responsible for the high technology boom and rapid economic development.

(4) U.S. and other European countries invest large amount in Israeli industries.

(5) On 18 December 2007, Israel became the first non-Latin American country to sign a free trade agreement with the Mercosur Trade Bloc.

(6) British Mandate of Palestine came into effect in 1920 which prohibited land purchases by Jewish immigrants. The Jewish population was initially more urban and had higher share in the industrial operations.

(7) The first survey of the Dead Sea in 1911, by the Russian Jewish engineer Potash Novomeysky led to the establishment of Palestine Potash Ltd. In 1930 later named Dead Sea Works. Palestine Electric Company was founded in 1923.

(8) After statehood, Israel faced a deep economic crisis. To recover from the divesting effects of 1948 Arab-Israel War, it has to absorb hundreds of thousands of Jewish refugees from Europe and almost a million from the Arab World. To face economic crisis, austerity measures were implemented from 1949 to 1959. Unemployment was high and foreign currency reserves were scarce.

(9) In 1952, Israel and West Germany signed an agreement stipulating that West Germany was to pay Israel for Jewish property stolen by Nazis. Over the next 14 years (upto1966) West Germany will pay \$111.5 billion to Israel. This became a decisive factor in Israeli's income, comprising as high as 87.5% Israeli income in 1956.

In 1950, Israeli government launched Israel Bonds to American and Canadian Jews to buy. In 1951, the final results of the bond program exceeded \$52 million. American Jews made private donations to Israel which were \$100 million a year which covers 35% of the Israel's special development budget for investment in agricultural and industrial development projects.

(10) Economic growth rate exceeded 10% annually between 1950 and 1963, the expenditure among the wage earner's families rise 97% in real terms.

(11) The developments have helped to transform Israel's economy since the beginning of the 1990s. The first is the Jewish immigrations. The second development benefiting the Israeli economy. Peace process began and the Madrid Conference of 1991 led to the signing of accords and later to a peace treaty between Jordan and Israel in 1994.

(12) Many Starts-up bankrupted in the early 2000s which was downturn of Israeli economy. Unemployment was in double digit in Israel.

(13) There has been unprecedented inflow of foreign investment totaled \$13 billion.

(14) While Israeli's total gross external debt is $95 billion or approximately 41.6% of GDP. Since 1991, it has become a net lender nation in terms of external debt (total value of assets vs liabilities in debt instruments owed abroad) which stood on June 2012 as a significant surplus of $ 60 billion. The Country also maintains a current account surplus in an amount equivalent to about 3% of its GDP.

(15) Israel became a full member on 07-09-20110 in spite of Palestinian objection of OEDC membership to Israel.

(16) Short term and long term challenges faced by Israel. Small Term challenge is the inability to duplicate its success in the telecommunication industry into other growing industries which hampered its economic outlook.

On the long term, Israel is facing challenges of high dependency of the growing number of ultra-orthodox Jews who have a low level of official labour force participation among men which leads to materially low employment to population ratio and high dependency ratio in future.

(17) In 2007, 2.3% of the country's GDP is derived from agriculture of a total labour force of 2.7 million, 2.6% are employed in agricultural production while 6.3% in services for agriculture. Israel imports substantial quantities of grain (80% of local consumption). It is largely self-sufficient in other agricultural products and food stuff like citrus fruits (grape, oranges and lemon). It is major agricultural export. The country exports more than $1.3 billion worth of agricultural products every year. It also exports agricultural inputs and technology worth $2 billion every year.

(18) Israel has over 100 active venture capital funds operating through the country with $10 billion under management. In 2008, Venture Capital investment in Israel rose 19 per cent to $1.9 billion. Between 1991 and 2000, Israel's annual venture capital outlays rose 60 fold from $58 million to3.3 billion. Companies rose from 100 to 800 and information technology revenues rise from $ 1.6 billion to $12.5 billion.

(19) In 2009, there were 63 mergers and acquisitions in the Israeli market worth a total $ 2.54 billion- 7% below that of 2008 levels and 33% lower than 2007 proceeds of $3.79 billion.

(20) Number of active hedge fund between 2007 1nd 2012 doubled to 60 currently managed with total value of $2 billion and employing 300 people.

(21) Historically, Israel relied on external imports for meeting most of its energy needs, spending 5% of its GDP in 2009 on import of energy products.

(22) In 2002, a modest discovery was made when a 32 billion cubic metric or 1200 billion cubic foot natural gas field was found.

(23) Israel is one of the major centers of polished diamonds alongwith Belgium and India. Israel's net polished diamond exports fell to 15.56 billion in 2002 from $ 7.2 billion in 2011. Diamond imports slipped 24.9% to $4.3 billion while net rough diamond imports dropped 12.9% to $3.8 billion due to Global Finance Crisis in Europe & US.

(24) Israel is the exporter of military equipment 10% of the world total in 2007. Israel Aerospace industry and RAFAEL. Defence industry is strategically important sector with large employees in the country.

(25) Israel is major player in the global market with 11th largest arms exporter in the world as of 2012. Total arms transfer agreements topped $12.9 billion between 2004 and 2011. 150 active defence companies in the country combined revenue $3.5 billion annually. Israeli defence equipment exports reached $7 billion in 2012 which was 20% higher than 2011. India is the major country for Israel's arms exports.

(26) Arab League boycott trade with Israel from 1948 i.e. independence of Israel statehood. It also boycott any company cooperating with Israel (tertiary boycott) as the financial sanctions.

(27) Currency : Israeli Shekel

(28) Fiscal year: Calendar year

(29) Trade Organizations: AIIB, UN, OECD, WTO

(30) Country Group: Developed/ Advanced, High Income Country

(31) GDP $387.717 billion Nominal & $ 354.197 billion PPP in 2019

(32) GDP Growth: 3.6% in 2017, 3.4% in 2018 3.1% in 2019 3.1% in 2020 forecast

(33) Population 90.53 lacs or 9.053 million.

(34) GDP per Capita: $ 42823 Nominal & $39121 PPP in 2019

(35) GDP by Sector: Agriculture2.3%, Industries 26.61% & Industries 69.5% in 2017

(36) Inflation 1.3% - 2020 Forecast

(37) Population below poverty line: 24.8%

(38) Labour Force 4.162 million or 41.62 lacs

(39) Labour Force by Occupation: Agriculture 5.1%, Industry 17.3% and 81.6%

(40) Unemployment: 3.4%. It is fluctuating and at times rises to double digit

(41) Main Industries: High Technology, Telecommunication, textiles, Diamond cutting and polishing, aerospace and defence, pharmaceuticals, chemical products.

(42) Exports: $60.6 billion

(43) Export Goods: Cut diamonds, refined petroleum, pharmaceuticals, machinery & equipment, textiles and aerospace, military equipments

(44) Imports: $66.76 billion. Trade Deficit $6.16 i.e.1.59% of GDP

(45) Imports Goods: raw materials, rough diamonds, military equipment, crude petroleum

(46) FDI $82.82 billion in 2011

(47) Gross External debt: $97.463 i.e.25.18% of GDP

(48) Public debt: 59.8% of GDP

(49) Budget Balance -3%

(50) Revenue $68.29 billion & Expenses $ 75.65 billion. Fiscal deficit 1.9% of GDP

(51) Foreign Reserves: $115.782 million

(52) Current Rating: S& Ps AA-, Outlook Stable, Moody's A1, Outlook Positive. Finch A1, Outlook Stable

Conclusion

Israelis have established a statehood on the heart of Arab Gulf states which are its traditional enemies. Arab Countries want to destroy existence of Israel state from the Arab land. There are missile attacks on Israel by Iran and other countries. Israel has a strong military and having advanced defence equipments to retaliate such military attacks and destroy the military base, storage of military weapons of Iran. Israel has strategic military partnership with US and US helps them directly in retaliation action on Arab Countries by Israel. Israel has most advanced military equipments including Naval ships, Rafael, aerospace and well discipline army. But there is constant unrest in the country on fear from military attack. On this point, the outlook of the country should be negative. But the country is well equipped for retaliation of any military action by any country and has proved it many times in the past. Therefore the financial outlook is awarded by the

International Credit Agencies to Israel as Positive or Stable which looks comfortable.

Arab League has prohibited trade with Israel and the company which cooperate Israeli in the trade. This is the financial Sanctions.

Constant dispute between Israel and Palestine, West Bank and Gaza Strip should be settled amicably. Israel should not forcibly and unilaterally construct residential buildings for accommodating refugee Jews in Gaza Strip area by forcibly removing the Palestinian residents there. In fact, all countries including US have strongly protested Israel on this issue. Israel should recognize that they were ruthlessly treated by the Arab countries so that Israel should treat them sympathetically and settle the issues including Jerusalem as the Capital of Palestine. This will reduce the tension of Israel in attacks of suicide bombing and missiles from Hamas and Fatah.

22

Economy of Gaza City

Critical Observations on Present Status of Economy of Gaza City

(1) From 2014, Gaza Strip came into light on account of illegal and residential construction of building forcibly by Israel to accommodate Israel people in this buildings. In fact, this is a disputed issue which should have been resolved amicably by the negotiation between Israel Prime Minister and President of Palestine

(2) Palestine of Fatah Party Mr. Mohammed Abbas. But like Chinese President Mr. Xi Jig Sing, Prime Minister of Israel took aggressive action in Gaza Strip construction.

(3) In 2018, President of USA Mr. Trump unilaterally declared that Palestine is the Capital of Israel and right of Palestine was snatched. This was opposed by all countries but Mr. Trump did not amend its decision and instructed Mr. Mohammed Abbas to negotiate and settle other disputed issues with Israel. Hamas Party and Extremists did not agree to this order and refused to settle this issue with Israel.

(4) In fact, Israel captured these provinces in war with Saria and Jordon. As per war regulations in force, the Palestine should have been handed over to Saria/Jordan. But Israel did not hand over the province to Saria that time.

(5) Gaza city economy is backward economy. The economy was dependent on small industries and agriculture. After years of decline, economic growth in Gaza is now on the rise, boosted by foreign aid.

(6) As per IMF, economy grew by 20% in 2011 and the per capita GDP increased by 19%.

(7) In the 19th century, Gaza was among soap producing cities in Levant, overshowed city by Nablus. Its factories purchased gill from merchants from Nablus and salt in Jordon. Gaza's part was eclipsed by the parts of Jaffa and Haifa, but it returned its fishing fleets.

(8) Although its port was inactive, land commerce thrived because of its strategic location

(9) Most caravans and travelers coming from Egypt stopped in Gaza for supplies.

(10) Bedouin from Malan, east of Wadi Araba, bought various sorts of provisions from the city to sell to Muslims pilgrims coming from Mecca. Bazars of Gaza were well-supplied for better than those of Jerusalem. Principal crop was cotton which was sold to the government and local Arab tribes.

(11) Many Gaza worked in Israeli services industries while the boarder was open. In the wake, of Israel's 2005 disarrangement plan, Gazans could no longer do so.

(12) Gaza suffered from serious shortage in housing, educational facilities, health facilities, infrastructure and an inadequate sewage system, contributing to serious hygiene and public health problems.

(13) Food prices rose during the blockade with wheat flour going up 34% and rice up 21%. The number of poor Gazans increased sharply, with 80% relying on humanitarian aid in 2008 compared to 63% in 2006. In 2007, household spent 62% of their total income on food compared to 37% in 2004. In a decade, the number of families depending on UNRWA food aid increased ten-fold.

(14) Increasing prosperity has held to the widespread replacement of donkey cart with tut-tuts.

(15) Economy of Gaza grew by 16% in the first half of 2010, almost twice as fast as the economy of the West Bank.

(16) European Union paid euro 420 million in aid to the Palestinians territories in 2001.This was in additional to contributions by individual member states. Germany contributed euro 55 million, France euro 67 million and UK pound 63.6 million (euro 76 million) in 2007.

(17) Unemployment in Gaza was 29% in 2011. Qatar donated $400 million towards construction projects in the Gaza Strip.

(18) In November 2012, a report by the Palestine Chamber of Commerce called for Gaza Strip to be recognized as an economic disaster area after it concluded that the Israeli operation Pillar of Defence caused approximately $300 million in economic damages.

(19) Major agricultural products are strawberries, dates, olives, flowers, various vegetables.

Pollution and massive population pressure on water have revealed the productive capacity of the surrounding farms.

(20) Small scale industries include production of plastics, construction materials, textiles, furniture, pottery, tiles, copper ware, carpets. Thousands of residents were employed in the various government ministries and security services. Others were employed UNRWA and other important Organizations.

(21) In 2012, 250 trucks passed through Kreme salons, Border crossing. Transporting goods from Israel to Gaza Strip City was capable of handling 950 trucks per day.

(22) In 2010, Gaza experienced a boom in construction industries, recreation facilities not aimed at tourists but at residents, new amusement parks, restaurants, crazy water and All Boston resort (Gaza) etc.

(23) Several hotels in Gaza including the hotel at Gaza Museum of Archaeology and the Palestine hotel is located along the coast. UN has Beach Club. It is not a frequent destination of tourists. Most foreigners are journalists who stay in hotels.

(24) In 2007, unemployment is Gaza Strip reached 40% Government Sector employed 53% of all working Gazans was devas led and many businesses went bankrupt. Out of 110000 workers 75000 lost jobs and 95% of the city's operations were closed.

23

Economy of the United Arab Emirates

United Arab Emigrate is the second largest economy in the Middle East after Saudi Arabia. It is concentrating on growth of its Economy. But sometimes, however, it involves itself to the political affairs of other counties. For example, in case of Yemen, there is a fight between Hathi and Hothi. It takes side of Hathi and provides them military assistance with Saudi Arabia. Recently Saudi Arabia suffered heavily when Hothi attacked Saudi's biggest Oil storage. The country should apply this military strength to self - protection.

Secondly, UAE economy is dependent on petroleum and natural gas. In the times, the petroleum products prices go down, their economy suffers badly. The country should therefore keep some reserves for the emergency time like fall in price of crude oil. The country should keep 20% reserves of their oil and gas income for future calamities to avoid economic crisis during recession. UAE has however diversified its economy in tourism and construction industries and will not be much affected today from dropping of oil prices to the bottom though its 85% of revenues come from exports of crude oil and natural gas. The low population i.e. 96 lacs is again advantageous for its high income and stable economic status.

The economy of the United Arab Emirates (or UAE) is the second largest in the Middle East (after Saudi Arabia), with a gross domestic product (GDP) of USD 414 billion (AED 1.52 trillion) in 2018.

The UAE has been successfully diversifying its economy, particularly in Dubai, but still remains heavily reliant on revenues from petroleum and natural gas, which continue to play a central role in its economy, especially in Abu Dhabi. More than 85% of the UAE's economy was based on the oil exports in 2009. While Abu Dhabi and other UAE emirates have remained relatively conservative in their approach to diversification, Dubai, which has far smaller oil reserves, was bolder in its diversification policy. In 2011, oil exports accounted for 77% of the UAE's state budget.

Tourism is one of the bigger non-oil sources of revenue in the UAE, with some of the world's most luxurious hotels being based in the UAE. A massive construction boom, an expanding manufacturing base, and a thriving services sector are helping the UAE diversify its economy. Nationwide, there is currently $350 billion worth of active construction projects.

The UAE is a member of the World Trade Organization and OPEC.

The UAE government has long been investing in the economy to diversify and reduce their dependence on oil revenue.

Historical Background

Prior to independence from the UK unification in 1971, each emirate was responsible for its own economy. At the time, pearl diving, sea farming and fishing were together the mainstay of the economy, until the development of Japanese cultured pearls and the discovery of commercial quantities of oil. Previous UAE President Sayed Bin Sultan Al Nanyang is credited with bringing the country forward into the 20th century and using the revenue from oil exports to fund all the necessary development. Likewise, former UAE vice-president Rashid Bin Saeed Al Actium had a bold vision for the Emirate of Dubai and foresaw the future in not petroleum alone, but also other industries.

In the 1980s Dubai's diversification is central around trade and the creation of shipping and logistics centres, notably Port Rashid and the port and Free Zone of Jebel Ali as well as Dubai International Airport, leading to a number of major global plays in shipping, transportation and logistics (DP World, Emirates, and DNATA). The emergence of Dubai's lively real estate market was briefly checked by the global financial crisis of 2007-8, when Dubai was bailed out by Abu Dhabi. The recovery from the overheated market led to tighter regulation and oversight and a more realistic market for real estate throughout the UAE with many 'on hold' projects restarting. Although the market continues to expand, current market conditions for developers have been characterised as 'tough'.

Overview

UAE has the second-largest economy in the Arab world (after Saudi Arabia), with a gross domestic product (GDP) of USD 414 billion (AED 1.52 trillion) in 2018. A third of the GDP is from oil revenues. The economy was expected to grow 4–4.5% in 2013, compared to 2.3–3.5% over the previous five years. Since independence in 1971, UAE's economy has grown by nearly 231 times to AED1.45 trillion in 2013. The non-oil trade has grown to AED1.2 trillion, a growth of around 28 times from 1981 to 2012.

The UAE's economy is one of the most open worldwide, and its economic history goes back to the times when ships sailed to India, along the Swahili coast, as far south as Mozambique.

International Monetary Fund (IMF) expected UAE's economic growth to increase to 4.5% in 2015, compared to 4.3% in 2014. The IMF ascribed UAE's potentially strong economic growth in World Economic Outlook Report to the increased contribution of non-petroleum sectors, which registered a growth average of more than 6% in 2014 and 2015. Such contribution includes banking, tourism, commerce and real estate. Increase of Emirati purchasing power and governmental expenditures in infrastructure projects have considerably increased.

Internationally, UAE is ranked among the top 20 for global service business, according to AT Kearney, the top 30 on the WEF "most-networked countries" and in the top quarter as a least corrupt country per the TI's corruption index.

External trade

Emirati exports in 2006

With imports totaling $273.5 billion in 2012, UAE passed Saudi Arabia as the largest consumer market in the region. Exports totaled $314 billion, which makes UAE the second largest exporter in the region.

UAE and India are each other's main trading partners, with the latter having many of its citizens working and living in the former. The trade totals over $75 billion (AED275.25 billion).

The top five of the Main Partner Countries of the UAE in 2014 are Iran (3.0%), India (2.9%), Saudi Arabia (1.5%), Oman (1.4%) and Switzerland (1.2%). As for the top five of UAE suppliers are China (7.4%), United States (6.4%), India (5.8%), Germany (3.9%) and Japan (3.5%).

Diversification

Although UAE has the most diversified economy in the GCC, the UAE's economy remains extremely reliant on oil. With the exception of Dubai, most of the UAE is dependent on oil revenues. Petroleum and natural gas continue to play a central role in the economy, especially in Abu Dhabi. More than 85% of the UAE's economy was based on the oil exports in 2009. While Abu Dhabi and other UAE emirates have remained relatively conservative in their approach to diversification, Dubai, which has far smaller oil reserves, was bolder in its diversification policy. In 2011, oil exports accounted for 77% of the UAE's state budget.

Dubai suffered from a significant economic crisis in 2007-2010 and was bailed out by Abu Dhabi's oil wealth. Dubai's current prosperity has been attributed to Abu Dhabi's petrodollars. In 2014, Dubai owed a total of \$142 billion in debt. The UAE government has worked towards reducing the economy's dependence on oil exports by 2030. Various projects are underway to help achieve this, the most recent being the Khalifa Port, opened in the Emirate of Abu Dhabi at the end of 2012. The UAE has also won the right to host the World Expo 2020, which is believed to have a positive effect on future growth, although there are some skeptics which mention the opposite.

Over the decades, the Emirate of Dubai has started to look for additional sources of revenue. High-class tourism and international finance continue to be developed. In line with this initiative, the Dubai International Financial Centre was announced, offering 55.5% foreign ownership, no withholding tax, freehold land and office space and a tailor-made financial regulatory system with laws taken from best practice in other leading financial centres like New York, London, Zürich and Singapore. A new stock market for regional companies and other initiatives were announced in DIFC. Dubai has also developed Internet and Media free zones, offering 100% foreign ownership, no tax office space for the world's leading ICT and media companies, with the latest communications infrastructure to service them. Many of the world's leading companies have now set up branch offices, and even changed headquarters to, there. Recent liberalization in the property market allowing non-citizens to buy freehold land has resulted in a major boom in the construction and real estate sectors, with several signature developments such as the 2 Palm Islands, the World (archipelago), Dubai Marina, Jumeirah Lake Towers, and a number of other developments, offering villas and high rise apartments and office space. Emirates (part of the Emirates Group) was formed by the Dubai Government in the 1980s and is presently one of the few airlines to witness strong levels of growth. Emirates is also the largest operator of the Airbus A380 aircraft. As of 2001, budgeted government revenues were about AED 29.7 billion, and expenditures were about AED 22.9 billion. In addition, to finding new ways of sustaining the national economy, the UAE has also made progress in installing new, sustainable methods of generating electricity. This is evidenced by various solar energy initiatives at Masdar City and by other renewable energy developments in parts of the country.

In addition, the UAE is starting to see the emergence of local manufacturing as new source of economic development, examples of significant government-led investments such as Strata in aerospace industry, under Mubadala are successful, while there are also small scale entrepreneurial ventures picking up, such as Zarooq Motors in the automotive industry.

Foreign trade

With reference to foreign trade, UAE's market is one of the world's most dynamic markets worldwide, placed among the 16 largest exporters and 20 largest importers of commodities. The top five of the Main Partner Countries of the UAE in 2014 are Iran (3.0%), India (2.9%), Saudi Arabia (1.5%), Oman (1.4%) and Switzerland (1.2%). As for the top five of UAE suppliers are China (7.4%), United States (6.4%), India (5.8%), Germany (3.9%) and Japan (3.5%).

In 2014, the United Arab Emirates managed to export 380.4bn dominated by four products which are Petroleum oils and oils obtained from bituminous. (19.8%) Diamonds, whether or not worked, but not mounted. (3.4%) Gold, incl. gold plated with platinum, HYPERLINK "https://en.santandertrade.com/analyse-markets/united-arab-emirates/foreign-trade-in-figures"unwrought. (3.2%) Articles of jewellery and parts thereof, of. 2.8%). In the same year, the United Arab Emirates imported 298.6 bn dominated by five countries which are China (7.4%), United States (6.4%), India (5.8%), Germany (3.9%), Japan (3.5%).

On one hand, the United Arab Emirates managed in 2013 to export 17 bn USD services exported in 2013 dominated by travel (67.13%), transportation (28.13%), Government services (4.74%). On the other hand, it imported 63.9 bn USD of services imported services dominated by transportation (70.68%), travel (27.70%) and government services (1.62%)

Work Force

Emiratization is an initiative by the government of the UAE to employ more UAE Nationals in a meaningful and efficient manner in the public and private sectors. While the program has been in place for more than a decade and results can be seen in the public sector, the private sector is still lagging behind with citizens only representing 0.34% of the private sector workforce.

While there is general agreement over the importance of Emiratization for social, economic and political reasons, there is also some contention as to the impact of localization on organizational efficiency. It is yet unknown whether, and the extent to which, employment of nationals generates returns for MNEs operating in the Middle East. Recent research cautions that localization is not always advantageous for firms operating in the region, and its effectiveness depends on a number of contingent factors.

In December 2009 however, a positive impact of UAE citizens in the workplace was identified in a newspaper article citing a yet unpublished study, this advantage being the use of networks within the evolving power structures.

Overall, however, uptake in the private sector remains low regardless of significant investments in education, which have reached record levels with education now accounting for 22.5% – or $2.6 billion – of the overall budget planned for 2010. Multiple governmental initiatives are actively promoting Emiratization by training anyone from high school dropouts to graduates in a multitude of skills needed for the - essentially Western - work environment of the UAE, these initiatives include Tawteen UAE, ENDP or the Abu Dhabi Tawteen Council.

There are very few anti-discrimination laws in relation to labour issues, with Emiratis – and other GCC nationals – being given preference when it comes to employment. Unions are generally banned and workers with any labour issues are advised to be in touch with the Ministry of Labour, instead of protesting or refusing to work. Migrant employees often complain of poor workplace safety and wages based on nationality, although this is being slowly addressed.

Beyond directly sponsoring educational initiatives, the Emirates Foundation for Philanthropy is funding major research initiatives into Emiratization through competitive research grants, allowing universities such as United Arab Emirates University or Dubai School of Government to build and disseminate expertise on the topic.

Academics working on various aspects of Emiratization include *Paul Dyer* [12] and *Natasha Ridge* from Dubai School of Government, *Ingo Forstenlechner* [13] from United Arab Emirates University, *Kasim Randaree* from the British University of Dubai and Paul Knoglinger from the FHWien

Investment

The stock market capitalisation of listed companies in the UAE was valued at $109.9 billion in October 2012 by Bloomberg.

Outward investment

An investment institutions were created by the government to promote manage investments made by the UAE abroad:

Abu Dhabi Investment Authority (ADIA)

- Abu Dhabi Investment Council (ADIC)

- Mubadala Development Company (MDC)
- International Petroleum Investment Company (IPIC)
- Dubai World
- Dubai International Capital (DIC)

Inward investment

The UAE is in the 17th position in term of the Global Competitiveness Index (GCI). The report says that the UAE competitiveness stems from "high quality [...] infrastructure" and "highly efficient good markets."

Corporate Governance Code

The Securities and Commodities Authority (SCA) introduced a new corporate governance regulation (the Corporate Governance Code), which applies to all joint stock companies and institutions whose securities are listed on Dubai Financial Market (DFM) and Abu Dhabi Securities Exchange (ADX) in 2009.

Real estate

The development in the real estate and infrastructure sectors during the recent year has contributed in making the country a global touristic destination. The contribution of tourism in the Emirati GDP increased from 3% in the mid-1990s to more than 16.5% by the end of 2010. This trend is supported by the huge public investments in touristic projects (47 Billion Dollars per annum) carried mainly to expend airports, increase their capacity, set up new airports and ports.

The real estate sector have a positive impact on development, job opportunities, investments and tourism as estate projects were launched to meet the needs of market and the increasing demand for housing and commercial units especially in Dubai and Abu Dhabi. The UAE has 18 tour hotels out of the 155 (150 meters high) that exist around the world. This makes the UAE the third destination with such tours after China and America in 2014. These buildings are among the UAE's attractions for tourists. Dubai has adopted dazzling ideas in construction and design of these tall tours.

The leap in real estate sector along and infrastructure development in the UAE during the recent year has contributed in making this country a global touristic destination par excellence. Therefore, the contribution of tourism in the Emirati GDP increased from 3% in the mid-1990s to more than 16.5% by the end of 2010. This trend is supported by the huge public investments in touristic projects (47 Billion Dollars per year) carried mainly to expend airports, increase their capacity, set up new airports and ports.

The UAE has about 37% of the region's petroleum and gas industries, chemical industries, energy and water and garbage projects. The UAE's government have been injecting huge funds in tourism and real estate projects, especially in Abu Dhabi and Dubai. Al Saadiyat Island in Abu Dhabi and Burj Khalifa in Dubai, the tallest tower in the world, world central near "Jebel Ali" are a point in case of the milestones that have given the UAE its high profile of a global tourist destination. According to 2013-2014 Global Competitiveness Report, the UAE ranked fourth worldwide in terms of infrastructure quality.

Critical Observations of the present status of Economy of UAE

(1) Economy of UAE is the second largest economy after Saudi Arabia.

(2) Though 85% of its economy is supported in exports of crude oil and natural gas, UAE has been successfully diversifying its economy, particularly in Dubai, in tourism and construction industry especially in constructing large international airports and largest luxurious hotels in UAE.

(3) Though Dubai in particular has diversified its economy and Ab Dhabi which was conservative in diversification, Abu Dhabi assisted Dubai for bail-out and Dubai's economy is based on Abu Dhabi petrodollars.

(4) Tourism is one of the biggest non-oil resources of revenue in the UAE with some of the World's most luxurious hotels are based in UAE.

(5) Since Independence from England in 1971, UAE's economy has grown by about 231 times to AED 1.45 trillion in 2013.

(6) A massive construction boom, an expounding manufacturing base, and a thriving service sector are helping the UAE diversify its economy. Nationwide, there is currently $350 billion worth of active construction projects.

(7) In the 1980s, Dubai's diversification is central around trade and creation of shipping and logistics centres, notably Port Rashid and the port and free and Free Zone of Jebel Ali as well as Dubai international Airport. Dubai is also, leading to a number of major global players in shipping, transportation and logistics. Dubai also

emerged as lively real estate market. This was checked by the global financial market.

(8) There is increased contribution of non-petroleum sectors, which registered a growth average of more than 6% in 2014-15. Such contribution includes banking, tourism, commerce and real estate. Internally, UAE is recognized among top 20 for global service business.

(9) With imports totaling $ 273.5 billion in 2012, UAE passed Saudi Arabia as the largest consumer market in the region. Exports totaled $ 314 billion – is second exporter in the region.

(10) Emigration is the largest operator of Airbus A380 aircraft. Government revenue is AED 29.7 billion and expenses AED 22.9 billion.

(11) Emiratization is an initiative by the government of UAE to employ more UAE nationals in a meaningful and effective manner in public and private sector.

(12) Stock Market Capitalization was $ 109.9 billion in October 2012. There are few non-discrimination laws in relation to labour issues. Unions are generally banned and worker with any labour issues are advised to be in touch with Ministry of Labour instead of protesting or reusing to work. Emigrates complained about bad atmosphere in the working places.

(13) Beyond directly sponsoring education initiatives, the Emigrates Funding for Philanthropy is funding major research initiatives into Emiratization through competitive research grants education investment 22.5% or $2.6 billion.

(14) The leap in real estate sector along and infrastructure development in the UAE during the recent year has contributed in making this country a global touristic destination par excellence. UAE has 180 tour hotels out of 155 that exist around the world. Hugh public investments in tourism projects $47 billion per year. UAE ranked fourth worldwide in terms of infrastructure quality.

(15) Currency of UAE is United Arab Immigrate Dirham AED 3.67 =$1

(16) Fiscal year Calendar year

(17) Trade Organizations: OPEC, WTO

(18) Population: 96 lacs - 2018

(19) GDP $405.771 billion Nominal. $ 746. 50 billion PPP - 2019

(20) GDP Growth: 0.5% in 2017, 1.7% in 2018, 1.8% in 2019 2.6% in Forecast 2020

(21) GDO per Capita : $ 37750 Nominal, $ 69435 PPP in 2019

(22) GDP by Sector: Agriculture 0.9%, Industry 49.8% and Services 49.2%

(23) Inflation 1.2% in 2020 forecast

(24) Labour Force: 69.05 lacs

(25) Labour force by Sector: Agriculture 7%, Industry 15% and Services 79% in 2020 Forecast

(26) Unemployment: 2.5% in 2017

(27) Man Industries: crude oil, natural gas, tourism, construction, aluminum, textiles

(28) Exports: $208.5 billion in 2017

(29) Goods for exports: crude oil, nature gas, re-export dried fish and dates

(30) Imports: $ 229.2 billion in 2017

(31) Import Goods: Machinery and transportation equipment, chemical and food

(32) FDI Stock: $129 billion. Abroad 1244 billion

(33) Current Account $26.47 billion

(34) Gross External debt: $237.6 58.33% of GDP in 2017

(35) Public debt 19.7% of GDP

(36) Revenues: $110.2 billion and Expenses $ 111.1 billion in 2017

(37) Foreign Reserves : $95.37 billion

(38) Credit Rating: S & Ps AA Outlook: Stable, M00dys:
Arab Outlook Stable Finch AA Outlook Stable

(39) UAE has large natural resources and its Population is only 96 lacs. It is therefore a very rich and high income country. UAE has diversified in various other sectors like tourism and construction though 85% of its income derives from crude oil and natural gas exports. It is therefore unlikely to be in economic crisis if oil prices drastically dropped in recession as it is happening today on account of Corona Virus and OPEC countries and Russia not agreeing to reduce oil production.

24

Economy of Palestine

Critical observations of present status of economy of Palestine

(1) Economies of Palestine, Gaza Strip and West Bank are dependent on each -others. Israel political and economic policy mainly result in growth or decline in the economy of Palestine, Gaza Strip and West Bank. Restrictions on land in Gaza Strip decline the economic growth of these countries. Israel assists Gaza Strip, Palestine and West Bank by giving them permit to work in Israel and thereby reduces the unemployment of these regions. It is also important to note that Israeli economy also suffers from restrictions which Israeli imposed on Gaza Strip, West Bank and Palestine including Eastern Jerusalem.

(2) Recently Palestine was in light on account of US President Mr. Trump unilaterally declaring Jerusalem as the Capital of Israel. This was opposed by all European Countries, Palestine, USSR, China and United Nations. In fact, during 1990s Israel conquered the countries which it never handed over to Syria/Jordan as per the war rules. As a part of US attempts to create a Peace Agreement between Israeli and Palestinians, Us granted $4 billion to Palestine that will help grew the Palestinian economy by 50% and bring unprecedented wealth to the region. The Plan was coordinated in conjunction with former Prime Minister Tony Blair. In this Peace Agreement Palestinians should agree that Eastern Jerusalem is the capital of Israel. Palestine President Mr. Mohammed Abbas of Fatah Party refused to agree to this condition and the so called unilateral Agreement failed. It was rightly declared by Palestinian Authority that Palestinian Authority's priority is not economic but rather a political framework for the creation of Palestinian State based on in 1967 lines with Eastern Jerusalem as its capital that ensures the rights of refugees and a political compromise, the Palestinian news agency added. US President

Trump's unilateral declaring Jerusalem as the capital of Israel will not make any political peace agreement in future. This will be permanent dispute which will never be settled in the short time.

(3) Economic conditions in the West Bank and Gaza Strip was governed by the Paris Economic Protocol of April 1994, between Israel and Palestinian Authority, deteriorated in the early 1990. Real per capita for West Bank and Gaza Strip declined by 36.1% between 192 and 1996. The downturn in economic activities was due to extensive corruption in the new governing Palestine Authority and to Israeli closure policies in response to terrorist attacks in Israel, which disrupted previously established labour and commodity market relationships. The most serious effect was the emergence of chronic unemployment. Unemployment rose from 5% in the 1980s to over 20% by mid 1990s. After 1997, Israel's use of comprehensive closures decreased and new policies were implemented in October 1999. Israel permitted the opening of a safe passage between the West Bank and Gaza Strip in accordance with 1995 Interim Agreement. This changes in the conduct of economic activity fueled a moderate economic recovery in 1998-99.

(4) As a result of Israeli blockade, 85% of factories were short or operated at less than 20% capacity. It is estimated that Israeli business lost $2 million per day from the closure of Gaza which approximately works out to $1million a day. World Bank estimated Nominal GDP of the territories at $4,007,000 and of Israel $ 66,822,000-. Per capita are worked out $ 1036 and $22563 per year.

(5) For 30 years, Israel permitted thousands of Palestinians to enter the country each day to work in construction, agriculture and other blue color jobs. During this period, the Palestinian economy was significantly greater than the major of Arab States. Until the mid -1990s, upto 150000 people entered Israel each day. After Palestinians unleashed a wave of suicide bombings, the idea of separation from the Palestinians took root in Israel. Israel found itself starved for labour, and gradually replaced most of the Palestinians with migrates from Thailand, Romania and elsewhere.

(6) In 2005, Palestinian Ministry of Finance stated the Israeli West Bank barrier, whose construction began unilaterally like aggressive China in the second half of 2002, as one reason for the depressed Palestinian economy activity. Real GDP growth in the West Bank declined substantially in 2000-2002, and increased modestly in 2005 and 2004. The World Bank attributed the modest economic growth since 2003 to

diminished level of violence, fewer curfews and more predictable closures, as well as adaption by Palestinian business to the constrained West Bank economy. Under a "disengagement scenario, the West Bank predicted a real growth rate of 0.2% in 2006 and 0.6 % in 2007.

(7) In the wake of Israel's unilateral disengagement from Gaza, there was shortage of bread and basic supplies due to the closure of Mentor/Karni border crossing into Israel's office. To open other crossings was turned down by the Hamas-run Palestinian Authority.

(8) In January 2006, legislative elections won by Hamas. Palestinian Authority led by Prime Minister Ismail Haniyah. The Palestine has monthly cash deficit \$60- \$70 million after it received \$55 million per month from Israel in taxes and customs duties. After election, Palestine Stock Market fell by about 20% and Palestinian Authority exhausted its borrowing capacity with local banks. Israeli ceased transferring \$55 million in tax receipts to the Palestinian authority. These funds accounted for a third of the Palestinian Authority's budget and paid the wages of 160000 Palestine civil servants. UN and EU halted direct aid to Palestinian authority, while US imposed a financial blockade on Palestine banks, impending the transfer of some of the Arab League's Funds (Saudi Arabia & Qatar). In May 2006, hundreds of Palestinians demonstrated in Gaza demanding payment of their wages. Tension between Hamas and Fatah rose as a result of this "economic squeeze" on the Palestinian authority.

(9) In 2009, the Israeli military removed its checkpoint at the entrance of Jennie in a series of reductions in security measures. In September 2012, EU countries stated that the Palestine economy lost access to 40% of the West Bank, 82% of its ground water and more than two-third of its grazing land due to the occupation and settlement construction. The first planned Palestinian City named Rawabi is under construction north of Ramallah, with the help of funds from Qatar. In 2013, commercial trade between Israel and Palestinian territories was valued at \$20 billion annually.

(10) In 2007, economy in the West Bank improved gradually. Economic growth reached about 4.5% and unemployment dropped by 3%. Wages rose more than 20% in 2008 and trade rose by 35%. Tourism in Bethlehem increased to about twice its previous levels. Tourism increased by 10% in Jericho. Life expectancy is 73. IMF Report for the West Bank forecast 7% growth rate in 2009. The Bethlehem Small Enterprise center opened in early 2008 funded by Germany to promote computer literacy and marketing skill.

(11) In 2009, efforts continued to build Palestinian local institutions and governments from the ground up. Much of the work was done by Tony Blair and US General Keith Dayton. In 2009, economic boom began with growth reaching 8% but inflation rose 9.9% and economic growth became negative.

(12) East Jerusalem is the first business and shopping hub of West Bank. Since the advent of Israeli Security checkpoints and separation barrier starting over a decade ago, it has become isolated from the customer base leading the serious economic decline. This resulted in unprecedented poverty, with 80% of the Palestinian population living below poverty line. Political and physical barriers separated it from West Bank. The cumulative effects of annexation, neglect, rights violations and completion of the separation barrier, housing situation Israeli Government has facilitated extensive construction for Israeli settler neighborhoods but has severally restricted development and building for Palestinian population which is strongly opposed by the Palestinians and all European counties. US has also asked Israel to restrain aggressive and make negotiation with Palestinians whose most important demand is to protect migrates.

(13) In case of Gaza Strip, Israeli's closure policy which was extended when the Hamas administration came to power in 2007, was responsible for high level of poverty and unemployment and a significant disclose of the private sector which was heavily reliance upon export markets. Israel blamed Hamas for taking action that led to the closure policy. A large part of the population is dependent on humanitarian assistance, primarily from UN Agencies. Israel is mercilessly and with cruelty is trying to treat the Palestinians, Gaza Strip and West Bank with its mighty military power and blind support from US President Mr. Trump.

(14) Primary currencies used in West Bank are new Israeli Shekel and Jordan dinar. Shekel is used in most transactions. While dinar is used more for savings and during goods transactions. US dollar is also used for savings and purchasing foreign goods.

(15) In Palestinian territories, it is complex system of taxation. In 2005, the Palestinian Authority collected approximately $34 million per month. Israel collected about $75 million per month in tariffs.

(16) Council for European Palestinian Relations, agriculture employed 13.4% of the population. In Gaza Strip, 41% were unemployed in 2008.

High unemployment in the Palestinian economy led about 100000 Palestinians to work in Israel. 45000 permits are issued for work in Israel with further 25000 permits were issued for work in West Bank settlements. 35000 Palestinians work through illegal channels and without a permit. Increased Permit quota reduced age from 26 to 24.

As of 2013, average daily wages in Israel is nearly 2.2 times higher than in private sector in West Bank and 4 times that of Gaza Strip. Palestinian monthly wage is 1450, almost third of that Israel which is 4300.

(17) Agriculture is mainstay in the economy. Agriculture sector formally employs 13.4% of population. 183 hectors land is cultivated. Handcrafts is the most impoverishment sector in Palestine. Handicrafts are mostly have been produced by Arabs in Palestine since hundreds of years, continue to be produced today. Embroidery work, pottery making, soap making, weaving gas-making and mother of pearl. Sale and export of such items is forming a key part of each city's economy.

(18) Traditional source of income from Palestinian economy is stonecutting. Annual average output per worker in the stone cutting industry higher than in any other sector. There are 650 stone production outlets in the West Bank, 138 of it in Belt Fajjar. The quarried material is cut into a rich of pink, sand and golden.

(19) World Bank estimated that in 2016, restrictive measures placed by Israel on telecommunication operators in the West Bank have had a notable negative impact on the development of the Palestinian which is sustaining losses in the range of 41 billion. Restrictive measures include denial to operate 60% of the West Bank under Israeli military administration.

During in 2000s, high-tech sector emerged in the Palestinian territories supported by its proximity to Israel. By 2013, 4500 Palestinians worked in the IT sector.

It grew from 0.8% of GDP in 2008 to 5% in 2010. Industry has seen 64% increase in foreign business since 2009.

According to World Bank Report in 2018, Palestinian technology, there were 241 active start-ups in Palestinian territories, created a total of 1247 jobs. 51 active investors in Palestinian Technology Company (annual 75 per cent angel investors and 2 per cent venture capital firms).

(20) In 2010, 4.6 million tourists visited against 2.6 million in 2009. Out of $.6 million tourists, 2.2 million were foreigners, 2.7 domestic.

Israeli Minister and Palestinian Authority attempted to work together on tourism in the Palestine. Recent co-operation is not successful in Palestine. Foreign tourism has restricted to Eastern Jerusalem and West Bank. There is essentially no tourism flow from Gaza since 2005. Access to Jerusalem and West Bank are controlled by Israel and access to Gaza controlled by Hamas. Entry to the occupied Palestinian territories requires only a valid International Passport but entry to Israel may be denied to Palestinian or Arab visitors.

(21) In 2008, West Bank and Gaza Strip economies were highly reliant on foreign aid which stood at $1.8 billion i.e. 31% of GDP or 487 per capita Palestinian income per year from foreign aid. Foreign aid provided essential services in nearly half of the Palestinian people. In 2010, Arab states cut financial aid to Palestinian Authority. Palestine received $583 million in budget supported by August 2010. 22% only came from Arab States.

There was budget support of $ 58.5 million from Arab states which works out to 22%.

As a part of US Government attempt to create a peace agreement between Israelis and Palestinians, US granted $ 4billion plan on the understanding that Palestinian Authority will recognised East Jerusalem as the capital of Israel. The plan of US4 billion would help grow the Palestine economy by 50% and bring unprecedented wealth to the region. The plan was coordinated in conjunction with former Prime Minister Tony Blair. Palestinian Prime Minister Mr. Mohamad Abbas forthwith rejected the Peace Plan on the ground that Palestine will not agree to recognize Jerusalem as Capital of Israel. Palestinian News Agency announced as follows:

"Palestinian Authority's priority is not economic but rather a political framework for the creation of Palestinian state based on in 1967 lines, with East Jerusalem as its Capital that ensures the rights of refugees and a political compromise."

(22) Israeli – Palestinian Relations: Conflict – In 2006, the unity of Palestinian economy was threatened when Israeli ties to West Bank were severed. In 2008-2009, all economic infrastructure in Gaza was destroyed leaving the Palestinian economy without any remaining activity and owning $1.4 billion. Oslo Accords aimed to prevent this but failed. Palestine economy was fluctuating. Presently economy lives on foreign aid and customs revenues between Israel and Palestine. But Israel restrictions caused increased in unemployment. By 2008, 71% of Gaza Strip's population was unemployed. Import

and export prosperity in Palestine was impacted by the boarder restrictions. Israeli constant control of Gaza and West Bank weakened the industrial and agricultural sectors. Restrictions on Palestinian land should be removed. In order to be Palestinian economy to be prosperous, the restrictions on Palestinian land must be removed. In the West Bank, Israeli restrictions caused Palestinian economy to lose $3.4 billion (35% of the annual GDP)

Unemployment in Gaza & West Bank:

Year	Percentage
2000	12.5%
2001	21%
2002	32%
2003	26%
2007	27.5%
2008	26.5%

(23) GDP $10 billion

(24) GDP per Capita $ 1924(West Bank), $870 (Gaza)

(25) GDP Growth: 3.1% in 2017, 0.9% in 2018, 0.5% in 2009 2.5% in 2020 forecast

(26) GDP by Sector : Agriculture 5.5%, industry 23.4% Services 71.4% in 2014

(27) Trade Organization: OIC, Group of 77

(28) Country Group: Developing/Emerging, Lower-middle income economy

(29) Population 45.69 lacs

(30) Population below poverty line 25.8%

(31) Inflation 2.7%

(32) Work Force: 13.16 lacs

(33) Labour Force by Occupation: Agriculture 12%, industry 23% services 65%

(34) Unemployment 27.5% very high. This is because the economy fully dependent on the policy of Israel. Arrangement to issue work permit is frequently canceled by Israel. Israel dominates this country with full support from US

(35) Main Industries: Cement, quarrying, textiles, soap, olive-wood, carving, food processing, mother-of-pearl souvenirs.

(36) Exports: 720 million

(37) Export Goods: Oliver, fruits, vegetables, limestone, citrus, flowers, textiles

(38) Imports: 4.2 billion

(39) Import Goods: food, consumer goods, construction materials

(40) Trade Deficit: $ 3.480 billion i.e. 34.8% of GDP Very high. Country is dependent from financial aid from foreign countries.

(41) Revenue: $2.2 Billion

(42) Expenses: 3.54 billion

(43) Fiscal deficit: $ 1.34 billion 13.4% of GDP

(44) Foreign Reserves: $464 million Public debt: $4.2 billion

(45) Country's annual Budget is dependent upon taxes it collects plus taxes and tariffs collected by Israel and handed over to Palestine and foreign aid from IMF, EU, US, Saudi Arabia, Qatar and others. Country's economy and especially country's unemployment level substantially depends upon employment arrangement made by Israel. Israeli dominance on the country economy is very wide. Gaza Strip is used for construction of Israeli residents unilaterally by Israel and fully supported by US. Israeli's disarrangement also affects Israeli economy. Recent declaration by US President Trump Jerusalem as the Capital of Israel has created clashes between Palestine and Israel. No Peace Agreement and Settlement is at sight between these two countries in near future. Israel is militarily very strong when Palestine has terrorists which attacks Israel with suicide bombing and that spoils the cordial relationship between 2 countries and Sanctions imposed by Israel completely scatters the Palestinian economy.

(46) Since both countries' economies are dependent on each other, these countries should cooperate with each other to strengthen their economy. Israel should not be too adamant in its attitude and Gaza, West Bank and Palestine should abandon their terrorist activities against Israel to stabilize its economy. Compromise and Peace agreement should be signed by both countries at the earliest.

Section - III

Conclusion

In this Section, we shall briefly describe the political policy of each country and weakness of that policy on the economy of that country.

(1) **Economy of USA**: USA is known to be economic super power. Its GDP is $20 trillion. It has also international debt of $21 trillion. As per American regulation, if this international debt goes beyond prescribed limit, there will be the financial shutdown imposed by the House of Commons. There are many occasions on which the shut - down was ordered by the House of Commons and observed by the state.

USA spent about $750-$800 billion on defence. US has most sophisticated military weapons, F22 fighting aircrafts, supersonic missiles and advanced equipments made by leisure technology. CBI has most powerful spy machinery. US has many submarines of advanced stage and naval advance Vessels.

US spent substantial amount on social welfare activities such as education, research of technology, unemployment compensation and health insurance.

USA financial institutions assist many countries by trade concession and financial aid to regularize economy of these less developed countries. By giving aids, USA also dominates those countries. It is the super power and interferes with the political affairs of all countries. In Syria, it wants to oust the present president Assad and the fresh election in that country from the inception of civil war in that country. It has imposed sanctions on Iran thereby making its country's economy vulnerable. In Venenzua, it stopped giving financial assistance to that country supported militarily by Iran, Russia and China. In Iraq, President Saddam Hussein was charged for serious offences by US. US invaded that country and ousted Hussein. Thereafter he was caught and killed ruthlessly.

In a competition of political supremacy over Russia and China, USA gives political support to some countries by substantial financial assistance and military assistance which loses peace in such condition and there is unrest arising out of the competition.

(2) **Economy of China:** China is a communist country and wants to grab the entire world as its empire. Its present President XI Jig Pong is most powerful and treats all people in the state ruthlessly. The citizens are not happy with him and Hongkong has started Freedom fight against China's ruler. Taiwan has declared itself as independent nation from China. President has become so powerful that he has assumed the power of what religion the citizens should practice. He ordered that every citizen in China will practice the religion as he preaches. China has taken full advantage of Dr. Kissinger's politic wrong diplomacy in declaring China as a most favorite nation and made competition with USA in trade and won the monopoly of USA in the foreign trade with USA trade deficit reaching to $250 billion yearly. Recently, Trump has started trade war against China and European countries on this issue. China has ruthlessly captured Tibet and claims some parts of India which are integral part of India. This policy of China is against the Welfare of state and against the whole mankind. China has large surplus on exports-imports trade. It takes advantageous of surplus and offers loans to all countries under "One Belt One Road" policy. But if country does not pay the debt in time, it captures its profitable land till the income from that with interest is repaid. Economically poor countries and rich countries do not take loans from China under "One Belt One Road" policy which is oppressive and dominating.

In order to widen their external trade to this extent, China has large industries where the production is taken at full capacity. Workers get higher salary and their standard of living is raised. Though gap between poor and rich is increased, more persons are becoming rich. There is no unemployment in the country and everybody is given the guarantee for work, food and medical treatment.

(3) **Russian economy:** Countries like Russia support the family of the workers by giving them enough food daily and by giving financial assistance to them. Every member of the state is assured of the job and is given food, shelter (home), clothes and assistance for the medical treatment. Russia is also guarantees education to its members. It has instituted IIT in Pavai which is the best technology institution in the world. It helped India in developing

nuclear weapons by giving it the Nuclear Rectos. Russia is the super power but it does not compete alone with USA. It is therefore taking assistance from China to defeat USA. Russia is developing AS 400 as its strongest fighting equipment. It has built up strong naval equipment and military weapons for ground fighting. It has military bases in Venenzua, Syria, Cuba and other countries. Russian President Putin has recently assumed all powers and shall be the President /prime Minister till his death. He is very experienced politician and strewed. It is alleged in USA that Russia interfered in the democratic elections in other countries like USA to bring President of USA as its choice but it is not officially proved. Russians have strong hydrogen bombs which will destroy the world. Instead of world destruction, Russia should strive for welfare of state in the world for the benefit of entire mankind.

(4) USA, Russia and China have potential to promote the welfare state but they are at present engaged in the competition of super power. Every country is trying to develop most sophisticated weapons by using latest technology such as leisure technology.

(5) **Japan:** Japanese are very sincere and laborious in producing maximum in the factory production. They are proud of their country. In fact, in Second World War country was completely destroyed on drop of Bombs on Hiroshima and Nagasaki. Japan has learned not to interfere in the political affairs of other countries. Japan has thereafter become a powerful country and is sometimes threatening China on South China occupation it has the right of ownership in some of the area in the South China. In fact, China has no right whatsoever to interfere in this area. But China expects that there are lot of petroleum mines and storage of minerals. International Court has asked China not to interfere in this area. But China refused to do so. Japan has a strategic partnership with USA to fight against China.

China's interference in Indian Ocean and Pacific Ocean has compelled the Strategic Partnership between India, USA, Australia and Japan.

(6) **Australia:** Australia is a nuclear country for self defence. Recently, it has reduced the China's pressure on making Chinese as its resident on the retirements. It is not taking financial assistance of China on "One Belt One Road" policy. It has good relationship with USA on financial and military matters.

(7) **Germany:** Germany suffered substantially on end of Second World War. Germany is the founding member of EU and recognizing euro as the official currency of EU. Germany has recently some conflict of interest with USA and it is firm on constructing gas pipe line between Germany and Russia in spite of strong opposition from USA. Germany was the strong supporter of entry of the refugees in European countries by quota system which was opposed by the country like Greece, Italy and others. This policy failed ultimately.

(8) **UK:** UK's economy is not stable. It was the world emperor and oppressed the Colonies like India for 150 years. It lost heavily in World War II. It does not usually interfere in the political policies of other countries.

(9) **India:** India is following non-alignment policy from independence. It has to prepare on military front to be vigilant to fight two neighbouring enemy countries Pakistan and China. It has fully made itself self-sufficient by importing military equipment from Russia, USA. Recently it has ordered 36 Rafael from France. It has been now preparing Military weapons with Russian technology in its own country. With import of the weapons, it buys the technology from that country so that India can make those equipment in its own country. It has taken sub-marines and naval Vessels from Russia on rental basis. It has also ordered AS 400 air equipment from Russia. It is now strong strategic defence partner of USA. UK is assisting India in constructing naval vessel in India's own shipping dockyards. India is becoming self-sufficient in defence to fight with both enemy countries successfully. India has also introduced welfare measures such as pension to Non-organized workers, financial assistance of Rs. 6000- annually to all farmers, residential houses and subsides gas to the poor, Farmer's loans waiver in case of drought, failure of monsoon etc. It is financially assisting Ceylon, Afghanistan and Nepal for the economic development of these countries.

(10) **France:** France economy was sufficiently damaged during Second World War. France then started building its economy and defence strong. It is now manufacturing advanced technology to prepare Rafael Airplane for defence. France is the founder member of EU and strong supporter with Germany on entry of refugees in large numbers to European countries on quota system. It supports India on Kashmir issue in UN all the times.

(11) **Argentina:** It is volatile economy and fluctuated widely. Its inflation is high @40% and has asked for bail-out package from IMF for $30 billion. Since its economy is not strong. Bail-out package $57 billion was given by Trump. In spite of this, Argentina wanted to stall the Military Base of China in Argentina. Trump objected to it strongly. Therefore it was postponed. Military dictatorship in the country does not interfere with other countries political affairs.

(12) **Mexico:** There was Mexico Revolution during 1910-20. The economy was scattered on account of unemployment and recession. There is elicit trade which earned billions of dollars. Prostitute trade was going on in Mexico. Mexico immigrants are not able to enter USA as USA constructed a Wall on Mexico border. Bail -out package was given by President Clinton to Mexico in early 2000s.

(13) **Venezuela:** Under the President Nicolas Maduro, the country was in worst financial conditions. Most of the companies abandoned the country. Value of the Currency was beyond the control People had no food to eat and no electricity and water. People left the country and took shelter in other countries as refugees. Maduro treated US as his enemy and took shelter of Russia and China. Oil was only resource but no country had faith in Venezuela. US was ready to help the country but Maduro refused to take help. There were military bases of Iran, Russia and China. But none of them were giving financial help because the country has gone to bankruptcy. Maduro was unable to withdraw Gold reserves in the Bank of England.

Under these circumstances, Maduro should have changed its attitude and took financial and food assistance from USA and should have kept aside his own personal political views. But he did not do that and made the country bankrupt. This is the glaring example of what country should not do to promote as welfare state.

(14) **South Africa:** South Africa adopted apartheid policy> country was previously a colony of Dutch, French, Portugal and U.K. Country got independence in 1948.

In 1948, SA got independence. In 1948, National Party election was conducted. After winning the election, National Party started implementing an ever stricter race-based policy named apartheid effectively dividing the economy into a privileged White one and an impoverished Black one. The policy was widely criticized and laid to crippling sanctions being placed against the country in 1980s. Sanctions had resulted in great set back to South African economy.

SA held first multi-racial election in 1994 leaving newly elected African National Congress (ANC) to restore order to the economy harmed by sanctions while integrating previously disadvantaged segment of the population into it.

New government tried to reduce the apartheid policy. President Mbeki vowed to promote economic growth and foreign capital by relaxing restrictive labour laws, and stepping up the pace of privatization, raising general spending, cutting interest rate sharply from 1998 levels. There was strong opposition from organized labour. From 2004, economic growth picked up significantly. Employment and Capital formation increased.

Refugees from other African country include many immigrants from the Democratic Republic of the Congo, Mozambique, Zimbabwe, Malawi and others, with the high unemployment levels amongst poor SAs. These migrated labour deprived the jobs of South African labors. Employers in SA have employed migrates from other countries for lower pay than South African citizens. South African skilled labour was employed by UK, France, and Germany. These skilled personnel are for managerial jobs. These labour have emigrated overseas since 1990s.

Its population is 5.877 crores with labour force 2.31 crores. Its GDP in 2017 was $385 billion and per capita GDP is $6550- Fiscal deficit was $ 16 billion which is 4.1% of GDP Unemployment was high at more than 25%. Challenges of government were: (1) in efficient government bureaucracy, (2) restrictive labour legislations, (3) shortage of skilled workers, (4) political instability and (5) Corruption.

There are racial inequality called apartheid. Whites are earning 6 times more than Blacks. 57% of Blacks are unemployed. International sanction and crippling economy has compelled the government to change its attitude. Reforms were introduced since 1994 which showed significant results. 40% Social Spending were directed towards Whites. This changed and in mid- 1980s, Social spending was 43% for Blanks. By 1990, 80% of total spending was assigned to Blacks and less than 10% to Whites which resulted in reducing the gap between rich and poor. University of Cape Town observed in 2011 that richest 10% were consisting of 40% Blacks while this figure was entirely of Whites previously.

Russia and China are recently showed interest in the economy of SA in order to dominate that country by huge investments, US is also in competition. SA like other African countries adopted non alignment policy and does not interfere in the political affairs of other countries. SA should not come into traps of China, Russia or US and should continue to follow its non-alignment policy.

In April 2017, political tensions in the country arise over the sacking of nine cabinet ministers including Minister of Finance Pravin Gordhan by the President Jacob Zuma. Finance Minister was seen as a central to efforts to restore confidence in SA. This resulted in S & P Global curt SA's credit rating to junk status on Monday 03-04-2017. Fitch rating followed suit on 07-02-2017 and the credit status to the sub-investment group of BBB-. African Rand lost more than 11% in the week following cabinet reshuffling.

South Africa is making sincere attempts to reduce the inequality between White and Blacks but to abolish it completely will take lot of time. Secondly, inflation is very high and there are weaknesses in inefficient government bureaucracy, corruption, political stability, restrictive labour regulations and shortage of skilled labour. This with apartheid for a long time prevailing for about 2 centuries has created inequality between Whites and Blacks. To abolish it completely is difficult in foreseen future. Government should make honest efforts to administer the available resources to optimum use to reduce inequalities, reduce inflation, continue to adopt non alignment policy and should not come into trap with the Russia, China or US. If this policy is followed in administrating the country sincerely, then SA will be able to achieve its citizen's growth, comforts and happiness which will lead to achieve its aim of making the SA as a welfare state and achieve the ultimate goal of mankind.

Other African Countries

(15) Angola:

(1) The country was ruled as a Portugal colony and Dutch colony. Portuguese and Dutch were buying slaves from Angola and selling them to Brazil for working on sugarcane cultivation plants.

(2) There was war of Independence from 1961 to 1975. In 1975, Angola got independence but Angola's hardships did not end there. After Independence, there was Civil War in Angola from 1975 to 2002. UN provided financial assistance of $ 5 billion to settle the civil war. But the war continued thereafter till 2002.

(3) After the civil war, government started effective administration for the welfare and prosperity by repairing and improving infrastructure, strengthening political and social institutions. But high inequality and corruption were big challenges.

(4) Crime and social unrest were further additional challenges for the government.

(5) Country has adopted non- alignment policy. It does not involve itself in the internal affairs of any country to show its supremacy. The country administration requires to proper distribution of its resources, substantial reduction of inequality, reduction in crimes and promoting peace among the people and reduction in inflation. These changes will lead the country to achieve its ultimate goal of the welfare state.

(16) **Malawi:**

(1) Malawi is the least developed country in the South Central African region. Population is 20 million and Labour force is 8 million.

(2) 90% of the population is living on agriculture. Production are tobacco, 30% of exports and cotton, coffee and tea 50% of exports. Since unemployment is high, nationals leave the country and enter South Africa for employment as refugees.

(3) Country is dependent on economic assistance from IMF, World Bank and other individual donors.

(4) Country does not interfere in the internal affairs of other

(17) **Mauritius:**

(1) Mauritius is a small tiny island in sub-Saharan African country. It is a mixed economy based on agriculture, financial services, and tourism. It got independence in 1968.

(2) Government of Mauritius made good progress by diversification the country's economy beyond dependence on just agriculture, particularly sugar-cane production. It achieved better progress than other sub-Saharan African countries due to the sustained progress in economy conditions. During

1977 and 2008, growth averaged annually 4.6% compared to average 2.9% in sub-Saharan Africa.

(3) It achieved the most equitable income distribution and inequality fell from 45.7% to 38.9% between 1990 and 2016. This remarkable achievement has been reflected in increase life expectancy, lower infant mortality and much improved infrastructure. The country is well governed by the leaders/administrators. Sugarcane is produced on 90% of cultivated land and amounts to 25% of exports.

(4) Government's development strategy attracted $10.9 Billion in FDI inflows in electric equipment, telecommunication, fuels, cement and gypsum products and service sector.

(5) Exchange rate of Mauritius Rupee was 30.12 =$1 on 26-03-2014 from MR 29.96 =$1 in 2002 and MR 29.13 =$1 in 2001.This was no large devaluation of Mauritius Rupee per Us Dollar during 2001-2014.

(6) It is a small country with population of 1.265 million with labour forces 600 thousands Unemployment was 6.8% and inflation 3.21%.

(7) GDP is $14.277 billion and GDP per capita $11280-.

(18) **Mozambique:**

(1) Mozambique got independence in 1975 from Portugal. Portugal contribution to the countries growth was very high. But after the independence, Civil war started in 1977 and ended in 1992 i.e. 15 years. In the Civil War, Agitators destroyed most of the infrastructure and development made by Portugal. After end of Civil War in 1992, the country started making growth and development. In 1987, government started series of macroeconomic reforms. Through the donors' assistance, political stability was established after multi-party elections in 1994. Dramatic improvement was brought. Inflation was brought to single digit in 1990s but again rose to double digit in 2000-02.

(2) Foreign debts were reduced through forgiveness (moratorium) and rescheduling under the IMF Heavily Indebted Poor Countries and Enhancement Initiatives. External debt is now at manageable level.

(3) Portuguese participated in the trading network of East Africa in 16th century but did not establish total colonial dominance

over the entire territory that now comprises Mozambique until the 19th century.

(4) Mozambique got independence in 1975. But Civil War starts in 1977 and ended after 15 years in 1992. There was hasty exodus of 90% of the ethnic Portugal citizens. Civil War destroyed all developments made by Portugal.

(5) Country has nationalist Guerrilla which in Civil War destroyed all developments made by the Portugal. Unless Guerrillas are controlled effectively, there will be no guarantee that developments made by the country will be retained. The country adopted non-alignment policy and does not interfere in the internal affairs of any country. Its rulers are sincerely engaged in the growth and development.

(19) **Tanzania:**

(1) Tanzania is the second largest economy in the East African country and the tenth largest in Africa.

(2) Agriculture is the main occupation of the economy.

(3) It is transit economy from command to market economy.

(4) Domestic and foreign investments were encouraged. Adjustment programs were introduced in 1986 to distribute the socialist economic control to encourage more participation of the private sector, reduce budget deficit, improve monetary control, depreciation of exchange rate, liberized trade, free interest rate, ease restriction on marketing of food, crop, and restructuring of financial sector.

(5) In May 2009, IMF approved an Exogenous Shock Facility for Tanzania to help the country cope with the global economic crisis. Tanzania is also engaged with policy Support instrument (PSI) which commenced in February 2007. Second three year Poverty Reduction and Growth Facility (PRGF) completed in August 2003.

(6) Growth remained 4% on overwhelming donors Dependents. External debt was $7.9 billion. Servicing debt was 40% of the expenditure. Debt worth $6 billion cancelled by Paris Club as per Agreement of Moratorium.

(7) Chinese firms are showing interest to develop the project of increasing natural gas capacity from 4.6 trillion cubic feet to 8.8 trillion cubic feet by the mid2015.

(8) Country has non-alignment policy and it does not interfere with the internal affairs of other countries. It strives for growth, progress and happiness of all people with equality and controlling of inflation which leads to the development of the nation as a welfare state.

(20) **Zambia:**

(1) Zambia is one of the fastest growing economy in Africa and its capital Lusaka is fastest growing city in South Africa Development Countries (SADC)

(2) One half of the population i.e. 8 million is residing in urban areas and rural areas are underpopulated. Zambia is one of the sub-Saharan Africa's most highly urbanized country.

(3) Unemployment and underemployment are serious consistent problems. High birth rate and AIDs have resulted in lower per capita annual income to about two-third of their levels at independence in spite of national GDP has actually doubled since 1964.

(4) In 2007, economic growth reached 6% - 7% though the average growth rate was 4.3% from 2017 onwards. Copper is the main export (64% of total exports) and agriculture is only 20% of GDP. There is no diversification of economy.

(5) Co-operation continues with international bodies on programs to reduce poverty, including new pending arrangements with these bodies.

(6) Zambian government's plan to gain control over insurance companies and building was successfully resisted by banks like Barclays, Standard Chartered and Grindlays.

(7) By mid-1980, Zambia was most indebted nation in the world, relative to its GDP. IMF was insisting that Zambia government should introduce programs aimed at stabilizing economy and restructuring it to reduce dependence on copper. The proposed measures included: the ending of price control, devaluation of kwacha, cut-backs in government expenditure, cancellation of subsidiaries on food and fertilizers, and increase farm production.

(8) After independence in 1964, country was ruled by Kaunda till 1991, then by Frederick Chiluba (1991-2001). They introduced reforms under planning and privatized many state industries, maintained positive interest rates, eliminated exchange controls and introduced free market principles.

(9) Zambian Kwacha was floating currency. To stabilize the exchange rate, foreign reserves were utilized and kwacha was devalued to resolve the Balance of Payment issue.

(10) Zambia qualified for HIPC debt relief in 2000 contingent upon the country meeting certain performance criteria and this should offer a long term solution. In 2003, the Zambia government informed the IMF and World Bank that it wishes to renegotiate some of its agreed performance criteria calling for privatization of Zambia National Commercial Bank, national telephone and electricity companies.

(11) Country's economy is crippling. Though the country is adopting non-alignment policy in respect of other countries in their internal affairs, Zambia will not be able to develop the welfare state unless it resolves all above highlighted issues.

(21) **Zimbabwe:**

(1) Currency RTGs dollar was volatile. During 1980-2000, there were fluctuations in exchange which led to economic crisis.

(2) Mugabe was the dictator who introduced the redistribution of land which failed miserably. Other economic reforms were also miserably failed. Share prices of mining companies fell when government implemented laws which required local ownership of mining companies. These led to imposing economic sanctions on Zimbabwe by USA, UK and EU. Zimbabwe was highly indebted and was eligible to get assistance from IMF on HIPC program. But IMF and UK, USA and EU refused to give Moratorium for $6 billion debt which these institutes approved for other countries under highly indebted countries program.

(3) Zimbabwe is developing/emerging country with low income economy.

(4) Adequate transport and electrical power network but maintenance is lacking.

(5) Democracy is lacking. Mugabe was responsible for economic meltdown.

(6) Bonus to Independence War veterans was announced in 1997(3% of GDP) followed by unexpected spending due to

the involvement of the Second Congo War in 1998, drought in 1999 weakened the economy and led to the country's bankruptcy.

(7) Land reforms by Mugabe, recurrent interference with judiciary, failure to maintain price controls and exchange rates led to the sharp drop in investors' confidence.

(8) Sanctions led to the crippling economy. Because of sanctions, no debts were cancelled. It also stopped food and forced the government to borrowing from local sources.

(9) Taxes and tariffs are high, government spending is 29.7% of GDP. State enterprises are strongly subsidized. Starting or Closing of business is slow and costly. Hiring a worker is cumbersome and firing is difficult. By 2008, unemployment was 94%.

(10) In doubling GDP, it took 190 years.

(11) Unemployment was high at 10.3%. Country was not able to pay weekly wages to the employees frequently compelled the government to reduce employment adding to the unemployment.

(12) Main industries are mining - coal, gold, platinum, copper and nickel.

(13) Exports $4.53 billion Imports $5.472 billion Trade deficit 0.942 billion i.e.4.48% of GDP.

(14) Revenue$3.8 billion Expenses$ 5.5 billion Fiscal deficit $1.7 billion i.e. 8.10% of GDP

(15) Foreign Reserves: $431.8 million.

(16) Country's economy is crippling. Mugabe is involved in Second Congo War in 1998, IMF refused to waive $ 6 billion loan as HIPC program on account of sanctions from US, UK and EU on account of failure of reforms introduced by Mugabe resulted in bankruptcy of the economy. Under Mugabe Country is not well managed and is incapable to promote a welfare state.

(22) **Economy of Canada:**

(1) Canada had clashes with India when Sikhs in India has formed Khalistan as the independent state from India at the instigation of Pakistan Army. These activities initiated in Canada and Canadian government had supported it. India registered a strong protest against Canada for anti-Indian

activities. Except this issue, the relation of India with Canada is cordial.

(2) Canada does not show political dominance on other countries by interfering in the political affairs of that country. It has adopted non-alignment policy. Its administrators are engaged to promote the welfare and economic growth of their country. There are no wasteful resources for military interference in the affairs of other countries and all available resources are used for promoting welfare state.

(3) Canada is the staunch follower of USA. Apart from the high trade partnership between Canada and USA under NAFTA, there is a strategic military partnership between USA and Canada. USA provides advanced military weapons including nuclear weapons and has built up a strong military base in Canada to protect the country from the military attack by any country especially from Russia or China. Canada has dispute over North Atlantic area where Russia has built up the Military Base which may result in escalation of dispute between two countries.

(4) The economy of Canada is highly developed market economy. The economy is dominated by Services industry which employs 75% of Canadian workforce.

(5) It has the third largest proven petroleum resources and is the fourth largest exporter of the natural gas. It has the natural resources worth $33 trillion.

(6) Canada is main trading partner of USA. NAFTA was unfavorable to USA. In 2016, USA stopped implementing NAFTA with Canada. In 2017, fresh NAFTA was signed with Canada which provided favourable terms of trade to USA and its adverse trade balance with Canada was substantially reduced.

(7) Main Industries are Transport equipments, chemicals, minerals, food products, wood & paper, fish

(8) Exports $585 billion, Imports $ 607 Trade deficit $22 billion

(9) Country has ample resources and is well managed. It strives for comforts happiness of its citizens It adopts non-alignment policy. It is well prosperous nation striving for the Welfare State which is the ultimate goal of the entire mankind.

(23) **Economy of Italy:**

(1) Presently as at 15-04-2020, Italy is known to the world for widespread and dangerous spreading of the virus known as Coronavirus. More than 20000 people died and there are 3 lacs Coronavirus patients under treatment.

(2) 1922. In order to improve economy, Mussolini abandoned leissez faire and free trade in favour of government intervention and protectionism.

(3) Mussolini fought against France and Ethiopia and supported Nazi aggressive policy in World War II which resulted in imposing various restrictions on Italy and it was administered by the wining countries. Tremendous war expenditure resulted in falling growth of the Italian economy. 7 lacs soldiers were killed and 5 million army was built up and there were economic crisis after the war.

(4) When the country diversifies its attention from the good administration and the Ruler starts dominating and interfering the internal affairs of other countries like Mussolini, the country suffers and economic crisis occurs. To avoid this, Ruler should always concentrate on the country's progress and should not support wrong aggressive Nazis as Mussolini did and led the country to the economic crisis after World War II. This is also happening to Iran as Shias are showing their mighty strength to the Super power USA and is under economic sanctions of USA. Italy should learn lesson from Fascist ideology and should concentrate on the growth and development of its economy.

(24) **Economy of Greece:**

(1) Country is at present in light due to the country's clashes with Turkey. Recep Erdogan, Turkey's President, had accepted refugees from the other countries like Syria, Libya, and Venenzua etc. on the basis of Agreement of Turkey with EU on terms that EU will provide financial assistance to Turkey as a compensation to Turkey for accepting these refugees.

Turkey has recently dispute with Syrian President Assad on Syrian army supporting Kurdish tribes of Iraq against the Turkey's fight with Kurdish tribes. In this dispute, Turkey's soldiers are killed in large number. Erdogan thereafter has proposed that European countries should assist militarily to resolve this issue. European countries did not respond to the Turkey's proposal positively. Erdogan then threatened the European countries that he will release the Turkey's border and will send refugees to the European countries in lacs. He released the Turkey's Border thereafter near to Greece Border and send thousands of refugees to Greece. Greece strongly opposed these refugees by military interference which led to ruthless opposition from refugees. There was ferrous fighting between Greece soldiers and refugees who protested for not allowing them to Greece entry, there were stone throwing etc. Erdogan criticized Greece for this protest and compared it with Nazi's action of killing hundreds of thousands Jews during World War II. This criticism was unwanted and false. This issue has not yet been resolved and Greece has kept military on the Border to prevent refugees to enter its Border. Refugees are forcibly tried to enter Greece but because of strong military action, refugees are not able to enter Greece. Erdogan has meantime closed Turkey's border on the ground of coronavirus. This has further added fuel to the fire.

(2) Greece is a developed country with an economy based on the Services (80%), Industry sector (16%) and Agriculture (4%)

(3) Important Greek industries are tourism and shipping. !8 million international tourists visited Greece recently.

(4) Greece Merchant Navy is the largest in the world with Greek owned vessels accounting for 15% of global deadweight tonnages of 2013. On account of increased demand for international maritime, transport between Greece and Asia resulted in un-precedent investment in the shipping industry.

(5) Country joined EU in 1981. Greece adopted the Euro as its currency. Currency rate 34075 Greece Drachma =euro 1

(6) Greece was accepted on the Economic and Monetary Union of the EU by the European Council in June 2000 based on number of criteria such as inflation rate, budget deficit, exchange rate, long term interest rate using 1999 as the reference year. It was observed in 2004 that this criteria

was not complied with by Greece while admitting it as a member of EMU. Budget deficit was under reported.

(7) Economic crisis resulting from huge public debt and fiscal deficit and increased borrowing rate made it impossible for the country to finance its debt since early 2010. In order to avert a default in 2010, the European countries and IMF agreed to a "rescue package" which involved giving Greece an immediate euro 45 billion bail-out package, with more funds to follow totaling euro110 billion. Greece was to adopt austerity measures to bring its loan, with more funds to follow totaling euro 110 billion. Austerity measures implementation was to be monitored and evaluated by the European Commission, European Central Bank and IMF.

(8) Austerity package met with anger by Greek public leading to riots and social unrest. There were labour strikes in the industry on account of unemployment, reduced wages etc. Austerity measures did not reduce the government deficit because of subsequent recession. Second bail-out package was given in 2014 for $1.36 billion and third bail-out was given in 2017 with credit $9.5 billion and $8.5 billion. Bail-out resulted in 25% of GDP. This increased debt to GDP ratio. Unemployment was 14.8% in 2012. Poverty was 15% in 2015 from 8.9%. Unemployment of young youth force was 60% and for others 25%.

(9) High spending on budget coupled with recession and debt crisis resulted in economic crisis.

(10) Greek labour force was working 1900 hours per year followed by Spaniards 1800 per year.

(11) On account of persistent economic crisis, industrial production in the country went down by 8% between 2010 and 2011. Building construction reduced by 73% Unemployment skyrocketed from 7.2% in late 2008 to 27.9% in June 2013 leaving millions jobless. Corruption and tax evasion added fuel to the fire.

(12) GDP $214.012 billion Nominal and $324.128 billion PPP

(13) Population was 1.07 crore GDP per Capita was $19974-Nominal & $30252 –PPP

(14) Labour Force 46.56 lacs. Unemployment was 16.3% in 2019 and 39.5% in 2018. Average Gross Salary euro 17512- and Net Salary euro 7863 in 2018

(15) Main Industries: Shipping and ship building, tourism, food and tobacco processing, textiles, chemicals, metal products.

(16) Country adopted non-alignment policy and does not interfere in the internal affairs of other country. But the country is poorly economically managed and is not capable to promote welfare state.

(25) **Economy of Afghanistan:**

(1) There is politically constant unrest in Afghanistan. Country is militarily attacked by Taliban continuously. It is an example how continuous unrest occurs in a country where many outside countries interfere in the internal political affairs of the country. Terrorists Taliban were rulers of Afghanistan. Taliban were first defeated by American troops with the military assistance of Pakistan in 1990 against Soviet Russia. Soviet Russia withdrew the troops from Afghanistan in 1990. Thereafter American troops protected Afghanistan against Taliban. There were elections periodically and Gunny was the President of Afghanistan. American soldiers gave military training to Afghanistan army. India has been investing in Afghanistan to improve Afghan conditions in education, industry building, construction transport facilities and infrastructure development. Pakistan and Taliban are protesting India's economic support to Afghanistan.

(2) Recently, America had negotiation with Taliban on peace and permanent cease-fire. But Taliban is unreliable and may not keep up their promise. USA troops in Afghanistan should be alert at all times. USA should not hastily withdraw their troops from Afghanistan.

(3) Economy of Afghanistan has improved significantly due to the infusion of billions of dollars as international assistance and remittances from Afghan expatriates. Unemployment was 23.9%. In 1979, Soviet Union Russia invasion and ensuing civil war destroyed much of its infrastructure and disrupted normal pattern of economic activities.

(4) Illicit trade in opium was destroyed. This was giving lot of funds to illegal tribes.

(5) Coal and iron mines infrastructure was built up. Afghanistan is planning to build up refinery within next three years.

(6) Country began facing several problems during 1970s when Pakistan closed border crossing on account of increasing political ties with northern neighbour i.e. Soviet Union. Pakistan and USA relationship and military ties were built up. USA started giving defence annual aid to Pakistan $1.3 billion till 2017 which was used by Pakistan to fund Terrorists tribes for attacking India on Kashmir issue. USA, and USA Secretary Dr. Kissinger were aware of this utilization but they ignored these activities since Soviet Union was India's friend and provided India with nuclear reactors. Kissinger was mad to disintegrate Soviet Union and took many wrong decisions which had bad impact on US economy for a long time.

(7) There are copper mines worth $33 billion. China invested $2.8 billion and Canada for copper exploration and SAIL in India expected to invest $14.6 billion developing untapped iron ore mines.

(8) It is estimated that Afghanistan has untapped minerals worth $1 to $3 trillion. Untapped rare earth minerals are estimated 1 million metric tonnes.

(9) In construction field, it is constructing green houses. It is self-sufficient in food except that it has to import 1 million ton wheat per year.

(10) Afghanistan is building up a strong military force to fight against Taliban. For building army for self-protecting is the appropriate action. It does not interfere with internal affairs of any country. It has adopted non-alignment policy.

(11) GDP is $17.734 billion Nominal & $76. 486 billion

(12) Population 3.45 crore GDP per capita $513.26

(13) Unemployment: 23.9%

(14) Main Industries: Small scale production of textile, soap, furniture, shoes, fertilizers, apparel, food products, nonalcoholic beverages, mineral water, cement. Untapped copper, iron ore mine, rare earth minerals 1 million metric ton and other minerals worth $ 3trillion. If untapped minerals worth $3 trillion are tapped and abstracted, the country will become self-sufficient and rich.

(15) Country is continuously facing problems internally and is expected to make many infrastructural changes to promote

the growth and development of the country and making it a welfare

(26) **Economy of Israel:**

British mandate of Palestine came into effect in 1920 which prohibited land purchases by Jewish immigrants. Jewish population was initially urban and had higher share in industrial operation.

Jews had no empire before World War II. After World War II, Western Countries and USA created a new nation on the heart of Arab Gulf known as Israel as Jews' Nation.

The first Survey of the Dead Sea in 1911, by the Russian Jewish Potash Novomeysky led to the establishment of Palestine potash Ltd. In 1930 later named the Dead Sea Works.

After statehood, Israel faced a deep economic crisis. To recover from the deviating effects of 1948 Arab-Israeli war on establishment of Israel as an independent nation on the heart of Arab's territory by USA and others after World War II, it has to absorb hundreds of thousands of Jewish refugees from European and million from the Arab World. To face economic crisis, austerity measures were implemented from 1949 to 1959. Unemployment was high and foreign currency reserves were scarce. Israel had to continuously fight with Arab countries for existence from 1948. Most of the Arab countries had vowed to destroy Israel from the Arab Territory. There was complete unrest in this territory. But Israel army and Intelligence unit has strong spy machinery. Jews were brave, strewed and prepared for any war. Israel was therefore survived from continuous attacks by Arab countries.

In 1952, Israel and West Germany signed an Agreement stipulating that West Germany was to pay for Jewish property stolen by Nazis, over the next the next 14 years (till 1966) 300 billion marks to Israeli i.e. $111.5 billion. This became a decisive factor in Israel's income, comprising as high as 87.5% of Israel income in 1956.

Israel conflict with Palestine and Gaza Strip also continued till date. Palestine declared that Eastern Jerusalem is and will be the Capital of Palestine in 1967 and there would be no compromise on this issue. Israel also wanted the Jerusalem as its Capital. Recently Mr. Trump, President of USA unilaterally declared that South Jerusalem will be the Capital of Israel and later on established its Israeli Embassy in Jerusalem. This was wrong decision. This agreement should have been reached by negotiation between Israel and Palestine on negotiation table. All countries and UN opposed the decision of USA and it was widely criticized. In fact, except

Democratic President Mr. Omana, hardly any President of USA has spoken against Israel. Though USA has so much support for Israel, it did not offer Israel a separate 51st state status in USA but created Israel nation on the heart of Arab Gulf. Israel was treated as an enemy by the Arab world from the inception and it goes back to 18th century.

Mr. Trump offered a Peace Compromise proposal to Palestine that it will give $4.5 billion to Palestine or its economic growth on the condition that Palestine will give up its right to treat the South Jerusalem as its Capital which obviously Palestine refused on the ground that the issue is not economic but it is a political issue. Israel had already illegally constructed residential buildings in Gaza Strip for Jews' accommodation forcing refugees from that site out of Gaza Strip. The Peace proposal of USA was turned out by Palestine on the ground that refugees in Gaza strip should be protected. The act of illegally constructing residential buildings in Gaza Strip to Jews' residence by Israel was opposed by President Omana of USA and EU, Russia, China and UN.

(1) Country's major economic sectors are high technology and industrial manufacturing. Israeli diamond industry is popular for diamond cutting and polishing accounting for 23.2% of its export.

Its imports are petroleum, raw materials, wheat, motor vehicles and uncut diamonds and production inputs.

(2) Israel's quality university education and establishment of highly motivated and educated populace is highly responsible for the technology booms and rapid economy development.

(3) In 1950, Israeli government launched bonds for Americans and Canadian Jews to buy. In 1951, the final result of the bond program exceeded $52 million. American Jews made private donations to Israel which were $100 million a year which covers 35% of Israel Special development budget for investment in agricultural and industrial development projects.

(4) Economic growth rate exceeded 10% annually between 1950 and 1963, expenditure among the wage earners' families rose to 97% in real terms.

(5) The developments have helped to transform Israel's economy since the beginning of 1990s. The first is the

Jewish immigration. The second development benefiting the Israeli economy is the peace process began and the Madrid Conference of October 1991, which led to the signing of accords and later to a Peace Treaty between Jordan and Israel in 1994.

(6) There has been unprecedented inflows of foreign investment in Israel. In 2006, foreign investment totaled $13 billion.

(7) Israel was unable to duplicate its success in Telecommunication industry.

(8) Its polished diamonds exports fell to $5.56 billion in 2012 from $7.2 billion in 2011.Diamond imports slipped 24.9% to $4.43 billion. Rough diamond imports dropped 12.9% to $3.8 billion due to Global Finance Crisis in Europe and US.

(9) Israel is exporter of military equipment 10% of the world total in 2007. Israeli defence equipment exports reached $7 billion in 2012, 20% higher than 2011.

(10) External Trade: There is moderate trade deficit in Exports and imports. Arab League boycott trade with Israel and any company doing the business with Israel. It is known as tertiary boycott.

(11) Economy of Gaza Strip and Palestine depends upon the policy of Israel in employing Palestine and Gaza Strip people. Many times, Israel issues work permit to them to work in Israel. The wages in Israel are higher than in Palestine and Gaza Strip.

(12) Main Industries: High technology products, telecommunication equipment, computer hardware, aerospace and defence contracting, medical devices, fiber optic, pharmaceuticals, potash & phosphates, chemical products, diamond cutting & polishing

(13) Overall, the country is managed well. It has conflict with Arab countries in the Gulf. Iran is main enemy of Israel. It has conflict with Gaza Strip, West Sea and Palestine. Country has strong support from super power USA. There are air attacks, suicide bombing and missiles attacks by Hamas terrorists in Palestine and Gaza Strip. Country is not prepared to resolve issues with Palestine by negotiation. Country is retaliating Iran and Palestine terrorists. It has a strong spy mechanism. Sometimes country attacks Iran in

Syria causing conflict with Russia. It is a country which administers the country well, but people are constantly under fear for military attacks from Arab Countries including Iran, Palestine terrorism and Syria's conflict area. Israel will not lead the world for the welfare state on account of a lust of power and grab of Gaza Strip and dominance on Palestine by the Israel rulers.

(27) **Gaza Strip:**

(1) The economy of Gaza Strip was dependent on small industries and agriculture. After years of decline, economic growth in Gaza is now in the rise, boosted by foreign aid.

(2) As per IMF, economy grew 20% in 2011 and per capita GDP increased by 19%.

(3) Many Gazans worked in Israeli services while the border was open. In the wake of Israel's 2005 disagreement plan, Gazans could no longer do so.

(4) Gaza suffered from various shortages in housing, educational facilities, health facilities, infrastructure and an inadequate sewage system, contributing to serious hygiene and public health problems.

(5) EU paid euro 420 million in aid to Palestinians territories in 2001.This is in additional to contributions by individual member states. Germany contributed euro 55 million, France euro 67 million, and Great Britain Sterling pounds 63.6 million in 2007. US paid $7.7 billion in 2008-2010.

(6) Unemployment in Gaza was 29% in 2011. Qatar donated $400 million towards construction projects in the Gaza Strip.

(7) In November 2012, a report by the Palestinian Chamber of Commerce called for the Gaza Strip to be recognized as an economic disaster area. It concluded that the Israeli operation Pillar of Defence caused approximately $300 million in economic damages.

(8) Gaza experienced boom in construction industry. Recreation facilities, not aimed at tourist but at residents, new amusement parks, restaurants, crazy water parks resorts were constructed. Many Hotels including the hotel at Gaza Museum were also constructed. Unemployment was 40% in Gaza Strip in 2007. Private sector employed 53% of all

working Gazans but because of bankruptcy, 95% of cities operations were suspended and 75000 workers out of 110000 lost their jobs.

(9) Israel has treated Gaza Strip and Palestine as its own property. Israel is grabbing these territory as its own like China grabbing South China Sea, Taiwan. Israel has constructed recently residential building for Israelis staying there. Israel is forcibly expelling the refugees staying there for long time. This creates conflict of interest as Gaza wants to protect refugees in this territory. This is illegal act of Israel protested by all countries and UN but Israel is refused to honour UN order. Since Israeli rulers have greed and lust of power, the country is unable to promote a welfare state. Gaza Strip has continuous unrest and has no happiness and growth. It is not a welfare state under the control of Israel.

(28) **Economy of Palestine:**

(1) The first Survey of the Dead Sea in 1911, by the Russian Jewish Potash Novomeysky led to the establishment of Palestine Potash Ltd. In 1930 later named the Dead Sea Works.

(2) Economic conditions in the West Bank and Gaza Strip was governed by the Paris Economic Protocol of April 1991 between Israel and the Palestinian Authority deteriorated in early 1990s. Real per capita GDP for the West Bank and Gaza Strip declined 36.1% between 1992 and 1996. The downturn in economic activities was due to extensive corruption in the new governing Palestine Authority and to Israel's closure policies in response to terrorist attacks in Israel which disrupted previously established labour and commodity market relationships. The most serious effect was the emergence of chronic unemployment. Unemployment rose from 5% in 1980s to over 20% by mid-1990.

(3) After 1997, Israel's use of comprehensive closures decreased and new policies were implemented in October 1999. Israel permitted the opening of a safe passage between West Bank and the Gaza Strip in accordance with the 1995 Interim Agreement. This changes in the conduct of economic activity fueled a moderate recovery in 1998-99.

(4) As a result of the Israeli blockade, 85% of factories were shut or operated at less than 20% capacity. It is estimated that Israeli business lost $ 2 million per day from the closure of Gaza lost approximately $1 million per day. World Bank estimated that Nominal GDP of the territories at $4,007,000- and of Israel $166,822,000- per capita are respectively $1063 and $22563- per year.

(5) In the wake of Israel's unilateral disengagement from Gaza, there were shortage of breed and basic supplies due to the closure of Mentar/ Karn border-crossing. Israel's offer to open the crossings was turned down by Hamas-run Palestine Authority.

(6) In January 2006, legislative elections were won by Hamas. Palestine Authority appointed the Prime Minister Ismail Haniyah. The Palestine has monthly cash deficit $60 -$70 million after it received $50-$55 million per month from Israel in taxes and customs duties collected by the Israel officials at the borders. After election, Palestine stock market fell by about 20% and Palestine Authority exhausted its borrowing capacity with local banks. Israel ceased transferring $55 million in tax receipts to the Palestine Authority. These funds accounted for a third of the Palestine Authority's budget and payment of wages to 160000 Palestine civil servants. UN and EU halted direct aid to Palestine Authority, while US imposed a financial blockade on Palestine Authority Banks, impending the transfer of some of Arab League's Fund (Saudi Arabia and Qatar). In May 2006, hundreds of Palestinians demonstrated in Gaza and the West Bank demanding payment of their wages. Tension between Hamas and Fatah rose as a result of this "economic Squeeze" on the Palestine Authority.

(7) East Jerusalem: It is the first business and shopping hub of West Bank. Since the advent of Israeli security checkpoints and the separation barrier starting over a decade ago, it has become isolated from the customer base leading the serious economic decline. This resulted in unprecedented levels of poverty, with 80% of the Palestine living below the poverty line. Political and physical barriers separated it from West Bank. The cumulative effects of annexure, neglect, right violations and completion of separation barrier and housing

situation. Israeli government has facilitated extensive construction of Israeli settler's neighborhood but has severally restricted development and building for the Palestine population.

(8) According to Hamas, Israeli's closure policy which was extended when the Hamas administration came to power in 2007, was responsible for high levels of poverty and unemployment and a significant decline of the private sector which was mainly reliant upon export merchant. Israel blamed Hamas for taking air attack and suicide bombers that led to the closure policy. Large part of the population is dependent on human assistance primarily from UN.

(9) Primary currency in West Bank was Israeli Shekel and Jordan dinar. Shekel is more used in most transactions while Jordan dinar is used more for savings.

(10) In 2005, Palestine Authorities collected approximately $34 million In Palestinian territories, taxation is the complex system. Israel collected about $75 million per month in tariffs.

(11) Council for European Palestinian Relations reports that agriculture employs 13.4% of the work force Unemployment was 41% in 2008 in Gaza.

(12) AS of 2013, average daily wages in Israel is nearly 2.2 times more than in private sector in the West Bank and 4 times that in Gaza. Palestinian monthly wage is 1450 almost third of Israel 4300.

(13) In 2008, West Bank and Gaza economies were heavily reliant on foreign aid which stood $1.8billion i.e. 31% of GDP. $487 per Palestinian per year came from foreign aid. Foreign aid provided essential service in nearly half of the Palestine people. In 2010, Arab states cut financial aid to Palestinian authority. Palestinian authority received $583 million in budget support by August 2010. 22% only came from Arab countries.

(14) In 2019, US President Mr. Trump unilaterally declared South Jerusalem as Capital of Israel. In fact, Palestine had declared that Eastern Jerusalem is and will be Capital of Palestine. There was dispute on this issue. Instead of

resolving this issue by mutual negotiation, Us President should not have declared Eastern Jerusalem as capital of Israel Not only the President declared the Capital but he established US Embassy in East Jerusalem. This action was protested strongly by all countries and UN. Palestinian present President Abbas refused and strongly protested the US President action and he declared that the Palestine will not sit for negotiation with Israel. Trump then submitted a proposal to Palestine that US will grant $4 billion to Palestine to improve its economy. This will help grow Palestine economy by 50% and there will be unprecedented wealth to the region. The Plan was coordinated in conjunction with former UK Prime Minister Tony Blair. But Palestinian Authority President Abbas disapproved it on the ground that Palestinian priority is not economic but rather a political framework for the creation of Palestinian state based on in 1967 lines, with East Jerusalem as its capital. That will ensure the rights of refugees and a political compromise, the Palestine new agency added.

(15) Main Industries: cement, quarrying, textiles, soap, olive-wood curving, food processing, mother of pearl

(16) The country is set up in 1967. There are disputes between Israel and Palestine. Economy of Palestine depends upon Israel. There is the difference with Israel on closing of Israeli borders, Jerusalem as Capital, rights of refugees. Israel is strongly supported by US all the times and US neglects Palestine with the result that Israel has become very aggressive and has illegally constructed buildings in Gaza strip and West Bank for residents of Jewish. Refugees are driven away and the refugees' rights are not protected. There are serious problems of unemployment. But the closure has heavy economic losses for Israel also. Israel's business loss is estimated at $2 million per month. Israel and Palestine economies are partly interdependent with each other. Palestine is relied on economic aids from Saudi Arabia, Qatar, US, taxes recovered by Israel on borders of Gaza, Palestine amounting to $55 million per month. It is a country administered at present by Hamas and Fatah. Present President is Mohammed Abbas. Country is low income group and is not able to give happiness and comforts

to all people in the state. It is not administered as a welfare state on account of many conflicts issues the Palestine faces.

(29) **Economy of Syria:**

(1) The economy of Syria has deteriorated considerably since the beginning of the Syrian Civil War. Moreover, Syria's economy has been turbulent. In 1963, the Arab Socialist Ba'ath Party came to power and instituted socialist policies of nationalization and land reforms.

(2) In 1970, General Hafiz al-Assad took power. The restrictions on private enterprise were released, but substantial part of the economy was still under the government control. By the 1980s, Syria found itself politically and economically isolated, and in the midst of a deep economic crisis. Real per GDP capita fell 20% between 1982 and 1989. In 1990, Assad government instituted a series of economic reforms, although the economy remained highly regulated.

(3) The Syrian economy experienced strong growth throughout the 1990s and into the 2000s. Syria's GDP per capita was $4058 in 2010. There is no official GDP data available after 2012, due to Syrian Civil War. Before the civil war, agriculture and oil were two pillars of the Syrian economy accounting for 50% of the GDP. However, poor climatic conditions ran severe drought badly affecting the agriculture, thus reducing its share in the economy to about 17% of 2008 GDP, down from 20.4% in 2007. On the other hand, crude higher prices countered declining oil production and led to the higher budgetary and export receipts.

(4) In 2011, Bashar al-Assad became President of Syria. There was outbreak of civil war on account of mismanagement of Assad family. Protesters were protesting against Bashar al-Assad and demanding its ouster from Presidential position. USA and its allies also wanted Assad to resign and go. But as usual Russia wanted Assad to stay. US, Russia and Iran set up Military Bases with their armies in Syria. There was a severe military attack by Al Qaeda. USA, Russia and Iran came together and defeated Al Qaeda.

(5) Economy suffered from hyperinflation and corruption. Economic sanctions added fuel to the fire by restricting trade with the Arab league, Australia, Canada, the EU

(including countries of Albania, Iceland Moldova, North Macedonia, Norway, Serbia and Switzerland), Georgia, Japan, South Korea, Taiwan, Turkey and US. The Sanctions, destruction and dislocation associated with the civil war have devastated Syrian economy.

(6) By the end of 2013, the UN estimated total economic damage of civil war at $143 billion. This reached $237 billion by end of 2015. With the Syrians Opposition's capture of Nasib border, crossing costing the government a further $500-$700 million a year on the top of this. In 2018, the World Bank estimated that about one-third of Syria's housing stock and one half of its heath and economic facilities has been destroyed by the conflict. According to the World Bank, a cumulative total of $ 226 billion in GDP was lost due to the conflict between 2011 and 2016. Syrian economy suffered from conflict-related hyperinflation. Syrian annual inflation rate was 30% which is one of the highest in the world.

(7) Bashar al-Assad was adamant. He did not resign but ruthlessly handled the demonstrators and this conflict. USA charged Assad for having using chemical missiles against the agitators and killing thousands of the citizens. USA therefore attacked Assad army with US army assisted by Iraq's Kurdish army. Russia also threatened US to counterattack US in Syria. Israel also retaliated by attacking Iran Military Base in Syria in retaliation of Iran's attack on Israel. Once, accidently, Russian fighting aeroplane was dropped and destroyed by Israel. Russia took this very seriously and retaliated Israel. Since there were constant fighting in Syria, Syrians found unsafe to stay in their country. They left the country and become refugees and took shelter in European countries as asylum. EU prescribed certain quotas for taking refugees from other countries by its members. Germany and France were strong supporters for migrating the refugees in European countries but after some time, all other countries like Italy, Greece strongly opposed to this policy and after strong opposition from the other countries, EU had to amend its migration plan.

(8) Syria has heavy-grade oil from fields inside the northeast since late 1960s. In the early 1980s, light-grade, low

Sulphur oil was discovered in eastern Syria. This needed Syria to import light oil to mix with domestic heavy crude in refineries. Syria's oil production is 379000 barrels per day. Oil reserves are 2.5 billion barrels in 2009. By end of next decade, Syria will become importer of petroleum.

(9) Government established an official parallel exchange rate to provide incentives for remittances and exports through official channels. This action improved the supply of basic commodities and contained inflation by removing risk premiums on smuggled commodities.

(10) Foreign aid was $199 million in 1997. World Bank committed $661 million for 20 operations in Syria in 2004.

(11) Agriculture and oil were two main exports earning $1 billion.

(12) Syria had been original contracting party of the formal General Agreement on Tariff and Trade but withdrew in 1951 on account of Israel joining. It has signed an Associate Agreement with the EU that would encourage both sides to negotiate a free trade agreement before 2010.

(13) The bulk of Syrian imports have been raw materials essential for industry, agriculture, equipment and machinery.

(14) Major exports are crude oil, refined products, raw cotton, clothing, fruits and cereal grains.

(15) Poor development of capital markets and lack of access to international market and capital markets, monetary policy remains captive to the need to cover the fiscal deficit. In 2003, Syria lowered interest rates for the first time in 22 years and again in 2004, rates remain fixed by law.

(16) National debt was 152% of GDP in 2002 and it was 30.02% in 2010. Syria has made progress in easing its heavy foreign debt burden through bilateral rescheduling deals with virtually all of its key creditors in Europe. In 2004, Syria & Poland reached an agreement by which Syria would buy $27 million out of the total $261.7 million debt. In January 2005, Russia and Syria signed a deal that wrote off nearly 80% of Syrian debt to Russia approximately euro 10.5 billion ($13 billion). Agreement left Syria with less than euro3 billion ($3.6 billion) owed to Moscow. Half of which would be paid in next 10 years. IN 2006, Syria

reached agreement with Slovakia and Czech Republic to settle debt estimated at $1.6 billion. Syria was forgiven the bulk of its debt, exchange for a one-time payment of $150 million.

(17) Syria abandoned its plans to build VVER-440 reactor after the Chernobyl accident. The plans for a nuclear program were revived at the beginning of 2000s when Syria negotiated with Russia to build the nuclear facility that would include nuclear power plant and a sea water atomic desalination plant.

(18) The industrial sector includes mining, manufacturing, construction.

(19) Since the start of civil war in 2011, there has been capital flight to nearby countries. Syria has been subjected by US, Canada, EU, Arab League and Turkey Sanctions because of civil war. Syrian pound devalued from SYP 47 per dollar in 2011 to SYP 515 per dollar in July 2017.

(20) US sanctions may have increased the role of Lebanese and European banks on account of ban on transactions between US financial institutions and Central Bank of Syria. This resulted in need for intermediary to US$ transfer. In addition to US, EU, Arab League and Turkey also imposed sanctions on the Central Bank because of the civil war.

(21) Syrian population is 21 million (2.1 crores). Population growth was 2.37%. 65% of population is under age 35 years and more than 40% under the age of 15. 200000 new jobs seekers enter the Syria job market every year. But the country has not been able to absorb them. In 2017, the labour force was 47.67 lacs. Labour force was classified as 17% in agriculture, 16% in industry and services 67%.

(22) Inflation 30% and Unemployment 50%

(23) Assad has now been pursued by Russia to conduct fresh election Assad agreed to conduct fresh election which were scheduled in April-May 2020. On account of sudden spread of Coronavirus, the elections have been postponed. Let us hope that after the election, the country shall get good ruler, sanctions by all countries will be removed and the present turmoil will be over.

(24) There is unrest in the country and rulers are unable to administer the country properly. There are Military Bases

of Iran, Russia and USA in Syria. Israel air-attacks on Iran Military Base destroys the deference ammunition of Iran and constant bombing frightened Syrians who fled from Syria and took shelter as refugees in other countries.

(30) **Economy of Libya:**

(1) The economy of Libya depends primarily on revenues from the petroleum sector, which represents over 95% of the export earnings and 60% of GDP. These oil revenues and a small population have given Libya one of the highest Nominal per capita GDP in Africa.

(2) Libya is not peaceful. Libya's administrator Saraj and Ex-Military General Haftar are fighting with each other since 2011 to date regarding acquisition of political power in the state. Countries like US and its allies have sympathy for democratically elected Saraj but these countries and UN do not take any side officially and insist that the dispute should be mutually settled among these two parties by negotiation. No official information has been given by the economy of Libya on this disputed issue harming peace in Libya.

(3) Presently, the country came to light because of Recep Erdogan, President of Turkey, supported Saraj by providing military equipments such as fighting planes, missiles etc. to Saraj government to fight against Haftar militant group. UN objected to Turkey's action and ordered Erdogan to refrain from supporting Saraj. UAE and Egypt threatened to train the Haftar group with naval war skills and other war skill area. The matter has not yet been settled.

(4) Since the oil is the main export, Libya's fantastic growth rate proved unsustainable in the face of global oil recession and international sanctions. Consequently, the GDP per capita shrank by 40% in the 1980s. Successful diversification and integration into the international commodity helped current GDP per capita to cut further deterioration to just 3.2% in the 1990s.

(5) Libyan GDP per capita was about $40 in the early 1920s but it rose to $1028 by 1967 alone, per capita GDP rose by 42%.

(6) It is to be noted that GDP PPP per capita was $27894 in 1980 and came down to $9986 in 2017. Inflation rate was

also 14.4% in 1980 which rose to 28% in 2017. Budget deficit was 12.5% of GDP in 2010 and rose dangerously to 43.2% in 2017.

(7) Libyan dinar 1 equals to US $0.77 and mean wage were $9.51 per hour in 2007.

(8) Although UN sanctions were suspended in 1999, foreign investment in the Libyan gas and oil sector were severally curtailed due to the US, Iran & Libya Sanctions Act capped the amount the foreign companies can invest in Libya yearly at $20 million (lowered from $40 million in 2001). As of May 2006, US removed Libya from its list of states that sponsor terrorism and has normalized ties and removed sanctions. This clears the road for US oil companies to exploit Libyan oil and is expected to have a passive impact on the Libyan economy.

(9) Production of oil raised from 1.8 million bpd in 2006 to 2 million bpd by 2008.

(10) In November 2005, Libya discovered a significant oil deposit of light, sweet crude in the Murzuq Basin.

(11) Oil wealth has enabled Libya to pursue extravagant projects such as agriculture and the Great Manmade river in the Sahara Desert.

(12) In 2007, Mining and hydrocarbon industries accounted for well over 95% of the Libyan economy. Diversification of the economy into manufacturing industries remain a long term issue.

(13) Libya depends on imports in most food. Climatic conditions and poor soil severally limit farm output, and domestic conditions limit output while higher incomes and a while higher incomes and a growing population have caused food consumption to rise. Because of the low rainfall levels in Libya, agricultural projects rely on underground water source. Libya's primary agricultural water source remains the Great Mandate River, but significant resources are being invested in desalinization research to meet grooving demand. Libyan agricultural projects and policies are overseen by a General Inspector.

(14) Libya posted a 3.3% rate of population growth during 1960-2003. In 2003, 86% of the population was urban

compared to 45% in 1970. Unemployment is reportedly acute. 50% of the population under the age of 20 years. Labour market regulations favour Libyan workers. Mismatch of the education system with market demand has produced a large pool of expatriate workers, with typically better suited education and high productivity. However, because of shortage of manual labour, Libya has attracted important numbers of less skilled immigrants. Expatriate workers represent an estimated fifth of the labour force.

The proportion of expatriate workers is below oil producing countries in the Persian Gulf. Foreign workers came from Egypt, Turkey, Sudan and Bosnia. Share of expatriates earning was LD 300 ($230) per month was 20% compared to 12% to the Libyan nationals.

(15) Population: 66.79 lacs (6.679 million)

(16) GDP: $40.951 billion Nominal & $74.719 billion PPP in 2018

(17) Unemployment: 30% very high. Education system should be improved to suit the market demands and skilled workers.

(18) Main Industries: Petroleum, steel, iron, food processing, textile, cement.

Conclusion

(1) Gaddafi ruled the country for a long time. Gaddafi was a cruel monarch who ruled the country ruthlessly. He had constant clashes with many countries like USA, EU member countries and UN members' countries. This resulted in imposing international sanctions by USA, EU and UN. This resulted in vulnerable economy of Libya. GDP and national growth crippled. GDP was the most volatile and widely fluctuating.

(2) There were constant civil war in the African country Libya under Gaddafi and presently between Saraj government and Ex-General Haftar. Due to the continuous unrest in the country, citizens left the country as refugees and immigrated in European countries where they got shelter.

(3) Country's main resource of revenue is oil and its economy depends upon oil prices. Country has not diversified its activities in other fields. But country has large foreign reserves. Country is not properly administrated by the rulers/government as a welfare state.

(31) **Economy of Yemen:**

(1) The economy of Yemen is one of the poorest and the country least developed in the world.

(2) South Yemen and North Yemen were two parts which were vastly different but both were equally struggling underdeveloped economic system.

(3) South Yemen and North Yemen were unified in 1990. Political trouble and civil war started between Hathi government and Hothi opposition thereafter.

(4) Unified Yemen supported Iraq in Persian War in 1990-91. This was a blunder as Saudi Arabia and Kuwait were granting huge economic aid to Yemen.

(5) After the Persian War, Saudi Arabia retaliated Yemen by expelling almost one million Yemen workers in Saudi Arabia. Saudi Arabia and Kuwait also significantly reduced economic aid to Yemen. This resulted in scattering the Yemen economy. Yemen economy was in crisis and vulnerable.

(6) In 1994 Civil war, Yemen's economy was further drained. As a consequence, for the last 26 years Yemen has relied heavily on aid from multilateral agencies to sustain its economy.

(7) In 1997, IMF approved two programs to increase Yemen's Credit significantly. Enhance structural adjustment facility (now known as Poverty Reduction and Growth Facility or PRGF) and Extended Fund Facility (EFF). In the ensuing years, Yemen's government attempted to implement recommended reforms-reducing the civil service payroll, eliminating diesel and other subsidies, lowering defence spending, introducing a general sale tax and privatizing state- run industries. However, limited progress led the IMF to suspend funding between 1999 and 2001.

(8) In late 2005, the WB which had extended Yemen a four year $2.3 billion economic support package in October 2002 together with other bilateral and multilateral lenders, announced that as a consequences of Yemen's failure to implement significant reforms, it would reduce financial aid by one third over the period of July 2005 through July 2008. A key component of the $2.3 billion package - $300

million in concessional financing – has been withheld pending renewal of PRGF with IMF, which is currently under negotiation. However in 2006, the WB adopted the an assistance strategy for Yemen under which it will provide approximately $400 million in International Development Association (IDA) credits over the period of FY 2006 to FY 2009. In November 2006, at a meeting of Yemen's development partners, a total of $4.7 billion in grants and concessional loans were pleaded for the period 2007-2010. But in spite of significant oil and gas resources and considerably agriculturally productive land, Yemen remained the one of the poorest of the world's low-income countries.

(9) The influx of an average 1000 Somali refugees per month into Yemen looking for work is an added drain on the economy. Yemen has already unemployment rate of 20% to 40%. Yemen is under constant pressure to implement economic reforms or face the loss of badly needed international financial support.

(10) Continuous disruption on account of civil war and frequently droughts had severed blows for previously prosperous agricultural sector. Citizens of Yemen left their country and became refugees and were migrated to European countries.

(11) In agriculture, coffee which was significant share of foreign exchange declined as the cultivation of khat increased. Low domestic industrial output and a lack of new materials made the Yemeni Arab Republic dependent on a wide variety of imports.

(12) Yemen's civil war between Hathi and Hothi was supported by various countries: US, EU, UAE, Saudi Arabia and allies supported Hathi government as it was the democratic elected government while Iran and Russia supported Hothi opposition for their claims. Recently in 2020, Hothi with the active military support from Iran air attacked and dropped missiles on Saudi Arabia's important oil tankers and refineries. This resulted in heavy damages to Saudi Arabia which had to close crude oil exports for some weeks to overcome the damages caused to oil tankers and refineries. After the air attack, UAE reduced the support to Saudi Arabia on issue of Hothi. UAE has, however, not given its occupation of Socotra Island which it has taken from

Yemen government on rental basis for 95 years. In fact, UAE plans to take this Island from Yemen on permanent basis. It is in the middle of Arabian Sea and Aden's gulf and very important as a commercial centre. Russia and China have also eye on this Island. But US Marine has visited this Island and US has given Patriot Missile System to UAE and these missiles have been installed in this Island. US plans to set up Military Base in Socotra Island to control aggressive activities of China and Russia in this area.

(13) Yemeni Civil War and air bombing campaign by the coalition during the Saudi led intervention has divested the Yemen economy further. As a result of civil war, Yemen is suffering from inflation and devaluation of Yemeni Riyal. Yemen's economy has contracted by 50% from the start of the civil war in 19-3-2015 to October 2018. In 1989, Yemeni Riyal was 11.70 per dollar. But in 2005, Yemeni riyal was 191.37 per dollar. For purchasing power parity comparison, the US dollar is exchanged at 150.11 Yemeni riyals. Mean wages were $1.06 per man-hour in 2009.

(14) US government estimates that Yemen's industrial sector constitutes 47.2% of GDP. Together with services, constructions and commerce, industry accounts for 25% of the labour force. Oil refining is the largest contributor of manufacturing sector consists of 9.5% of GDP in 2005. Yemen had 134000 institutions establishments with 115000 workers.

(15) Following unification, Yemen experienced a very high average rate of inflation about 40%. Economic reforms brought down this to 5.4% in 1997 but high oil prices and cut in fuel subsidy in recent years had a negative impact on the inflation rate. In 2004, Central Bank of Yemen tightens the money supply which was offset by a weakening US$ to which the Yemeni Riyal is linked in a managed float. This rose global commodity prices and inflation rate was 12.5%. Sale tax was reduced to 5% in July 2005 resulting in inflation rising to 15% I 2006.

(16) The large volume of non-performing loans, low capitalization and weak enforcement of regulatory standards hamper Yemen's banking sector as a whole.

(17) Population: 29 million.

(18) GDP: $ 27.591 billion Nominal & $69.439 billion PPP in 2018

(19) GDP per Capita: $951 Nominal $2394 PPP

(20) Inflation: 27.6% High

(21) Work force: 68.14 lacs

(22) Industries: crude, petroleum refining, aluminum, leather goods, food processing, ship repairs,

(23) There are constant unrest in the country. Civil war in the country disrupted its progress. Conflict between Hathi and Hothi still continues resulting in unrest among nationals. IMF wanted to introduce austerity measures but substantial reduction in subsidy resulted in wide protest from public and have to be withdrawn. Country's government is unable to give happiness, growth and inflation control. Citizens are leaving the country as refugees and taking asylum in EU and other countries. Corruption is heavy. Administrators are not capable to administer the country properly.

(32) **Economy of Turkey:**

Turkey is an emerging industrial economy and has made progress in all sectors including agriculture, construction, telecommunication, textiles, motor vechicles, transportation equipment, armaments, satellite etc. In 2018, Turkey went through a currency and debt crisis, characterized by the Turkish Lira plunging in value, high inflation, rising borrowing cost and correspondingly rising debt defaults. This crisis was caused by the Turkish economy's excessive current account deficit and foreign currency debt, in combination with the ruling Justice & Development Party's increasing authoritarianism and President Recep Erdogan's unorthodox ideas about interest rate policy. With policy of Recep Erdogan fueling the construction sector, where many of his business allies are active, Turkey as of May 2018 had around 2 million unused houses, blocking worth three times average annual new housing sales.

On 10-08-2018, Turkish lira nosedived following Trump's tweet about doubling tariffs on Turkish steel and aluminum that day. Currency weakened 17% and has lost nearly 40% of its value against $ till that time. The crash of Lira has sent ripples-through global markets, putting more pressures on the euro and increasing investors' risk aversion to emerging market currencies across the board. On August 13, South African rand slumped nearly 10%. Lira crisis spotlighted deeper concerns about the Turkey's economy that have long signaled turmoil long along. By end of 2018, Turkey went in recession. Turkish economy reduced by 2.4% in the last quarter of 2018. Lira shrunk down to 30% against US dollar in 2018. Present economy of Turkey is as follows as per the financial data:

Population: 8.20 crores

GDP: $743.708 billion Nominal, $2.347 trillion PPP in 2019

GDP per capita : $8958 Nominal $28264 PPP

Inflation: 12.6% high on account of increased borrowing of foreign currency debts and high spending. Austerity measures required.

Population below poverty line: 41.3%

Labour Force: 3.3 crores (40.24% of population. Very low)

Labour Force by Occupation: Agriculture 17.7%, Industries 29% Services 53.3%

Unemployment 13.3% in 2019 27.4%. Youth unemployment in 2019 was too high. May be causing unrest in the country. President Erdogan to look into this issue.

Conclusion

From the above description of Turkey's economy, it is clear that Turkey has made progress in many fields. But President Erdogan is very dominating, aggressive and short temper personality. He wants to be the leader of all Islamic countries inclusive Saudi Arabia, Iran, Iraq, Qatar, UAE, Malaysia, Pakistan etc. He also is very ambitious to dominate the political and economic policies of other countries.

As a member of EU, he made an agreement with EU that Turkey will accommodate refugees in the country and he will get monetary compensation for the same.

After announcement by USA to withdraw the troops from Syria, Erdogan attacked the Kurdish to drive them away from Syria. Syrian army supported Kurdish opposition to Iraq government. Turkey lost about 40 soldiers and Erdogan's plan failed. He then asked for military support of EU countries but these countries never supported Turkeys in this conflicting issue. There-after Erdogan threatened these countries that Turkey will release its border and will send refugees to the European countries. He did so. Refugees then wanted to enter Greece Border but Greece protected its border by keeping large military on the border. Refugees were not allowed by the army to enter in Greece. There was fierce fighting between refugees and Greece army. Erdogan criticized Greece as giving treatment to refugees as Nazis had given to Jews in World War II. This was unnecessary and false criticism by the short tempered Erdogan. In order that refugees should not enter again in Turkey, Erdogan closed the Turkey's order under the pretext of Coronavirus spreading in Turkey. Matter is not yet settled.

Turkey has 8 crore population and Turkey is developing/emerging and middle income economy. There was currency and debt crisis in Turkey in 2018. Turkey President should effectively manage Turkey's economy.

Turkey President Mr. Recep Erdogan is however very aggressive in nature and he wants to control the political policy of the other countries. He is a dominated personality and interfere with the affairs of some countries.

Erdogan sent his military to Syria for attack on terrorists thereby spent lot of energy and financial resources which result in economic crisis in that country.

There is no reason for Erdogan to offer military weapons and armament to Saraj Government to fight against Haftar military. This is prohibited by UN. In-spite of this Erdogan interferes in this affairs but country like Egypt and UAE are strongly opposing to Turkey's aggressive policy and they threatened to give naval and military training to Haftar sliders and will fight supporting Haftar army. Erdogan hasty decision failed here also.

Erdogan is trying to have good relationship with Russia on Syrian issue and with USA on military assistance issue. He, however, is not successful. Erdogan took AS400 advanced fighters from Russia. USA strongly opposed to this movement. In spite of that Erdogan was firm on his agreement with Russia. USA imposed financial sanctions on Turkey. Turkey's economy was vulnerable in 2018 on currency and debt crisis. USA Sanctions fueled fire to this economic situation and country's economic position has become more vulnerable.

In order to show his authority and control over Islamic countries like Pakistan, Iran and others, Erdogan took Pakistan side on abolition of Article 370 in Kashmir by the Government of India. Secondly, Citizen Amendment Act and NRR were also opposed by Erdogan and has conflict with India on political issues. Erdogan has no right to interfere with India's matter. He has spoiled relation with India on these India's internal issue unnecessarily. This will result in India imposing ban on trade with Turkey in which Turkey will suffer more financial loss than India.

Erdogan should concentrate on his country's internal matters instead of interfering in the internal matters of other countries. He should cut unnecessary spending in the budget, reduce the foreign currency loans to avoid default in external debt servicing, monitor interest rate, inflation and unemployment. Unnecessary construction of houses should be stopped and should concentrate on selling of unsold houses to improve the Turkey's economy. His policy should be the country's interest first instead of implementing his personal political ideology. By change in his policy, Erdogan will make his country and should make his country economically and financially strong with country's highest economic growth and by making Turkey as a welfare state.

(33) **Economy of Iraq:**

(1) Economic sector of Iraq is dominated by oil sector which has provided 99.7% of exports earnings to Iraq. Iraq has, however, not diversified its economy to other industries/ other fields.

(2) In the 1980s, Iraq faced financial problems on account of massive expenditure $80 billion in the Iraq-Iran War (1980-88).

(3) In the 1980s, massive expenditure of Iraq- Iran War and damages to Iraqi oil exports facilities by UN International Sanctions as well as sabotage by the Islamic State damaging refineries, pipes and infrastructure led government to austerity measures which include borrowing heavily and later rescheduling foreign debt payments.

(4) In 1988, oil exports gradually increased with construction of new pipelines and restoration of damages facilities.

(5) Gulf War in 1990 resulted in conquering Kuwait which was wrong decision. This resulted in UN international Sanctions on export of oil from 1990 to 2003. This was slightly relaxed in 1997 by export for food programme facility given by UN.

(6) US invaded Iraq in 2003 and defeated Saddam Hussein which costed heavily to US as the unemployment in various IT companies spread dangerously. Cost of the war is reported $500 billion to US.

(7) Post Hussein efforts were made to modernize economy through privatization and reducing in foreign exchange debt. Economy continued to decline due to continuance violence, economic mismanagement and oil shortage caused by outdated technology.

(8) Inflation has decreased consistently since 2006 as the security has improved but unemployment remain a consistent problem.

(9) Iraq's seizure of Kuwait in August 1990, consequent international economic sanctions on Iraq, and damage from military action by international coalition beginning in January 1991, drastically reduced economic activity. The regime exacerbated shortages by exporting large military and internal security forces and by allocating them reduces to key supporters of Ba'ath party. The implementation of the UN's oil for food program in December 1996 helped improve economic conditions. For the first six-month phases of the program; Iraq was allowed to export increasing amount of oil in exchange for food, medicine and other humanitarian needs. In December 1999, the UN Security Council authorized Iraq to export as much as oil as required to meet humanitarian needs.

(10) Iraq changed its oil reserve currency from US dollar to euro in 2000. However, 28% of Iraq's export revenues under the program were deducted to meet UN Compensation fund and UN administration expenses. GDP supported in 2001 on account of fall of oil prices and global economic slowdown.

(11) One of the key economic challenges was Iraq's immense foreign debt, estimated $125 billion. Although some of this debt was derived from normal export contracts that Iraq had failed to pay for, some was a result of military and financial support during the Iraq's war with Iran.

(12) Iraq's agriculture suffered substantial physical disruption from the Gulf war, and economic disruption from Sanctions imposed by UN in August 1990. Sanctions curtailed imports by cutting off Iraq's petroleum exports and embargoing those agriculture production. Inputs deemed to have potentially military applications. The Iraq Government responded by monopolizing grain and oil seeds marketing,

imposing production quotas, and instituting a public Distribution System for basic foodstuffs.

(13) Under an Oil for Food Program, Iraq started exporting petroleum and importing food three months later. Grain imports averaged $828 million in the years 1997-2001, 180% from the previous five year period.

(14) Population: 3.84 crores

(15) GDP: $224.228 billion Nominal & $ 669.906 billion PPP in 2018

(16) GDP per Capita $ 5882 Nominal $17572 PPP in 2018

(17) Labour Force: 1.0378 crore

(18) Main Industries: Petroleum, chemicals, textiles, construction materials, food processing, fertilizers, crude oil

Conclusion:

Country has faced Iran-Iraq War for 8 Years which costed $80 billion. Gulf War resulted in winning Kuwait which was very costly as UN imposed sanctions on Iraq from 1990-2003. Country's only income was from export of crude oil. Since there was no diversification and the country was prohibited from exporting crude oil on account of UN Sanctions, there was economic crisis

Invasion of Iraq by US in 2003 further deteriorated the economy. There was civil war. There are many militant tribes which fought with each other. Kurdish has its own independent, de facto, state. Kurdish do not obey President's orders. Sabotage is done on petroleum pipe lines and infrastructure which resulted in difficulties to export crude oil.

Crude petrol is the only resource of income of Iraq. But it has not diversified its economy in other fields. Country has to depend on imports for foodgrains from other countries.

At Present, Iran and the US have military bases in Iraq. There are clashes between two countries which results in air attacks including missiles. Recently on 03-01-2020, on Baghdad airport, Sulemani, highest military head who was Iran's religious Guru Mr. Khomeini's most favourable military Head was killed in Motor accident outside Baghdad Airport on account of air attack on the Sulemani car by USA military in Baghdad. This was a great blow to Iran.

This has resulted in Iran attacking US with ballistic missiles in the USA military Base in Baghdad.

Iraq is not able to control various tribes in its country. Only to some extent, President Saddam Hussein was controlling these tribes and ruling the country. But US attacked, on the pretext that Saddam Hussein is dropping chemical missiles on tribes and killing them ruthlessly. This allegation proved wrong after the war. After the war, USA arrested Saddam Hussein and killed him ruthlessly.

Iraq has a titular ruler supported by USA. There are Military Bases of US and Iran in Iraq which are constantly fighting with each order. Nationals of Iraq are frightened by the constant air and missile attacks by Iran and USA. They are leaving the country and taking shelter in other countries as refugees.

Future rulers of Iraq should concentrate in growth and welfare of the economy as well as establishing a tight security to control sabotage of the Islamic country and various tribes in Iraq including Kurdish. Iran should diversify its economy from oil income to other income like telecommunication, construction, tourism etc. Rulers should not interfere in the internal matters of other countries to show their supremacy on the other countries at the cost of damages to the interest and growth of Iraq.

(34) **Economy of Iran:**

Iran's economy is constantly affected by USA sanctions from 1979 on account of the civil war in 1979 and Iran-Iraq war thereafter from 1980-88. Again in 2006, on account of issue of nuclear creation by Iran, Sanctions were imposed by USA, UN and EU. Iran whose 60% economy is based on Oil was prohibited since 1979 to 2014 to export oil to the importing country on account of sanctions. This led to the economic crisis of Iran. There were some relaxation from 2015-2017 on account of joint Agreement on nuclear issue in 2015 between Iran and EU, Russia and USA. But these were again withdrawn by USA in 2018 on the ground that Iran is not complying with terms of Agreement of 2015. USA withdrew from Agreement in 2018 but other countries were party to this agreement. This time, USA sanctions were stringent whereby India who was given concession to import oil from Iran till then, was prohibited to import oil from Iran. There was economic crisis in Iran on account of USA constant sanctions. Iran had large foreign exchange reserves $17 billion in overseas banks which were frozen. Still Iran managed the economy well and administered its country systematically.

Iran's main source of income is oil. 60% of Iran's economy is centrally planned. Iran has well diversified its economy from oil exports to other sectors such as tourism, construction, telecommunication, arms production etc.

On account of stringent sanctions by USA, India was compelled to import oil from other countries like Saudi Arabia, Qatar, US. India declared in 2020 that its import with Iran has come to zero level by 2019.

(1) Iran's economy has been hit hard since US sanctions which came into effect in mid-2018 and resulted nearly half of its import and exports estimated at 600000 bbd of oil being slashed.

(2) Iran's economy has the presence of large religious foundations called Bonyad whose combined budgets represent more than 30% of central government's spending.

(3) Iran's supreme Religious priest and Ruler Khomeini always treated US as his enemy and opposed the negotiations on compromise with USA all the times. He should compromise with USA to promote the interest of Iran, setting aside his personal opinion and ideology about USA.

(4) Export aided self-sufficiency and domestic investment, Iran's educated population, high human development, constrained economy and insufficient foreign and domestic investment prompted an increasing number of Iranians to seek overseas employment resulting in a significant "brain drain".

(5) Rising fuel prices in 2019 led to a grave economic crisis and widespread protest, which the government ruthlessly crushed resulting in hundreds of death.

(6) The government's long term objectives were stated as economic independence, full employment and comfortable standard of living but Iran's population increased more than double between 1980 and 2000 and its maiden age declined by two third population (74 million) was less than 30 years age. Though many Iranians are farmers, agricultural

production has constantly fallen since 1960. By 1990, Iran imported much of its food. Economic hardship forced many people moving cities.

(7) Expansion of public healthcare and international relations are other major objectives of the plan which includes subsidy reforms, banking, recapitalization, currency, taxation customs construction, employment, nationwide goods and services distribution, social justice and productivity. To make the country self-sufficient by 2015 and replace the payment of $100 billion in subsidies annually with targeted social assistance.

(8) Since the 1979 revolution, government spending has averaged 55% on social policies, 17% on economic matters, 15% on national defence and 13% on general affairs. Payments averaged 39% on education, health and social security, 20% in other social programs, 3% on agriculture, 16% on water, power, and gas, 5% on manufacturing and mining, 12% on roads and transportation, 5% on other economic affairs. Iran's investment was 27.7% of GDP in 2009. Around 55% of government revenue earned came from oil and natural gas, 31% from taxes and fees. Millions of people virtually do not plan taxes.

(9) Iran had $110 billion in foreign reserves in 2011 and its balances in external payments by pricing oil at appropriately $75 per barrel. As of 2011, only $30 million to $50 billion of these reserves are accessible on account of current sanctions.

(10) Following the hostilities with Iraq, government declared its intention to privatize most industries and to liberalize and decentralize the economy. Sale of state-owned companies proceed slowly, due to the opposition by nationalist majority in the parliament. In 2006, most industries, some 70% of the economy remain state owned. The majority of heavy industries including steel, petrochemicals, copper, automobiles and machine tools remain in the public sector. Most light industries were privately owned.

(11) Labour force had lack of education. After the revolution, the government established a national education system that improved literacy rates. In 2008, 85% of the population was literate. In order to avoid Arab Spring, the government

should quickly accomplish its target of making 100% educated which will match with their work.

(12) Around economic growth of about 5% is necessary to absorb 750000 new labour force entrants each year.

(13) Although Iranian workers have a theoretical right to form labour unions, there is no union system in the country. Ostensibly, worker representation is provided by the Workers House.

(14) Iran's defence budget was $7.31 billion in 2007 i.e. 2.7% of GDP or $102 per capita. Since 1992, Defence Industries Organization (DIO) has produced its own tanks, armed personnel carriers, guided missiles destroyer, military vessels, radar system, submarines and fighting planes. Iran exported weapons to 57 countries in 2006 including NATO members and export reached $100 million. It is also developing a sophisticated mobile air defence system dubbed as Bavar 373.

(15) Mineral production contributed to 0.6% of the GDP in 2011. Figure reached to 4% when mining relating industries are included. Although the petroleum industry provides the majority of revenues, there are other minerals like coal, iron ore, copper lead, zinc, aluminum, salt, gypsum, uranium and gold.

(16) On 15-11-2019, Iran raised the oil prices by 50% and imposed a strict rationing system. Prices per liter gasoline rose to 15000 riyals, where only 60 liters were permitted to private cars per month. Oil purchase beyond this limit will cause 30000 riyals per liter. The policy changes came in effect to the US sanctions, and caused protests across the country. Protesters began to demand the ousting of President Hassan Rouhani. The protest began to grow violent, where people began setting fire to public property. On 17-11-2019, the Iranian Supreme Leader Ayatollah Ali Khomeini called these protesters "thug" amidst the talks with clerics. He signaled a potential crackdown killing hundreds of protesters, while the internet access was also shut down for the entire nation.

(17) After the Iranian Revolution in 1979, the US ended its economic and diplomatic ties with Iran, banned Iranian oil imports and froze approximately $11 billion of its assets.

(18) Iran may be using as much as $60 billion annually in energy investment. Sanctions are making imports 24% more costly on average. Latest round of sanctions could cost Iran annually $50 billion in lost oil revenues. Iran is increasingly used the barter trade because its access to the international dollar payment system has be denied.

IEA estimated that Iran export fell to a record of 860000 bpd in September 2012 from 2.2 million bpd at the end of 2011. This fall led to a drop in revenues and clashes on the street of Teheran when the local currency, the riyal, collapsed. Iran had the lowest output in September 2012 since 1988.

In January 2019, Iran's President Hassan Rouhani blamed the US for Iran's declining economy. Following the US pullout from the international nuclear deal with Iran and re-imposed sanctions, Iran faced toughest economic situation in last 40 years.

(19) Population: 8.18 crores

(20) GDP: $458.50 billion Nominal $1.471 trillion PPP in 2019

(21) GDP per capita $ 5506 Nominal & $17663 PPP in 2019

(22) Inflation: 31%

(23) Labour Force: 2.74 crores

(24) Main Industries: Petroleum, Petrochemicals, fertilizers, Caustic soda, car manufacturing parts, pharmaceuticals, home appliances, electronics, telecom, construction, ferrous & non-ferrous metals.

(25) Credit Rating: Economic Intelligence Unit : CCC (Sovereign risk) CCC (Currency risk), CC (Banking Sector risk), CC (Political Risk), BB (economic Structure Risk) CC (country Risk) Iran is continuously under financial sanctions from US and EU since 1979 except for 2015, 2016 and 2017 where the Nuclear Agreement was signed in 2015 which withdrew main sanctions on Iran by US. This is a golden period for Iran's economy. Sanctions were again imposed by US in 2018 when it withdraws unilaterally from the Nuclear Agreement in 2018. Under constant sanctions, Iran economy became vulnerable. It has therefore potential Sovereign risk, currency risk and Country risk. Economic structure is sound as its oil exports earned revenues of

$50 billion and it has $120.6 billion as foreign reserves. It is in conflict with Israel, Saudi Arabia, Iraq and UAE. Only it has Qatar as its friend in Arabian Gulf. In other to establish its supremacy on other countries, it interferes in the political affairs of Syria, Yemen, Iraq and Libya. Clashes in these country results in losing amenities and military weapons stored in its military Bases in these countries. In Iran-Iraq War in 1980-88, it lost 300000 soldiers, another 500000 were injured and cost of the war was $50000 billion. Political risk is therefore potential.

(26) Iran should not interfere in the internal affairs of other countries. It should avoid fighting with Israel and conserve its energy from keeping aloof in Yemen's Civil War, Syria civil war and Libya's Saraj and Haftar conflict and other issues.

It is to be noted that in spite of continuous sanctions from USA and EU, Iran has made good progress in administering its country and help the nationals to improve their standard of living by planned economy.

(35) **Economy of UAE:**

(1) Economy of UAE is the second largest economy after Saudi Arabia.

(2) Though 85% of its economy is supported in exports of crude oil and natural gas, UAE has been successfully diversifying its economy, particularly in Dubai, in tourism and construction industry especially in constructing large international airports and largest luxurious hotels in UAE.

(3) Though Dubai in particular has diversified its economy and Ab Dhabi which was conservative in diversification, Abu Dhabi assisted Dubai for bail-out and Dubai's economy is based on Abu Dhabi petrodollars.

(4) Tourism is one of the biggest non-oil resources of revenue in the UAE with some of the World's most luxurious hotels are based in UAE.

(5) Since Independence from England in 1971, UAE's economy has grown by about 231 times to AED 1.45 trillion in 2013.

(6) A massive construction boom, an expounding manufacturing base, and a thriving service sector are helping the UAE

diversify its economy. Nationwide, there is currently \$350 billion worth of active construction projects.

(7) In the 1980s, Dubai's diversification is central around trade and creation of shipping and logistics centres, notably Port Rashid and the port and free and Free Zone of Jebel Ali as well as Dubai international Airport. Dubai is also, leading to a number of major global players in shipping, transportation and logistics. Dubai also emerged as lively real estate market. This was checked by the global financial market.

(8) There is increased contribution of non-petroleum sectors, which registered a growth average of more than 6% in 2014-15. Such contribution includes banking, tourism, commerce and real estate. Internally, UAE is recognized among top 20 for global service business.

(9) With imports totaling \$ 273.5 billion in 2012, UAE passed Saudi Arabia as the largest consumer market in the region. Exports totaled \$ 314 billion – is second exporter in the region.

(10) Emigrate is the largest operator of Airbus A380 aircraft. Government revenue is AED 29.7 billion and expenses AED 22.9 billion.

(11) Emiratization is an initiative by the government of UAE to employ more UAE nationals in a meaningful and effective manner in public and private sector.

(12) Beyond directly sponsoring education initiatives, the Emigrates Funding for Philanthropy is funding major research initiatives into Emiratization through competitive research grants education investment 22.5% or \$2.6 billion.

(13) The leap in real estate sector along and infrastructure development in the UAE during the recent year has contributed in making this country a global touristic destination par excellence. UAE has 180 tour hotels out of 155 that exist around the world. Hugh public investments in tourism projects \$47 billion per year. UAE ranked fourth worldwide in terms of infrastructure quality.

(14) Currency of UAE is United Arab Immigrate Dirham AED 3.67 =\$1

(15) Population: 96 lacs - 2018

(16) GDP $405.771 billion Nominal. $ 746. 50 billion PPP - 2019

(17) GDP per Capita : $ 37750 Nominal, $ 69435 PPP in 2019

(18) Labour Force: 69.05 lacs

(19) Man Industries: crude oil, natural gas, tourism, construction, aluminum, textiles

(20) FDI Stock: $129 billion. Abroad 1244 billion

(21) Credit Rating: S & Ps AA Outlook: Stable, Moody's: Outlook Stable Finch AA Outlook Stable

(22) UAE has large natural resources and its Population is only 96 lacs. It is therefore a very rich and high income country. UAE has diversified in various other sectors like tourism and construction though 85% of its income derives from crude oil and natural gas exports. It is therefore unlikely to be in economic crisis if oil prices drastically dropped in recession as it is happening today on account of Corona Virus and OPEC countries and Russia not agreeing to reduce oil production. UAE is cautious in interfering in the internal matters with other countries like Hothi in support of the Saudi Arabia.

It should continuously adopt this policy and concentrate on administration of the country properly.

(36) **Economy of Qatar:**

(1) Being abundant storage of proven petroleum oil, the economy of Qatar is one of the richest in the world.

(2) Petroleum and natural gas are two cornerstones of Qatar economy. It earns 70% of total government revenue, 60% of GDP and 85% of total exports.

(3) Before the emergence of petrol-based industry, Qatar was poor pearl diving country. Exploration of oil and gas fields began in 1939. In 1973, oil production and revenues increased dramatically. It was in downturn from 1982 to 199O. OPEC quotas on crude oil production, lower price of oil, negative outlook on international markets reduced oil earnings. Spending plan cut to match lower income. The resulting recessionary local business climate caused many firms to lay off the expatriate staff. With the economy recovering from 1990s, expatriate population from Egypt and South Asia have grown again.

(4) Oil production was 500000 bpd. Storage of oil is expected to last 2023. Natural gas located off Qatar's northeast coast. These are significant oil and condensate reserves. Gas condensate can be refined to usual oil products in specialized refineries. In June 2016, oil production was 670000 bpd down from 692000 bpd.in February 2016.

(5) Qatar's proved reserves of gas is 250 trillion cubic feet (7000km). Economy was boosted in 1991. Liquefied natural gas exported to Japan.

(6) Qatari Banking Sector managed to escape the direct impact of the global surprise fall out, but was not together unscathed by its after- shocks. Issue of liquidation declining customer confidence and forced reluctant to lend.

(7) Government encouraged banks to lend by buying the investment portfolio of the banks. Loan to deposit ratio was as high as 90%.

(8) In August 2019, Qatar Central Bank stated that Qatari economy will boost on account of stable oil prices and strong exports.

(9) In addition to Islamic banks, Conventional banks were also entering in Qatar with sophisticated instruments/

(10) Stock Market capitalization was $95.487 billion in 2007.

(11) Under the ambitious five year development plan, Qatar Tourism and Exhibition Authority (QTEA), government aimed to boost the number of visitors from 964000 in 2007 to 1.5 million in 2010. The funding required to meet this goal was present in sufficient amounts. In 2008, the state allocated 17 billion for tourism development. Hotels, Exhibition Space and Infrastructure were developed. Hotel capacity raised to 400% by 2012 to help rising number of visitors. Qatar eased the business regulations to increase private sector activities. Hamad International Airport has the capacity of handling 24 million passengers on its completion phase I in 2012.

(12) With fast expanding population and substantial economic growth over the past decade, extensive transportation network is becoming necessary within Qatar.

(13) Public Works Authority underwent major reorganization in order to streamline and modernize the preparation of major project expansion across all segments.

(14) Fisheries is a minor sector. Fishery output is exclusively used for domestic consumption.

(15) Road network is the major focus. Multi billion dollars spent to develop Doha Expressway and Qatar Bahrain Causeway to connect Qatar to Bahrain and Saudi Arabia. This will be milestone in regional interconnectivity. Doha International Airport will accommodate 50 million passengers. Port infrastructure is Qatar's integral part.

(16) Exchange rate for Qatari Riyal is 3.65 Riyals per US dollar. PPP US dollar rate is Riyals 3.67 =US dollar 1.

(17) Population: 2.782 million

(18) GDP: $191.849 billion Nominal & $365.835 billion PPP in 2019

(19) GDP per Capital: $69688 Nominal & $ 132886 PPP

(20) Labour Force: 2.129 million. Labour force of the country should be 1.5 million domestic and 0.6 million from expatriate in other countries like Egypt and South Asia

(21) Main Industries: liquefied natural gas, crude oil, ammonia, fertilizers, petrochemicals, steel, cement, construction, ship repair

(22) Credit Rating: S&P's AA (Domestic), AA (Foreign)

AA+, Outlook: Stable (T&C), Moody's Aa2, Outlook: Stable.

(23) Qatar was isolated by Saudi Arabia and UAE on account of secretly assisting Iran but it has no impact on Qatar. Qatar employs large amount of expatriate labour from Egypt and South Asia as its labour force may not exceed 1.4 million out of the small population of 2.782 million.

(24) Qatar gives financial aid to many African economically weak countries to raise their infrastructure and development projects.

(25) Country is well managed as a welfare state.

(37) **Economy of Saudi Arabia**

(1) Saudi Arabia was a subsistence economy till 1930. In 1933, Saudi government signed an oil Concession agreement with Standard Oil Company of California. Development of oil fields continued in Saudi Arabia, managed by Saudi Armco formed by partnership of Texaco and Chevron.

Production was 500000 bpd in 1949 and raised to 1 million in 1954.

(2) Foreign ownership of business was allowed by mid-1980s. In mid-1990s, foreign ownership rules were relaxed with investment sought in telecommunications, utilities and financial services. In 2000, 100% foreign owned businesses were allowed in the kingdom.

(3) In the Report of UNCTAD released in June 2018, Saudi's FDI was $ 1.4 billion only in 2017, down from $ 7.5 billion and in 2016, and $ 12.2 billion in 2012.

(4) Diversification from 1970s, fishing villages of Jubal on Persian Gulf and Yanbu on Red Sea were developed. Total length of paved highways tripled. Power generation increased by multiple of 28. Capacity of seaports grew tenfold.

In third plan (1980-85), emphasis changed. There was less spending on infrastructure. Spending rose markedly on education, health and social services.

In forth plan (1985-90), infrastructure was completed but education and training remained area of concerns.

The main investing countries in Saudi in 2016 were USA, UAE, France, Singapore, Kuwait and Malaysia. They mainly invested in real estate, tourism, fossil fuels, automobiles and machinery. As a part of diversification, Refinery contracts with Chinese and other companies were made.

(5) In 2008, two-third workers employed in Saudi were foreigners. Private sector employed 90% of expatriates. This was lowered by compelling private sector to double the Saudi nationals to 1.5 million. (10 million foreign workers were working in Saudi). Economists estimate only 30-40 percent of working age Saudis hold jobs or actively seek work although official unemployment rate was around 12%. Most Saudis with jobs are employed in government. IMF warned no support for such government large bill in the long term. Foreign workforce and employment grew. Heavy fee on expatriate resulted in 677000 foreigners leaving the jobs. Unemployment rose to 12.9%.

(6) Real estate plays a fundamental role in the country's non-oil economy. In 2016, value of real estate transactions including sale of existing units accounted to $74.91 billion

from October 15 to September 16. In 2017, there was major drop. In earlier decade, it was \$239.97billion. Ownership of land property is restricted to Saudis, Gulf Corporation Council nationals and companies have certain rights to own land. Foreigners are entitled to ownership with conditions.

(7) There are two handful of business i.e. construction and real estate.

(8) Halting or reversing the decline in capital income, improving education to prepare youth for work force, providing them employment, diversifying the economy, stimulating private sector and housing construction, diminishing corruption and inequality are challenges before the Saudi government.

(9) The UN Arab Development Report blamed stunted social and economic development inhibited by the lack of personal freedom, poor education and government hiring based on factors other than merit, and exclusion of women.

(10) Income per capita dropped from \$18000 in 1981 to \$7000 in 2001 due to rapid growth of population during the period.

(11) Saudi population is young with 51% of population is under age of 25. Only 1.6 million nationals are employed. Private sector jobs are 600000 but only for expatriate from Persian Gulf. This will result in unrest among the Saudi nations. Government should give education to all nationals speedily to match with knowledge of jobs to avoid giving employment to expatriates from Egypt and South Asia.

(12) Saudi government forced the private sector employers to take 30% of the Saudi nationals in their employment. But these employers complained bitterly about lack of skills among young locals. Quota system was dropped and flexible system was introduced. Kingdom depends on huge numbers of expatriate workers to fill technical and administrative positions.

(13) Number of applications are required to be made to get permission to start new business and favors required from many ministries.

(14) Cost of maintaining Royal family is estimated @ \$10 billion per year. 77% of businessmen felt they had to "bypass" the law to conduct their operations. To tackle money laundering

and interacts, the country is not sufficiently investigating and prosecuting individuals involved in money laundering for tourism financing.

(15) Population below poverty line is estimated between two million and 4 million of the country's natives live in less than about $530 per month and $17 per day –considered poverty in Saudi Arabia.

(16) 50% of Saudi Arabians own house. Government Real Estate Development Fund which provides 81% of all loans for housing has waiting list of 18 years for loans due to pent up demand. Maximum loan is offer at SR 500000- ($133000-). High cost of land in urban area makes it difficult to buy a house at SR500000-. In order to encourage the nationals to buy house, the government gives further loan on mortgage of new house in additional to maximum loan SR 500000 –provided by the Real Estate Development Fund.

(17) 5% value added tax halted private sector growth. 75000 private enterprises left and departed.

(18) Rich Saudis are reluctant to invest due to inquiry.

(19) Stock Exchange capitalization is $646 billion in 2005.

(20) Saudi Arabian Basic Industries Corporation was established by a royal decree in 1976. To produce chemicals, polymers and fertilizers. It was Asia's profitable publicly listed non-oil company in 2008.

(21) Population 34.173 million (3.42 crores)

(22) GDP: $ 779.289 billion Nominal (2019) & $1.899 trillion PPP in 2018

(23) GDP per capita: $ 22865 Nominal & $55704 PPP

(24) Labour Force: 13.8 million - 3.1 million Saudis (about 10% of Population), 10.7 million non-Saudis 52.4% employment rate in 2018

(25) Main Industries: Crude oil products, petroleum refineries, petrochemical, ammonia, industrial gases, sodium hydroxide, cement, fertilizers, plastic, metal, ship repairs, aircraft repairs, construction, foodstuff

(26) Revenue $181 billion & Expenses 241.8 billion in 2017 Fiscal deficit: $60.8 billion i.e.7.80% of GDP high

(27) Foreign reserves: 4500.588 billion

(28) Current rating: S & P's A- (Domestic & Foreign), A (T&C), Outlook: Stable Moody's A1 Outlook Stable. Fitch A+ outlook: Stable

Conclusion

There are internal conflict between Royal family members especially Princes about who will become the next king. Recently it was reported that there was fierce fight internally between the present King Prince Mr. Mohammad Bin Salman who is the son and the successor of the present King and other ambitious princes. Other aggressive princes were punished and locked-up in jail. They were then released on their agreement not to contest the King position.

Royal family is not administrating the country properly. Why the country requires foreigners to work in its country. Why they cannot educate and train skilled workers. Why only 50% of the Saudis own house when country is one of richest in the world. Why real estate is in the hands of Royal family. Why the prices of house cannot be brought down. Why there is population under poverty line of 20% and 40% as per the country's standards of poverty. These challenges should be addressed and resolved speedily by the country. Otherwise there will be unrest like Arab Spring in the country.

Saudi is unnecessarily involving in the internal affairs of many countries. Hothi in Yemen air attached with dropping missiles with the military assistance of Iran recently on the Oil refinery and oil storage tanks. It resulted in heavy losses to Saudi and has to stop exporting oil for some days. Saudi should divert its attention to the challenges before it as mentioned above and should not dominate other countries. Present King's son i.e. Princess is supposed to be the next king. He shows the power and take many important decisions for the present king. He is the most powerful personality in the Saudi kingdom.

King Prince is most powerful and he generally looks after the policy of the state. Saudi is not complying with Human Rights imposed by the World's Human Rights Committee. But present Prince has given concession to women not to cover their faces by mass and to drive cars, motor-cycles on road. Recently he has abolished hanging to death punishment for minor children under the age of 18. He also stopped the physical punishment on body by hunter.

Of late, it was reported that 15 Royal members are Corona virus patients.

Final Conclusion

After World War II, All countries met and took the decision to form the institutions for the welfare of mankind. Accordingly, IMF, World Bank, UN, WTO, WHO and many others were formed. USA had the lion's share in this activities. These Institutions have assisted the mankind for peace in many occasions when there is a conflict between two strong superpower countries which may possibly result in world war with serious effect. In conflict between Russia and USA on Latin American country Quaba recently, UN intervened. In Corona virus, WHO started taking steps to avoid wide spreading of the disease by advising countries about taking preventing measures

USA, Russia and China are three super power countries. They have the potentials to make their country as welfare state and direct and guide other countries to develop their countries into welfare states.

But at present, they have been concentrating in competition with each other 0ther showing who is the highest supreme power. For that purpose, these countries are developing most sophisticated war missiles, hydrogen and nuclear bombs. If any accident to their storage of nuclear weapons will occur like Chernobyl, we can image what disaster will happen. These countries have so strong nuclear weapons that it will destroy the whole world ten times.

From the above observation of the various countries' economies, it is found that India, though have 125 crores as their population and per capita GDP only little more than $2000 has potential to develop its country as a welfare state and direct/encourage other countries who do not interfere in the internal affairs of other countries and rulers in these countries are concentrating on economic growth, equality of resources, making optimum use of the available resources and restricting unemployment and inflation to develop their countries as welfare states which is the ultimate goal of entire mankind.

But unless above three upper power countries are keen to promote their states as Welfare States and encourage the other countries to promote Welfare states, the target of the Welfare states in the world is not able to be accomplished which is the ultimate goal of the entire mankind.

During the last six months i.e. from December 2019 to May 2020, whole world is suffering from new epidemic disease known as Corona virus. The disease spread all over the world such as China, Italy, Japan, Arabian Gulf, Turkey, USA, Greece, France, UK, Germany, India etc. There is no medicine or vaccine to cure this disease. To avoid the spread of disease in the country, "lockdown" is the only preventive remedy. As mentioned above, China suffered first from Corona virus. It then spread all over the world. China and all other countries adopted the "closedown" of their cities which resulted in paralyzing the economies of these countries and economic growth of these country is zero or negative.

At present more than 150 countries which are suffering from this disease. About 3300000 patients are suffering and there are 257000 patients dead and 900000 patients have recovered as at 07-05-2020. USA suffered worse with 1130000 patients with 78000 dead during the said period. WHO has declared financial aid to the countries to fight Corona virus. It has given $2 billion to India. USA also gave financial aid of $1 billion. India has declared two social welfare packages of Rs 1. 70 trillion each ($45.32 billion) to fight this disease. These social welfare measures include giving food to poor citizens free of cost for 3 months, giving lunch at concessional rate Rs. 5 known as Shivthali" in Maharashtra, postponing EMI and Monthly maintenance of Co-operative societies etc. Providing free travel to interstate labors to go to their native places etc. and giving financial assistance to all workers Rs. 2000- for three months.

Various countries are suffering serious economic loss of the lockdown. In India 12 crores are unemployed in April 2020 which means 21% was the rate of unemployed. In USA 2 crores lost their jobs in April 2020. Since there is no medicine/vaccine to cure this disease and rate of spreading of this disease is volatile and fluctuating, nobody can predict when the post lockdown period will start.

At least period of two years from the post lockdown will be crucial. All nations and their nationals have to face courageously the situation for this period as there will be dangerous recession, unemployment will be at the highest level about 30%-35% of the present level. There will be no demand for various commodities. The factory/industries will work with much lower level. The economic growth will be negative or @ zero level. This recession business cycle will last at last more than two years.

Then the recovery period will start. Economies of the country will start gradually recovering, Economic growth will be gradually positive and GDP will increase. Thereafter, there will be economic boom during this period.

We are optimistic that meantime Super powers such as USA, Russia and China will realise their mistake and they will strive to make their countries as fully welfare states. These countries will also take initiative and encourage other countries to be welfare states. There will be the welfare states known as "Ram Rajya" all over the world which is the ultimate goal of all mankind. This will be accomplished by end-2025.

Second alternative is that at present USA is suffering the maximum from Corona virus. USA is blaming China and WHO for this disaster. USA has withdrawn its membership of WHO. USA is planning to take serious military action against China with other European countries and Japan, Australia. Like India, USA is also planning to ban apps. President Trump has recently closed commercial embassy of China in Houston in USA. The relation of China and USA are becoming worse with both closing each other embassies.

China is very much adamant in his attitude with India on East Ladakh border issue. It has created conflict with India in the Ganwan valley region of the eastern Ladakh. Confrontation resulted in military attack by China on Indian soldiers killing 20 Indian soldiers. In retaliation, India killed 43 Chinese soldiers. This resulted in Peace talk of Chinese military commanders with India several times but China is not withdrawing its troops from the present position to original position along LOC. It is claiming some part across LOC which India has firmly refused. This may result in further military clashes between India and China. India has banned 59 Chinese apps and has cancelled all Road and Railways construction projects with China resulting in heavy financial loss to China. Recently, India has changed rules to enable curbs on bidders from countries that share land order with India on the grounds of defence and national security. This is imposing curbs on Chinese investment. This seeks to block supply of stationary, turbines telecom equipment award of road and power contracts to companies that have a link with China.

Prime Minister of Nepal Mr. Sharma Oli has also created boarder dispute with India on instigation of China and has claimed boarder areas such as Lipukekh, Limpaiya and Kalapur of Uttarkhand border. India has protested strongly against these claims but Nepal is adamant in not negotiating talks with India. Internally, Oli has clashes with other leaders of Communist Party of Nepal such as Prachanda on political power issue. Oli has support from China. Nepal population is against Oli policy. In spite of that Oli managed to pass legislation in Nepal Parliament and revised Nepali map to include above provinces in it. Oli is so aggressive that it militarily attacked Bihar Border of India and killed innocent citizens of India. India is watching the situation and will retaliate on appropriate time.

Iran has also spoiled relationship with India on oil export issue and has recently withdrawn Indian participation in Chabahar Agreement on the ground that India is delaying payment of this project and declared that Iran alone will carry on this project with full cost of the project without assistance from any country. Iran has recently executed an Agreement with China for $ 4 billion for supplying petrol oil to it on long term basis. Clearly, Iran is instigated by China on its relationship with India.

Pakistan is also enemy of India. It is reported that China has agreed with Pakistan that it will develop most sophisticated laboratory in Pakistan to fix epidemic virus in various military weapons to spread like Corona virus when these weapons are used and thrown on the enemy country. Clearly, it is pointing finger at India.

Political situation in India and the world is very explosive and if it continues, it will result in horrible third war. USA, India, European countries, Japan, South Korea and Australia will be fighting against China probably supported by Russia, Iran, Pakistan, Bangladesh and Nepal.

There will be expenditure of multiples of trillion dollars to all countries. Casualty will be in tens of crores and same amount of people in the world will be seriously sick, handicapped and disabled. World will be on the verge of collapse/destruction. All countries will require badly world welfare and peace in the world. These countries will then come together and set up WHO, UN, IMF, World Bank and other Welfare Institutions on more refined basis. Powerful countries will develop full welfare states in their countries and will encourage other countries to make up their countries as welfare states. There will be welfare states all over the world which is "Ram Rajya" which is the ultimate goal of all mankind. This will be accomplished by end 2025.

References

WIKIPEDIA, FREE ENCYCLOPEDIA

- Economy of Qatar with references
- Economy of Saudi Arabia with references
- Economy of Yemen with references
- Economy of Canada with references
- Economy of Zambia with references
- Economy of Angola with references
- Economy of Malawi with references
- Economy of Mauritius with references
- Economy of Mozambique with references
- Economy of Zimbabwe with references
- Economy of Tanzania with references
- Economy of South Africa with references
- Economy of Afghanistan with references
- Economy of Italy with references
- Economy of Greece with references
- Economy of Iran with references
- Economy of Libya with references
- Economy of Syria with references
- Economy of Iraq with references
- Economy of Turkey with references
- Economy of Israel with references
- Economy of Gaza Strip with references
- Economy of UAE with references

- Economy of Palestine with references

Introduction to the Book (on Front page of hard cover of the book)

Ultimate target of the entire mankind is the promoting the world as a welfare state. USA, Russia and China and to some extent to India have the potential to promote a welfare state and guide other countries to promote their countries as a welfare state.

The name of the book is "Critical Analysis of political policy on national economies" clearly highlighted how the political action of one country impacts on its national economy.

For example, aggression in Iran in 1979 and thereafter the Iran-Iraq War in 1980-88 resulted in Sanctions imposed by USA on Iran which resulted in exporting petroleum to other countries and foreign exchange reserves of Iran in overseas banks were made inoperative resulting in economic crisis in Iran. Iran lost $ 500 billion in war, 300000 soldier were killed and 500000 injured.

For the purpose of happiness and welfare of the entire mankind, we have internationally set up Institutions such as IMF, WB, WHO, UN.

Country such as USA, Russia and China are super power and they are engaged in competition to create most sophisticated weapons. USA and Russia have 90% of the nuclear weapons. We can imagine what disaster will be created if their storages are accidently exploited like Chernobyl. During this last six months, new disease "Corona virus' spread all over the world which killed 250000 and there are 3350000 patients and 900000 patients are cured in 193 countries resulted in closedown many countries in the world resulting in great recession following thereafter.

India has potential to promote its country as welfare state and encourage others who have non alignment policy to promote their states as the welfare states which is the ultimate goal of the entire mankind.

Index

D

G

J

K

L

N

S

U